Looking at Ourselves:
An Introduction to Philosophy

Looking at Ourselves:
An Introduction to Philosophy

Vincent Barry
Bakersfield College

Wadsworth Publishing Company, Inc.
Belmont, California

ISBN 0–534–00464–4
L.C. Cat. Card No. 76–8111
Printed in the United States of America

1 2 3 4 5 6 7 8 9 10—81 80 79 78 77

Philosophy Editor: Kenneth King
Designer: Carolyn Braun
Production Editor: Larry Olsen
Cartoonist: Tony Hall
Cover Photographer: Elaine Faris Keenan, 1976 NEST, S.F.

Preface

This book has a three-fold purpose: (1) to introduce readers to traditional philosophical problems in a way that will help them to define and shape themselves; (2) to expose readers to philosophical argumentation in such a way that they will feel confident in handling abstract concepts; and (3) to help readers recognize philosophical problems in an everyday context and to deal with everyday problems philosophically.

These purposes suggest the value of *usefulness* which was very much in my mind when writing *Looking at Ourselves*. For a number of reasons, many of today's students have to be shown the importance and applicability of philosophy. In recent years I have felt challenged to meet the needs and interests of contemporary students without sacrificing traditional philosophical content. It seems to me that an introductory philosophy text which tries to meet this problem must dramatize the usefulness of philosophy in defining oneself, including one's goals, values, attitudes, and conceptual framework. *Looking at Ourselves* is an attempt to do just this.

Toward this end I have used a number of instructional techniques. First, as a student and teacher I have observed that beginning philosophy students often have difficulty reading the material. A major reason for this is the stiffly formal textbook style, muscle-bound with technical jargon. A study as vital as philosophy need not make dull or labored reading, and it is unpardonable for a prose style to suggest that philosophy is an "elitist" pursuit. To ensure a vigorous, engaging presentation, I have tried to be as informal as intelligent conversation allows, while minimizing the use of technical language. My chief criterion for including philosophical terms was whether such terms were widely and frequently used. At the same time I realize that some instructors and readers may desire a more inclusive philosophical lexicon. For those readers I have included an extensive glossary at the end of the book. Terms defined in the glossary are set in bold face type at their first appearance in the text.

Another instructional technique I have used are fictional dialogues among ordinary people. These dialogues are intended not only to illustrate and clarify philosophical concepts, but also to help readers recognize philosophical problems in the context of everyday life.

Another device included in *Looking at Ourselves* is what I have termed "Reflections." These sections are not designed to be "busy work" or homework; rather, they are intended to provide a thought-provoking pause in the reading. Those desiring formal exercises will find them at the end of each chapter. They are grouped according to each subject considered in the chapter, so the reader may turn to them immediately upon completing a section.

Each chapter, furthermore, is preceded by an outline of subjects to be considered. At the end of each chapter appears a summary, as well as a list of main points. I hope these features will be useful to readers in organizing and summarizing the content of each chapter.

At the end of each chapter also appears a list of recommended paperbacks for further reading. The list is annotated, and it includes fiction as well as non-fiction. At the end of the text is an extensive bibliography consisting of works that are "pure philosophy."

Finally, a word about the organization of the text. Few instructors cover any course the same way, especially one as personal as philosophy. I have tried to anticipate this by writing as comprehensive a text as possible, one that includes the often omitted subjects of language, logic, science, esthetics, and social philosophy, together with the traditional subjects of epistemology, metaphysics, ethics, and religion. The particular sequence of topics is not an important issue. Rather than organize the material sequentially, I have organized it radially, like the spokes of a wheel, with the notion of self at the hub. Since we return to the center with each chapter, the only logical connections which need be made are between the self and the material discussed.

Nevertheless, for those wishing to take a linear approach in dealing with these topics, there is a rationale for their sequence. Since language plays such a fundamental role in defining who and what we are, and because all philosophy is conceived and expressed in language, I have dealt with this subject very early, in Chapter 2. The subject of language naturally led me into one facet of language expression, the problem of knowledge, and epistemological issues are discussed in Chapters 3, 4, and 5. Because what we know or claim to know is ultimately bound up with what we consider real, I decided to take up metaphysics next, in Chapter 6. In preparing this chapter it struck me that two major movements in recent centuries have vied for our loyalties on the issue of what is ultimately real: science and religion. So, I considered these subjects next, in Chapters 7 and 8. Finally, whether our bias is scientific or religious, we are still faced with value decisions: socially and politically, ethically and esthetically. These subjects I considered in Chapters 9,

10, and 11. Again I wish to stress that omitting or reordering any chapters will not detract from the text's effectiveness.

The two chapters I have yet to account for are the first and last. The first introduces readers to philosophy, sets the theme of self-identity, and provides general direction for the rest of the text. This chapter should be read first. The last chapter attempts to aid readers in formulating their own personal philosophies and should be read last.

I would like to acknowledge the encouragement and helpful assistance of those who have helped to shape this book. Especially deserving of thanks is editor Ken King, whose remarkable ability to stroke and poke at just the right times ensured the completion of this text. For their constructive criticism I am also indebted to Professors Marie-Louise Collinsworth, Canada College; Walter Douglas, San Bernardino Valley College; Ralph Hallman, Pasadena City College; Eva Konrich, East Los Angeles College; Clarence Parker, Central State University, Oklahoma; Richard Voight, Northampton County Area Community College; and Peter Wheatcroft, Grossmont College. Finally, a hearty thank-you to Susan Bain for her helpful assistance in preparing the manuscript.

Vincent Barry

Contents

Looking at Ourselves:
An Introduction to Philosophy

Human Nature and the Self

1

Indeed it is of the essence of man . . . that he can lose himself in the jungle of his existence, within himself, and thanks to his sensation of being lost can react by setting energetically to work to find himself again.
—José Ortega y Gasset

Have you ever felt out of touch with yourself? Not long ago there was a popular expression that described the effort to order one's life, to define or redefine oneself. It was "getting your head together."

Perhaps you have heard a friend say "I've got to get my head together," or maybe you have felt this way. It is not an uncommon feeling. Often events seem more than we can bear. Demands at home, at school, or at work can build until we fear we are losing our identities, losing touch with ourselves.

Well, just what is this **self** that we can seem to "lose touch" with? Some believe the self is everything that has ever happened to a person, that it is synonymous with one's experiences. We are what we are, they say, because of genetic and environmental influences. Others claim that the self is always something more than a person's experiences, that it is some nonmaterial quality: a **soul**, spirit, mind, or the like. Still others deny the existence of the self, insisting that it is an illusion. Whatever the view, all are agreed on this: the question of personal identity, of who or what we are, is as fundamental and difficult a question as we can ask.

This book raises that question. In so doing we make several assumptions. First, we assume that to a large extent we are what we believe. All our opinions, convictions, ideals, and attitudes are an expression of who and what we are. It follows, then, that much of self-discovery lies in discovering and formulating our beliefs. This book focuses on these beliefs, while, of course, acknowledging such other obvious aspects of self-identity as our physical make-up.

3

Another assumption we shall make is that our intellectual heritage influences our beliefs. The main currents of Western thought, founded in Judaeo-Christian and Greco-Roman cultures, are expressed in our educational, social, and religious institutions, all of which play a role in defining us. Unless we are aware of these influences, we cannot fully understand ourselves and the alternatives to being what we are.

A third assumption is that we can exercise some control over our beliefs. Despite our intellectual heritage, our heredity, and our environment, we can alter our beliefs and ourselves. To do this requires that we become aware of the intellectual influences in our lives and of the options available to us.

In this opening chapter we will use these assumptions specifically by considering how various traditional views of human nature pertain to self-discovery. We will see that, although outside the classroom we may seldom give these views much thought, we do interpret many aspects of our lives through these traditional views. To illustrate this point we will consider one question important for every individual, the issue of personal freedom. How we perceive human nature strongly affects whether we see ourselves as totally free, partially free, or not free at all; and our view of freedom in turn affects how we manage our lives. As an example we will meet a young college woman trying to decide what to do with her life, struggling with her identity. Although like many of us she has never before thought much about how her intellectual heritage has molded her own self-concept, she does now. The result is an intellectual crisis that cuts to the assumptions of her life—and perhaps our own.

FIVE VIEWS OF HUMAN NATURE

One factor that complicates the search for self-identity is the several ways of viewing human nature we have inherited. Before discussing them we should note the connection between these views of human nature and views of self.

Have you ever witnessed a hypnosis? People under hypnosis often do strange things. A common hypnotic exercise, for example, is to suggest that a person act like an animal, perhaps a dog. Invariably the person starts barking and growling, and may even fetch a stick. By affecting those characteristics that apparently apply to all dogs, the person does what is proper to canine nature.

In a similar way, we live our lives by what we believe to be proper to **human nature,** by what we believe makes us as a species different from anything else. For example, because we believe humans have a sense of right and wrong, we often admire or despise ourselves and others on that basis. In other words, since we view moral choice as

"A third assumption is that we can exercise
some control over our beliefs."

uniquely human, we tend to view ourselves as capable of making moral choices, of doing good or bad, of acting in a praiseworthy or blameworthy way. So, qualities we believe to be essentially human influence how we see ourselves and others. And, as in the case of hypnotic suggestion, we may not even be aware of these influences that are affecting our perceptions. If we wish to exercise some control over our lives, it is important that we at least be aware of the more prominent of these influences.

In this chapter we will examine five important theories of human nature. Four of these views spring from our Western tradition: the views of the human as a rational, divine, mechanical, or existential being. The fifth is primarily an Oriental view and is unique in that it denies the existence of any self. Here the treatment of these views and their inevitable influences on our self-concepts will be intentionally sketchy and noncritical, for these views will re-emerge periodically throughout the text, at which time we will analyze them. Here we simply wish to trace the main currents of thought that are affecting our lives.

The Human as a Rational Being

One theory of human nature, held by the ancient Greeks, views the human primarily as a thinker capable of reasoning. Plato (427?–347 B.C.), for one, contended that the highest part of the self is **reason**. But he did not believe that reason was the sole constituent of the self.

To understand Plato's view, consider this illustration. Suppose you are very thirsty. Before you is a glass of poisoned water. One part of you, what Plato called Appetite—located in the abdomen—invites you to drink. By Appetite he meant thirst and hunger, as well as sexual and other physical desires. But a second part of you, Reason, forbids you to drink. By Reason Plato meant the uniquely human capacity for thinking reflectively and drawing conclusions—the ability to follow relationships from one thought to another in an orderly and correct way. This rational part, said Plato, has its center in the brain. In this illustration a conflict arises between Appetite and Reason. But Plato claimed conflict could arise in another way, as when our emotions or passions flare up.

Suppose someone cuts you off on the highway. You become enraged; you begin to blow your horn and shake your fist at the driver. You are even tempted to tailgate him for a few miles just to vent your spleen. But what good would that do? Besides, it would be downright dangerous. Nevertheless, you surely would like to. Plato would say that the conflict you feel here is not between Reason and Appetite, but between Reason and what he variously calls anger, indignation, or Spirit. Spirit is like self-assertion or self-interest, and, according to Plato, it resides in the breast.

Thus, in Plato's view, Reason, Spirit, and Appetite characterize human nature. Depending on which part dominates, we get three kinds of people, whose main desires are knowledge, success, and gain. But Plato leaves no doubt about which element should dominate: Reason. True, each element plays a part; but Spirit and Appetite have no principle of order of their own. They must be brought under the control of Reason. It is through Reason that we can discover the truth about how we ought to live. This truth, claimed Plato, exists outside ourselves in some objective state. It is not, he argued, a matter of opinion or feeling; neither is it something we make for ourselves. It is not relative.

For Aristotle (384–322 B.C.), too, reason is the human's highest faculty. It is our distinguishing characteristic, the one that sets us apart from all other creatures of nature. Likewise, the Stoics, members of a school of thought founded by Zeno in 308 B.C., regarded the ideal person as the one able to suppress passion and emotion through reason. Only in this way could humans discover knowledge and be in harmony with cosmic reason, or **logos.**

Although there are many differences among Plato's, Aristotle's, and the Stoics' views, they all stress reason as the human's most important feature. This view generally would have us perceive the self as consisting of a body and a mind. The body is physical and subject to the laws that govern matter. The mind is immaterial; it is conscious and characterized by reasoning. Unlike the body, the mind has no extension; it is not part of the world of matter. Neither is it subject to its laws.

We might even view ourselves as a field of conflict between these two aspects of our nature, the physical and the mental. And, since we are the only creatures with a rational mind, we would tend to experience conflict in relation to nature; for we might perceive ourselves as distinct from the matter of the world and as potential masters of it. In short, our mind enables us to stand apart from our environment, to find meaning and sense in the events around us. Moreover, we are capable of learning the truth about how we ought to live. The way to this truth, in this classical view, is through reason.

So the implications of the view of the human as primarily rational for self-perception and identity are widespread. This classical view is one of the two most influential theories in Western civilization. The other is the view of the human as essentially a divine being.

The Human as a Divine Being

According to the Judaeo-Christian tradition, humans are made in the image of God. They are essentially divine beings. What makes them divine is that they contain something of the self-consciousness and ability to love that characterize their Creator.

This ability to love is the distinguishing characteristic of the Judaeo-Christian divine view. Whereas the Greeks held that only those capable of attaining theoretical and moral knowledge could realize the purpose of living, the divine view contends that the two purposes of life—loving God and serving God—are open to all regardless of intelligence. As St. Paul writes, "If I understand all mysteries and all knowledge . . . but have not love, I am nothing" (*Corinthians* 13:2). Being given by God, this love is divine, and so allows humans to share in divinity.

At the same time, the divine view is hardly a denial of the classical view. On the contrary, Plato strongly influenced Christian thought through philosophers such as the Roman Plotinus (205?–270?) and the early Christian St. Augustine (354–430). We observe in their philosophies a similar dualism of mind and body and a belief in the uniqueness of the human mind. But the divine view also holds that a single personal God created humans in His own image; that is, He endowed His creation with self-consciousness and the ability to love. This ability is what makes human beings unique.

What views of the self is this divine view likely to foster? First, since the universe is the expression of an intelligent mind (God), the believer is likely to see himself as being part of a universe in whose meaning and purpose he personally shares through fellowship with God. One's purpose in life, therefore, is found in serving and loving God.

For the Christian, the way to serve and love God is by imitating the life of Jesus of Nazareth. There we find a living expression of the highest virtue: love. We love when we perform selfless acts, develop a keen sense of social-mindedness, and realize that people are creatures of God and are thereby intrinsically worthwhile.

For the Jew, one serves and loves God primarily through expressions of justice and righteousness. One also develops a sense of honor, derived from a commitment to the ideals of truth, humility, fidelity, and kindness. Commitment to these ideals produces a sharp sense of responsibility to family and community.

The divine view also fosters the concept of a moral self. In this view each of us is capable of great good, but also of great evil. When we refuse to serve and love God, we commit our greatest evil. There exist various expressions of this refusal, such as injustice, vanity, pride, and dishonesty. Whenever we commit these offenses to the will and nature of God, we lose touch with ourselves by retreating from alliance with God. In contrast to the Greek belief that we must develop our rational powers to perceive the moral order in the universe, the divine view holds that intelligence is no prerequisite for a moral sense. We do good when we make God the center of our lives; we do wrong when we retreat from this commitment.

That we can make moral decisions implies that we are *free* to make them. Moral freedom, then, is another feature of the self fostered by the divine view. As a divine creation we are supposedly free to choose a course that will bring us closer to or take us away from our Creator. As a result, we bear full responsibility for our moral choices and cannot blame external factors for our failure to love and serve God.

As we noted, the views of the human as a rational and as a divine being have been the most influential in Western civilization. In them we find the intellectual emphasis of the Greeks and the religious emphasis of the Jews and Christians. From them we inherit the view that there exists an essential human nature shared by all individuals. In this sense human nature precedes any particular human being; the universal human prototype (Adam and Eve) precedes the individual human experience.

In the twentieth century two additional views have arisen, both of which deny any essential human nature. As a result, their influences on one's self-concept are different in emphasis from those of the rational and divine views. One of these views holds that the human is a mechanical being; the other holds that the human is an existential being. Apart from their common belief that there is no essential human nature, these two views share very few other beliefs.

Reflection   You are standing before a mirror. Suddenly some strange changes begin to occur. Your limbs begin to change their size and their spatial relationships to one another. Your face becomes like silly putty and distorts; hair sprouts all over your body. You no longer see *you* but a monkey. Yet in all other respects, you remain the same. You can speak to communicate your shock, to tell others you are really the same person, to assure them you can recall your pre-monkey state. In short, except for looking precisely like a monkey, you remain unchanged. Are you *you*?

The Human as a Mechanical Being

Because of science's increasing impact on our outlook, a strong contemporary tendency is to view the human scientifically—as being subject to the same scientific laws that inanimate life is subject to. In brief, this view contends that humans are mechanical.

Proponents of this view acknowledge that the human is more complex than other mechanisms, but that ultimately he or she will be explained in terms of the natural sciences, physics and chemistry. In their opinion there is no essential "human nature" in the classical or religious sense; there is no so-called mind or ability to love that makes us unique. Neither is there any way that we are *supposed* to be. Rather, we are the sum total of our experiences.

Thus, when proponents of the mechanical view use the term *self*, they are referring to an integrated system of responses that genetics and environment cause. Although they often differ among themselves on other points, those holding this view insist that the individual is basically a passive object—something acted upon, something that really cannot help acting in any way but the way it does. This position has been advanced particularly by the emergence of the social sciences (the studies of society and of individual relationships in and to society), generally including sociology, psychology, anthropology, economics, political science, and history.

Even a cursory reading of the social sciences reveals the widespread belief that humans are somehow "driven" beings; that is, they are moved by outer and inner needs or urges to behave the way they do. Historically there has been debate over precisely what those needs are.

For example, political philosopher Karl Marx (1818–1883) rejected the primacy of reason and the divine origins of humankind. According to Marx, material forces produce both human nature and societal tendencies. What changes social structure is the production and reproduction of life. The primary need, said Marx, is to survive. How we make a living, therefore, is of utmost importance, for the primary social characteristic that drives humans is their productive capacity. Because we are economic animals, to a large extent we are driven and ruled by our need to produce in order to survive. We can influence our life and history to a degree by altering the conditions under which we live, but this capacity does not reside in our brains, wills, ideas, or desires. It exists, said Marx, mainly in the means of production and the class dynamics of society.

Philosopher Friedrich Nietzsche (1840–1900) also believed that humans are "driven," but not so much by economics as by power. Even on the subconscious level, thought Nietzsche, we express our will to power by trying to dominate the weak. Because society frequently disapproves of this drive, we inhibit it and express it through socially acceptable channels. Even when people appear free of power drives, said Nietzsche, they are invariably engaged in a power-struggle relationship. Thus, the "humility" that an employee shows to his employer is an expression and further reinforcement of the relationship between them, which is one of inferior to superior. In Nietzsche's view, many of the values preached by classical Greece and Christianity, such as justice, charity, and humility, are part of a "herd morality," exaltation of the virtues of the weak based on antagonism for the strong.

Much twentieth-century psychoanalytic literature, in its examination of inner drives, has further advanced the view of the human as mechanical. Psychoanalyst Sigmund Freud (1856–1939), for example, held that nothing we do is haphazard or coincidental but that everything we do results from mental causes, most of which we are unaware of. For Freud the mind is not synonymous with what is conscious or potentially conscious, but includes forces of which we are ignorant. This "unconsciousness" is a deep level of human motivation in which resides a reservoir of instincts. In general, most of what we think, believe, and do is the result of unconscious urges, especially as they develop in the first five years of life in response to traumatic experiences.

Although there is a tendency in Marx, Nietzsche, and Freud to view the human mechanically, they still seem to support the notion of a basic human nature. But as the social sciences have continued to grow, and with the increasing influence of the natural sciences, the belief in an essential human nature has steadily declined. As a result, today the tendency is to view humans as strictly mechanical. This view has received impetus from psychological **behaviorism**, a school of psychology that restricts the study of humans to what can be objectively observed— namely, human behavior.

Founded by John B. Watson and popularized by B. F. Skinner, behaviorism is not concerned with human motives, goals, purposes of speech, or action. As Watson puts it, a human being is simply "an assembled organic machine ready to run." As a result, behaviorists view all humans as empty organisms equipped with the same neural mechanisms, awaiting conditioning and programming. Phenomena such as will, impulse, feeling, and purpose find no place in psychological behaviorism. We are, in effect, mechanisms that are shaped and controlled by our environment. By facing this fact, say the behaviorists, we will better cope with the human condition by concentrating on the outer factors that mold human behavior, not on the nonexistent inner ones.

In discussing the rational and divine theories of human nature, we saw that they insist that mind and body are essentially different—that the mind is immaterial, the body material. In contrast, the mechanical view makes no such distinction, but insists that all is matter. Neither does it distinguish between humans and other creatures of nature. Mechanists would argue that human phenomena are as much the products of material forces as are other organic and inorganic phenomena. This position leads to a concept of self decidedly different from that springing from the rational and divine views.

According to the mechanical view, the self is not primarily mind and certainly not unique. Rather, everyone is essentially the same empty organism awaiting the input of environmental forces. In effect, the individual's behavior is not free but determined.

Determinism is the theory that everything in the universe, humans included, is totally ruled by causal laws. In other words, nothing happens in the universe without a natural cause. Determinists claim that what happens in any given moment is the result of what occurred at some previous time; that is, the present is always determined by the past. The view of the human as mechanical would apply determinism to people, claiming that such sciences as physics, chemistry, biology, psychology, and sociology can show us how humans, like everything else, are ruled by cause and effect. The inevitable conclusion, they insist, is that humans are not free; that there is no individual freedom. Lacking freedom, we cannot view ourselves as morally responsible for our actions, as both the classical and the religious views require. As Skinner puts it, "The free inner man who is held responsible for the behavior of the external biological organism is only a prescientific substitute for the kinds of causes which are discovered in the course of a scientific analysis. All these alternatives lie outside the individual."[1]

Another twentieth-century view, which differs from psychological behaviorism, denies any essential human nature but contends that humans are ultimately free of their genetic and environmental influences to control what and who they will be. This view sees humans as agents actively engaged in the world around them.

---

[1]B. F. Skinner. *Science and Human Behavior*. New York: Free Press, 1965, p. 285.

Reflection It is the year 2050. Human brain transplants have become a reality. You have a terminal brain disease and must have a brain transplant. The operation is so successful that you no longer have any consciousness of who you were before the operation. In fact, you must take the word of the surgeons that you were indeed ill and had such a transplant. Just who are you?

The Human as an Existential Being

Although the theory that humans are agents actively engaged in determining what they will be is not new, it appears full blown in our century in a philosophy called **existentialism**. Existentialists focus on individual existence and its problems. They deny any essential human nature, insisting that individuals create their own characters throughout their lifetimes through free, responsible choices and actions. Humans are active participants in the world, not determined mechanisms. Although they recognize outside influences, existentialists insist that each self determines its own "human nature."

The chief exponent of atheistic existentialism is Jean-Paul Sartre (1905–), who sees humans as "condemned to be free." We are free because we can rely neither on a nonexistent God nor on society to justify our actions or to tell us what we essentially are. We are condemned because without absolute guidelines we must suffer the agony of our own decision-making and the anguish of its consequences.

Although he believes that there are no "true" universal statements about what humans ought to be, Sartre does make at least one general statement about the human condition: we are free. This freedom consists chiefly of our ability to envisage additional possibilities to our state, to conceive of what is not the case, to suspend judgment, to be different from what we are.

To illustrate, many believe that we have little or no control over our emotions. If we're depressed, we're depressed, and there's little we can do about it. Sartre argues that if we're depressed it's because we've chosen to make ourselves depressed. Emotions, he says, are not moods that come over us but ways we freely choose to perceive the world. It is the consciousness of this freedom and its accompanying responsibilities that cause our anguish. The most anguishing thought of all is that ultimately we don't know how we will behave next. Sometimes we escape this anguish by pretending we are not free, as when we pretend that our genes or our environment is the cause of how we are or act. When we so pretend, says Sartre, we act in "bad faith." To guard against acting in bad faith, he cautions us to make individual choices fully aware that we are the ones making them. This includes taking full responsibility not only for our actions but also for our beliefs, feelings, and attitudes.

Existentialism obviously puts great emphasis on the individual. The self in this view is not necessarily rational, divine, or mechanical. It is neither a creature of God nor a "kind of moss, or a fungus, or a cauliflower." The self is "a project which possesses a subjective life"; it is the sum total of everything it ever does. "We are our choices. Man is freedom."[2]

In addition, existentialism gives the inner life and experience a new emphasis. Whereas those seeing the self as a response to stimuli ignore the inner world of feelings, sensations, moods, and anxieties, existentialists focus on it. Indeed, this inner life is precisely what the self experiences, and thus it is the self. In it are found our feelings of despair, fear, guilt, and isolation, as well as our uncertainties, especially about death. There, too, we confront the meaninglessness that is at the core of existence. And when the self confronts this meaninglessness, this "sickness unto death," it discovers a truth that enables it to live fully conscious of what it means to be human.

Despite existentialism's assertion of self and its wide contemporary influence, many argue that the self is really an illusion, that it is attachment to this illusion that causes so much existential sorrow, anguish, and ultimate absurdity. Psychological behaviorists would probably so argue. But this reaction has become increasingly popular in the West with the spread of Oriental philosophies and religions that deny the existence of an essential human nature and of the self.

The Human as No Self

Oriental thought offers many views of human nature. It is impossible to mention them all, but Buddhism's view is particularly noteworthy for several reasons. First, it represents a large number of Eastern thinkers. Second, it has converted many Westerners to its view. Third, it contrasts sharply with most Western views.

Central to Buddhist thought is belief in constant movement and change characterizing all existence. Since "all is change," there is no fixed or static human nature. Nevertheless, like existentialists, Buddhists do make statements about the human condition. These can be summed up in the Buddhist doctrine of the Four Noble Truths.

The first of these truths is the existence of suffering. From birth to death, life is a succession of physical and psychological torments that

---

[2]Jean-Paul Sartre. "Existentialism," in W. Kaufman (Ed.), *Existentialism from Dostoevsky to Sartre.* New York: World Publishing, 1965, p. 291.

"'We are our choices. Man is freedom.'"

leaves no one untouched. Yes, for a time we may ward off suffering with youth, health, and riches, but ultimately we experience it. Suffering is a universal problem in a finite and ever-changing world.

The Second Noble Truth concerns the cause of this suffering. We suffer because we desire or crave all sorts of things. The insidious nature of these "thirsts" is that the more we try to satisfy them the worse they become. The more we get the more we want and the more we must have. When these desires run unchecked they leave us frustrated and unhappy. But they need not control us. When we master them we attain a peace and serenity that no amount of appetite-feeding can match.

The Third Noble Truth is that release from this seemingly endless round of pleasure-pursuit is possible. We gain this release by realizing that the true nature of self is not found in trying to satisfy our desires. Rather, we must fortify ourselves with values that are contrary to these desires. When we do, we will ease pain, suffering, and unhappiness.

The values that express the true nature of self are found in the Fourth Noble Truth: that we gain release from suffering through the Noble Eightfold Path. This path consists of the following steps:

1. *Right understanding.* Humans must realize that the only way out of pain and suffering is to know their true selves, abandon ignorance about the self, and eliminate craving and desire. Without understanding we do not know how to escape our predicament.
2. *Right intention or purpose.* We must want release from our dilemma and commit ourselves to discovering self-knowledge. Without purpose we will not do what we must to find peace.

3. *Right speech.* One sign that we are serious about attaining enlightenment is that our speech is above reproach. We must never lie, gossip, slander, boast, flatter, or threaten.
4. *Right conduct.* Just as speech reflects the quality of our intention, so does conduct. Seekers of enlightenment never kill or harm any living creature. Neither do they pollute their bodies with meats and liquors.
5. *Right way of livelihood.* How we earn a living must be compatible with our goal of enlightenment. For example, seeking material self-enrichment, such as money and status, further excites desires and leads us from the path of true self-knowledge. Working in the service of other people, on the other hand, helps to quell these desires and keep us directed toward our goal.
6. *Right effort.* Speech, conduct, and way of living are not substitutes for discipline. Right effort involves constantly checking desires and cravings and conceding no morsel of gratification to them.
7. *Right mindfulness.* The interior life is as important as the exterior; what we think is as important as what we do. Just as we must not give in to desires, so we must not even think about them. All action originates in thought. When the thought is right, so will the action be.
8. *Right concentration.* The best way to ensure right mindfulness is through meditation and concentration, the spine of the Eightfold Way. Through reflective practices and concentrated voyages into the interior self, we can gain enlightenment.

Enlightenment, in Buddhist doctrine, is the state of "pure joy." This joy may come after long-practiced meditation and is not dependent on other people or on our own egos. We are enlightened when we are no longer selves or egos but a part of all that is, part of the flow of universal energy. We so merge with this flow of energy that we are one with it. Nothing can still or limit the joy of this merging, not even thoughts of death; for there is no death for the energy of the universe. And since we are one with this energy, we too will always exist, not as particular human beings but as embodiments of eternal Being. When we realize this, we abandon self-centered concerns and gain release from the endless round of change and impermanence.

Although to ease explanation even Buddhist scholars must use the word *self*, Buddhists contend that there is no self as we are accustomed to viewing it. In fact, any attempt to characterize the self as a rational, divine, mechanical, or existential being is destined to fail. Likewise, any attempt to affirm our egos is doomed to misery.

Instead of a self, Buddhist teaching poses a merging of five "streams" of physical sensations, feelings, perceptions, ideas, and consciousness. These streams, called *skandhas*, comprise being and *an-atta*, the "no self." In denying self and ego, Buddhists assert that there is nothing permanent, everlasting, or absolute. According to the Buddha, the idea of self is an imaginary, false belief that produces harmful thoughts of "me," "mine," desire, vanity, egoism, and ill will.

SOME OBSERVATIONS ABOUT THE VIEWS OF HUMAN NATURE

In examining any one view, there is a tendency to see it as excluding others. But it is rare that any of these theories does that. The rational, divine, and existential views, for example, all agree on the human's essential freedom. The mechanical and Buddhist views are agreed that the self does not exist in the way that traditional Western thought would have it. Nietzsche, while perhaps advancing the cause of the mechanical view, at the same time viewed humans as active agents, as existential beings.

You yourself might hold a traditional view that the human is a combination of mind and body. You might consider the mind immaterial and immortal, the body material and mortal. You would probably view yourself, then, as rational and mechanical. So these traditions do overlap, and "combination" views are not only common but seemingly necessary to account for the full range of human experience. Where differences in views do appear, they are differences of emphasis more often than of content.

Thinkers obviously disagree about which aspect of the human experience deserves the most emphasis. Differences in emphases have produced these different positions about human nature. But no position is watertight. Each offers a different aspect of what it means to be human, but none completely describes that phenomenon. Nevertheless, the tendencies of recent decades have been to view the human as a mechanical being or as an existential being.

A corollary to the mechanical view is the denial of mental states— that is, conscious experiences like thought, feeling, and sensation. Mechanists choose to view what we traditionally have called mental states as brain states—conditions of the brain produced by neural impulses. Thus thought, feelings, and sensations, they claim, are really conditions of the central nervous system. Other mechanists, although not denying the existence of mental states, speak of them in terms of physical states. For them, mental states are secondary phenomena that sometimes accompany physical processes. Feelings, thoughts, sensations, emotions, and other mental states are shadows or reflections cast by material phenomena. They are to the brain as smoke is to fire. Only the brain and fire cause anything; mental states and smoke are a kind of glow or shadow that appears under certain physical conditions.

On the other hand, existentialists claim that such positions unjustifiably deny the self, that they remove from the series of total events the most necessary element: the individual person. It is impossible to talk about experiences, they argue, without experiencers. In other words, every event must belong to some individual self that experiences it. Without the individual "I" it is impossible even to talk about experiences.

In the last analysis, it is unlikely that any one theory will or can fully describe and explain human nature. The most reasonable position seems to be one that does not oversimplify by allowing its own focus to distort and ignore other aspects of human experience, and one that can accommodate additional data about the human condition. Although we cannot say which view this is, the acceptance or rejection of a particular view can and does influence our lives and the way we interpret other issues. The issue of freedom, which we have already referred to, is a good example. Whether we consider ourselves free, partially free, or not free at all depends to a large extent on what view of human nature we hold. Whether we consider ourselves free also influences how we live.

Reflection   Write a detailed verbal profile of yourself. Which characteristics could you lose and still be you?

FREEDOM AND SELF

Freedom is an extremely complex issue that requires more pages here than we can give to it. So let us simply define freedom as the ability to choose for yourself from among alternatives.

Defining freedom this way, you probably consider yourself free. After all, if you set out to buy a new car, you can choose for yourself from among alternatives. And yet you are not absolutely free, for there are factors operating that appear to limit your freedom. For example, suppose you have little money. This factor so limits your freedom to choose that you may be inclined to buy an "economy car," one that needs little upkeep and gets good gas mileage. And if your friends all show a preference for a particular car, that may be a further factor in your choice. Even your own physical build could pose a limitation. If you are a particularly tall or stout person, you obviously must consider that fact in your selection.

After making a list of all the influences affecting your decision, you may be tempted to conclude that you were choosing far less freely than you at first thought. Realizing the multitude of psychological and physiological factors involved, you may even conclude that you yourself are not choosing at all, but that the decision is determined for you. If you do reach this conclusion, you may feel like a computer that can do only what it is programmed to do. Although the question of your choice of car is probably not very important, the one it illustrates is: Are you free? If so, how free?

Whether or not you have ever seriously thought about the question, you have already acted innumerable times as if you were certain of the answer. Right now you perceive yourself as free, not free, or somewhere in between. And it is likely that the views of human nature we have mentioned have had some influence in your evaluation. Take, as one example, the view of the human as a divine being. Typical of this outlook is the belief in **free will**.

Freedom as Free Will (The Divine View)

The divine view of the human believes in free will as the God-given capacity to make voluntary decisions, to choose freely from among alternatives. This free will is considered a uniquely human characteristic. Given this religious tradition, we may live much of our lives in the comfortable assumption that we are free, responsible masters of our lives.

To illustrate this aspect of a self-concept, consider the case of Doris, who has grown up in this religious tradition. Like many of us, Doris has never really given the issue of freedom much thought. She takes freedom for granted. But something has happened to cause her to question her assumptions.

Having begun college, Doris must start thinking about what she is going to do with her life. Had she lived a generation or two ago, she probably would not have even debated the question. She most likely would have become a wife and mother and not given the matter too much thought. But times have changed; circumstances are different. "It's just not that simple anymore," she tells her tradition-minded parents, who still are not convinced that college is the proper place for their daughter. But if it is, why shouldn't she take something "practical," like business or nursing? A woman can always find work as a secretary or nurse, they tell her, or perhaps as an elementary school teacher.

The fact is that Doris has begun to major in elementary school education. But she is dissatisfied. She finds the curriculum not challenging enough for her and the prospect of life in a classroom not particularly attractive. Lately she has begun to think about law. She has always been extremely good in the humanities, and she enjoys working with people. But studying law hardly seems the "practical" thing to do. It is expensive, gruelling, and uncertain. And even if she does complete law school, what is the future for a female lawyer? Prospects are improving, but they are still uncertain. And what about all the pressure along the way? Already many of her friends are married; others are set on traditional "female professions."

In brief, Doris is in a quandary. Everything tells her to do the "practical" thing. And yet more than anything else she wants to feel that she alone is making the choice and not her parents, friends, or society. She wants to feel free. She is convinced that making the decision is tough enough without feeling that she is not really making it herself. Doris's problem cuts to the very assumption on which she has based her life, in this case the assumption that springs from the view of the human as a divine being.

It is true that other theories of human nature support concepts of human freedom; but, again, because their emphases are different they foster different outlooks. For example, the view of the human as primarily rational agrees that we are free but does not hold that this freedom is a God-given quality. Rather, freedom springs from our nature as beings who can use reason to achieve self-awareness and subsequently make choices. Similarly, the existentialist view stresses freedom, but freedom as an essential part of being human. In other words, because we are human we are free. Contrasting with these two views are the mechanical and the Oriental views, both of which generally deny the existence of personal freedom. Let us illustrate these different emphases by seeing how Doris attempts to deal with her problem.

Reflection   What influences do you perceive operating in your career choice? If you could do anything you wanted, what would you choose? If it is different from your intended career, why?

Freedom as Self-Awareness (The Rational View)

Feeling the pinch of her dilemma, Doris seeks advice from a friend, Jane. Jane does not believe in the religious concept of free will. Rather, she considers herself primarily a thinker, a person who through commitment to thought and reason tries to solve her problems as a rational being. Let us see what advice Jane gives Doris.

Doris: I've decided to be a teacher.

Jane: Are you sure that's what you want to do?

Doris: No, but I'm tired of weighing the pros and cons. It's decided, and that's the end of it.

Jane: *It's* decided? A second ago you said *you* decided.

Doris: I mean I. *I* have decided.

Jane: Okay, why do you want to be a teacher?

Doris: Look, Jane, I really don't want to go through all this again.

Jane: I really think you should.

Doris: But what good will it do?

Jane: It might stop you from doing something you'll regret.

Doris: Whatever I do I'm going to regret.

Jane: Okay, so you have two unpleasant alternatives. By thoroughly examining them, at least you'll have the comfort of knowing why you made the decision.

Doris: Is that so important—to know why?

Jane: Well, just think. If you don't know why you're choosing something, how do you know *you* are choosing it? Remember when you bought your car?

Doris: Sure.

Jane: Did you know why you bought it?

Doris: Of course. I needed transportation.

Jane: And you wanted something small, cheap, and dependable.

Doris: Right.

Jane: You knew why you were buying the car. And if someone asked, you could have told him.

Doris: So?

Jane: Well, isn't this choice as important as buying a car?

Doris: Of course it is.

Jane: Then why do you want to be a teacher?

Doris: For a lot of reasons. For one, my parents think it's a good idea.

Jane: Sure they do, but for their reasons.

Doris: What do you mean?

Jane: Well, *they're* not becoming a teacher—you are. They're not the ones who must spend the rest of their professional lives in a classroom—you are.

Doris: You make them sound terrible.

Jane: I'm sorry, I don't mean to. I'm just trying to help you see sides of the question that you don't seem to be aware of.

Doris: Do you really believe I'm not being honest with myself about this?

Jane: I don't know. But I do know that if *you* are really going to choose, you should be aware of *why* you're choosing. Otherwise you're having the choice made for you. And that's what's really going to hurt over the long haul—much more than if you make the so-called right choice.

Doris: You know, Jane, you've got me thinking.

Jane: In what way?

Doris: Well, I'm just wondering how many things that I'm not aware of are influencing this choice.

Jane: Right. Now you're reaching for some self-insight. You've taken the first step toward choosing for yourself.

Doris: I don't know if that's so good. After all, I can never be aware of everything.

Jane: Of course not.

Doris: And I can't even be aware of what has limited my self-awareness.

Jane: I don't follow.

Doris: Look, you're saying that I'm not really making my own choice unless I'm aware of the hidden influences in it, right?

Jane: Right.

Doris: Well, what about my awareness itself? Couldn't it also be a victim of the same influences? How much of my own awareness has been limited by the very things you're asking me to look at?

Jane: I see what you mean.

Essentially, Jane's view is that of the human as a reasoning being. So she encourages Doris to think and reflect, to develop insightful awareness. Jane sees herself as someone who is free only to the degree that she is aware of the factors affecting her choice. The less aware, the less free she is; the more aware, the more free she is.

Jane seems to be saying that Doris must *learn* to be free. Doris points out that this is begging the question. After all, Jane admits there are many factors affecting Doris's decision. Aren't these same factors affecting how well she can learn and how much awareness she can have? How much self-insight can she develop? Suppose Doris was never encouraged to be self-aware. Suppose self-awareness was not a value in her upbringing. Can she all of a sudden develop self-awareness? Then there's another problem. If we are to become self-aware for self-awareness's own sake, there seems to be little point in making any decision at all. Just become aware of the factors affecting a decision. But presumably we become self-aware to reach the "right" decision. Jane seems to imply that if Doris just thinks hard and long enough she will see the "right" thing to do. True, the universe seems to be governed by physical laws, like the laws of motion and gravity, and through thought and reason we discover them. But are there other laws at work as well that await our discovery?

The ability to reflect seems a double-edged sword. On the one hand, it can lead us to valuable self-insights, to an understanding of the factors influencing our decisions. On the other, it can make us acutely aware of so many of these factors that it may confirm in us the suspicion that we are not free at all, which can lead us to the position that there is no freedom. The belief that freedom is an illusion is an integral part of the mechanical and Buddhist views.

Reflection   Make a detailed list of all the factors you can think of that have brought you to read this book at this time. Begin with the obvious ones—"because it was assigned." Then move to the less apparent ones—"because I went to this college."

Freedom as Illusion
(The Mechanical and No-Self Views)

At the conclusion of her conversation with Jane, Doris wonders whether those very influences Jane mentioned as affecting her choice are also influencing her ability to be aware of those influences. Taking Jane's advice to think, introspect, and become self-aware, Doris examines the factors bearing on her choice. What she discovers is a whole list of influences: parents, home life, education, friends, and so forth.

For example, she recalls how as a little girl she was given dolls and doll houses to play with, encouraged to think of marriage and family, and sheltered from considering professional possibilities like medicine, engineering, or law. In fact, she can't think of a single instance when someone asked her "What are you going to be when you grow up?" although she recalls that they often asked that of her brother. What she would be seemed a foregone conclusion: a wife and mother.

Such considerations set her to thinking about just how free any person is in light of all the environmental and hereditary influences affecting us. She wonders if we can behave any differently from the way we are programmed to. Thinking along this line, Doris concludes that she cannot help acting as she will, for her past is determining her future.

This view of freedom smacks of the human as a mechanical being. But it also seems consistent with the Buddhist concept of freedom. The Buddhists view everything that exists as interconnected; everything depends on and is influenced by everything else. Indeed, no thing can be fully understood except in relation to everything else—in terms of the principles of conditionality, relativity, and interdependence. This interdependence of all things is summed up in the Buddhist formula of **conditioned genesis**, which consists of 12 factors:

1. Through ignorance are conditioned volitional actions.
2. Through volitional actions is conditioned consciousness.
3. Through consciousness are conditioned mental and physical phenomena.
4. Through mental and physical phenomena are conditioned the six faculties (i.e., five physical sense organs and mind).
5. Through the six faculties is conditioned (sensorial and mental) contact.
6. Through (sensorial and mental) contact is conditioned sensation.
7. Through sensation is conditioned desire, "thirst."
8. Through desire ("thirst") is conditioned clinging.
9. Through clinging is conditioned the process of becoming.
10. Through the process of becoming is conditioned birth.
11. Through birth are conditioned . . . (12) decay, death, lamentation, pain, etc.[3]

Therefore, nothing—physical or mental—is absolutely free, because everything is relative and conditioned. Since the whole of existence is relative and conditioned, there can be no freedom, for freedom implies something independent of conditions.

Many claim to see in our society a trend toward viewing freedom as illusion. They point to judicial decisions that frequently find the environment guilty rather than the defendant, to schools that are disinclined to hold students academically accountable, or to welfare programs that appear calculated to destroy initiative and personal responsibility. These trends, they say, suggest that we do not really believe that individuals are free to alter the conditions of their lives. In contrast, those who view the human as an existential being claim that we are by nature free and self-determining.

Freedom as a State of Being (The Existential View)

Discontent with the idea that she is not at all free, Doris confides in another friend, Fred. Fred sees humans as active participants in the world around them. They are by nature free to choose and direct the courses of their lives. Although this sounds like the concept of free

---

[3]Wahola Rahula. *What the Buddha Taught*. New York: Grove Press, 1962, p. 55. Copyright © 1959 by W. Rahula. Second and Enlarged Edition © by W. Rahula. All rights reserved. Reprinted by permission of Grove Press, Inc.

will, Fred's sense of freedom poses no God from whom freedom springs. Rather, it contends that freedom is an integral part of being human.

Doris cannot quite believe that she is free in the way Fred says she is. She asks him whether, if she introspects enough, she will discover the "right" thing to do. Fred points out that it isn't a question of the "right" thing to do. If there were a right decision to be made, he says, we would be under an obligation to discover it. But obligations are the opposite of freedom; they restrict and limit rather than liberate. Her job, Fred tells Doris, is not to discover the so-called right decision but to *make* it. And in making it she will make herself. Doris doesn't quite understand.

"Right now," says Fred, "you're like an empty canvas that sits waiting for the artist to put shape and color and form on it for meaning. It sits awaiting its real identity."

"But the paints, what about the paints? Aren't they just everything that's ever happened to me? Aren't they what give 'me' meaning?"

"No. It's the painter who does that. What paints are used—color, tone, perspective—are left to the artist, to you in this case. And if no painting ever appears on the canvas, that too is up to the artist, up to you."

Fred sees Doris as an agent engaged in her own self-definition. He admits that the past influences the present and the present the future. But humans are not mechanical, they are not objects. They are subjects; they are acted upon, but they act as well. It is this dimension, the "I" as agent, that provides us with freedom. Simply by being, we are free. This freedom allows us to determine what we will be, to fashion meaning out of experience. There are no "shoulds" or "musts," for these would bind us to obligations not of our own making. There is no right or wrong waiting to be followed or found. There just *is*. We exist, and why we exist is up to each of us to say. The whole meaning of our lives lies in creating our own reasons for being.

Reflection   Pretend you are a surgeon preparing to operate on an important political leader. A terrorist group kidnaps the person you love the most and threatens to murder him or her unless you cooperate with them by killing the leader. After great anguish you turn the affair over to the authorities. The terrorists murder your loved one. You console yourself with the thought that there was nothing else you could have done. Precisely what do you mean, and are you accurate?

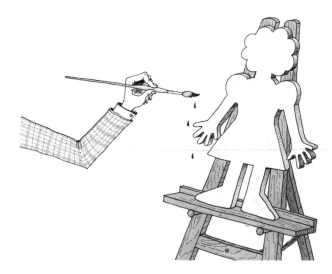

"'. . . you're like an empty canvas that sits
waiting for the artist to put shape and
color and form on it for meaning.'"

CONCLUSIONS

Doris's predicament illustrates how various theories of human nature influence our views of one aspect of self, personal freedom. It also reinforces the fact that these views do not exist in isolation, that they often melt into one another. We seldom find ourselves acting exclusively according to one school of thought; more often we must deal with the influences of several. Finally, it should provoke some personal reflections about what we believe and why.

But how we view personal freedom is only one aspect of who and what we are. There are others: what we know, what we consider to be ultimately real, what we cherish as objects of ultimate loyalty, what we hold to be morally right, what we regard as beautiful, and so on. All are fundamental expressions of how we see ourselves. And, as with the issue of personal freedom, our beliefs in these areas betray many influences. We will explore these influences in further chapters, for these subjects are among those that constitute the study of **philosophy.**

Over 2000 years ago the Greek philosopher Socrates (469–399 B.C.) claimed that "the unexamined life is not worth living." When humans begin to examine life, they begin to philosophize. Philosophers are persons who perceive to some degree the ways that the many experiences and insights of their existence form a pattern of meaning. Philosophy, then, is an activity undertaken by those who are deeply concerned with who and what they are and what everything means. You are about to undertake that activity.

SUMMARY

We opened the chapter by raising the issue of self as it applies to personal identity: who and what am I? What you believe is at least part of the answer to that question. Our beliefs are strongly influenced by our intellectual heritage. If we are to identify ourselves, we should be aware of this heritage. How we see ourselves has been influenced by at least five theories of human nature. Although it is impossible to say which theory is the most accurate, we frequently interpret aspects of our lives through them, as we do with the issue of personal freedom. In the chapters ahead we will examine various aspects of the self-identity question through the study of philosophy.

MAIN POINTS

1. "Human nature" refers to what it means to be one of our species, what makes us different from anything else.
2. The view of the human as a rational being, dating from the ancient Greeks, contends that humans are primarily reasoning creatures. This view fosters a concept of the self as something existing apart from and above the objective world around it and as capable of discovering truth, beauty, and goodness. It also fosters a view of freedom as self-awareness.
3. The view of the human as a divine being, rooted in Judaeo-Christian thought, claims that humans are unique because they are made in the image of God, their Creator, who has endowed them with self-consciousness and an ability to love. This concept fosters a view of self that is purposeful and moral and that possesses free will.
4. The view of the human as a mechanical being denies any essential human nature. It asserts that humans are driven by inner needs and that they are the products of their experiences. Twentieth-century psychological behaviorism has advanced this view by making no distinction between body and mind or between humans and nature. Concepts like purpose, morality, and will are, say the behaviorists, the results of prescientific thinking. Everything is determined; that is, everything can be explained in terms of cause and effect. There is no personal freedom.
5. The view of the human as an existential being, while denying the existence of any essential human nature, also denies that we are only products of our environment. Rather, it asserts that, although

there is no essential self, there is an existing self, and that the self is a freely choosing, active agent. Self, as Sartre argues, is choice.

6. The human as no self is the Buddhist doctrine that denies both a human nature and a self. These concepts are imaginary and arise from deep-seated psychological needs for self-protection and self-preservation. Freedom is an illusion.

SECTION EXERCISES

The Human as a Rational Being

1. Some people argue that the fact that nonhuman animals can think proves that humans are not unique at all. What is the difference between thinking and reasoning? What mental states would you say indicate a thinking process? Would you say that reasoning presumes thinking, but that thinking does not presume reasoning?
2. What historical evidence would you say indicates we are rational animals? What evidence would you say indicates we are not?

The Human as a Divine Being

1. How do the rational and divine views foster a concept of the human as at odds with nature? Does history indicate that we have lived up to this concept in the Western world? Does contemporary experience confirm or challenge the wisdom of this concept?
2. Do you think that in general religions have not emphasized the God-given capacity to love so much as other concepts, such as sinful human nature, reward and punishment, and adherence to dogma?

The Human as a Mechanical Being

1. Psychological behaviorists claim that the human can be measured experimentally. Are there any human characteristics that defy this claim? What human qualities cannot be measured?
2. Behaviorists also argue that there are techniques and engineering practices that can so shape behavior that people will function harmoniously for everyone's benefit. What questions would you raise about such a proposal?

The Human as an Existential Being

1. Sartre's existentialism leaves us without moral rules or behavioral guidelines, yet it holds us ultimately responsible for all our choices.

Do you find such a view appealing? Contradictory? Unsettling? Liberating?

2. To what degree and in what ways, if any, do you experience your life as free, as Sartre describes freedom?

The Human as No Self

1. Both the Buddhist and the mechanical views deny the existence of self. But how and why they do are quite different. Describe the contrasts.
2. Does the view of no self have anything to offer the Western world? In what areas?

Freedom as Free Will

1. Political polls and projections are often said to influence the outcome of elections. What control, if any, does a forecast exercise over an event (for example, the astrological prophecies of Jeanne Dixon)? Assuming the existence of God, if He already knows how things are going to turn out, can any of us alter that result? If we cannot alter something, are we free?
2. In the *Crito*, Plato shows Socrates refusing to break out of jail, even though he has been imprisoned unjustly, because such an action would violate the principles of a life dedicated to upholding the law. As a result, Socrates drinks the hemlock and dies. Was he free to choose differently? Was he a victim of his past?

Freedom as Self-Awareness

1. Jane claims "By thorough self-examination, at least you'll have the comfort of knowing *why* you made the decision. . . . If you don't know why you're choosing something, how do you know *you* are choosing it?" Relative to the problem of self, how important would you say it is to know *why* you do something? In what sense are you less "yourself" by not knowing? Can you think of an instance in which it may be better not to know why you're doing something? Would it be better in the long term as well as the short?
2. Point to examples in your own life that show you doing things for other people's reasons. Perhaps your choice to be in school or to study a particular subject would be a good place to begin. How susceptible to peer pressure do you think you are? Do you detect the pressure affecting the views you hold? In what area of life do you feel you can truly express yourself?

3. Doris suggests that the very faculty of self-awareness may be a victim of the same influences Jane claims might be affecting Doris's decision. Can you illustrate Doris's suggestion?

Freedom as Illusion

1. Are we strictly mechanical, as Doris suspects? Can you think of qualities we possess that computers do not? Are they qualities computers *can never* possess, or qualities they do not possess now but could in the future?
2. **Fatalism** is the belief that events are fixed, that there's nothing we can do to alter them—that what will be, will be. Is Doris a fatalist? Are you? Does the view of the mechanical human necessitate fatalism? Is fatalism consistent with the doctrine of free will? Is it consistent with the view of the human as thinker? As an existential being?

Freedom as a State of Being

1. If Fred believed that the "right" decision lay buried in us like a treasure to be discovered, he could not believe we were truly free to make our own decisions. Why?
2. The difference between "making" yourself and "finding" yourself is partially one of chronological order. Does "making" yourself precede or follow your coming into existence? Does "finding" yourself suggest that something precedes your existence? Relate your explanations to each of the five views.
3. Can you think of any instance in which you would have no freedom at all? If we are essentially free, how does this freedom lead to uncertainty?

ADDITIONAL EXERCISES

1. Do you agree with this statement? "If everything that can be said of you can also be said of me, and everything that can be said of me can also be said of you, then we're identical."
2. In what sense are you the same person you were ten years ago? In what sense are you different?
3. Demonstrate the role that one of the five views of human nature is playing in your life in defining who you are. Show how you might think, believe, and act differently in the context of an alternative view.
4. Shakespeare claimed that all the world is a stage and that we are all actors upon it. To what extent do roles and role-playing influence how we perceive the self?

5. What implications does the mechanical view have for the area of human values?

6. Consider some important films of the last ten or 15 years: *Easy Rider, Midnight Cowboy, Butch Cassidy and the Sundance Kid, Serpico, The King of Marvin Gardens, Five Easy Pieces, A Woman Under the Influence.* How do the characters in these films see themselves? In your opinion, are their views accurate?

7. In what sense would you be the same person if:
   a. You lost all recollection of your past.
   b. Your brain was replaced with another one. (Would you or the other person be the doner? What if the donor were of the opposite sex?)
   c. Tissue was taken from your tongue, and a clone—an exact replica of you—was produced, and the "original you" was then killed.

8. Remembering that determinism is the belief that everything has a cause, evaluate these arguments:
   a. "To hold that human choice is determined is foolish, because we know that humans often act spontaneously."
   b. "If determinism is not true, science by necessity collapses."
   c. "If determinism is true, there's no point in debating whether to stop smoking. I simply will or won't."
   d. "In my bones I feel I'm free. This is the best proof of my freedom."
   e. "Looking back, I couldn't help doing what I did. Although I couldn't see it at the time, everything pointed to the course I took. If I had it to do over again, I'd do—in fact, *I couldn't help but do*—the same thing."
   f. "The best proof that we're really free to choose from among alternatives is that we mull over choices. A frog can't mull over whether to eat insects. It just does or doesn't. But we do. Should I have pizza or lasagna? Ravioli or spaghetti?"
   g. "If determinism is true, we should open the jails and let out the inmates, because we're imprisoning people for things they couldn't possibly have avoided doing. And that's certainly unjust."

PAPERBACKS FOR FURTHER READING

Ellison, Ralph. *Invisible Man.* New York: Vintage, 1951. Launching this novel with an explosive opening chapter, Ellison has written a compelling tale of the quest for self-discovery.

Sartre, Jean-Paul. *Nausea.* New York: New Directions, 1964. A less systematic presentation of his philosophy than his formal works, *Existentialism and Humanism* and *Existentialism and Human Emotions*, this novel nevertheless illustrates Sartre's views on freedom, ambiguity, anxiety, and nothingness.

Skinner, B. F. *Walden II.* New York: Macmillan, 1962. Psychologist Skinner presents his behavioristic utopia governed by principles of stimulus and response, positive reinforcement, and aversive conditioning. The novel is a good introduction to the ideas spelled out in Skinner's *Beyond Freedom and Dignity.*

Thoreau, Henry David. *Walden and Other Writings.* Joseph Wood Krutch, Ed. New York: Bantam, 1971. *Walden* is Thoreau's classic autobiographical statement of how he avoided a life of "quiet desperation" and found personal freedom and identity, as well as joy, in nature.

Watts, Alan. *The Book: On the Taboo Against Knowing Who You Are.* New York: Collier Books, 1966. In a thoroughly readable work, Watts examines what he considers the West's mistaken focus on ego and self. He argues for the Oriental position of no self and the interdependence of all things. In addition, Watts raises questions of love, suffering, death, and the meaning of existence.

Language and Perception

2

Every language is also a way of looking at the world and interpreting it.
—Clyde Kluckhohn

Language may seem an unusual topic to be considering in a philosophy text, especially one that aims at helping us discover ourselves. Why not proceed directly to those beliefs in religion, ethics, or politics that partially express who and what we are? The answer is simple: how we perceive the world around us cannot be divorced from the language we use to express ourselves.

Language seems both to reflect and to shape the way we see things. As a simple example of how language reflects a society's viewpoint, consider that we have only one word for snow and many different words for things that fly. Having just one word for snow would astound an Eskimo, who has a separate word for each kind of snow: soft snow, slushy snow, wind-driven snow, hard-packed snow. And whereas English is precise in distinguishing among flying things—birds, flyers, airplanes, blimps, rockets—Hopi, an American Indian language, has just one noun for everything airborne other than birds. Such distinctions or lack of them reflect the interests of a society. In studying our language, then, we should discover something of how we see things. But language seems to affect as well as reflect our interests.

To understand the way language can influence perception, suppose a journalist had to report the presence of 5000 nonstudents living along Telegraph Avenue in Berkeley, California. The journalist might write "Five thousand nonstudents are living in the buildings along Telegraph Avenue." Or he might write "Five thousand nonstudents are holed up in the warrens along Telegraph Avenue." If you read the second version, you would undoubtedly see a different image from the image the first version would give you. Because *holed up* and *warrens* suggest

33

rodent-like creatures, you would probably get the feeling that the non-students were perhaps unclean, or a source of violence and upheaval. If you read the first version of the sentence, on the other hand, you would probably form no such opinion. How the journalist chooses to report an event influences our experience of it. The point is that language is a powerful tool in shaping how we see the world around us.

If language influences how we view things, then it affects our ideas, beliefs, attitudes, and even behavior. In brief, the positions we maintain on questions of religion, ethics, politics, knowledge, reality, and art may find a philosophical basis in our language. For this reason we are investigating language before we explore any of the more traditional subjects of philosophy.

Specifically, this chapter deals with the connection between language and perception. By **language** we mean an aspect of human behavior that involves the use of vocal sounds and corresponding written symbols in meaningful patterns to formulate, express, and communicate thoughts and feelings. And by **perception** we mean the act or process by which we become aware of ordinary objects—trees, cars, cups—when our sense organs are stimulated. Because how we perceive things is a large measure of who and what we are, the connection between language and perception directly relates to the issue of self. We will examine this connection by focusing on the main aspects of language: words and structure.

Words can be used persuasively to get us to think and perceive in prescribed ways. To understand this we shall first try to nail down what a word is, whether a word simply stands for a thing or whether it stands for the behavior or feelings the word elicits. We will see how frequently the unwritten meaning of a word gets us to buy anything from toothpaste to political candidates and, more important, influences our self-image. Then we will examine sentence structure and learn how it establishes the framework in which we think, a framework that helps order experience but that may limit and distort it as well. Examining these aspects of language should provide further insights into the ways we see ourselves.

WORDS

How would you define a word? Perhaps by giving an example of one, or by pointing to a word in a newspaper. But what if you had to give the characteristics of a word, features that make a word a word and not something else?

One feature of a word is that it can be spoken or written. But what about *hippenspoofen, grendelgreek,* and *twod*? These can be spoken or written, but they are not words. Apparently, in addition to being spoken or written, words must have meaning; that is, they must stand for something beyond themselves. Whatever stands for something beyond itself is a sign. Clouds are a sign of rain; smoke is a sign of fire. But these are natural signs. Signs that humans have devised to stand for something beyond the signs themselves are called symbols. A red traffic light, a wailing siren, and a written musical note are all symbols. So are words. These symbols are arbitrary; there is nothing necessary about them. If we chose, we could allow *hippenspoofen* to symbolize house, or *grendelgreek* to symbolize depression. But it is essential that we all agree on the meaning of the word. Otherwise, we could not communicate. We may define a word, then, as a written or spoken symbol that is arbitrary and agreed upon.

Of all the characteristics of a word, its meaning sparks the most debate. Although a word represents something beyond itself, this meaning is not always so clear and precise as the meanings for other symbols. Consider, for example, the red traffic light, which symbolizes the command to stop. When we see a red traffic light, we stop. No confusion there. Neither do we experience confusion with the mathematical symbols for addition (+), multiplication (×), and subtraction (−). But consider *justice, goodness, reality, love, beauty, from, through, which.* The meanings of these words, their definitions, are not precise. In fact, the meaning of any word often depends on what we mean by definition itself—whether we mean designation, denotation, or connotation.

THREE KINDS OF DEFINITION

Designation

When we defined a word above, we listed its essential features. We decided a word must be spoken or written, symbolic, arbitrary, and agreed upon. Such characteristics that are necessary to make an entity what it is are called **defining characteristics**. Whenever we list an entity's defining characteristics we are providing its **designation**.

You could designate *rectangle* by listing its defining characteristics, the features without which a figure would not be a rectangle. You would probably say that a rectangle must (1) be a plane figure, (2) contain right angles, (3) have four sides, and (4) have opposite sides parallel. It is clear that in designating a word—providing the defining characteristics of what a word stands for—we are giving a precise definition.

But designations are not always easy to formulate. Designating *dog*, for example, is much harder than designating *rectangle*. Many dictionaries list domesticity and carnivorousness as characteristics of *dog*. But are they *defining* characteristics? If a dog were not domesticated, it would still be a dog. Even if it were a vegetarian, it would remain a dog. One thing that makes designations tricky is that characteristics that always appear to accompany an entity are not necessarily

". . . if a dog did not bark, it would not cease to be a dog."

defining ones. For example, a bark generally accompanies a dog. But if a dog did not bark, it would not cease to be a dog.

Characteristics that accompany an entity but are not necessary to make it what it is are called **accidental** or **accompanying characteristics.** When an accidental characteristic is absent, a thing does not lose its identity. Thus, some triangles are equilateral; that is, their sides are equal. But in the absence of this characteristic, a figure could still be a triangle. On the other hand, if a defining characteristic is absent, an entity loses its identity. Thus, in the absence of three sides, a figure cannot be a triangle.

The difference between defining and accidental characteristics may seem only technical, but in some cases a technical difference has wide social implications. Consider for a moment the movement to break down sexual discrimination. One of the movement's goals is to redefine sex roles. So accustomed have we become to viewing homemakers, secretaries, nurses, and assistants of every sort as female that we seem to accept "female" as a defining characteristic of these roles. Conversely, executives, physicians, attorneys, and breadwinners of every sort we designate "male." We then reinforce these notions when we train, hire, and promote people at all levels of education, business, and government. Recall the week of August 11, 1974, when President Ford was seeking a Vice President. When asked what he thought of a possible female Vice President, Senator Barry Goldwater replied that the idea was all right with him, "as long as she could cook." Facetious, perhaps, but nonetheless revealing.

The early-childhood roles we play often increase the confusion between defining and accidental characteristics as they pertain to sexual identity. Interest in dolls, houses, and babies are for many not accidental characteristics of being a girl but defining ones. Imagine the consternation of the father whose son prefers dolls to football. Although few boys may prefer dolls to football, interest in football is an accidental and not a defining characteristic of being male. But we can become so far removed from the essence of our own sexuality that the results are sometimes pathetically humorous, as in this case of a 5-year-old asking his father some pretty sticky questions.

Son: Dad, what's a boy?

Dad: A boy? Well, you're a boy.

Son: I know. But why?

Dad: Well, you're a boy because . . . see . . . a boy is . . . uh . . . let me put it this way . . . first off, I mean if you really want to get right down to it . . .

Son: Yeah?

Dad: A boy is different from a girl.

Son: How?

Dad: A lot.

Son: But how?

Dad: Well, they like different things, for one. I mean, boys like baseball.

Son: Stephanie Robbins likes baseball. Is Stephanie Robbins a boy?

Dad: No. No, Stephanie isn't a boy.

Son: And her brother Bobby hates baseball.

Dad: That may be.

Son: I thought all brothers were boys.

Dad: They are. All brothers are definitely boys—no question about that. But, you see, it's not just a matter of liking baseball, exactly.

Son: It's not?

Dad: No. In fact, the big thing—I mean, if you want to get right down to it—the big thing is that, well, boys—how can I put it?—boys can't have babies.

Son: And girls can?

Dad: That's right—when they get bigger, they can.

Son: Can boys when they get bigger?

Dad: No, only girls.

Son: All girls?

Dad: No . . . no, not all girls. Some. Many. A lot, a lot can—but not all.

Son: The ones who can't—are they boys?

Dad: Oh no. No, they're girls, all right.

Son: Then what's the difference between girls who can't have babies and boys?

Dad: Well, the main difference—you want the main difference, right?

Son: Yeah.

Dad: Well, the main difference is that . . . well, boys can *help* have babies.

Son: All boys?

Dad: Yes—well, no . . . no, it's true there are some boys who can't help have babies. That's true.

Son: Are they girls?

Dad: Well, no, they're not girls . . . they're still boys.

Son: Just like the ones who can help?

Dad: That's right.

Son: I see.

Dad: You do?

Son: Sure. A boy *can* help have babies . . . and a boy *can't* help have babies.

Dad: Does that make sense?

Son: No, but that's okay, Dad. When I find out I'll explain it to you.

Presumably Dad knows what defines a boy, but you would never know it. Notice that his initial reply to his son's question is "You're a boy." He simply pointed to a boy. We often define things this way. And frequently we merely name them: "Bobby Robbins is a boy," "Stephanie Robbins is a girl." Next, let us consider these kinds of definitions, which are not so precise as designations but which are useful.

Reflection   In Chapter 1 you wrote a verbal profile of yourself and determined which characteristics you could eliminate and still be you. What *defining* characteristics of yourself were you left with?

Denotation

Whenever we give an example of the group a word signifies, we *denote* that word. If we wished to denote *word* itself we could say *is, house, time, carriage,* or any other word—even the word *word*. What about *bridge*? *Golden Gate, Brooklyn, Verrazano Narrows,* and *London* are all **denotations** of *bridge*. A word is said to denote every single member of the group it symbolizes. *Bridge* denotes every single instance of a bridge—past, present, and future. Obviously, it is extremely difficult to list a complete denotation of a word; in most cases we must be satisfied with a partial one. But there are times when a complete denotation is easy. Proper names, for example, symbolize one particular person or thing. *Golden Gate Bridge* denotes the particular bridge that connects San Francisco with Sausalito, California.

We must be careful about using denotations. Recall the point about how confusion between defining and accidental characteristics can so distort our views that we allow roles to designate gender. The problem is actually rooted in a confusion between denotation and designation. Take, for example, the term *U.S. President. U.S. President designates* a natural-born U.S. citizen, at least 35 years old, elected President according to U.S. Constitutional procedures. Now consider this term's *denotation: Gerald Ford, Richard Nixon, Lyndon Johnson, John Kennedy, Dwight Eisenhower,* and on back to *George Washington.* Notice that they are all males. But being a male is *not* a defining characteristic of being a U.S. President. Yet, if we relied only on the denotation of *U.S. President,* we might think it was. What makes denotations potentially misleading is that they frequently embody accidental characteristics that we think are defining.

Sometimes in defining we neither designate nor denote. We simply point to an instance of what a word denotes. This is an **ostensive definition**. Showing someone a house would provide an ostensive definition of *house*. Recall that when the child asked the father "What's a boy?" the father replied "You're a boy." He was defining ostensively—by showing. When we define ostensively, we indicate a word's meaning without relying on words. Through this type of definition we come to understand the meaning of words signifying states that must be experienced: *hate, envy, purple, love, headache, desperation.* There are some words that defy ostensive definition. Since the United States had no Vice President during the week of August 11, 1974, it would have been impossible to provide an ostensive definition for *U.S. Vice President*.

Again, because a denotation frequently embodies accidental features, the ostensive definition is limited. It can be used to manage and manipulate. For example, if you wished to disparage the legal profession you might ostensively define *lawyer* in terms of the many lawyers indicted and convicted in the Watergate affair. They would hardly be representative, but they could serve as ostensive definitions of *lawyer*. But nowhere is the persuasive value of such definitions seen more vividly than in advertising. Ostensive definition for an *STP user*? Robert Blake. Ostensive definition for a *milk drinker*? Pat Boone. The advertising rule of thumb here is: identify the product with a noteworthy person. The advertisers are attempting to use a famous consumer to define *a product worth buying*.

Nor is education free of such devices. Many U.S. history texts still define *blacks in America* in terms of Booker T. Washington and George Washington Carver, and *women in America* in terms of Susan B. Anthony and Carrie Nation. Every *American Indian* who ever lived seems to be embodied in everybody's favorite Indian, Tecumseh.

The point is that an ostensive definition can be used to confer unearned integrity on a product or to misrepresent a group of people. As a result, it can distort perception and understanding. But perhaps even more persuasive is the third kind of definition, connotation.

Connotation

In his book *The Running of Richard M. Nixon*,[1] Leonard Lurie recounts how a friend and investment partner of Nixon's one day visited the White House. He was trying to prevail on Nixon to sell his shares in some Key Biscayne land for the price Nixon had paid for them rather than for the price Nixon then wanted. "Please, Dick," the man implored. But Nixon abruptly ordered the man to call him not "Dick" but "Mister President." Nixon obviously wished the man to use not the informal and familiar tone that "Dick" struck, but the more formal and authoritative "Mister President." The incident illustrates the power of word connotation.

The **connotation** of a word is everything a word suggests, the images and feelings it arouses. *Dove* is a bird, but it also suggests peace; *hawk* suggests war; *owl* suggests wisdom; *ox* suggests stupidity.

Clearly, the connotations of a word are not part of the word's designation. An ox could be bright and quick-witted, an owl stupid and easily fooled. Nor do a word's connotations necessarily lie in its denotation. Paul Bunyan's mythical ox Babe was hardly stupid.

The denotations of two words may be the same, but their connotations may differ. *Woman* and *broad* are good examples. They both mean "adult female," but they carry different emotive impact. They could denote the same person, as, "If you want to promote a woman, it's all right with me"; "If you want to promote a broad, it's all right with me." Because of *broad's* connotation, however, the second statement imparts information beyond its literal meaning. Probably the speaker disapproves of promoting females; possibly the speaker disapproves of females in general or sees them less as people than as sexual objects. Just such implicit feelings sometimes sway a decision or introduce emotion where reason should rule. So, although it is debatable whether connotation

---

[1]Leonard Lurie. *The Running of Richard M. Nixon.* New York: Coward, McCann, 1972.

should be considered part of a word's meaning, connotation frequently influences thought by using language persuasively.

Whenever we use word connotations to win over or convince, we are using **persuasive language**. Consider the ad: "Show her you love her; give her Arpege." The ad equates showing love with giving Arpege perfume. The favorable connotations of *love* are obvious. What may not be so obvious is how the ad extends the designation of *love* to the act of giving Arpege perfume—adds the act to its defining characteristics. Another example: suppose a lawyer insists "any fair and open-minded person will find my client innocent." Capitalizing on the positive connotations of "fair and open-minded," the lawyer extends the designation of these words to include "find my client innocent." A variation of persuasive language is seen in the advertising technique known as "positioning." In positioning an advertiser tries to sell a product by capitalizing on the earned reputation of the competition. The advertiser identifies his product with its successful competitor. Thus Avis is "the other rental car" (besides Hertz). Seven-Up is "the uncola" (as opposed to Coke and Pepsi); Goodrich is "the one without the blimp" (Goodyear has the blimp); Honeywell is "the other computer company" (besides IBM); and Sabena is the airline that "started flying four years ahead of the world's most experienced airline" (Pan American). Not very rational, but persuasive.

Sometimes persuasive language takes an intense form known as **propaganda**, which further capitalizes on the emotional impact of words. Propaganda strongly influences perception, as we shall see.

Reflection   Suppose you are a press agent for a committee of the House of Representatives. What words in the following sentence would you select to ensure that the committee's viewpoint gets a positive airing?

> The chairman met (privately, secretly) with (colleagues, cronies) of the Steering Committee today to (devise, formulate) (reprisals, responses) to the President's (threat, promise) to (veto, fight) the Committee's (demand, recommendation) for increases in defense (spending, expenditures) to (combat, answer) increased (enemy, foreign) (military, defense) spending.

Explain your selections.

PROPAGANDA

Propaganda is the systematic advancing of a doctrine. Because of its own connotations, the word *propaganda* is often associated with lies. But propagandists just choose their facts; they do not necessarily manufacture them.

In almost every war in which the United States has been engaged, the government has had a well-designed propaganda machine functioning at home and abroad. Our recent engagement in Vietnam saw us drop thousands of propagandistic leaflets, as well as bombs, on the countryside. In our first war, Thomas Paine produced a classic piece of propaganda in his *Common Sense.* So it is incorrect to think that propaganda comes only through TASS (the Soviet news service), the writings of Mao, or the letters of Che Guevara.

Propagandists invariably select facts according to their views of reality. Then they use language designed to produce a favorable emotional response to that view. For example, in his opening paragraph of "The American Crisis," Paine, alerting his compatriots to their peril and need to respond, includes the emotive words *patriot, crisis, shrink, service, country, love, tyranny, hell, conquered, conflict, glorious, triumph, heaven, celestial, freedom, tyranny, bind, slavery,* and *impious.* These words succeeded in helping to arouse a revolutionary spirit within the colonists.

We can see similar propagandistic value in the rhetoric of today's social movements. Although the denotations of *Negro* and *black* are the same (and probably their designations as well), *black* is preferred. For the black person this word helps develop a new view of reality and of self founded on pride, equality, and identity. A similar example is the term *Ms.,* which some have used to replace *Mrs.* and *Miss. Ms.* suggests that the female has the same marital anonymity as the male. The term also implies that there is nothing so sacred about marriage that an unmarried female should be stigmatized because she lacks the title *Mrs.*

Nor has the propagandistic value of language been lost on the gay revolution. It hardly seems coincidental that shortly after the word *gay* became pervasive, the American Medical Association ruled that homosexuality should no longer be considered a disease but rather an alternative life-style. It is impossible to assess the role that the word *gay* played in producing such a decision, but the previously used term *homosexual* was associated with the alleged abnormal sexual nature of such a person, much as *Mrs.* or *Miss* referred to a woman's marital status. When *homosexual* fell from use, so did much of the disapproval and fear of this group.

As used in these movements, persuasive language can alter our perception by calling attention to new aspects of an issue. Seeing things differently is the first step toward new and sometimes more rewarding and constructive forms of personal and social behavior. In this sense language can be a catalyst for social change.

But language's influence on our perception is not confined to its verbal aspects. One linguist has observed that language—and not just language that is patently connotative—can affect thinking by causing

"We can see similar propagandistic value
in the rhetoric of today's social movements."

the hearer to notice those aspects of the environment that pertain to
the application of the term and to neglect others. So far we have concentrated on just one aspect of language: words. But language is more.
It is also the way words are linked together to convey thought—that
is, language's structure. So we should consider how the structure of a
language can influence thought and conceptual reality the way words do.

SENTENCE STRUCTURE

Have you ever found yourself in a rut—doing the same old things, thinking the same old way, seeing the same old people? Our behavior can
become so habitual that we often do not even recognize the ruts we are
in until someone points them out to us: "How come you always want
to eat at the same old place?" "Why must we always watch the same
old programs?" "Isn't there anything else to do around here on Friday
nights but drag Main Street?" One reason ruts are so difficult to leave
is that, no matter how dull and monotonous they are, they are secure,
comfortable, and predictable ways of behaving. For most of us such
security dies hard, even though it may bore us to death.

Language is like a rut in that it is a learned and practiced way of
behaving (speaking and writing) of which we are seldom conscious. But
because the word *rut* has negative connotations that do not strictly apply
to language, let us call language ruts language "patterns"—that is, ways
we speak and write our language. For most of us these patterns go unno-

ticed because we constantly use them. So fixed and comfortable are they that we slip into them automatically, just as we might into an old pair of shoes. There are three elements of language structure that reveal these patterns: word order, word form, and function words.

Word Order, Word Form, and Function Words

Examining a sentence with no sensible meaning will demonstrate how important these elements of language structure are in understanding. In the nonsense sentence "The zite dwart twarily oilated blurtses near an ach grul," you know that it is the dwart who oilated and not the blurtses; and that the grul the dwart oilated near was an *ach* grul. How do you know this? Surely not through word meaning, because these words have no dictionary definition. You know it because of the position of the words relative to each other in the sentence—that is, **word order.**

Generally, English sentences fall into the pattern "The dogs ate," "The children finished," "The dwart oilated." This pattern is the kernel of the English sentence. One word names something; another word reports an event in which the first participates: "dog ate" and "child finished." We generally call words that name entities nouns; those that report events, verbs. So, even though the sentence is nonsense, we recognize that *dwart* patterns like a noun and *oilated* patterns like a verb. Frequently, of course, the pattern uses two nouns, one *performing* in an event and another *receiving* in the same event. Thus, "The dog devoured food," and "The child finished lunch." "The dwart oilated blurtses" follows this pattern. Because *dwart* precedes *oilated* and *blurtses* follows it, we know that it is the dwart that did the oilating and not the blurtses, just as we know that it is the dog that ate the food and the child that finished lunch. Of course, grammatically we designate the subject as the performer (the dwart) and the object as the receiver (blurtses) of the sentence. But we can recognize the order of a sentence pattern before we know grammar, before we even begin school, since we fall into such language patterns by the time we are just a few years old.

In the preceding nonsense sentence, we can also recognize that *zite* and *ach* pattern like *green, bright, tall, narrow, heavy,* and *big*; that is, they function like words we commonly find describing nouns, which we call adjectives. *Twarily,* on the other hand, patterns like *quietly, warily, nearly*—like words we commonly find describing verbs or adjectives, which we call adverbs. Over 99 percent of all English words fall into these four classes: nouns, verbs, adjectives, and adverbs. This is one reason that, when we come upon a sentence composed mostly of meaningless words that occupy positions regularly reserved for these four classes, we are able to see obvious structural meaning in the sentence.

But would we be able to tell from word order that only one dwart oilated? Or that the dwart has finished oilating? No. The endings these words have, what we call their *inflections*, report that. When we speak of a word's inflection, we are speaking of its form. *Dwart*, for example, has the form of *wart, heart, meat,* and *cat.* Since these words show plurality by adding an *s,* we infer that any noun form ending in *t* forms its plural by adding *s.* Hence in the nonsense sentence there is only one dwart. *Blurtses,* on the other hand, has the form of *messes* and *kisses,* or perhaps *houses* and *shoes.* Since these words show plurality by adding *es* or *s,* we infer that any noun form ending in *s* or *e* shows its plural by inflecting an *es* or an *s.* Therefore, in the nonsense sentence there are more than one blurts or blurtse. And from the inflection *ed* in oilated we know that the action of the verb is completed. If the action were still occurring—that is, the dwart were still performing—the inflection *ing* or *s* would be evident. As with word order, we learn such **word forms** very early.

These are some of the technicalities of word order and form. But alone they do not allow us to understand just any nonsense sentence. Consider this one: "Uc zite dwart oilated druz clut ach grul." Missing from the original nonsense sentence are *the, near,* and *an.* These words obviously were connecting the other words in the sentence and establishing a sentence pattern. Words like these, which show relationships between other words in a sentence, are called function words. *So, because, since, therefore, consequently, of, by, within, between, among, under,* and *in* are all function words. Without function words many sentences would carry no meaning.

In summary, the pattern of a sentence conveys much meaning through word order, word form, and function words. We learn these patterns very early in life simply by hearing English spoken and imitating what we hear. We strengthen these language habits later when we learn to read and write.

There is an unpleasant feature connected with most ruts, perhaps including language patterns. They allow us to see only what we have become used to within their limitations. Is language like this? Perhaps we begin by saying what we think, but we may end up by thinking what we say. We have already seen how one aspect of language, words, can get us to perceive in prescribed ways. Now we are wondering whether this other aspect of language, its structure, also distorts perception.

Reflection   Remember the poem "Jabberwocky" from *Through the Looking Glass?*

'Twas brillig, and the slithy toves
  Did gyre and gimble in the wabe;
All mimsy were the borogoves,
  And the mome raths outgrabe. . . .

Substitute meaningful words for the nonsense ones. Compare your version with others'. What do they have in common?

SENTENCE STRUCTURE AND PERCEPTION

We have seen that structure provides any sentence, even a nonsense one, with meaning. Word order and function words, two elements of sentence structure, allow us to designate the job a particular word is doing. Although we do not know what *dwart* names, it seems that word order so influences how we perceive that we confidently say that *dwart* names something. In effect, we have classified *dwart* before we really know anything more about it than its position in the sentence. **Classification** is important in understanding the relationship between sentence structure and perception.

Anytime you speak you are probably classifying. Suppose you say "I saw President Ford on television the other night." Notice you said *President*. That word labels Ford; it classifies him as one of a group of 36 U.S. Presidents. You could have referred to him as *Republican, swimmer, father, husband, lawyer, former House minority leader, Michiganite, national leader,* or *politician,* among other things. When we classify we group like things. Because nouns name classes, they are often called "class words." So *dwart* is a noun, or class word, because it classifies some entity.

Even though we do not know what a word denotes, sentence order predisposes us to classification, or putting things into classes or categories: *dwart* is a noun, *zite* an adjective, *oilated* a verb, *twarily* an adverb. Indeed, since classification requires that we name things, we can say that our word order predisposes us to think in terms of things. Remember that we do not even know what *dwart* stands for, what it denotes. Still, we can and do classify it; we can and do attribute the property of ziteness to it; we can and do attribute an action or state of being oilated to it. In other words, this nonsense sentence encourages us to see in terms of the thing *dwart.* But the structure of this sentence, as we know, is typical of English sentence structure. It appears, then, that our sentence structure predisposes us to perceive reality in terms of things. The philosophical implications of this tendency will appear as we examine this subject of classification further.

CLASSIFICATION

Whenever we name something we classify it. *Tree, house, woman, man, lion, school* are all names—all classifications. An individual instance or member has no classification until we provide it. For example, a child is born in New York City. He is therefore labeled a *U.S. citizen*. Was he a U.S. citizen before he was born? No. Circumstances surrounding his birth permitted such a classification. If he was born in Australia, he would be labeled an *Australian citizen*. What if his parents were U.S. citizens and the child was born in Australia? He would then fall under both classifications: *U.S. citizen* and *Australian citizen*. Naturally, no two *U.S. citizens* or *Australian citizens* are the same. Neither, for that matter, are any two members of any classification. But the effect of classification is to get us to *perceive* the individuals as the same and, consequently, to treat them the same. "No U.S. citizen may hold citizenship elsewhere." "All U.S. citizens have the right to practice the religion of their choice." The nature of classification, then, blurs individual differences and may affect how you perceive the world around you. But before considering its influence on perception, let us discuss the importance of classification.

The Importance of Classification

First, classification simplifies our lives. Imagine if every time we came upon a tree we had to name it and then remember that name. Our lives would soon become unmanageable.

Second, classification provides psychological security. Recall the last time you walked into a room full of strangers. You probably felt anxious. That is only natural; after all, you did not know *who* or *what* they were or anything about them. They were unknown, unlabeled, unclassified—and you were uncertain. On the other hand, suppose that just before you entered the room a friend informed you "Jean Davis is in there." "Jean Davis?" you ask. "Yes, you know, *Doctor* Davis." "Oh, the dentist." "Right." "Oh, great. I've been wanting to meet her to find out how tough it is to get into dental school." Having been classified, Jean Davis would have become a *known* quantity, and you would have entered the room a little more at ease. For the same reason, you sleep better when you can *name* the sound out back that goes bump in the night.

FLINDERSIA BRAYLEYANA!

"Imagine if every time we came upon a tree
we had to name it and then remember
that name."

So potent is the psychological value of being able to name something that some African tribes still believe that to know someone's name is to control that person's life. And recall how the ancient Jews dared not name their God, for to name was to know and to know was to limit. Thus, when Moses on Mt. Sinai asks with whom he shall tell his people he has spoken, he is told to tell them *Yahweh*, "I am that I am."

A third desirable feature of classification is that it directs activity. Even if you were really thirsty you would not swig a bottle of Clorox, because you know it is a poison; you have classified it. Or take the case of a dog mooching out of your trash can. At first you just hear the sound. Then you identify it as the neighbor's dog. Armed with this knowledge you can then act: invite him in for a snack or throw a sneaker at him.

Finally, classification permits us to relate classes of things. Suppose a child plays with matches. He strikes one and presto—fire! He might do it again and again. If he survives he will eventually conclude "Matches cause fire." Think of the classifications in that statement: matches, causation, fire. Notice that he does not conclude "This *particular* match causes fire." Instead, he **abstracts**—moves from particular instances to classifications—and sees relationships between those classifications. As far as we know, we are the only animal that can do this.

Simplicity, security, direction, and relationship: classification provides us with each of these necessary life-preservers. Without classification our lives would be what William James called an "empirical sand heap." But classification is not without its pitfalls, pitfalls that spell trouble for perception.

Classification and Perception

If someone asked you to name (denote) three trees, you might reply *elm, oak,* and *maple.* Although these are all trees, they are different kinds of trees. Similarly, if you were to name three Republicans, you might say *Gerald Ford, Lowell Weicker,* and *Barry Goldwater.* Again you would be right, although these three certainly represent different schools of Republican thought. The point is that we can forget these differences when we start labeling indiscriminately, which we often do.

Radical, conservative, reactionary, liberal, progressive: just consider how casually we use these labels to identify the people, movements, and events around us. But labeling is not confined to politics. Consider *women's liberationist, male chauvinist, hard-hat, bureaucrat, schoolteacher, C student, big spender, hero, coward, treason, love, murder, crisis*—the list is endless. One thing all classification labels confer is a partial and therefore incomplete view of any of its members. Gloria Steinem may be a *women's liberationist,* but she is also a *voter,* a *licensed driver,* a *taxpayer,* a *consumer,* and so on. If we perceive her strictly in terms of a single classification, we distort our perception of her.

Yet we do perceive in terms of things, and classification aids this tendency. As linguist Gordon Allport says, "It brings many grains of sand into a single pail." But Allport also points out that classification disregards "the fact that the same grains might have fitted just as appropriately into another pail."[2] Consider this study as an example:

Thirty photographs of college girls were shown on a screen to 150 students. The subjects rated the girls on a scale from one to five for *beauty, intelligence, character, ambition, general likeability.* Two months later the same subjects were asked to rate the same photographs (and fifteen additional ones introduced to complicate the memory factor). This time five of the original photographs were given Jewish surnames (Cohen, Kantor, etc.), five Italian (Valenti, etc.), and five Irish (O'Brien, etc.); and the remaining girls were given names chosen from the signers of the Declaration of Independence and from the Social Register (Davis, Adams, Clark, etc.).

---

[2]Gordon Allport. *The Nature of Prejudice.* Reading, Mass.: Addison-Wesley, 1954, p. 178.

When Jewish names were attached to photographs, there occurred the following changes in ratings:

    decrease in liking
    decrease in character
    decrease in beauty
    increase in intelligence
    increase in ambition

For those photographs given Italian names there occurred:

    decrease in liking
    decrease in character
    decrease in beauty
    decrease in intelligence

Thus a mere proper name leads to prejudgment of personal attributes. Individuals are fitted to the prejudiced ethnic category, and not judged in their own rights.

While the Irish names also brought about depreciated judgment, the depreciation was not as great as in the case of the Jews and Italians. The falling likeability of the "Jewish girls" was twice as great as for "Italians" and five times as great as for "Irish." We note, however, that the "Jewish" photographs caused higher ratings in *intelligence* and in *ambition*. Not all stereotypes of out-groups are unfavorable.[3]

Of course, such stereotypes are boomerangs: eventually they victimize us. After all, we are all members of ethnic groups, as well as holders of occupations and members of religions.

To understand the implications classification holds for one's self-concept, consider the word *black*. If you look up *black* in a dictionary, you will find that it has almost no positive connotations. In fact, many of its connotations are sinister. Such a classification label would probably have a negative influence on a black person's self-perception. Similarly, classification can negatively affect a female's perception of her own sexuality. Note that unmarried men are forever classed as *bachelors*. Not so for women. They "descend" from *bachelor girl* to *spinster* to *old maid*. If you are a man, how would it feel to see yourself comparably labeled rather than as a *bachelor*? And no doubt other titles affect how the female perceives herself: spokes*man*, chair*man*, church*man*, business*man*, congress*man*, jury*man*, and, ultimately, wo*man*. True, we now frequently substitute "person" for the male form; but inequalities remain, as in the ceremonial language of the marital rite: "I now pronounce you *man* and *wife*,"

---

[3]Gordon Allport. *The Nature of Prejudice*, pp. 180-181.

not *husband* and *wife*. Also, the female in most cases still assumes her husband's surname when she marries. Does a husband own a wife? Is she to see herself as property? Is he encouraged to see her this way? We raise these questions as part of an inquiry into how we view the world, including other people and ourselves, and how the classification process of language structure influences those perceptions.

So, word order encourages classification. When you classify an entity, you generally recognize it as existing outside yourself: tree, dog, house, school, building. This entity occupies a position in time and space. You can see, feel, touch, smell, or taste it; in the case of an intangible entity, you can imagine or conceive of it; you can take account of it and thus classify it. Why classify? Mostly to gain a measure of control over your life. But be alert to two features of classification: (1) it blurs individual differences and (2) it often treats a person in terms of some thing the person is.

Classification raises further problems for perception. The nucleus of the English sentence is the subject and verb. Lacking either, stated or implied, we have no sentence. We still have meaning, of course, but it is a safe bet that if we spoke and wrote completely in nonsentences we would not remain intelligible very long. So the structure of our language rests on this subject-verb classification, this bipolarity. Yet this bipolarity is hardly confined to our language structure. It is also reflected in the way we see things, which is often in erroneous either/or terms. So pervasive is this tendency that we should take a closer look at it.

Reflection   Picture in your mind a "liberated woman." Now try to pass this test. Most likely,

1. She is wearing
   a. a gingham dress
   b. hot pants
   c. slacks
2. She reads
   a. *Good Housekeeping*
   b. *Ms.*
   c. *Playboy*
3. The adjective that best describes her is
   a. submissive
   b. aggressive
   c. industrious
4. She is
   a. for
   b. against
   c. indifferent to
   the traditional concepts of family and child-rearing.
5. She thinks the worst crime anyone could commit is
   a. murder
   b. rape
   c. blackmail
6. She
   a. shaves her legs
   b. does not shave her legs
   c. either answer is correct

Answers: 1. c, 2. b, 3. b, 4. b, 5. b, 6. b.

If you got all or most of these "right," how did you do it? What would you say is the source of this stereotype? What does this exercise show you about labels?

LANGUAGE STRUCTURE AND BIPOLARITY

"Should we ban offshore drilling for oil, or allow the oil companies to drill as national demand warrants it?" "Should the United States support the Jews or the Arabs in the Middle East?" "Should you pursue a career that offers money or one that offers free time?" Notice that these questions reduce your choices to just two. There is nothing wrong with that, providing that there really are only two choices. But, in question 1, there could be a ban on *some* offshore drilling and/or *some* control over oil drilling. In question 2, the United States could support *both* the Jews and the Arabs, or neither. In the final question, there are careers that offer *both* free time and money. In short, the choices provided in the questions do not exhaust all the possibilities available. Whenever we treat many alternatives as if they were just two, we create a **false dilemma.**

The modern public-opinion poll frequently relies on the false dilemma to influence our perception of the running of government and the activities of politicians. Consider the following questions taken from Gallup polls:

1. In general, do you think the U.N. organization is doing a good job or a poor job in trying to solve the problems it has had to face?
2. Do you think there will be more people out of work or fewer people out of work in this community in the next six months?
3. Which political party do you think can do a better job of handling [the problem]?
4. When new appointments are made by the President to the Supreme Court, would you like to have these people be liberal or conservative in their political views?

Each of these questions sets up a false dilemma by presenting two alternatives that do not exhaust all the possible ones. In question 1, the U.N. may be doing an average or mediocre job. In question 2, there may be the same number of people unemployed. In question 3, the word *better* implies only two political parties, presumably the Democratic and the Republican, although there are others: American Independent, Socialist, Libertarian. In question 4, the appointees might be moderates, radical leftists, or reactionaries. Although the choices presented in these questions did not exhaust all possible alternatives, at least 88 percent of those polled chose one of the alternatives offered. This fact suggests that most of us do not object to operating within the constraints of a false dilemma, to choosing from between "either/ors" when in fact there are more choices, to seeing things in black and white when there are a myriad of other colors. Perhaps this is true at least partly because of our language structure—especially our word order, which predisposes us to see in terms of **bipolarity.**

Remember that English would have us perceive mainly in terms of two classes: nouns and verbs. Also, English sentences would have us perceive primarily in terms of two sentence functions: subject and action. We have already seen our own language's tendency to classify, to put entities into compartments. Now we are suggesting an additional tendency: to view entities in terms of only two classes. It is curious to compare such a bipolar tendency with the tendencies of a culture that uses a non-Indo-European language. (Indo-European is the name designating the family of languages that includes Germanic, Celtic, Italic, Slavic, and Greek.)

For example, consider Nootka, a non-Indo-European language of Vancouver Island. In Nootka all words are verbs. Therefore Nootka has just one class. The Nootka people literally perceive in terms of events, not things. Thus, *a house occurs* or *it houses* is how Nootka expresses "house." By adding a suffix to the verb, Nootka indicates the length of the event: *long-lasting house, temporary house, future house, house that used to be, what started out to be a house.* In Nootka, then, it is literally impossible to express yourself outside a stream of happenings. Things are constantly moving, shifting, changing. Nootka language structure both reflects and affects such a perception.

If the ways we have traditionally perceived reality are indications of language's influence on perception, then there is much evidence to suspect that we are to a degree prisoners of the language we speak. For example, a bipolarity appears in almost every major Western philosophical movement from Plato through Sartre. Beginning in Chapter 3 we shall see this. Suffice it to say here that, even before Plato, the earliest Greek philosopher-scientists were preoccupied with the question of how the universe might better be described: in terms of unity *or* diversity, one *or* many. Plato himself saw things in terms of opinion *or* knowledge, the world of matter *and* the world of form. The Christian thinker St. Augustine observed tension between the city of man *and* the city of God. The empirical movement of the seventeenth and subsequent centuries wrestled with the question of objective *versus* subjective reality.

Georg Hegel's absolute idealism of the nineteenth century, although clearly identifying absolute reality as "becoming," did posit conflict between being *and* nothing, thesis *and* antithesis. In the twentieth century Jean-Paul Sartre distinguishes between being-in-itself *and* being-for-itself, Martin Buber between the "I-it" *and* the "I-thou" kinds of knowledge, and linguistic analysts between propositions *and* non-propositions, propositions themselves being *either* analytic *or* synthetic. We mention these ideas here just to note the pervasiveness of bipolarity in Western thought. In fact, in the twentieth century, linguistic analysts ask the trenchant question: is language usage actually a bane to our attempts to philosophize? As we will see later, these analysts believe that our language and our usage are inadequate not only to answer philosophical inquiries but even to formulate the proper questions. As a result, they say, no philosophical inquiry can begin until language is clarified and refined. Otherwise the results of such an inquiry will be only more confusion and obscurity.

CONCLUSIONS

By influencing how and what we perceive, language plays a vital role in formulating self-identity. Specifically, persuasive language can get us to see only a limited aspect of an issue, as well as mold our opinions, influence our actions, and incline us to see the world of objects in sharply defined classes. This aspect of language is enough to influence what we perceive, think, and do.

How language structure influences perception is more subtle, because it provides a framework within which we function. Usually it is difficult to imagine what lies outside a frame of reference. For example, before someone sailed around the world, it was very difficult for most people to imagine a round world. It is similarly hard for us to conceive of things in terms other than the ones our language allows. It is as if our language structure provides territorial boundaries in which we formulate, comprehend, and express our experiences. Sometimes we permit these boundaries to limit and distort our view of things, as in the cases of classification and false dilemma. At other times the intrusion of language structure is more subtle.

As an example, consider the use of function words. Given our use of these connectives—prepositions, conjunctions, articles, and conjunctive adverbs—it is logical for us to perceive "logical relationships" among things. When after examining a body of evidence someone says "Therefore, I believe the defendant is guilty," the function word *therefore* indicates a result relationship between evidence and judgment.

Function words also indicate another kind of relationship. When we speak of "a branch of the tree" the word *of* expresses a relationship between branch and tree. *Branch* and *tree* are names of things with a definite outline or shape; that is, they are *individual* nouns. Function words like *of* permit us to communicate relationships between individual nouns. But function words also allow us to make relationships between what are called *mass* nouns. A mass noun denotes bodies of indefinite shape; *water, air, heat, time,* and *space* are mass nouns. Although these nouns are of indefinite shape, we casually set boundaries around them. Thus, *glass of water, degree of heat, six minutes of time, miles of space.* It is as if we put our mass nouns into containers that provide them with shape or form. But not all peoples do. The Hopi Indians, for example, always use the individual sense of nouns. They allow for no division of mass nouns. This aspect of their language influences how they perceive things.

Suppose you are a Hopi. A government official informs you "In the spring your land will end at the waterfall." The statement baffles you, for in Hopi there is no *your land*. Land cannot be fractured any more than air can be. There is just land, everybody's land. Does the official want to use the land? To hunt buffalo on it? Fine. But why is he even asking permission? And what is this *waterfall*? Hopi speaks of no waterfall, or for that matter of no *pond, lake,* or *stream*. There is simply *pahe*, the water of rivers and natural lakes, and *kevi*, the water found in jugs and canteens. As for *spring*, there is no telling what this means. Hopi does not allow such treatment of time as if it were a loaf of bread to be sliced into *summer, fall, winter,* and *spring*. Distinct ways of speaking, distinct ways of perceiving.

So function words fix relationships between things. We use these relationships in reasoning about the world. But the question is: are the relationships actually so fixed as our language reports them?

The ancient Greek philosopher Heraclitus (about 500 B.C.) once said "It is not possible to step twice into the same river." He meant that the constant flow of the water makes the river different each time we step into it. But Heraclitus also said "Into the same river we both step and do not step, we are and we are not." In other words, we, too, are different each time, if in no other way than because each of us is a study in constant molecular motion. Is our language structure inclined to report this change, this motion, this flux? It appears more likely to fix reality, to freeze it.

As a result we may view ourselves as not dynamic but static; as organisms not in a state of development but finished and complete. If we do, then we probably see our personal values as fixed and unchanging and our social and political institutions as rigid and inflexible. Such a view misreads experience, for reality, in the broadest sense, is forever changing like the river of Heraclitus. Failure to perceive this change in our world and especially in ourselves may preclude knowing much of the nature of either.

SUMMARY

We opened the chapter by suggesting that language may not only reflect how we see ourselves and the world around us but also affect that world. Words are one aspect of language. After defining *word* we discussed three theories of word meaning and three different kinds of definition. We also saw how widely used are persuasive language and propaganda. Another aspect of language is sentence structure. Language has a recognizable structure that may predispose us to classification and bipolarities. Because language influences our perception of things, it affects how we see ourselves.

MAIN POINTS

1. Language is an aspect of human behavior that involves the use of vocal sounds and corresponding written symbols in meaningful patterns to formulate, express, and communicate thoughts and feelings.
2. Perception is the act or process by which we become aware of ordinary objects.
3. A word is a written or spoken symbol that is arbitrary and agreed upon.
4. There are three kinds of definition: designation, denotation, and connotation.
5. Whenever we use word connotations to win over or convince, we are using language persuasively.
6. An intense form of persuasive language is propaganda, the systematic advancing of a doctrine. Because persuasive language focuses on one aspect of reality, it can distort.
7. Another aspect of language is structure. Language structure is a pattern of speaking and writing that we recognize and adopt early in our lives.
8. Language structure consists of word order, word form, and function words.
9. Word order presumes a classification system. Language structure predisposes us to classification, to the grouping of like things.
10. Although necessary for simplicity, security, direction, and relationship, classification gives a partial and incomplete view of reality. It tends to "thingify."
11. Language structure, relying as much as it does on linguistic bipolarity, may tend to impose bipolarity on our perceptions. A bipolarity consists of two contrasting alternatives. When there are additional possibilities, the bipolarity is a false one.
12. Many contemporary philosophers believe that the proper functioning of philosophy requires a clarification of language usage.

SECTION EXERCISES

Three Kinds of Definition

1. List five words from contemporary political rhetoric whose meanings are very vague.

DESIGNATION

a.   Column B contains characteristics of the things listed in column A. Which characteristics are defining? Which are accidental or accompanying?

A	B
triangle	three sides
mother	female
word	sound
pen	ink
elephant	trunk
zebra	stripes
human	omnivore
ammonia	nitrogen
equilateral	equal angles
U.S. Vice President	Republican or Democrat
New York	Empire State Building

b.   Defining characteristics are not always easy to devise. Can you give at least one for each of the following?

wristwatch	automobile
homicide	death
truth	cup
table	star

DENOTATION

a.   For each of the following words, provide a denotation.

soldier	novel
statesman	celebrity
father	poet
adjective	U.S. Senator

b.   For every denotation you listed in the preceding exercise, provide a word for which the same denotation applies.

c.   Is there any way you can define the following words other than ostensively? Explain.

red	queasy
sour	anxiety
bitter	charisma

d. You are interested in influencing someone through ostensive definition. For the words that follow, suggest an ostensive definition that would influence the person favorably, then one that would influence him or her unfavorably.

novelist	football player
women's liberationist	liberal (as in "liberal politician")
actress	conservative (as in "conservative politician")

e. Select any area—education, politics, consumerism, sports, or religion, for example—and give three illustrations of how ostensive definition is used to mold thought. Note whether or not ostensive definition is used to define accurately.

CONNOTATION

a. What connotations do these ten words for animals have?

snake	pigeon
rat	lamb
lion	sheep
ostrich	wolf
possum	eagle

b. List ten pairs of words that have the same denotation but different connotations.
c. List a word of positive connotation, then one of negative connotation, to describe each of the following:

a person who says what is on his mind
a person who is persistent
a person who cries easily
a person who is hard-working
a person who remains eternally young

Word Order, Word Form, and Function Words

1. The basic word order of an English sentence is subject, verb, object. There are, however, exceptions: in "The fish we finally caught," the order is object, subject, verb. List at least ten examples of such

deviations from the norm. What is the effect of these variants? In being exceptions to the norm, what do they say about how the speaker or writer perceives the content? Does he or she convey this perception to you through the unusual word order?

2. The stress we give to words and the pauses we make between them are essential vocal structural signals that are missing in writing. Without proper stress and pause, we can create ambiguity in communicating our perceptions. With the appropriate stress or pause, show how the following phrases or sentences may be taken in at least two different ways:

   She has a daughter Robin who's an engineer.
   Where did they go then?
   A mad dog killer
   Jones is an outdoor lover.
   It was dark enough to play "On Top of Old Smokey."

3. Mark Twain once concocted from the French a word-for-word translation of his short story "The Jumping Frog of Calaveras County." Sample absurdity: "I no saw not that the frog has nothing of better than each frog." What does this sample illustrate about the importance of structural meaning? How does it underscore the limitations of a dictionary?

4. To understand the importance of function words and their precise usage, consider these three statements: "That's true of you," "That's true for you," "That's true to you." What different meanings are expressed by the three prepositions *of, for,* and *to*?

Sentence Structure

1. Two common speech ruts we fall into are *you know* and *uh*: "I think the best thing to do, you know, is to, uh, leave right now." Listen for these in the next lecture you hear. How many do you detect? How many similar speech ruts can you think of?

2. Determine the definitions of *euphemism, slang,* and *jargon*. In what way can these be language ruts? Name some slang expressions we chronically rely on to communicate.

3. The first English-class assignment of a fall semester often illustrates an English-instruction rut: "Write an essay entitled 'How I Spent My Summer Vacation.'" List other academic ruts you have discovered.

Classification

THE IMPORTANCE OF CLASSIFICATION

1. Make a list of the classification labels that now apply to you. How many of these satisfy one or more of the functions of classification: simplicity, security, direction, relationship? In what sense do they violate any of these?
2. Linguist S. I. Hayakawa has said "Society regards as 'true' those systems of classification that produce desired results." Do you agree? Why or why not?

CLASSIFICATION AND PERCEPTION

1. Briefly describe a common stereotype: a professor, an athlete, a clergyman, or a doctor, for example. Now contrast this stereotype with an actual person of this category. Does the person fit the stereotype?
2. Linguist Irving Lee demonstrates the cutting edge of classification:

> I knew a man who had lost the use of both eyes. He was called a "blind man." He could also be called an expert typist, a conscientious worker, a good student, a careful listener, a man who wanted a job. But he couldn't get a job in the department store order room where employees sat and typed orders which came over the telephone. The personnel man was impatient to get the interview over. "But you're a blind man," he kept saying, and one could almost feel his silent assumption that somehow the incapacity in one aspect made the man incapable in every other. So blinded by the label was the interviewer that he could not be persuaded to look beyond it.[4]

Do you know of similar instances in which someone has been so victimized?

Language Structure

1. Cite six examples of false dilemmas from newspapers, magazines, or textbooks (including this one!).

---

[4]Quoted by Gordon Allport in *The Nature of Prejudice*. Reading, Mass.: Addison-Wesley, 1954, pp. 178-179.

2. Illustrate how, historically, we have viewed ourselves as *apart from* and not *a part of* nature. Can you point to any Biblical injunctions that foster this attitude?

ADDITIONAL EXERCISES

1. Using what you know of defining and accidental characteristics, take a position on the following issues.
    a. A person who has had a heart transplant *is/is not* the same person as before the transplant.
    b. If a tree falls in the forest and no one is there to hear it, it *makes/does not make* a sound.
    c. *Since/Although* this watch has lost its hands, it is *no longer/still* a timepiece.
    d. An android that manifests all the behavioral characteristics of a human *is/is not* a human.
2. Demonstrate how these words may have different designations but the same denotations.

    man—senator
    song—hymn
    drink—soda
    digit—prime number
    molecule—atom
    square—rhombus

3. Each of the following pairs of words usually has the same denotations; some even have the same designations. Considering the connotations of each, which would you say are *full* equivalents?

    shrewd—astute
    loose—promiscuous
    sophisticated—worldly
    partisan—biased
    objective—disinterested
    capricious—whimsical

4. The British philosopher Bertrand Russell once conjugated an "irregular verb" as "I am firm, you are obstinate, he is pig-headed." Can you write two similar conjugations that illustrate such connotative shift?
5. List a half-dozen words that can be defined only ostensively.
6. Skim through a magazine or newspaper and locate five examples of positioning.
7. How is persuasive language used to influence your perception of self? Cite examples.

8. Examine the rhetoric of sports. Would you have any reason for saying that we perceive sports as warfare? As sexual activity? Explain.
9. "The Greek philosopher Heraclitus believed that reality could be accounted for best in terms of change: things are in constant motion and flux. Similarly, the nineteenth-century German philosopher Hegel claimed that things were in a state of 'becoming.' Although these ideas are close to the scientific picture of the universe we now have, our language structure is not really equipped to deal with such a reality." Explain this argument.
10. In what sense is the Austrian philosopher Ludwig Wittgenstein correct when he says, "The limits of our language are the limits of our world"?
11. Make a list of all the terms you can think of that show how we quantify time. Do you think these terms represent an accurate description of time? Explain.

PAPERBACKS FOR FURTHER READING

Boulding, Kenneth. *The Image: Knowledge in Life and Society*. Ann Arbor: University of Michigan Press, 1956. Much of what we know is the result of what images of self, other, and society we hold. Boulding does a remarkable job of portraying the impact of image in our lives. Image, as the author presents it, becomes a most communicative and persuasive language.

Hayakawa, S. I. *Language in Thought and Action*. New York: Harcourt Brace Jovanovich, 1972. This is a very readable treatment of the relationship between language and meaning. Hayakawa is particularly adept at showing how language habits affect values, attitudes, and behavior.

Herzog, William. *The B.S. Factor*. New York: Simon & Schuster, 1973. A former Peace Corps volunteer, Herzog presents an incisive and chilling study of how language misuse and abuse stymie governmental agencies.

Newman, Edwin A. *Strictly Speaking*. New York: Warner Books, 1975. Newman, an NBC news commentator, observes the depths to which correct language usage has sunk in contemporary society. Newman is especially good at focusing on the influence politics and technology have had on language.

Orwell, George. *1984*. New York: Harcourt Brace & World, 1949. This is the disturbing futuristic novel about a totalitarian state whose underpinnings are "newspeak." Recent commentators note that much of what Orwell anticipated has come to pass.

Orwell, George. "Politics and the English Language." In *Shooting an Elephant and Other Essays*. New York: Harcourt Brace Jovanovich, 1950. This essay is another Orwell classic, in which the author details the relationship between fuzzy language usage and politics. Immensely readable and humorous, it is also informative.

Plato. *Laches; Euthyphro; Meno; Cratylus*. These Platonic dialogues relate to the issues of language, knowledge, and reality. They are available in many economical paperback editions.

The Nature of Knowledge

3

Que sais-je? *What do I know?* —Michel de Montaigne

A great part of who and what we are is what we know or claim to know. This is so because knowledge forms the basis of the beliefs, values, and attitudes by which we express ourselves, direct and give meaning to our lives, and distinguish ourselves from others. Therefore, if we are to discover self, it is important to determine what we know. Just what do we know?

One thing you would no doubt say you know is that right now there is a book in front of you. Yet there is a question about the certainty even of a claim as apparent as this one.

Some night, as you gaze up into the heavens, consider that many of the stars you seem to see simply are not there; they have long since extinguished. What you do see is light arriving at your eye after having traveled millions of light-years through space. But all the data that reach our senses travel through space and time, however small. It is possible, therefore, that in that infinitesimally small interval it takes for your brain to register the impulse from the optic nerve that the book you are reading stimulates, the book itself has ceased to exist. Perhaps, then, it would be more accurate to say that you know the book *was* before you. But even if we do know only the past, can we be sure that our particular experiences or ideas of the past are the actual past?

In philosophy these kinds of questions about knowledge are termed epistemological. **Epistemology** is the branch of philosophy that investigates the nature, sources, limitations, and validity of knowledge. In this chapter we ask: what do we know, and what can we know? Epistemologically, then, we are studying the nature of knowledge. Although we shall not explore every facet of the nature of knowledge, we shall look at three germinal viewpoints that should excite further insights

"Are things what they appear to be?"

into the issue of self. These views go by various names. We shall term
them realism, idealism, and phenomenalism.

REALISM: COMMON-SENSE AND REPRESENTATIVE

Common-Sense Realism

If we ask a man how he knows that it is raining, he may tell us to go
outside and see for ourselves. If we ask him how he knows that today
is the hottest day of the year, he again may tell us to go out and *feel*
it, then *listen* to the weather report. If we ask him how he knows that
a lemon is bitter and sugar is sweet, he will tell us to *taste* them. The
question of knowledge, it seems, is bound up with what we perceive,
perception being the process by which we become aware of things
through sense stimulation. Through perception we become aware of
the rain and the heat, the lemon and the sugar. Through perception,
also, we feel confident that we *know*—that is, that we are in possession
of the way things really are.

Do you think there is any difference between things as they really
are and our perception of them? Are things what they appear to be?
To throw some light on these matters, let us introduce a couple of auto
workers, Marvin and Orval. About noon each day they break for lunch.
On the day we join them, Marvin is feeling a little testy because his
wife, Myrtle, has again packed his lunch pail with mushrooms.

Marvin:	I hate mushrooms!
Orval:	Oh, come on, we're not going through that again, are we?
Marvin:	She knows I hate mushrooms! Why is she doing this to me?
Orval:	Forget it. Here, have a fig newton.
Marvin:	I don't want a fig newton.
Orval:	Then eat what you want.
Marvin:	"What I want," he says. I have to eat what I've got, not what I want.
Orval:	Why?
Marvin:	Why? What are you, nuts or something?
Orval:	Look, what if you didn't know the pail was full of mushrooms?
Marvin:	I'd be a happy man, I can tell you that.
Orval:	All right, then. It's not full of mushrooms.
Marvin:	What?
Orval:	Look, you like shrimp, don't you?
Marvin:	Shrimp? Orval, I think I'd kill for a shrimp right now.
Orval:	All right then, shrimp you've got.
Marvin:	What're you talking about?
Orval:	As far as you're concerned that pail is bulging with fat juicy shrimp.
Marvin:	Are you nuts? Here, look at this pail. Mushrooms! Mushrooms, Orval, not shrimp!
Orval:	You sure?
Marvin:	Am I sure? You think I don't know a mushroom when I see one?
Orval:	You know what you see, is that it?
Marvin:	That's right.
Orval:	All right, fine. You see this?
Marvin:	That's a pickle. So what?
Orval:	Wrong.
Marvin:	It's not a pickle?
Orval:	No pickle.
Marvin:	What is it then?
Orval:	It's a Hershey bar.
Marvin:	A Hershey bar. Isn't that something! You work with a guy all your life; you think you know him. Then all of a sudden—boom! He goes bananas!

Orval: Chocolate, not bananas. I love Hershey bars. I could eat them for breakfast. I'm what you'd call a Hershey nut.

Marvin: You said it, I didn't.

Orval: Only trouble is, I break out.

Marvin: I think you have. I think this time you broke out so far they'll never be able to put you back again.

Orval: So now, whenever I want a Hershey bar, I have one of these.

Marvin: I bet you don't break out anymore.

Orval: No way. And you know the beauty of it?

Marvin: You're not even pregnant?

Orval: Go ahead, laugh if you want, but this *is* a Hershey bar. I mean, to me it looks like one, smells like one, and tastes like one.

Marvin: I don't believe it.

Orval: I don't care if you believe it or not. I'm telling you that as far as I'm concerned this *is* a Hershey bar.

Marvin: Is that right? Well I'm telling you that even if it looks like chocolate, smells like it, tastes like it—even if it sounds like it—it's not chocolate!

Orval: Thanks.

Marvin: For what?

Orval: For proving my point.

Marvin: What point?

Orval: A second ago you said you knew that your pail was full of mushrooms because you knew a mushroom when you saw one.

Marvin: So?

Orval: So now you're saying that a person could not only see something, but smell, taste, feel, and hear it as well, and it might not actually be what he's sensing.

Marvin: So what's your point?

Orval: My point is you can't trust your senses to tell you the way things really are.

Marvin: Now what's that supposed to mean?

Orval: It means there's a big difference between your experience of the thing and the thing itself.

Marvin: You mean I'm not really seeing a mushroom at all?

Orval: Could be.

Marvin: Then what am I seeing, wise guy?

Orval: Who knows? Just some stuff in the air your eyes are picking up, that's all.

Marvin: Is that a fact?

Orval: That's a fact.

Marvin: Hey, Orval, you know the stuff in the air my eyes are picking up?

Orval: What about it?

Marvin: It looks just like a mushroom.

Orval: Very funny.

Marvin: Yeah, and I hope your pickle makes you break out.

One thing Marvin believes is that mushrooms, pickles, and everything else exist apart from our awareness of them. No matter how Orval chooses to experience his pickle, Marvin believes that it exists independently of Orval's experience. Marvin is a realist. In epistemology, **realism** is the doctrine that objects of our senses exist independently of their being known by or related to the mind. A pickle is a pickle, no matter what Orval or anyone else thinks. But Marvin is a special kind of realist. Because he also believes that there is no difference between an object and the appearance of that object, he is a **common-sense realist**. Like all common-sense realists, Marvin comes to know things through sense experience. He would agree that, if he had never had a sense experience of mushrooms, he would have no idea what a mushroom is. But because he has had such experience, he knows a mushroom when he sees one. In effect, for a common-sense realist like Marvin, what he perceives coincides exactly with what exists, even though perceived objects exist independently of the perceiver.

Reflection   During a deep hypnotic state, a subject has the sensation of being burned on the finger. The subject actually sees a flame and feels the pain. Afterward, the subject's finger is blistered and must receive medication. Would you say that the subject was burned?

Representative Realism

John Locke (1632–1704), a leading British realist, objected to common-sense realism. Locke did agree that all ideas come from experience. "Let us suppose," he wrote, "the mind to be as we say, white paper, void of all characters, without any ideas: How comes it to be furnished? Whence has it all the *materials* of reason and knowledge? To this I answer in one word: EXPERIENCE. In that all our knowledge is founded."[1] And, like all realists, Locke believed that physical objects exist outside us, that they are independent of our perceptions of them. But at the same time he maintained that the ways entities appear to us should be distinguished from the entities themselves, for "since the mind, in all its thoughts and reasonings, hath no other immediate object but its own ideas, it is evident that our knowledge is only conversant about them."[2] In brief, our knowledge of things is more accurately our knowledge of our *ideas of things*, which in turn are *representative* of the things themselves. Hence Locke is called a **representative realist**. But just how are our ideas representative of things? In answering this question, Locke separated himself from the common-sense realists.

According to Locke, an object—say, a tree—has certain qualities distinct from our perception of it, qualities it would have even if it were not perceived. These he called **primary qualities**. Generally, primary qualities are those that can be measured, like size, shape, and weight. These qualities, said Locke, are in things "whether we perceive them or not; and when they are of that size that we can discover them, we have by these an idea of the thing as it is in itself."[3] Thus, even if an object such as a tree is not perceived, it still has a certain size, shape, and weight. For Locke, our ideas represent these primary qualities.

But Locke also believed that there are qualities that are not within an object itself. A tree, for example, has color, smell, texture, and maybe even a certain taste. In the fall the tree may be one color, in the spring another—as it may be one color at dawn and another at noon. Without its leaves, the tree may be odorless; with them, it may be fragrant. What is the actual color of the tree? Its real smell? For Locke there is no telling, for these qualities are not in the thing itself. Rather, they are ideas that we have. All the tree has is the power to produce in us certain sense experiences. As Locke puts it:

First our Senses, conversant about particular sensible objects, do convey into the mind several distinct perceptions of things, according to those various ways wherein those objects do affect them. And thus we come by those *ideas* we have of *yellow, white, heat, cold, soft, hard, bitter, sweet*, and all those which we call sensible qualities: which when I say the senses convey into the mind what produces there those perceptions; this great source of most of the ideas we have, depending wholly upon our senses and derived by them to the understanding, I call SENSATION.[4]

---

[1]John Locke. *An Essay Concerning Human Understanding.* A. C. Fraser, Ed. Oxford: Clarendon Press, 1894, Vol. 2, p. 2.

[2]John Locke. *An Essay Concerning Human Understanding.* Vol. 2, pp. 1–2.

[3]John Locke. *An Essay Concerning Human Understanding.* Vol. 2, p. 2.

[4]John Locke. *An Essay Concerning Human Understanding.* Vol. 2, p. 4.

According to Locke, therefore, a tree that we call "green" has no greenness; it has only the power to produce in us a sense experience we call "green." These powers that physical objects have to produce sense experiences in us Locke calls **secondary qualities**. They are secondary because the object does not really have the quality "greenness," for example; it has only the power to produce a certain sense experience in us, which we mistakenly presume to be a real quality of the object.

We know how things are, therefore, because of our ideas, which represent the primary qualities of the external world. For example, if we experience the tree as being a certain height, we can trust that idea to resemble the way the tree really is; if we experience it to have a certain circumference, we can trust that idea to resemble the way the tree really is. Thus, we come to know the things around us by having sense experiences of their primary qualities; these experiences resemble the entities themselves.

During the early part of this century a group of men composed a book entitled *Essays in Critical Realism*. Their contemporary realism shows a marked Lockean flavor. Like Locke, the critical realists do not believe that the perception of entities is so direct as the common-sense realists would have it. It is not the outer object that is present in the consciousness, they argue, but **sense data**. Sense data are the images or sense impressions—the immediately given contents of sense experience—which, according to the critical realists, indicate the presence and nature of perceived objects. Only by inference can we go beyond sense data to the object from which they are derived. Critical realists believe that sense data provide accurate contact with entities, that they reveal what objects are and thus what the external world is like. They believe that three factors operate: (1) a perceiver, knower, or conscious mind; (2) the entity or object, consisting of primary qualities; and (3) the sense data, which serve as a bridge between the perceiver and the object perceived.

Still, a question nags: how can we be sure that our perceptions are truly representative of the objects perceived? Locke tried to answer this question with his so-called copy theory.

LOCKE'S "COPY THEORY"

For purposes of understanding, consider the operations of the senses as so many cameras snapping pictures. The senses are "photographing" everything that comes in contact with them. The resulting "photographs" of our experiences are obviously not the things themselves but copies of them. These copies, claimed Locke, are so much like the actual things that through knowing and understanding the copies we come to comprehend the world around us. As Locke puts it:

When our senses do actually convey into our understandings any idea, we cannot but be satisfied that there doth something *at that time* really exist without us, which doth affect our senses, and by them give notice of itself to our apprehensive faculties, and actually produce that idea which we then perceive; and we cannot so far distrust their testimony, as to doubt that such *collections* of simple ideas as we have observed by our senses to be united together, do really exist together.[5]

He is insisting that the senses can do two things: (1) certify that things outside the self actually exist, and (2) provide an accurate picture of those things.

But no matter how representative a photograph, a photograph is still not the thing itself. There still remains a difference between copy and thing, between our idea of something and the thing itself. And if we are in touch with only our ideas of things, how do we know they are really like the things themselves? Furthermore, pictures are frequently distortions of reality. Perhaps the camera snapping them is malfunctioning. Are our senses perfect receivers of sensory data? Even if they are, it is not likely that your sense experiences are identical with mine. Whose, then, are more representative? Such unanswered questions have led philosophers to propose alternative views to Locke's.

Reflection   At lunch another day, Marvin informs Orval that he can prove to him that what he is seeing are actually mushrooms.

Marvin: The way I figure it, you're right and you're wrong.
Orval: Both?
Marvin: Why not? Listen—you see these mushrooms?
Orval: Sure.
Marvin: Okay. Now, the only reason you see them is that some stuff is hitting you in the eyes, right?
Orval: Right.
Marvin: So the eyes are acting like a little camera—snap, snap, all the time just snapping away, snapping pictures of everything that's out there.

Complete the dialogue, letting Orval criticize Marvin's Lockean theory.

IDEALISM

Another British philosopher, George Berkeley (1685–1753), raised similar objections to Locke's epistemological theory. Berkeley agreed with much of what Locke said, except on the question of what we can know.

---

[5]John Locke. *An Essay Concerning Human Understanding.* Vol. 4, pp. 1–2.

Berkeley, while accepting Locke's argument that secondary qualities are subjective, insisted that the same could be said of primary qualities. As Berkeley put it:

They who assert that figure, motion, and the rest of the primary or original qualities do exist without mind in unthinking substances do at the same time acknowledge that colours, sounds, heat, cold and such like secondary qualities, do not; which they tell us are sensations, existing in the mind alone, that depend on and are occasioned by the different size, texture, and motion of the minute particles of matter. . . . Now if it be certain that those original qualities are inseparably united with other sensible qualities, and not, even in thought, capable of being abstracted from them, it plainly follows they exist only in the mind. But I desire anyone to reflect, and try whether he can, by any abstraction of thought conceive the extension and motion of a body without all other sensible qualities. For my own part, I see evidently that it is not in my power to frame an idea of a body extended and moving but I must . . . give it some colour or sensible quality, which is acknowledged to exist only in the mind. In short, extension, figure and motion, abstracted from all other qualities, are inconceivable. Where therefore the other sensible qualities are, there must these be also, to wit, in the mind and nowhere else.[6]

Berkeley is asking: if heat or cold is a secondary quality, a quality only of the mind—as Locke insists—then why not figure and *extension* as well? For example, a coin appears round from one angle and linear from another, just as a tree appears taller from the bottom of a hill than from the top. Why? Because, says Berkeley, all qualities are mind-dependent. Indeed, to think of sensible qualities as existing in outward objects is ridiculous.

For Berkeley, only minds and their ideas exist. In saying that an idea exists, Berkeley means that it is being perceived by some mind. In other words, for ideas *esse est percipi:* "to be is to be perceived." On the other hand, minds are not dependent for their existence on being perceived, because they are perceivers. For Berkeley, therefore, what exists is the conscious mind or some idea or perception held by that mind.

According to Berkeley, then, what we know are our ideas or perceptions. Marvin knows only his idea of those mushrooms; that is all he can possibly know. Berkeley's claim that we can know only ideas is the core of **idealism**. Because Berkeley claims that we know only our own ideas, he is, epistemologically, a **subjective idealist**. The subjectivist contends that there can be no entity or any perception of it without a perceiver; that the perceiver to some degree creates the perceived object; and that everything that is real is a conscious mind or a perception by a conscious mind. When we say that an entity exists we mean that it is perceived.

---

[6]George Berkeley. *A Treatise Concerning the Principle of Human Knowledge.* In A. C. Fraser (Ed.), *The Works of George Berkeley.* Oxford: Clarendon Press, 1901, Vol. 1, p. 87.

"... all qualities are mind-dependent."

Carried to an extreme, Berkeley's thinking can become **solipsism**, the position that only "I" exist and that everything else is just a creation of my subjective consciousness. This position contends that there is only one perceiver—myself. When I stop thinking about it, the world ceases to exist. Other persons and objects have no independent existence but exist solely as creations of my consciousness when and to the degree that I am conscious of them. But it is unfair to push Berkeley's idealism that far, for he never did. To avoid such excesses as the belief that nothing exists if the individual stops perceiving it, Berkeley relied on an outside source for his ideas: God. Things continue to exist even when no conscious mind is perceiving them, because God is forever perceiving them. God always has them "in mind." But now other problems arise, of which the chief one is: if all that exists is a conscious mind and some perception by that mind, how do we know that God exists? If we cannot say that something material exists, how can we insist that something nonmaterial, like God, does? In one of his dialogues between Hylas (substitute "Locke") and Philonus (substitute "Berkeley"), Berkeley anticipates just such an objection.

Hylas: Answer me, Philonus. Are all our ideas perfectly inert beings? Or
             have they any agency included in them?
Philonus: They are altogether passive and inert.
Hylas: And is not God an agent, a being purely active?
Philonus: I acknowledge it.
Hylas: No idea therefore can be like unto, or represent, the nature of God.
Philonus: It cannot.

Hylas: Since therefore you have no idea of the mind of God, how can you conceive it possible that things should exist in His mind? Or, if you can conceive the existence of Matter, notwithstanding I have no idea of it? . . . You admit . . . that there is a spiritual Substance, although you have no idea of it; while you deny there can be such a thing as material Substance, because you have no notion or idea of it. Is this fair dealing? To act consistently, you must either admit Matter or reject Spirit.[7]

"Admit Matter or reject Spirit"—this was something Berkeley seemed unwilling to do. Some claim it was because Berkeley never intended to make such a rigorous criticism of Locke, that from the outset he disbelieved the existence of matter and tried to use the empirical method to prove it. When the empirical method seemed to disprove what he wanted to believe, Berkeley forsook it. Perhaps. In fairness to Berkeley, however, we should note the difficulty of defending the sense of the contention that there are objects that are *not* objects—objects that are unknown to subjects and that are unthought and unexperienced. Surely Berkeley at least anticipated this problem, with which another idealist, Immanuel Kant, would subsequently deal.

Finally, let us be certain about what Berkeley claims and what he does not. He does not deny that there are houses, books, trees, cats, and people. But he denies that these or any other physical objects exist independently of our minds. For Berkeley, there are not beds and then sense experiences of beds that copy or resemble beds, as Locke believed. There is only the sense experience of beds.

But if we talk of our experience of a bed, it seems that we are suggesting that there is a bed to be experienced. This is because our language is misleading. There simply is not an appropriate way to speak of the contents of our sense experiences without mentioning the name of the physical object we believe the experience to be of. But although the language suggests the existence of a physical object causing the experience, Berkeley would not have it. Yes, for Berkeley there are beds, but *not* experiences of beds caused by beds—that is, by physical objects existing outside and independently of us.

Berkeley held that *bed* and all other physical-object words are names of "recurring patterns" of sense experiences, and no more. Physical objects are groups of sense experiences that we are constantly aware of, since we are always having sense experiences that fall into ordered patterns or groups. The most important sense experience is touch, which allows us to distinguish between the imaginary and the real. For Berkeley there is a big difference between a real bed and an imaginary one.

---

[7]George Berkeley. "Three Dialogues Between Hylas and Philonus." In A. C. Fraser (Ed.), *The Works of George Berkeley.* Oxford: Clarendon Press, 1901, Vol. 1, pp. 447–479.

We can sit, lie, or jump on a real bed. We cannot do so on an imaginary one. He believed that, if we cannot have a tactual experience of an object, there is no physical object—even though we might have a visual experience. So, if you "see" a bed but upon going up to it you can't touch it, you must admit that what seemed to be a bed is really a hallucination. On the other hand, if you stumble into something invisible with the tactual shape of a bed, you must say it is an invisible bed, not a hallucination. Thus, Berkeley's ultimate criterion for deciding whether experiences are true perceptions or hallucinations is the sense of touch.

Reflection   Scholar Samuel Johnson, when asked what he thought of Berkeley's idealism, is said to have kicked a stone and declared "I refute it thus!" What do you think Johnson meant? Did he, in fact, thus refute Berkeley?

PHENOMENALISM

In the eighteenth century the German philosopher Immanuel Kant (1724–1808), not wanting to abandon idealism entirely, but acknowledging the problems with Berkeley's version, proposed a theory of perception known as **phenomenalism**. Although Kant's thought is extremely complex, we can at least provide a general outline of those aspects of it relevant to this discussion.

Kant contended that we do not perceive things as they really are. We never perceive the thing-in-itself—what he called the *noumenon*. All we ever know is how the thing appears to us—what he called the *phenomenon*. The noumenon stimulates the senses; the sensations that follow are translated by the mind into ideas or concepts, phenomena. Thus, what we eventually perceive are the ideas produced by our mind.

One element that makes phenomenalism unique is that Kant recognized a logical necessity for the existence of a nonphenomenal realm that is responsible for the existence of a phenomenal one. Unlike Berkeley, for whom what is perceived is all that exists, Kant claimed that, in addition to our experience of a thing, a thing has its own nature—that is, what it is really like. This thing-in-itself, the noumenon, is responsible for the fact that appearances exist at all. Although we can never know what these noumena are in themselves, the mind has the capacity to integrate and interpret sense data and thus make knowledge possible.

Kant distinguishes between the content of knowledge and the form of knowledge. For Kant, content comes from sense experience; form is provided by reason. Our senses provide data such as tastes, smells,

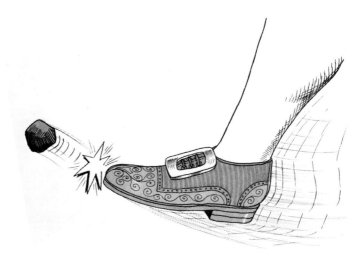

"'I refute it thus!'"

sounds, and shapes, but they do not reveal relationships, laws, or causes. It takes the mind to "make sense" of the data provided by our senses. Kant believed that the mind possesses ideas or conceptual molds by which it orders sense data so that knowing is possible. Because these conceptual molds must be present before any sense data are present, Kant claimed that these molds must be **a priori**; that is, they must precede any sense experience.

To draw out Kant's thinking, especially on this important point about conceptual molds, let us rejoin Marvin and Orval. After wrestling with the mushroom problem, Marvin believes that he has solved it. Now he can be sure that what he is experiencing is how things really are.

Orval:	Marvin, why are you taking off your shoe and sock?
Marvin:	To show you my toe.
Orval:	I don't want to see . . . wow! Your toe's all black and blue!
Marvin:	And swollen.
Orval:	What happened?
Marvin:	Well, the other night Myrtle and I had one of those pepperoni pizzas for dinner. But we couldn't finish it all, so in the middle of the night I got up to get another piece. I didn't want to wake up Myrtle, so I didn't turn on the light. That's when it happened.
Orval:	You stubbed your toe.

Marvin:	Boy, did I stub my toe! That's when I knew that something was really out there.
Orval:	You've got to be kidding.
Marvin:	No, I'm not. I really knew, I'm telling you.
Orval:	Did it make your toe feel any better?
Marvin:	The toe hurt like mad, if you've got to know, but the point is that in the dark I couldn't tell what it was I'd bumped into. But that didn't matter, because I knew I'd bumped into *something*.
Orval:	You mean you didn't know exactly what it was you stubbed your toe on?
Marvin:	Yeah, that's it. I figure living is the same way. We have these ideas and experiences because there's really something out there giving them to us. But all we're really in touch with are the ideas, not the things.
Orval:	Sure. Like I said the other day, there's a difference between your ideas of a thing and the thing itself.
Marvin:	Yeah, but at the same time I figure we can know things.
Orval:	How?
Marvin:	Because of mind. The mind does it by sorting stuff out.
Orval:	Sorting stuff out?
Marvin:	That's right. You see, I think the mind is a sorting machine. You know, one of those gizmos that sorts things out according to their size or shape?
Orval:	Like what they were using at the post office last Christmas to sort the mail.
Marvin:	Yeah, something like that. The mind sorts out all the stuff that comes in through the senses. It puts it all where it belongs; it makes sense out of everything.
Orval:	So what's all this got to do with your toe?
Marvin:	So I stub my toe on the way for a pizza, right? That's my sense experience. But no sooner do I do that than I'm cursing my head off! But what am I cursing?
Orval:	Whatever it is you bumped into.
Marvin:	But how did I know I bumped into something?
Orval:	Because you could feel it.
Marvin:	But Myrtle couldn't feel it, and she knew I bumped into something, because she woke up and right away wanted to know what was happening.
Orval:	Well, what do you expect? You were probably screaming like a stuck pig. You think she could sleep through something like that?
Marvin:	That's right. Even though she didn't feel what I did, she heard me yelling my head off, so she figured something had happened. Just like when I banged my toe *I* figured something was out there.

Orval: But so what?

Marvin: Well, doesn't it strike you as peculiar that both Myrtle and I figured out something in the same way?

Orval: What do you mean, "same way"?

Marvin: Look, she knows that if I'm screaming, something must have happened, right? And I know that if I banged my toe, I must have banged it on something. Just think about that, Orval. We're figuring that if something happened, something must've *caused* it.

Orval: Now wait a minute. Let's see if I've got this. Are you saying that your minds, yours and Myrtle's, took that sense stuff and sorted it out in terms of causes?

Marvin: I couldn't have said it better myself.

Kant believed that the mind has the inborn ability to order sense experiences, that humans come into existence with mental slots or compartments into which sense data fall, are interpreted, and are subsequently known.

The phenomenon we experience, said Kant, results in part from the workings of our senses and mind. The senses help provide the content or the stuff, and the mind provides the form or shape. So, as we noted, the senses provide things like tastes, feelings, and smells, for "all our knowledge begins with experience."[8] But the mind provides the relationships that exist among the sense data. Through an awareness of these relationships, we come to knowledge. The mind is able to impose these relationships because it consists of molds for organizing and interpreting experience. As Marvin says, one of these molds is the causation principle—that is, every event has a cause. Kant believed there were other molds, such as spatial relationships and time. It is through these many molds that we are able to know, claimed Kant— just as the mail-sorting machine is able to distinguish the long from the short, the square from the oblong.

Notice that Kant was trying to solve the same problem Locke was struggling with: how can we hold that an objective, physical world exists and at the same time claim to know it? Although, unlike Locke, Kant relies on idealism to answer the question, his phenomenalism is open to some of the same objections as Locke's realism.

---

[8]Immanuel Kant. *Critique of Pure Reason*. 2nd ed. N. K. Smith, trans. London: Macmillan, 1929, p. 1.

Orval:	But aren't you forgetting something, Marvin?
Marvin:	Yeah, I'd better get this shoe back on before I catch cold.
Orval:	I'm talking about your theory. Let me ask you this. Suppose for some reason that big ugly toe of yours was numb.
Marvin:	It is.
Orval:	I mean suppose it was numb back when you stubbed it.
Marvin:	What are you talking about? If it didn't have any feeling, I wouldn't have felt anything.
Orval:	That's right. In fact, you wouldn't even have known you had stubbed it or that anything was there for you to stub it on.
Marvin:	Sure.
Orval:	So, even if your mind sorts out all this sense stuff like you say it does, it can't do a thing until it gets the sense stuff. Just as that sorting machine can't start sorting until it has some mail to sort.
Marvin:	Get to the point, huh?
Orval:	The point is we're back where we started: everything's hanging on the senses. And we already know that they aren't that reliable. Just think. If you had no feeling in your big toe, you might stub it all over the place and never know it. Why, your toe could be black and blue and you wouldn't have the foggiest idea what happened. And even when you had feeling in your toe, you still didn't know what you'd bumped into; you were still in the dark, weren't you?
Marvin:	That's just a way of speaking, Orval. I could've turned on the lights and seen okay.
Orval:	And what would you have seen? A second ago you said that the thing and your idea of it are different. So turn on all the lights you want. Stare at the foot of the bed for as long as you want. Whatever you're seeing is different from what is actually there. So how do you ever know that what you're seeing is the way the thing really is?

In objecting to Locke's realism, we discussed the reliability of the senses. Orval rightly raises the same objections here. Are the senses all that reliable? Even more bothersome is the thought that, if our perceptions are fundamentally different from reality (phenomena from noumena), it seems we cannot be sure we are perceiving things as they actually are. And what about those mental categories into which sense data fall? Orval did not object to those, but we might—by asking how many of them there are and whether they are the same for everyone.

CONCLUSIONS

It is sometimes said that the only thing we can be certain of is uncertainty itself. We shall have reason to recall this observation again and again in our study of philosophy, and certainly as it applies to the question, "What do I know?"

But although there seem to be no certain answers, we should guard against thinking that questions like these are not worth asking. If this were so, we should not continue to ask: What should I do with my life? How should I deal with other people? What should I believe?—and all the other imponderables. But we do, and seemingly we must. Perhaps this is so because one of the factors that makes humans unique is not that we are problem-solvers but that we are question-askers. But, more to the point, the fact that no certain answers are possible does not mean that no answers are probable. To reason as if there were either certain answers or no answers is to fall into a false dilemma. Frequently there is ample middle ground. This discussion of knowledge is a good example of how adequate a probable answer or solution to a problem is.

Just what conclusions about knowledge and self can we draw from having listened to Marvin and Orval, and learned something about the thinking of three philosophers? First, the problem of knowledge is not so simple as we first may have thought. Although we constantly claim to know things and thereby express ourselves, underlying these claims is often a naïve assumption about the nature of knowledge: that through our senses we know things precisely as they are. According to this position, known as common-sense realism, things exist outside us but at the same time inside us in precisely the same way. Thus, the self is passive; it has no influence on its knowledge of entities but experiences them as they are. By making the knower the known, the common-sense realist would lose the self in an objective reality. We have heard enough criticism of this position to realize that it leads more often to a caricature of knowledge than to an accurate description of it.

Yet there is probably something "out there," and it is likely that individuals often report it accurately, if not precisely. It seems that we can know things. We should come to this conclusion because this assumption is more explanatory than the assumption that nothing is out there. To assume something is out there fits in with our experiences, the black and blue toes of our lives. It makes sense. Moreover, such an assumption can be tested by stubbing your toe or sending a man to the moon. And it allows us to predict the course of events, from the speed of a falling penny to the position of Jupiter on January 1, 2000. So there does seem to be an objective world with which we interact and over which we can exercise some control. But do we know it exactly as it is? That is another question.

Extreme subjectivism, or solipsism, would make a shambles of objective reality. In effect, it makes each self a creator of its own world. Things exist only as the subjective self perceives them. Whereas common-sense realism eliminates the self, solipsism eliminates all that is not self. But, again, there are unquestionably subjective elements in our knowledge. The self, in fact, perceives things from its own vantage point. It frequently sees things not as they are but as it would have them. Sense data do pass through the filter of subjective consciousness and eventuate in our ideas of things. To some degree, then, our knowledge of the objective world apparently does rely on our perceptions of things. Each self is unique in the sense that it probably sees things as no one else quite does or has or will, and in the sense that it alone can be aware of its own perceptions.

SUMMARY

We opened this chapter by noting that the issue of self is tied up with the question of knowledge. Questions about knowledge fall under the heading of epistemology, which, among other things, investigates the nature of knowledge. One answer to the question of what we know is that we know what we experience. This answer presumes that things have an existence independent of us. Such a belief is called realism. John Locke believed that we really know only our ideas of things, but that our ideas are truly representative of how things are. George Berkeley, a subjective idealist, claimed that physical objects exist only in the sense that they are our perceptions. Immanuel Kant believed that we know only our ideas of things—the phenomena—and not how things really are, the noumena. Nevertheless, the mind has the ability to impose certain relationships on objective reality; in this way we know what is objectively real. We concluded that extreme positions on the nature of knowledge seem untenable, that the nature of knowledge appears to be both subjective and objective.

MAIN POINTS

1. Epistemology is the branch of philosophy that investigates the nature, sources, limitations, and validity of knowledge.
2. There are at least three theories concerning the nature of knowledge: realism, idealism, and phenomenalism.
3. Realism is the doctrine that things exist independently of anyone's knowing them. A common-sense realist is one who sees no difference between an object and the experience of it. A representative realist is one who distinguishes between an object and the experience of it.

4. John Locke was a representative realist who held that objects have primary qualities, qualities distinct from our perception of them: size, shape, weight. He also believed that they had secondary qualities, qualities that we impose on them: color, smell, texture, and so on. We come to know the objective world through sense experience, which is a "copy" of reality.

5. According to Berkeley's subjective idealism, all we know are our own ideas, and all that exists is the conscious mind and what is perceived by it. Carried to an extreme, Berkeley's thinking can become solipsism, the position that only "I" exist and that everything else is a creation of my subjective consciousness.

6. Immanuel Kant distinguished between our experience of things (the phenomena) and things as they are (noumena). The mind, claimed Kant, has the ability to sort our sense data (phenomena) and posit relationships among the sense data. Through an awareness of these relationships, we come to knowledge.

7. Extreme epistemological positions like common-sense realism and solipsism seem untenable; the former eliminates the self, the latter eliminates all that is not the self. We help explain reality better by assuming that there probably is an objective reality than by assuming the opposite. But there also seems to be a subjective element in knowledge: each individual does experience things as no one else quite does.

SECTION EXERCISES

Realism

1. Orval has raised one serious objection to Marvin's common-sense realism. Can you describe it? Do you think it is valid?

2. What example can you think of that suggests that the senses are imperfect receivers of information?

3. Do you think Marvin's position is a sound one? If not, what would you substitute in its place?

Representative Realism, Copy Theory

1. For Locke, shape is a primary quality, color a secondary quality. Would you agree or disagree with the following statements, and why? As a result, would you agree or disagree with Locke's distinction?

    a. Even when something is not being perceived, it has shape; but it does not have color when it is not being perceived.

    b.   You can experience shape with more than one sense, but not color.

    c.   The shape of a thing never changes, but its color does so frequently.

    d.   A thing without color can have shape.

2.   Locke believed that we come into the world as a "blank slate." Ideas come after sense experiences. Would you agree that we can have no ideas without first having sense experiences? Or would you hold that at least some ideas (for example, everything must have a cause; there is a God; murdering a 2-year-old baby for your own pleasure is evil) do not depend on sense experience?

3.   Locke inspired a movement called British empiricism. **Empiricism** is the belief that all knowledge originates in sense experience. Empiricism accepts nothing as true that cannot be verified through sense experience. Would you subscribe to this position?

4.   What kinds of statements do you think Marvin and Locke would consider true? In other words, under what circumstances would they consider true the statement "It is raining"? How would they verify this statement? Do you think this verification process is sound?

Idealism

1.   Does Berkeley's idealism deny an objective reality?

2.   According to Berkeley, in what sense can we not know anything?

3.   Explain this statement: "Berkeley's idealism originates in a physical world and ends in denying knowledge of it."

4.   What evidence would you give to prove that while you were sleeping a physical reality outside you persisted?

Phenomenalism

1.   Says Marvin: "We get these ideas and experiences of things because there's really something out there giving them to us. But all we're really in touch with are the ideas, not the things." Show the influence of Berkeley and Locke in this position.

2.   Marvin claims that he and Myrtle arrived at their knowledge in the same way. Describe the process.

3.   **Skepticism** is the epistemological view that all assumptions must be doubted until proved true. The skeptic David Hume claimed that we can have no ideas without sense impressions. Would Kant agree?

ADDITIONAL EXERCISES

1. What bipolarities do you detect in Locke's, Berkeley's, and Kant's thinking? Do you think they are genuine bipolarities?
2. Which of the five views of human nature described in Chapter 1 do you think Locke, Berkeley, and Kant would subscribe to?
3. When you call someone a "realist" or an "idealist" in everyday talk, what do you mean? Is there any connection between these meanings and a philosophical "realist" or "idealist"?
4. How would you describe the fundamental difference between the role the mind plays in realism and the role it plays in idealism?
5. Imagine us in possession of more or fewer senses than we have now. In what respect would the world be the same? In what respect would it be different?
6. We have often heard the expression "You've got to see it to believe it." What things, if any, would you say must be experienced before they can be known?
7. Where do you get your ideas of beauty, justice, love, and the like? Plato, another idealist, believed that we receive these perfect ideas in a pre-life. As we live, then, we simply recall these ideas as the things of the physical world remind us of them (for example, a beautiful woman, a just man). In effect, we never learn; we simply remember. Are such ideas inborn? Or do we acquire them, as Locke would say, by first experiencing individual things that are beautiful and just and then formulating an idea from these?
8. How do you *know* you exist? What evidence can you point to?

PAPERBACKS FOR FURTHER READING

Berkeley, George. *A Treatise Concerning the Principles of Human Knowledge.* Colin M. Turbayne, Ed. New York: Liberal Arts Press, 1954. Turbayne's introduction is helpful for understanding Berkeley's major work.

Berrill, N. J. *Man's Emerging Mind.* New York: Dodd, Mead, 1955. A British zoologist argues that through senses, science, and our "inward nature," we have come to know the world around us. Love and hope, claims Berrill, are natural outgrowths of our evolution, and at our best we "represent the spirit of the universe."

Locke, John. *An Essay Concerning Human Understanding,* 2 vols. J. W. Tolton (Ed. Vol. 1) and A. O. Woozley (Ed. Vol. 2). New York: Dutton, 1973. Locke's classic on perception and knowledge is enhanced by helpful introductions.

Pirandello, Luigi. *It Is So If You Think So*, in Eric Bentley, Ed., *Naked Masks: Five Plays*. New York: Dutton, 1957. Italian novelist and playwright Pirandello concerns himself in this play with the mental state of a character called Ponza. Is Ponza insane and keeping his wife and her mother from seeing one another? Or is he sane, and the mother not really the mother at all, but a madwoman who has never accepted the death of her daughter? The play raises pertinent questions about the subjective/objective nature of truth.

Plato. *Republic*, Books 6 and 7. F. M. Cornford, trans. Oxford: Oxford University Press, 1945. These books from Plato's description of his classic utopia contain Plato's theory of the nature of knowledge.

Wooldridge, Dean E. *Mechanical Man: The Physical Basis of Intelligent Life*. New York: McGraw-Hill, 1968. Wooldridge, a research engineer, argues that human intelligence, consciousness, and behavior are explained solely through physical laws.

Truth

4

No one is so wrong as the man who knows all the answers.
—Thomas Merton

What we know or claim to know is a measure of who we are. But every claim to knowledge is also a claim to truth. If you say "I know that going to college will increase my earning potential," you are saying "It's true that going to college will increase my earning potential." You make a similar assertion of truth when you claim to know that democracy is the best form of government, that God exists, or that murder is wrong. Thus, what we consider true is as much an expression of self as what we claim to know.

Just as we asked what knowledge is, we now ask what truth is. In asking this, we inquire about the nature of truth—just what it means to say that "George Washington was the first President of the United States" is true and that "Abraham Lincoln resigned office" is false. An investigation into the nature of truth is important because it reveals the basis for the individual truths each of us holds and lives by. But it is difficult to appreciate the importance of the nature of truth without first understanding the problems involved in the nature of truth. So let us consider this problem by creating a courtroom situation.

THE PROBLEM OF TRUTH

The Prosecution has just called Wilbur Scaife, a witness whose testimony is sure to destroy the case of famous defense attorney Lamont P. Eveready. Never has he had a greater challenge than to discredit witness Scaife, and fast!

91

Bailiff:	Do you swear to tell the truth, the whole truth, and nothing but the truth, so help you God?
Scaife:	I do.
Eveready:	Objection, Your Honor.
Judge:	But the witness has not even taken his seat.
Eveready:	Defense objects, Your Honor, on grounds that the witness has perjured himself.
Judge:	Perjured himself? Why, he hasn't even answered a question yet.
Eveready:	Defense humbly begs to differ, Your Honor. The witness has sworn to tell the truth, the whole truth, and nothing but the truth. Defense contends that the witness Wilbur Scaife is in no position to meet that oath, since he knows nothing of the truth of which he speaks.
Judge:	Knows nothing of . . .
Eveready:	To put it simply, Your Honor: Scaife doesn't know the truth from a hole in the ground.
Scaife:	Oh, yeah? You want to step outside and say that?
Judge:	The witness will contain himself. Can Defense prove this contention?
Eveready:	Defense can and will, Your Honor.
Judge:	Then proceed.
Eveready:	Thank you, Your Honor. Now, Mr. Scaife, you have just sworn a holy oath before God Almighty to tell the truth, the whole truth, and nothing but the truth. Is that correct?
Scaife:	Yes.
Eveready:	Presumably, you have sworn this oath knowing full well what it means.
Scaife:	Yes, I have. It means I'm going to tell the truth.
Eveready:	The whole truth and nothing but the truth.
Scaife:	You said it.
Eveready:	Now, Scaife, what in your opinion is the truth?
Scaife:	The truth? The truth is the way things are.
Eveready:	The way things are. All right. *American flag*—is that the truth?
Scaife:	What about the American flag?
Eveready:	Oh, I must say something *about* it?
Scaife:	Well, sure. How else would you know if you got the truth or not?
Eveready:	I see. So what you're really saying is that the truth refers not so much to the ways things are as it does to a *statement* about the way things

are. In other words it would be silly to say "American flag" is true. But it would make perfect sense to say "There's a red, white, and blue American flag in this courtroom."

Scaife: Now you've got the truth, mister.

Eveready: You mean that statement is true?

Scaife: You bet your life it is.

Eveready: And tell the court, Scaife, how you know the statement "There is a red, white, and blue American flag in this courtrooom" is true.

Scaife: Because I see that flag right over there.

Eveready: Because you see it. Tell me, Scaife, does everything you see lead you to make a true statement?

Scaife: I don't get you.

Eveready: Let me illustrate. You've no doubt seen a pencil resting in a glass of water.

Scaife: Sure.

Eveready: How would you describe such a pencil?

Scaife: You mean that it looks bent?

Eveready: It looks bent. Your eyes report it as bent.

Scaife: But it's not.

Eveready: No, it's not. Consequently, the statement "That pencil is bent" is not true, is it?

Scaife: No way.

Eveready: And yet your eyes report it as true, don't they?

Scaife: But it's different here with the flag. The flag is actually here, the way you said it was. The pencil isn't. That's the difference.

Eveready: The flag is actually here, the way I said it was. . . . Your Honor, the Defense wishes to call from the gallery for one question only Ms. Bertha Moynier.

Prosecution: I object, Your Honor. Counsel's line of questioning has no purpose except to rattle, confuse, and intimidate the witness.

Judge: The irregularity of his request forces me to warn Defense that for his and his client's sake the Bench hopes all this has some constructive end.

Eveready: I assure the Bench it has.

Judge: Will Ms. Moynier please rise?

Eveready: Ms. Moynier, will you please tell the court whether the following statement is true: "There is a red, white, and blue American flag in this room."

Moynier:	I don't know.
Scaife:	What! She must be blind!
Eveready:	I compliment you on your powers of deduction, Scaife. Ms. Moynier is, in fact, blind.
Judge:	What's the meaning of this demonstration, Eveready?
Eveready:	Your Honor, the purpose of this exercise is to show the court that what the witness, Wilbur Scaife, *thinks* is truth is in fact nothing but hearsay. Indeed, what the witness *thinks* is truth consigns truth to the very dubious area of sense-data interpretation. Such interpretation must be purely subjective and need not have anything to do with the way things actually are.
Prosecution:	Your Honor, I have sat here patiently while the Defense has made a mockery of this court. I submit that he has gone beyond the role of court jester and is now showing open contempt for the Bench itself!
Eveready:	If the court will allow, the Defense would like to call from the gallery Mr. Bartholomew Peabody in order to prove the sincerity of Defense's cause.
Judge:	With great reluctance, the Bench asks Mr. Bartholomew Peabody to rise.
Eveready:	Thank you, Your honor. Mr. Peabody, will you tell the court whether the following statement is true: "There is a red, white, and blue American flag in this courtroom."
Peabody:	Well, if you want to know the truth, what you say is so and it isn't.
Eveready:	Would you explain to the court why my statement is true and not true?
Peabody:	First, you do have a flag, all right. Any fool can see that.
Scaife:	There! What did I tell you?
Judge:	The witness will restrain himself.
Peabody:	But it's not a red, white, and blue flag. It's red, white, and green.
Scaife:	Green! He must be color-blind!
Eveready:	Must he? Why? Because he disagrees with you?
Prosecution:	Your Honor, how long will the Bench allow this travesty to continue?
Eveready:	On the contrary, Your Honor, the court is hardly witnessing a travesty. Rather, in a matter of minutes, the court has heard three persons report different "truths" while supposedly observing the same object at the same time. Yet the witness Wilbur Scaife would have us believe that the truth characterizes that statement which reports an actual fact. I respectfully submit, Your Honor, that we can never know how things really are, because the only way we can come to such knowledge is through sense experience, which I have just demonstrated to be unreliable.

Judge:	Is Defense suggesting that in this case the testimonies of a blind and a color-blind person are equal to that of a normally sighted one?
Eveready:	Your Honor, may I respectfully answer with another question? Just what constitutes "normal sight"? Is it not a convention, a standard that the majority sets? Would the court submit the question of truth to a head count?
Judge:	On the question of whether there is in fact a red, white, and blue American flag in this courtroom, the court might seriously entertain such a proposal.
Eveready:	So be it, Your Honor. I submit the question to the gallery. Let a show of hands determine the truth of the statement "There is a red, white, and blue American flag in this courtroom."
Judge:	Nobody! Not a single hand?
Prosecution:	I object, Your Honor! The Defense has obviously stacked the gallery as a card shark would a deck of playing cards.
Eveready:	The Prosecution's powers of deduction are as astonishing as Wilbur Scaife's, Your Honor. True, the Defense has stacked the gallery, but only to demonstrate that, when we insist that truth is an agreement between a statement of fact and the fact itself, we play the game of life with a stacked deck.

Although Eveready claims that when we insist that truth is an agreement between a statement of fact and the fact itself we "play the game of life with a stacked deck," this is the most common way of ascertaining truth. Take the simple statement "It is raining." We know this statement is true if, in fact, it is raining—that is, if the statement "It is raining" agrees with the fact that it is actually raining. Yet Eveready's objections nag. They raise fundamental questions about the nature of truth and about our uncanny powers of self-deception. Is truth only that which can be empirically verified? Do we make our own truth? Is truth ultimately an illusion, a grand design that each of us chooses to abide by for purposes of order and sanity?

In this chapter we raise these questions. We investigate three theories on the nature of truth: the correspondence, coherence, and pragmatic theories. By the time we have finished, we should have some insights into how vital a role a theory of truth, whatever it may be, plays in the way we view self and that which is outside self. You may decide that what you believe is as close to the truth as you are likely to get. On the other hand, you may conclude that you have been living fraudulently, living a chronic low-grade self-deceit. Whatever you conclude, you should realize that your concept of truth helps form the basis of your self-concept.

THREE THEORIES OF TRUTH

Correspondence Theory

In the last chapter, we examined a typical view of the nature of knowledge: that knowledge originates in sense experience. Consistent with this position is the belief that truth is an accurate report of the way things actually are. Thus, we experience things and then make statements about them. A statement we make that reports how things actually are is a true statement. Thus, "Water boils at 212 degrees Fahrenheit at sea level" is a true statement because it corresponds to the fact that water does boil at 212 degrees Fahrenheit at sea level. This we have experienced directly. "Every U.S. President has been a male" is true because the statement corresponds to the fact that every U.S. President has been a male. This we have experienced indirectly, through reading and learning. This **correspondence theory** of truth, then, holds that truth is an agreement between a statement of fact and the fact itself. In general, epistemological realists such as John Locke hold this position. And the belief seems reasonable enough until someone like Lamont P. Eveready comes along and starts poking around.

Objections

In effect, Eveready is asking: since we know only our experiences, how can we ever get outside them to verify what reality actually is? It seems that the correspondence theory of truth assumes that we know not only our interpretations of things but also the way things actually are apart from our interpretations. Whether Eveready has "stacked" the courtroom is hardly so important as what he claims to have demonstrated: we cannot know the truth apart from our sense experiences. And since we are never in touch with anything but our own experiences, we can never know whether they actually correspond with how things really are.

Reflection   Suppose one of your senses was supersensitive. For example, suppose your hearing was so acute that you could actually hear a plant "breathe" or your own blood flow. How would your experience and understanding of things be different from the way they now are?

Coherence Theory

Exasperated by Eveready's protests, the Judge has summoned him and the Prosecution to the bench. Let us eavesdrop on these private remarks between Judge and counselors.

"... since we know only our experiences,
how can we ever get outside them to verify
what reality actually is?"

Judge:	Now see here, Eveready, this line of interrogation can't continue. It's making a shambles of my court.
Prosecution:	Amen!
Judge:	Eveready, aren't you at all interested in the law?
Eveready:	Of course I am, Your Honor. But I'm also interested in truth. Does Your Honor think the law and the truth are mutually exclusive?
Judge:	Stop putting words in my mouth! You think I'm Scaife?
Eveready:	I beg your pardon, Your Honor.
Judge:	Pardon not granted. Didn't they teach you in law school the kind of truth on which much of the judicial process is based?
Eveready:	*Kind* of truth? Are there *kinds* of truth, Your Honor?
Prosecution:	Stop sassing the Judge.
Judge:	I'll be judge of who's sassing me. Let me ask you something, Eveready.
Eveready:	Proceed.
Judge:	How are innocence and guilt determined?
Eveready:	By a trial.
Judge:	And what happens at a trial? I mean a normal trial, not this circus.
Eveready:	Well, at a normal trial, lawyers present cases.

Judge:	Exactly. And isn't it true that in theory the better case wins?
Eveready:	In theory.
Judge:	And what makes for the better case, Eveready?
Eveready:	Obviously, persuading the jury.
Judge:	Obviously. And which case, in theory, should persuade the jury?
Eveready:	The one that hangs together better.
Judge:	Precisely. Your job is to present the jury with pieces of a puzzle, isn't it? The jury's job is to take each piece and evaluate it. How? Well, let's see. They can't go back to the scene of the crime or to the circumstances that you describe, can they? No, they can't. So how do they figure out if a particular piece is true? I'll tell you how: usually by seeing how it fits in with all the other pieces. If it fits in, if it's consistent, if it doesn't contradict any of the other pieces, then it's true. At the very end, if you've presented a good case, all the pieces fit. The truth is right in front of their noses. "This person," they declare, "is guilty" or "not guilty."

Notice how the Judge's theory of truth differs from the correspondence theory. According to him, a statement is true if it is consistent with other statements that are regarded as true. The essential test is not correspondence between statement and actual fact but coherence between statement and other relevant statements. Notice that the Judge wants to know if the case hangs together, if all the pieces fit together. This **coherence theory** of truth, as it is called, insists that truth is a property of a related group of consistent statements. A particular statement is true if it is integrated within the framework of all the other statements already accepted as true.

Mathematics is a good example of the coherence theory in operation. Building upon a certain number of basic statements, mathematics constructs an entire system of "truths." In science, likewise, theories gain respectability when they are consistent with the body of already accepted judgments. Of course, there are exceptions. The Copernican theory and Darwin's theory of evolution were so powerful that they forced people to reconsider what they had already accepted. Generally, however, a scientific idea's respectability depends on its consistency with a previously established body of truth.

As you might imagine, the coherence theory of truth is particularly meaningful for the idealist. Since, as the idealist maintains, we cannot compare our ideas of the world with the actual world, we must rely for truth on a system of consistent statements. As an example of how a philosopher can build a whole world view on a coherence theory of truth, consider Plato.

Using Euclid's geometry as a model, Plato formulated a coherence theory of truth based on the belief that he had discovered a means of attaining truth without relying on observation or sensory experience. He was convinced he had discovered a perfect and true world of ideal (that is, non-sensible) Forms. These Forms, he claimed, are connected to one another by eternal and necessary relationships. Through thought, the mind can grasp this world of ideas, which, when understood, reveals a complete system of unchanging and necessary truth.

Unlike Berkeley, Plato believed that ideas exist outside us in some perfect form, in some objective state. This perfect world of Forms, said Plato, we experience in a pre-life. When we are born we forget them. As the nineteenth-century English romantic poet Wordsworth put it, "Our birth is but a sleep and a forgetting." During life we experience a physical world that reminds us of that perfect world. For Plato, therefore, we never really learn anything; we *remember* it. We recognize people as beautiful or as just because they remind us of the Forms of perfect beauty or justice.

The sense world, then, is just a shadow of the "real world," the world of perfect Ideas or Forms. For Plato, we know something only when we contact this ideal world, when we abandon the illusion that the physical world is the only reality.

It is true that Plato's judgment concerning the truth about physical things rests on how well our assertions about physical facts *correspond* with the Forms themselves. But his theory of Forms is itself a complex series of statements regarding the *coherent* relationships among the Forms. Underlying Plato's system is the assumption that a perfect world of Forms does exist. More importantly, it is on the basis of this assumption that Plato seems to justify his claims.

For example, Plato claims that poetry and drama are often morally objectionable. Just how can he "prove" that? Well, think of what these arts often do: usually they represent the physical world. But for Plato the physical world is a mere shadow of the perfect world of Forms. The arts, therefore, can distract us from knowing the "real world" of pure ideas; they draw us farther and farther away from it. Therefore, they are often morally objectionable. Consistent? Coherent? Very much so. In the *Republic*, in which he presents his utopia, Plato argues with similar consistency. Central to all his claims is the world of perfect Forms.

But is such systemic coherence alone a guarantee of truth? After all, what evidence is there for assuming a world of perfect Forms to begin with? It is hard for us to accept a form or idea as "more real" than what we can actually experience through the senses—to believe that what we actually see or touch is "less real" than what we cannot. True, the world of Forms may be logical; it may appeal to our minds. But is it experiential? Does it appeal to our senses as well? These reservations about Platonic idealism can be extended more generally to the coherence theory of truth.

Objections

Recall that, at one time, almost everyone believed that the earth was the center of the solar system. This belief stemmed back to the ancient Greek astronomer Ptolemy (of the second century A.D.). Why did everyone believe this? Because it made sense. It was part of Ptolemy's very *consistent* system of judgments, which, as a result of their consistency, held sway for 1500 years. In fact, the major difference between Ptolemy's theory and the one that replaced it, Copernicus's, was that the latter's was simpler. Yet both theories were consistent. The point is that coherence theory seems to make no distinction between consistent truth and consistent error. A judgment may be true if it is consistent with other judgments; but what if the other judgments are false? If first judgments are not true, they can produce a system of consistent error.

Furthermore, even within the coherence tradition, philosophers have disagreed over basic first judgments. We saw that Plato subscribed to a belief in pure Forms as his beginning postulate. These Forms are fixed and unchanging. In the nineteenth century the German idealist Georg Hegel (1770–1831) saw change, flux, and process as the fundamental characteristics of all things. Absolute reality for Hegel was not a world of pure Forms, as for Plato, but the process of "becoming." Both erected coherent systems based on their postulates. Which, if either, is true?

Another objection is that a coherence theory seemingly must, in the last analysis, rely on correspondence. After all, if a judgment is coherent it must cohere with another judgment. But what of first judgments? What do they cohere with? If they are "first," they cannot cohere with anything. It seems that their truth can be verified only by determining whether they report an actual fact. But this is the correspondence theory. Proponents of the coherence theory, however, insist that a judgment of fact itself can be verified only by the coherence theory. As contemporary idealist Brand Blanshard (1892–) illustrates it:

Suppose we say, "the table in the next room is round"; how should we test this judgment? In the case in question, what verifies the statement of fact is the perceptual judgment that I make when I open the door and look. But then what verifies the perceptual judgment itself? . . . To which the reply is, as before, that a judgment of fact can be verified only by the sort of apprehension that can present us with a fact, and that this must be a further judgment. And an agreement between judgments is best described not as a correspondence, but as coherence.[1]

---

[1] Brand Blanshard. "The Nature of Thought," in Sidney and Beatrice Rome, Eds., *Philosophical Interrogation.* New York: Holt, Rinehart and Winston, 1964, p. 210.

"If first judgments are not true, they can
produce a system of consistent error."

Reflection   Can you think of one thing about yourself that, although you
cannot prove through correspondence, you accept, because it "fits in"
with what is known about humans or what you know about yourself?

Pragmatic Theory

Because of the evident weaknesses in the correspondence and coherence
theories, philosophers of recent times have suggested another possibility, the pragmatic theory of truth. Let us see how it works by returning to the Judge's chambers.

Prosecution: Well, if you want my opinion, I think the whole discussion is silly.
I mean, if you want to know what's true, find out what works.

Eveready: What?

Judge: Are you saying that if something works, it's true?

Prosecution: What else can it be? How else can you judge what's true, except by
its results? Take the theory of the sun-centered solar system, for
example. What makes it true is that it works. It is true because it
accurately describes a situation in such a way that people can use
that description to produce desired results. That theory's allowed us

to plot the position of the heavenly bodies, estimate the distance between them, send satellites into space, and put men on the moon. Previous theories couldn't have produced these results. They just wouldn't have worked. That's why they were untrue, while this one is true.

Eveready: But if what works is true, what's stopping it from not working?

Prosecution: Nothing. Then it wouldn't be true any longer. The trouble with you, Eveready, is that you're hung up on the idea that truth is something absolute, something unchanging and unchangeable. Well, it's not so. You'd better get used to that. Where do you think truth comes from, anyway? It comes from you and me and the Judge. And every man, woman, and child who's ever lived or will live. It doesn't grow on trees for the picking. People make it! They change it and they make it again. We make our own truth!

Eveready: So, according to you, if something works, it's true.

Prosecution: Exactly.

Eveready: Well, it sounds to me as if you're saying that if I believe I'm Napoleon, I am Napoleon.

Prosecution: Your belief that you're Napoleon must face the test of truth: how does the belief work out in practice? Does it lead to satisfactory results? In your case, it wouldn't. People would be frightened by you, they'd avoid you, they'd probably lock you up and throw away the key. Your belief doesn't work. Therefore, it's not true.

Eveready: Well, what about the theory that the earth was once visited by astronaut gods? Presumably the belief worked for its author. It produced satisfactory results for him, just as you say the truth must. Now, does that make his theory true?

Prosecution: You make it sound as if the author were merely claiming to be happy or to have a toothache, Eveready. His claim isn't just a private one, you know. He's not just reporting his own internal state. He's making a public claim. So, as with all public claims, satisfactory results depend on more than just the results they produce for a single person.

Eveready: But how do you know if his claim works or not?

Prosecution: Test it. Try it and see if it works. What else does it explain? What else does it account for? What use can we make of it? That's how to find out if it works.

The Prosecution's idea of truth is different from both the correspondence and the coherence theories. He would admit that we can know only our experiences; as a result, truth cannot be what corresponds with reality. But he would also view the coherence theory as far too abstract and impractical to use to measure truth. Instead, he wishes to introduce usefulness as the measure of truth. Truth, he insists, can be defined only in relation to consequences. A statement is true if people can use that statement to achieve results they desire. There is no absolute truth, or truth that is unchanging. To verify a belief as truth, we should see if the belief satisfies the whole of human nature over a long period of time, if it can be proved scientifically, or if it aids us individually or collectively in the biological struggle for survival. In short, the Prosecution argues for a pragmatic theory of truth. This position essentially states: if something works, it is true.

The pragmatic theory of truth is the cornerstone of **pragmatism**, an essentially American philosophy that has grown up during the nineteenth and twentieth centuries, especially through the writings of Charles S. Peirce (1839–1914), William James (1842–1910), and John Dewey (1859–1942). Having tired of older European outlooks, especially those that viewed humans primarily as rational or mechanical beings, the pragmatists saw the human as one who must use the practical consequences of beliefs to determine their truth and validity. *"True ideas,"* says James, *"are those that we can assimilate, validate, corroborate and verify.* False ideas are those that we cannot."[2] Truth is what "happens to an idea." If you remember that traditional views saw truth as something fixed, you can appreciate the novelty of this statement. James wanted to know what concrete difference a belief would make in our lives. "A difference that makes no difference is no difference." Events make ideas true, and an idea that produces satisfactory consequences is a true idea. Truth changes; it is subjective and relative. It is "the expedient in the way of our thinking." Although pragmatism was a new and vigorous approach to the problem of truth that matched the youth and energy of nineteenth-century America, whose future seemed limited only by its ambition and imagination, it is not without flaws.

Objections

A potential weakness in the pragmatic theory arises in questions that cannot be resolved scientifically. Take, for example, the question of God's existence. Suppose the Prosecution believes in God, and that his belief produces satisfactory results for him. He is happy, well adjusted, and confident of life's meaning. In short, the Prosecution's belief in God works. Suppose, on the other hand, the same belief produces in Eveready guilt, fear, and general anxiety. For Eveready, a belief in God does not work. In the last analysis, there is no way these claims can be verified.

---

[2]William James. *Pragmatism: A New Name for Some Old Ways of Thinking.* New York: Longmans, Green, 1907, p. 199.

"Truth is what 'happens to an idea.'"

It appears that the pragmatist must say that for the Prosecution it is *true* that God exists and for Eveready it is *true* that God does not exist. But God cannot both exist and not exist. Evidently, one of these men believes not a truth but a falsehood. As a result, as critics suggest, pragmatists seem to be encouraging us to see things not as they are but as we would have them.[3]

Also noteworthy is a pragmatist tendency that pragmatists themselves would caution against: once having decided an issue such as God's existence, the tendency is to shut down intellectual scrutiny, to refuse to reconsider, even in the light of additional evidence. It is important to realize that pragmatists do not and surely would not advocate this action. What they are saying is that, on questions that empirical evidence alone will not resolve, we may feel intellectually respectable in following feeling, intuition, and emotion. But we must exercise care. Otherwise we can easily be confirmed in mistaken notions and ideas. We can glibly confuse belief with truth and forget that belief does not alter fact. We can conveniently forget that what happens to work and what is true are not necessarily the same, although what is true works. Finally, we can dangerously ignore the fact that countless theories in economics, religion, and science that "worked" for a period of time were ultimately proved erroneous.

---

[3]The value of James's position for religious belief is fully discussed in Chapter 8.

Reflection   Recall three instances in which you had to operate as if you knew the truth. In what areas did these instances occur? Did it turn out that you indeed knew the truth? Would you say that your belief in any way brought the truth to pass?

The Compatibility of the Truth Theories

Eveready, the Judge, and the Prosecution are not as opposed as they appear to be. If we take a closer look at the various positions that Eveready assumes in the dialogues, we shall notice that, rather than being contradictory, the three theories of truth are compatible with one another.

First, Eveready believes that truth is not something that changes or is relative or that we go around making. Yet, at the outset of Scaife's testimony, he went to flamboyant lengths to prove the opposite: that truth is relative. Eveready could object that what he was actually demonstrating was the relativity of belief, not of truth; that the statement "There is a red, white, and blue American flag in this courtroom" is in fact either true or false, that we just don't know which it is. Still, if we do not know which it is, then Eveready cannot claim to know that it must be one or the other. It seems, then, that Eveready has no recourse but to declare that truth must exist. Of course, he could also insist that although truth may exist we can never know it.

Some philosophers have been that skeptical. The ancient Greek Gorgias (483–376 B.C.) claimed that we could never know if there even was such a thing as truth. Consequently, he believed that seeking truth was futile. But most skeptics stop short of this conclusion. The best known is David Hume, who for all his skepticism nevertheless admitted, in his *Treatise on Human Nature*, "Whether I be really one of those sceptics who hold that all is uncertain . . . I should reply that this question is entirely superfluous, and that neither I, nor any person was ever sincerely and constantly of that opinion."[4] The fact is that extreme skepticism founders on self-contradiction, for to know you cannot know is to know something. Eveready must at least believe in the existence of truth; otherwise he could not claim to know that he does not know the truth. Ultimately, Eveready, like most of us, must operate as if truth does exist—if for no other reason than to dispose of patent falsehood.

Thus, despite his railing to the contrary, Eveready in fact holds as true a belief that gives his life meaning, produces satisfactory results,

---

[4]David Hume. *Treatise on Human Nature*. L. A. Selby-Bigge, Ed. Oxford: Clarendon Press, 1896, Vol. 1, p. 7.

and, in short, works. In other words, his belief that truth exists is founded in pragmatic theory. Furthermore, Eveready takes this belief as self-evident, as a first judgment with which he compares additional judgments and upon which he organizes his whole life. So he must subscribe to the idea that the truth is what hangs together—that is, to the coherence theory of truth. Such an assumption provides grounds for his claiming that the statement "There is a red, white, and blue American flag in this courtroom" is either true or false. Finally, on what basis is this statement to be judged true? It seems that Eveready must admit that there can be no other basis than whether there is *in fact* a red, white, and blue American flag in the courtroom. But here he calls on the correspondence theory.

CONCLUSIONS

In the last analysis, no one approach—correspondence, coherence, or pragmatic—is a complete and ever-reliable solution to the problem of truth. Each has its shortcomings and strengths. Equally important, each theory plays a part in the search for and discovery of self.

It is true that in everyday life we frequently use the test of correspondence to arrive at truth. From our earliest days in school, we are rewarded for reporting things "as they are": two plus two is four, Paris is the capital of France, two hydrogen atoms combine with one oxygen atom to form water. This is the primary way of gleaning information about the world. The correspondence theory also allows us to know about the quantifiable aspects of the self—height, weight, blood pressure, body temperature, and so on. This information, in turn, helps us to stay well: to know when to diet, when to relax, when to exercise. When we ignore these quantifiable aspects of self, we risk injury or illness.

But not all aspects of self are so easily quantified. In the complex area of personal experience, for example, the correspondence theory is not so useful. How would you verify the statement "He/she loves me"? You cannot verify it as you can verify "I have a temperature." You would probably evaluate it on the basis of the person's behavior toward you: "If he/she loves me, would he/she have said that?" In other words, you would test through coherence, asking if the person's actions were consistent with what it means to love somebody. Of course, you would be making an assumption about what it means to be in love.

Our assumptions frequently lead us to distorted views of self and the world. For example, a man who is ashamed to cry publicly because it isn't "manly" may be acting consistently with an assumption that is warping his personality. Likewise, a woman who refuses to call a man for a date because women shouldn't be "aggressive" is acting consistently with an assumption that may be inhibiting her. Just where we get all the assumptions we live by is less relevant here than the fact that we unconsciously measure our concepts, feelings, atittudes, and actions against them as if they were self-evident truths. Thus we do use the coherence theory of truth, but it is valuable only if our first judgments are accurate. This caution is especially applicable to those judgments concerning self or human nature.

If you were still wondering whether a particular individual loved you, you would frequently test pragmatically by asking, in effect, what practical difference the person's loving or not loving you makes in the person's life. Does it affect the way the person feels or thinks, what the person desires, how the person behaves? You might also ask the same questions of yourself. Suppose that even after you answered these questions you were still undecided. At this point, the pragmatic theory recognizes the nonmental aspect of the self, which can and should influence decisions in cases like these. At this point we often listen to the reasons of the heart that reason knows little about, to paraphrase the seventeenth-century French philosopher Blaise Pascal.

Thus, the correspondence, coherence, and pragmatic theories of truth really work together and are instrumental in unfolding the self and the world. They do not contradict but supplement one another. Truth may be that characteristic of a statement or judgment that describes things as they are (correspondence); but in cases in which we cannot determine how things actually are we must rely on how consistent that statement or judgment is with established truth (coherence), or how useful its consequences are (pragmatic).

SUMMARY

We opened this chapter by noting that every claim to knowledge is a claim to truth, and that what we consider to be true shapes who we are and how we act. There are three theories concerning the nature of truth: correspondence, coherence, and pragmatic. These theories supplement and are compatible with one another. We maximize our possibilities for self-discovery when we are prepared to use all three.

MAIN POINTS

1. The correspondence theory of truth claims that truth is an agreement between a statement of fact and the fact itself. Objection: if we know only our sense experiences, how can we ever get outside them to verify how reality actually is?
2. The coherence theory of truth claims that truth is a property of a related group of consistent statements. Objection: consistency is

no guarantee of truth. If first judgments are false, they produce a system of consistent error; there is much disagreement even among idealists over first judgments.

3.   The pragmatic theory claims that truth is what works. This theory is the cornerstone of pragmatism, an essentially American philosophy that germinated in the nineteenth century through the writings of Peirce, James, and Dewey. The pragmatist sees the human as one who must use the practical consequences of his beliefs to determine their truth and validity. Objection: in cases where empirical evidence is insufficient to determine truth, truth is left up to the individual; thus conflicting "truths" often arise without the hope of resolution.

4.   No theory of truth is complete in itself. In life we use all three, frequently at the same time.

SECTION EXERCISES

Correspondence Theory

1.   Do you think it is ever possible to tell "the whole truth"? Explain.
2.   Is describing truth as a correspondence between a statement and the way things actually are really begging the question? In what sense does such a definition not actually answer the question "What is truth?" but endorse a version of that question?
3.   Eveready claims: "Indeed, what the witness *thinks* is truth consigns truth to the very dubious area of sense-data interpretation. Such interpretation can only be purely subjective and need not have anything to do with the way things are." Cite instances or cases that illustrate Eveready's charge.
4.   Do you think there are two kinds of truth—subjective and objective, truth as an individual perceives it and truth as it actually is? Or is there just one objective truth, and everything else merely belief and opinion?

Coherence Theory

1.   Show how the following statements pass the test of coherence:
     a.   I am a rational being.
     b.   I am a divine being.
     c.   I am a mechanical being.
     d.   I am an existential being.
     e.   I am no self.
2.   Take some theory in psychology, anthropology, economics, or history, for example, and put it to the coherence test. Does it pass?

Can you find an opposing theory that passes as well? What might you conclude about the coherence theory of truth?

3. In what sense do claims of extrasensory perception not "fit in" with what we claim to know? In what sense do they?

4. Demonstrate how the coherence theory of truth ultimately seems to rely on the correspondence theory. How would proponents of the coherence theory object to this claim?

5. Do you believe in God? If you do, describe how this belief, working through the coherence theory of truth, influences how you see yourself, other people, the world around you, and the future of mankind.

6. Consider the fact that you are studying to enter some profession. Demonstrate how this intention is working as a "truth" in your life and serving as the cornerstone for a structure of other "truths."

7. Take some event from the recent past, such as the Vietnam war. Show how the coherence theory of truth operated in it to formulate policy and direct activity. Do you think our apparent failure in Vietnam is a vindication of the coherence theory of truth? An indictment? Both? Neither?

Pragmatic Theory

1. Cite a belief that you consider true primarily on pragmatic grounds.

2. Give an example of people's creating their own truth.

3. In a sense, truth for the pragmatist is an extension of belief. Illustrate how belief can "make truth." Do you detect dangers in this position? How would this position affect how you view yourself? In what sense will you be tomorrow what you decide to be today?

4. In opposition to the pragmatists and their theory of truth, critics charge "But don't you see that you're encouraging us to see things as we would have them and not as they are?" Do you agree with this criticism?

5. Can you think of anything that, although true, does not "work"? Something that, although it works, is not true?

ADDITIONAL EXERCISES

1. Cite an example from your own life that illustrates how you combined all three theories to arrive at the truth.

2. "Convictions are more dangerous enemies of truth than lies." Explain this statement. Can you point to historic examples that prove this?

3. "Ye shall know the truth and the truth shall make you free." Can the truth make you free? Does it always?

4. Defining *works* as "produces satisfactory results," can you think of an example to show that something works for one person but not for another? What bearing does this example have on the pragmatic theory of truth—truth is what works?

5. A **hypothesis** is a working explanation of a phenomenon. For example, the belief that cancer is caused by viruses is a hypothesis. Demonstrate how hypotheses figure prominently in the coherence theory of truth.

6. Demonstrate how your view of the opposite sex is based on a coherence theory of truth. What are your starting premises? Can these premises be verified by correspondence? In what sense does your view work? In what sense does it not? In what sense are you making realities of your working assumptions?

PAPERBACKS FOR FURTHER READING

Castaneda, Carlos. *A Separate Reality*. New York: Simon & Schuster, 1972. The author covers the first five years of his relationship with the Yaqui Indian Don Juan, whose truth and sources of knowledge defy conventional epistemological attitudes. A book sure to leave the reader asking just what truth is.

Huxley, Aldous. *The Doors of Perception*. Harper & Row, 1970. Huxley records his experiences with the drug mescaline. His account raises questions about the senses and the mind, but especially about knowledge and truth.

Russell, Bertrand. *Human Knowledge: Its Scope and Limits*. New York: Simon & Schuster, 1948. This is a clear, readable review of many philosophical topics, including science, language, and probability, as well as knowledge and perception.

Stoppard, Tom. *Jumpers*. New York: Grove Press, 1974. Stoppard, one of today's foremost dramatists, explores the difficulty of sustaining philosophical truth in the midst of the absurd, the comic, and the pathetic. In this play a philosopher delivers a lecture while bedlam reigns around him.

White, Alan R. *Truth*. Garden City, N.Y.: Doubleday, 1970. This book offers a thoughtful treatment of the different meanings of truth, including three traditional and three modern concepts.

Sources of Knowledge

5

Myself when young did eagerly frequent Doctor and Saint, and heard great argument about it and about; but evermore came out by the same door wherein I went.—Omar Khayyám

This chapter, like the last two, deals with an epistemological issue. We have previously stressed that what we know to a great extent determines who we are. But what we know is only as reliable as the sources we use to discover that knowledge. Now suppose someone asked you just how you come to knowledge, and thus to a vital element of your self-identity.

"Tell me something you know," this person says. "I know that Washington was at Valley Forge," you reply. "How do you know that?" You know it, you say, because you read it. "Do you believe everything you read?" he asks. No, but you believe this, because everybody who's written about it says it's so. "How do they know?" he asks. "Were they there?" No, they weren't there, you admit; but they've studied the subject. "Where did they study it?" In books, mostly.

"Let me see if I've got this straight," he says. "You claim to know from what you've read, right?" Right. "And they claim to know from what they've read. Presumably, the people they've researched have studied the matter, too. Is that right?" Sure. "Then where does all this stop? I mean, is there anyone who *knows* this without having read it somewhere?" Sure, you explain: the people who were there, the ones who were at Valley Forge with Washington; they know, they witnessed it.

"Have you ever been in a car accident?" he next wants to know. Sure, you tell him, but what does that have to do with Washington? "Were there any witnesses?" he asks. There were. "What about their stories—did they agree?" No, you admit, they didn't. But . . . "I'm

113

just asking you how reliable eyewitness testimony is to begin with." You grant that eyewitness testimony often isn't very reliable, but that doesn't mean it wasn't reliable at Valley Forge. "Of course not," he says, "but it does mean that it might not have been reliable. What you claim to know might not be true."

Just how *do* we know what we claim to know? Where do we get the information that influences how we see ourselves and the world around us? In this chapter, we focus on the sources of knowledge. First we shall consider the primary sources, senses and reason, and then two common secondary sources, authority and intuition. Finding out about these sources will show us how we have arrived at what we know and believe about things. In turn, this information will give us a basis for examining that knowledge and those beliefs, a basis for self-introspection.

PRIMARY SOURCES OF KNOWLEDGE: SENSES AND REASON

Senses

If you say "That lemon is sour," and someone asks you how you know, you say "I just tasted it." If you tell a child "Don't touch the stove, it's hot," and she asks you to prove it, you say "Touch it and find out." In both cases you appeal to senses, the most obvious of all the sources of knowledge.

We have already seen a number of attempts to discredit sense-data knowledge. Orval did it when Marvin claimed to know that there were mushrooms in his lunch pail. Eveready did it when witness Scaife claimed to know that a red, white, and blue American flag was in the courtroom. Berkeley did it when he questioned Locke's theory of knowledge and truth. Hume did it when he challenged the possibility of any knowledge. Just how reliable are the senses? Can we depend on knowledge we acquire through them?

Sometimes we have sense experiences that are highly inaccurate. The classic example is that of the thirsty person who "sees" water and trees just ahead when in fact there is only more desert. At other times what we witness actually is there, but it does not have the characteristics we think it has—as when the color-blind witness at Scaife's trial testified that the American flag in the courtroom was red, white, and green. It is the existence of these so-called perceptual errors that leads many to claim that the senses are fallible, that they cannot be trusted as sources of knowledge.

But it is more accurate to term such errors ones of interpretation or judgment, not perception. Our senses have not misled us. They have merely led us to make a judgment based on sense perceptions. Thus

"Sometimes we have sense experiences
that are highly inaccurate."

these errors are ones of judgment, not perception. Had we withheld judgment—had we not taken the spot at the top of the desert hill to be a pool of water—we would have made no error. What the senses do is provide us with experiences. They do not make judgments about those experiences.

It is noteworthy that, whenever we make such perceptual errors because of insufficient information, it is always additional sense experience that allows us to discover and correct the error. For example, we probably once thought that the pencil resting in a glass of water was actually bent, or that the shadow on the bedroom wall was that of a threatening intruder. It did not take long for us to learn, however, that both were illusions—that they appeared to be something they were not. We realized this when we withdrew the pencil and examined it, or turned on the bedroom light and saw nothing more threatening than a drape unfurling by an open window on a moonlit night. We were no longer "taken in" once we acquired additional sense information. Thus .it was not our senses but our interpretations of our sense experiences that were in error. After all, our senses still receive the same information: the pencil still appears bent, the shadow still appears threatening. But now our judgment is correct because all the information is "in."

So far we have spoken only of the so-called external senses, those through which we gain information about the outside world. There are, in addition, internal senses—those that acquaint us with our moods, feelings, pains, pleasures, and the rest of our internal states, as well as our mental operations such as thinking, believing, imagining, and dreaming. Although these internal senses do not involve sense organs, we are entitled to make certain statements on the basis of what they tell us. But the only statements we should make are those based on our internal states. Thus, "I feel sick," "I feel happy," "I feel anxious," and the like are legitimate claims based on internal senses. The fact that we are having the experiences we claim is, and need be, the only guarantee of the truth of our statements.

But contrast such claims with "I feel I've got a cavity" or "I feel the presence of God." These claims are more than expressions of internal states. True, in these statements we claim to "feel," and we are feeling something. But what we claim to feel presumably has an objective existence apart from our feeling it. In one case we claim to feel the presence of a cavity; in the other case we feel the presence of God. Do we have a cavity? Is God present? To answer these questions we must move from the realm of internal states into the arena of public **verification**. Just because we feel that we have a cavity does not mean we have one; just because we feel that God is present does not mean that God is present or, indeed, that God even exists. We are feeling something, all right, but we cannot assume that what we claim to feel is what we are actually feeling. Such claims must stand the test of public verification, which requires that other people verify the claims we are making. Thus, a dentist could prove that we have a cavity; other people must not only concur that God is present but first prove that God exists.

It is most important to distinguish, then, between statements that report only internal states and those that claim to report more. If we are taken in by statements disguised as ones of pure experience, we run the risk of admitting as true our own and others' claims simply on the basis of reports of internal states. When a statement involves more than a claim of an internal experience, it must stand the test of the **scientific method**—a method of inquiry based on the collection, analysis, and interpretation of sense information in order to discover the most likely explanation this sense information suggests. In other words, it must be empirically verifiable. In concluding this section on the senses, a brief word about empiricism and sense experience will be appropriate, since the empiricist relies so heavily on the senses as a source of knowledge.

Empiricism is the belief that all knowledge originates in sense experience. John Locke was one of the first empiricists. Along with Berkeley and Hume he represented the school of "British empiricists." Writing in the seventeenth century, Locke viewed the mind as a "blank slate" (*tabula rasa*) on which the outside world impresses itself. We know, he said, through sense experiences. What we never experience, we cannot know.

Contemporary empiricism, in the form of pragmatism, views the mind's role as a more active one. The mind selects and shapes its experiences in keeping with the needs, desires, and goals of the whole human organism. For pragmatists, experience is a growing, changing process in which the self plays an active role.

But whatever the brand of empiricism, there remains a deep-seated commitment to the doctrine that all knowledge begins in sense experience. Accompanying this belief is a commitment to science and the scientific method. But at the same time, empiricism recognizes that biases and emotions often taint sense experiences, and that if we are not careful we can stray by perceiving the world other than as it is. Nevertheless, empiricists feel that this caution applies even more to a careless application of another primary source of knowledge: reason.

Reflection   Is there anything that you claim to know that is not the result of some experience? Do you need a sense experience to know that the statement "The green grass is green" is true?

Reason

If A is greater than B and B is greater than C, then A is greater than C. You know this not through sense knowledge but through reason. Also through reason you know that seven times eight is fifty-six and that the city in which you live is either New York or not New York.

We may define reason as the capacity to think reflectively and draw conclusions. It is the process of following relationships from one thought to another and thereby discovering, when we perform this process correctly, what must follow if the evidence is true. Whereas the senses describe matters of fact, reason describes matters of logic; whereas the senses describe the world, reason describes the mind.

We reason by **deduction** and **induction**. In reasoning deductively we draw conclusions that are logically certain; that is, they must follow from the evidence provided. Thus:

> All voters are citizens.
>
> Smith is a voter.
>
> Therefore, Smith is a citizen.

From the first two statements the conclusion follows with logical certainty. Such an argument is said to have **validity**—that is, one whose evidence, or premises, provides enough grounds for a conclusion.

In reasoning inductively, on the other hand, we draw conclusions that are never logically certain but are probable. Thus:

> Since the first 450 dogs we examined in this pound all had fleas, all 500 dogs in this pound have fleas.

The conclusion here is only probable: any one of the remaining 50 dogs may not have fleas. In general, the inductive method is the method of the empiricists, who are committed to probable conclusions in the sense that they believe that "all" the evidence is never in; that the best we can ever say is that something is "most probably" the case.

As we have already seen, many philosophers have questioned the reliability of sense knowledge. They have attempted to discredit the senses as a legitimate source of knowledge, and certainly as the only source. In contrast, they maintain that reason alone is sufficient to arrive at certain knowledge and truth. Thinking that emphasizes reasoning as the main avenue to knowledge is called **rationalism**. The senses alone, the rationalists say, are insufficient to provide a system of consistent and universal truths. What the senses provide are just the ingredients of knowledge. It takes the reasoning mind to organize that data into coherent principles, laws, and concepts. In general, the rationalists rely on deductive reasoning to arrive at their judgments.

But by far the most distinguishing claim of the rationalists is that reason alone, without the aid of sense information, is capable of arriving at some knowledge. Notice that they are not only talking about the truth of such statements as "The green grass is green" or "My brother is a male." They have traditionally held as equally self-evident such statements as "Every event must have a cause," "The whole is the sum of its parts," "A thing cannot be in two different places at the same time," "Parallel lines never meet," "Everything that has color has extension." Any one of these statements, claim the rationalists, we know without sense experience. You can deduce any one of them from other truths. Thus:

> No thing can be in two places at the same time.
>
> This desk, a thing, is in this room.
>
> Therefore, this desk cannot be in any other place at this time but in this room.

The deductive system as the rationalists apply it seems harmless enough when we speak of desks and rooms. But consider this argument:

> If an entity thinks, then it exists.
>
> I think.
>
> Therefore, I exist.

Starting with what he considered an undeniable truth, "If an entity thinks, it exists," René Descartes, the seventeenth-century rationalist, reasoned his own existence. Starting with another "self-evident truth," he reasoned the existence of God:

Since an effect cannot be greater than its cause, the imperfect human mind cannot itself conceive of a Perfect Being.

Since the human mind can and does conceive of a Perfect Being, something perfect must have caused that conception.

If a thing is perfect, it must exist, because if it did not it would be "less perfect" than what does exist.

Therefore, a Perfect Being exists.

Empiricists have charged rationalists with confusing validity with truth. The following argument is valid, but not true:

All creatures with two legs are humans.

A cow has two legs.

Therefore, a cow is human.

Based on the first two statements (in other words, assuming they are true), the conclusion must follow; therefore, the argument is valid. But not a single statement of it is true. Validity—correct reasoning procedure—is different from truth. To test for truth, say the empiricists, we must turn to sense experience; reason alone will not lead us to truth. Go out and look around to see if "all creatures with two legs are humans." You'll find ostriches out there; they have two legs, and they're not human. And when you look at a cow, you'll see that it generally has four legs, not two. Therefore, the conclusion of this argument, although valid, cannot possibly be true. In effect, empiricists claim that any first premises not grounded in sense experience lead nowhere.

In life, we are constantly using both the inductive and the deductive processes. For example, before crossing a street we look both ways, because we figure that by looking both ways we shall ensure a safe crossing. Our reasoning follows this line:

If I look both ways before crossing, I'll ensure a safe crossing.

I do look both ways before crossing.

Therefore, I ensure a safe crossing.

This is a deductive argument. But notice that we arrived at the first statement inductively. From countless similar experiences of our own and of others, we have formulated this generalization, a statement that holds true all or almost all of the time. But there is nothing certain about it; it is just highly likely. It is possible that, despite our looking, our crossing will prove unsafe. So, although we operate daily in the realm of certain deductive conclusions, the evidence we use to arrive at such conclusions is itself tentative. When we forget this, we run the risk of substituting our rational deductive systems for empirical observation.

"... first premises not grounded in sense
experience lead nowhere."

How do we reason correctly? How do we ensure that our reasoning is valid? The answer is not simple. An entire study is devoted to it: **logic.** Logic is the branch of epistemology that studies the methods and principles of correct reasoning. Of course, that definition assumes that there is a correct way to reason. You may wish to ponder that assumption. The question is a fascinating one, as is the study. Although we can hardly explore logic here, we can mention some of the more common ways in which people seem to reason incorrectly.

Informal Fallacies

Broadly defined, a **fallacy** is an incorrect way of reasoning. We may also call a fallacy any attempt to persuade emotionally or psychologically but not logically. Suppose a political candidate rises and declares "My opponent is an unmitigated liar. So don't believe a word she says when she addresses you tonight." To discredit his opponent, the candidate has relied not on reason but on name-calling. By calling his opponent a liar, he has attacked the person, not the person's stand on the issues. In logic, such an attack is called "poisoning the well" or an *ad hominem* ("to the man") appeal. In effect, before anyone has had a chance to drink from the well, the candidate has poisoned the waters. This is one of many ways in which our minds are manipulated daily. Logicians call these illogical appeals **informal fallacies.** Since there are well over a hundred varieties of these, we can mention only those most frequently used.

1. ARGUMENT FROM IGNORANCE

Have you ever heard someone argue "God exists because you can't prove He doesn't"? Or "God doesn't exist because you can't prove he does"? When we claim that something is so because it cannot be disproved, we commit the fallacy called "argument from ignorance."

2. HYPOTHESIS CONTRARY TO FACT

Sometimes we claim to know something because we believe that something would not have happened if conditions had been other than they were. Thus: "If Edison had not invented the light bulb, we wouldn't have flash bulbs today." Having set up a condition contrary to fact, we then ignore other factors and draw a "certain" conclusion. Whenever we claim to know with certainty what would have happened if things had been different, we commit the fallacy called "hypothesis contrary to fact." Other examples:

Sportscaster:	"One thing's sure: if Smith had been in the lineup today, this game would have gone differently."
Historian:	"If Hitler had not invaded Russia, the Germans would have won the war."
Disappointed lover:	"I know she would have gone out with me if I hadn't been so brusque."

3. BEGGING THE QUESTION

The fallacy of hypothesis contrary to fact is frequently implied in a question (for example, "Would things have gone differently today had Smith been in the lineup?"). But even more common with respect to questions is the fallacy of "begging the question." To illustrate, we all have probably had the experience of being in a classroom when a student asks "Why do we have to study this stuff?" The teacher's customary reply is "If I have to tell you *why*, you shouldn't be here." The teacher is guilty of begging the question, the fallacy of endorsing a version of the very question asked. Rather than answering the question, the teacher lets it go begging. Another example:

Reporter:	Senator, do you think civil disobedience is ever justifiable?
Senator:	In a system that's responsive to public need and demand, there's no excuse for civil disobedience.

4. STRAW MAN

Frequently, in responding to an issue, we try to divert attention from it. For example, those arguing for increased national-defense spending sometimes paint the bleak and frightening prospect of a defenseless nation at the mercy of its enemies. Instead of defending the particular expenditures in the proposed budget—tanks, planes, ships, munitions— they choose to divert attention to the more manageable issue of the perils of being defenseless. When we so divert attention by presenting or attacking an argument similar to but significantly different from the one at issue, we commit the fallacy of setting up a "straw man."

5. APPEAL TO PITY

There is another effective device used to divert. Suppose a man applies to you for a job. You ask him for his qualifications. His reply: "I've been out of work for three months. My wife desperately needs an oper- ation, and my three small children are wearing rags. I can't afford to heat the house this winter, and I don't know what I'm going to do about paying next month's bills." Rather than answering your question, he has appealed to your heart, to your emotions. Whenever we rely on sympathy to persuade, we are guilty of making an "appeal to pity."

6. APPEAL TO FORCE

As frequently persuasive a device, although just as illogical, is the appeal to force. Thus, a lobbyist might persuade a politician not to vote for a bill by suggesting that he will lose his political support if he does. A nation might "persuade" another nation to its political ideology by arguing, in effect, "Our way is the best way, because we have the might to impose it on you." Whenever we rely on threat to persuade, we are guilty of making an "appeal to force."

7. REIFICATION

Suppose someone argued "National security demands wiretapping"? This approach seems more rational than a threat, but it is not. Who is *demanding*? National security. But national security cannot demand. It is not a person, not even a thing. Yet the speaker treats it as if it is. Whenever we treat an idea or a concept, such as national security, as if it were a thing, we commit the fallacy of "reification." Thus, "Fear persuaded him to flee the danger" and "The fuel crisis compels us to conserve our natural resources."

"Our way is the best way . . ."

8. POST HOC

In a later chapter we shall discuss the question of cause. Here let us just note a fallacy that frequently occurs in deciding the cause of an event. Because what we call a cause occurs before the event it effects, we can easily reason that, because something precedes an event, it is the cause of that event. A simple example: "Just after I walked under the ladder a car hit me. So walking under that ladder caused my misfortune." Only the hopelessly superstitious would reason that way. But who has not said something like "Last night I slept with the window open, and this morning I've got a cold. That open window must have caused it." Whenever we claim that one event is the cause of another simply because it preceded the other, we commit the *post hoc ergo propter hoc* ("after this, therefore because of this") fallacy. We can attribute false cause in other ways than *post hoc*, but discussion of these is better left until later.

9. HASTY CONCLUSION

Finally, we should note that drawing a conclusion based on insufficient evidence leads to the fallacy of "hasty conclusion." Thus: "Since the first 450 dogs I examined had fleas, all 500 dogs in this pound must have fleas." How many fallacies can you detect in the following exchange between a driver and a policeman who has stopped him for speeding?

Officer:	May I see your license, please?
Motorist:	Why? What did I do?
Officer:	May I see your license?
Motorist:	Sure, here.
Officer:	Thank you. Mr. Roberts, why were you traveling 70 miles per hour in a 55 zone?
Motorist:	I wasn't going 70!
Officer:	Yes, you were. I clocked you.
Motorist:	I couldn't have! This heap won't go that fast. Besides, did you see all the cars that were passing me? I was just trying to keep up with traffic.
Officer:	Maybe you shouldn't try to keep up if it means speeding.
Motorist:	Sure, and if I didn't you'd give me a ticket for obstructing traffic.
Officer:	What're you trying to say? I'm picking on you?
Motorist:	Well, it sure is funny that this van has been stopped three times in the last hundred miles, that's all.
Officer:	Is that right? Well, let me tell you something. In the last week I've stopped three of these vans, and on each occasion the occupants were transporting junk. Now isn't that a coincidence?
Motorist:	Okay, go ahead, search me, *and* this van. See if I'm carrying anything.
Officer:	I intend to, but first I'm going to cite you for speeding.
Motorist:	Oh, come on, will you? Give me a break. Another ticket and I'll lose my insurance.
Officer:	You should have thought about that earlier.
Motorist:	Okay, go ahead, give me the ticket. But I'm going to see you in court. It's your word against mine. I wasn't speeding, because there's no way you can prove I was.
Officer:	Mr. Roberts, I don't have to prove it. Fortunately, we haven't reached the point where the court's going to take the word of your kind over mine.

Notice that in answer to the motorist's denial of speeding, the officer replies "Yes, you were. I clocked you." The officer sets himself up as the authority on the issue: "*I* clocked you, so it must be so." So pervasive are the appeal to authority and authority itself as sources of knowledge that we shall consider them in detail below.

Reflection   State one of your religious, political, or moral beliefs. Can you trace the reasoning process that has led you to this position?

SECONDARY SOURCES OF KNOWLEDGE: AUTHORITY AND INTUITION

Authority

We often justify what we know by appealing to some outside source, perhaps to something we have read or someone we have heard. Thus we appeal to authority. **Authority** is a source of knowledge that exists outside us and that we use as an expert source of information. It is a safe bet that without relying on authority we would know very little. But we should use authority cautiously.

Since the invention of Gutenberg's printing press, the written word has served as our chief source of authority. Even today, what appears between two covers is often thought "gospel." We tend to forget that authority lies not in the print but in the individual behind it.

For many, newspapers and television programs are an authoritative source of news information. It is true that these media are often accurate and reliable sources of knowledge, but the cautious person should remember a few facts of journalistic life.

First, conventional newspapers and television news programs are sponsored. They receive commercial backing. This state of affairs is not necessarily undesirable, but remember that the sponsor, in return for its investment, expects appropriate public exposure. The greater the audience, the greater the sponsor's potential market; the smaller the audience, the smaller the market. We may infer, then, that a sponsor of a news program will take more than a passing interest in a program's content. Television and newspapers must be sensitive to this fact to survive. As a result, the news media may place commercial interests above comprehensive and accurate coverage of the news, above our true understanding of things.

Second, a quick glance at most papers indicates that the chief source of news is the wire services. But where do *they* get the news? Primarily from press releases, news conferences, bureaucratic announcements, and the like. In other words, for the most part the wire services record the daily doings of the "powers that be" as those powers would have them recorded. Naturally, there are glaring exceptions to this general practice. The Woodward and Bernstein Watergate stories in the *Washington Post* are an example of how vigorous a role investigative reporting can play. But more often the news media echo established views.

Third, for a variety of reasons, newspapers often engage in other practices that inhibit comprehensive and accurate news coverage. Often they rely on language that is intended more to sell papers than to inform. A headline reading RECESSION FEARED is sensational and will probably sell papers. But the accompanying story may prove much less threatening than the headline itself: "The President today said he feared a recession if the unemployment rate continues to rise, the GNP continues to fall, and the consumer price index continues to climb. But he hastened to add that his administration has taken steps to prevent just such an occurrence." Be careful also of the authoritative-sounding phrases "informed sources," "sources close to the President," and "reliable sources." True, reporters may be protecting their sources. But they may also be lending their stories an authoritative clout they do not deserve. Also beware the ubiquitous ellipsis, those three dots (. . .) that indicate something has been omitted. In the hands of a good editor the ellipsis is invaluable. But it can also conceal evidence. Did you ever read a film ad like this one? *"All the Sad Clowns*: a fantastic . . . film!" The reviewer's original sentence may have read *"All the Sad Clowns*: a fantastic mixture of poor photography, incompetent direction, sloppy editing, and appalling acting, the likes of which have never been seen on film!"

In recent years television has usurped the written word's position as chief authority for news. Because of time limitations and extraordinary production costs, television is even more beholden to commercial sponsorship than are newspapers. Also, the feverish competition that besets entertainment shows affects TV news programs as well: a program must be concerned with its ratings. Furthermore, a television station must be sensitive to the desires of the Federal Communications Commission, the governmental agency that supplies its broadcasting license. In the light of these facts, pause before claiming newspapers or TV as your source of knowledge.

When can you rely on what you read or hear? If you apply a few simple criteria, you will use authority validly. First, make sure the authority is in fact an expert in the area you are talking about. This precaution alone will make you leery of the "endorsement game" in advertising. Someone's being a celebrity does not ensure a quality product.

Second, ensure that there is agreement among the· experts. Take, for example, the question of whether marijuana usage leads to hard-drug addiction. Some experts say yes; some say no. The jury is still out; the people who should know are not yet agreed. So, reserve judgment. Regarding cigarette smoking and lung cancer, however, experts do seem to be agreed. Respect that agreement.

Third, ensure that the expert is in a position to know. If a film projectionist you meet at a party tells you that in the near future the

President will reverse our foreign policy in the Middle East, you would probably not take the projectionist's word as authoritative. The person is not in a position to know. But if at the same party a high-level State Department official tells you the same thing, you will rightly assume that this person is in a position to know.

Finally, ask yourself if you could verify the claim if you wanted to. Could you prove that our foreign policy is about to be reversed? Could you prove that cigarette smoking can cause lung cancer? Could you prove Einstein's theory of relativity? If you had the time, energy, interest, and intelligence, you could. What about historic events? Obviously, no amount of intelligence, energy, or wherewithal can take you back to Valley Forge to prove that Washington was encamped there. But in such cases you should easily be able to conceive of eyewitnesses to the event. *Notice that in the last analysis the claim to authority always relies on senses or reason, and must itself never be taken as a primary source.*

Reflection To what extent is submitting to authority currently necessary for you to be "successful"? Does the extent depend on your definition of "successful"?

Intuition

Do you believe in love at first sight? Have you ever unsuccessfully worked on a problem and later, when you were not "thinking" about it, discovered the solution? Have you ever felt that you were in direct communion with some spiritual being, with a higher being, with God? Have you ever felt that you knew something that you could not adequately express because it transcended sense experience and reason? If you answered yes to any of the preceding questions, you have probably relied on **intuition** as a source of knowledge. Carefully defined as direct awareness that does not rely immediately on the senses or on reason, intuition may be a creative source of knowledge.

In an article entitled "How I Write," the British philosopher Bertrand Russell tells of "planting" in his subconscious a problem that eventually worked itself out.

The most curious example of this process, and the one which led me subsequently to rely upon it, occurred at the beginning of 1914. I had undertaken to give the Lowell Lectures at Boston, and had chosen as my subject "Our Knowledge of the External World." Throughout 1913 I thought about this topic. In term time in my room at Cambridge, in vacations in a quiet inn on the upper reaches of the Thames, I concentrated with such intensity that I sometimes forgot to breathe and emerged panting as if from a trance. But all to no avail. To every theory I could think of I could perceive some fatal objections. At last, in despair, I went off to Rome for Christmas, hoping a holiday would revive my flagging energy. I got back to Cambridge on the last day of 1913, and although my difficulties were still completely unresolved I arranged, because the remaining time was short, to dictate as best I could to a stenographer. Next morning as she came to the door, I suddenly saw exactly what I had to say, and proceeded to dictate the whole book without a moment's hesitation.[1]

Russell seems to have "intuited" what bouts of labored thought were unable to produce. In fact, the more he intellectualized, the more confused he became. Some philosophers, skeptical of the often bewildering human capacity for analysis, have viewed intuition as a higher form of knowledge.

The French philosopher Henri Bergson (1859–1941) viewed intuition as the highest form of knowledge. He saw reason and intellect as leading us outward into the world of things, since analysis is the tool of science, and science classifies and quantifies. But intuition, claimed Bergson, leads inward to the nature of things. Follow intuition, he said, and it will reveal the life force of the world. That it supposedly can discover this life force is why intuition is the chosen method of mysticism.

Mysticism is the belief that we *know* only when we surrender ourselves to the divine unity that underlies all things. Mystics claim that intuition allows us to experience God directly. Almost all the major religions of the world have had their mystics: Zoroaster, Gautama Buddha, the Hebrew prophets, Jesus, Mohammed. But mysticism and intuition generally play a bigger part in Eastern thinking than in Western.

In fact, many Oriental philosophies put minimal store in the primary sources of human knowledge, since they have little confidence in human knowledge to begin with. They claim that any system of objective knowing invariably fragments and distorts because it is based ultimately on social agreement as communicated through language, which fractures, blurs, and confuses. As a result, what we claim to know is a matter of how well we have mastered social convention, not how things really are. In contrast, Zen scholar Alan Watts advises in *The Way of Zen*: "We must at least be prepared to admit the possibility of some view of the world other than the conventional, some knowledge other than the contents of our surface consciousness, which can apprehend reality only in the form of one abstraction . . . at a time."[2]

In short, Eastern thought has never made rationality the core of personal identity the way we seem to in the West. As a result, it looks

---

[1]Bertrand Russell. *Portraits from Memory and Other Essays*. New York: Simon & Schuster, 1956, pp. 211–212.

[2]Alan Watts. *The Way of Zen*. New York: Pantheon Books, 1957, p. 25.

"'We must at least be prepared to admit the
possibility of some view of the world
other than the conventional . . .'"

with hearty skepticism at our so-called truths of reason, and favors instead an intuitive process that unifies life's diversities: rationality and irrationality, mind and senses, morality and nature. The West, in contrast, emphasizes the objective world of the senses and uses the scientific method to verify claims about objective reality. When our knowledge transcends our immediate experience, we generally express it in some theoretical language—perhaps mathematics. In other words, we *rationalize* it. It is clear, then, that we rely primarily on empiricism and rationalism, on senses and reason.

Eastern thought, on the other hand, is generally more concerned with the inner world than with the outer. Therefore, it stresses the knowledge that comes from living—that is, knowledge by acquaintance. One discovers the nature of and the truth about things, not by reasoning to conclusions based on pieces of information, but through personal experience. Such wisdom is not easily attained without great self-discipline, which includes ridding the mind of unsettling feelings and base impulses.

In general, then, Eastern thinkers seek knowledge from three sources: experience, reason, and intuition. But intuition is valued above experience and reason. For this reason Gautama rejected the authority of the ancient Vedic scriptures, along with all claims to revelation. He counseled his followers to accept only what coincided with their own experiences, subjected to healthful rational scrutiny. In the last analysis it is the intuitive grasp of knowledge that is prized, for "those who know do not speak; those who speak do not know."

The problem with strict intuitionism is that, by definition, it defies verification. Since it relies on neither sense knowledge nor reason, it frustrates the scientific method. Admittedly, this objection is raised by the exponents of the scientific method themselves. But when mystics expect their personal intuitive insights to be accepted as public knowledge, their claims seem to deserve skepticism. After all, how seriously would you entertain the claim that the world will end on January 1, 2000, if the only evidence was that one person foresaw it in a dream? When intuition blossoms from previous experience, however, we have another matter. When Russell saw exactly what he had to say in his book, his "vision" came as a dividend to his creative intuition, which he had invested in the stuff of his experience. Still, after the flash came reality testing. Russell, like all who experience a flash of intuition, had to ask: Does what I'm writing hold water? Does it make sense? Can others understand it? Can I prove it? Naturally, if he were not interested in communicating his insight to the public or claiming objective respectability for it, he need not have asked any of these questions. But since he was, he could not expect the public to share his intuitive insight without demonstrating how it was grounded in empiricism.

Reflection   Can you cite a personal example of what you would call an intuitive experience?

CONCLUSIONS

In discussing these sources of knowledge, there is danger of overlooking precisely why we use them. True, we use them to acquire information, but primarily we use them to acquire self-knowledge and insight.

Perhaps most important, these sources can inform us of our needs. Our senses alone reveal physical needs. We must keep fed and clean. Along with reason, they inform us that we also need security and protection, that we must be and feel safe. But there are other heartfelt needs that we seem to "intuit"—needs that authoritative sources, especially in psychology and the social sciences, continue to corroborate: the needs for love and for self-esteem. As one psychiatrist puts it, "Psychiatry must be concerned with two basic psychological needs: *the need to love and be loved and the need to feel that we are worthwhile to ourselves and to others.*"[3] At the most refined level of needs is, perhaps, what psychologist Abraham Maslow calls "self-actualization," by which he means the need to function at our highest level.

---

[3]William Glasser. *Reality Therapy—A New Approach to Psychiatry*. New York: Harper & Row, 1965, p. 9.

Lacking a refined version of and an accurate application of the sources of knowledge, it is difficult to imagine anyone attaining "self-actualization." To understand why, consider the profile of the self-actualized person that Maslow drew after studying esteemed historical figures such as Lincoln, Beethoven, Einstein, and Eleanor Roosevelt.[4] Such an individual, he said, can perceive things effectively, judge others accurately, and tolerate uncertainty. All of these abilities require a sound application of empirical and rational methodology. Self-actualized people are neither dogmatic nor uncommitted. They do not blindly comply with the demands of their society or culture; they are often original and productive. They are not locked into their experiences, but often show spontaneity and creativity. In other words, they have a healthful although not constraining respect for authority and are willing to follow their intuitive impulse when it springs from a genuine intellectual encounter with a problem. Indeed, they are problem-directed, not ego-centered. They seek out privacy in order to view life with the detachment necessary for understanding it—that is, with the philosophic calm that accompanies tranquil analysis. Yet they recognize the limits of analysis. They are alive to the basic experiences of life, many of them having mystical experiences that cement their identity with humankind and leave them with intense social interests and interpersonal relationships. Finally, they learn for the sake of learning; that is, they continue to cultivate the sources of knowledge.

Without keeping in mind such an ideal human profile, we can easily forget the importance and worth of the sources of knowledge. Furthermore, we can easily ignore their complementary nature. One does not substitute for another, any more than one contradicts the other. Ultimately they form a kind of federation, through which we should come not to an encyclopedic mastery of the world but to a deep development and rich understanding of the self.

SUMMARY

We opened this chapter by asking: Just how do we know what we claim to know? What are our sources of knowledge? There are two primary sources: senses and reason. Empiricism is the belief that all knowledge originates in sense experience. Rationalism emphasizes reason as a source of knowledge and claims that reason alone—without the aid of sense information—is capable of arriving at some knowledge, at some undeniable truths. We reason deductively to logically certain conclusions, and inductively to probable ones. Informal fallacies often invalidate

---

[4]Abraham H. Maslow. "A Theory of Human Motivation." *Psychological Review* 50 (1943), pp. 370–396.

the reasoning process. In addition, we examined two secondary sources of knowledge: authority and intuition. We concluded by noting that these sources of knowledge must ultimately lead to self-knowledge and insight.

MAIN POINTS

1. There are two primary sources of knowledge: senses and reason.
2. Whereas the senses describe matters of fact, reason describes matters of logic; whereas the senses describe the world, reason describes the mind.
3. Validity pertains to the correctness of the reasoning process. An argument is valid when its conclusion follows with logical certainty —that is, when its evidence provides enough grounds for its conclusion.
4. Logic is the branch of epistemology that studies the methods and principles of correct reasoning.
5. A fallacy is an incorrect way of reasoning; it is also an argument that tries to persuade emotionally or psychologically but not logically.
6. Informal fallacies are common devices used to persuade emotionally or psychologically but not logically. There are well over 100 varieties of these.
7. Authority is a secondary source of knowledge that exists outside the person making the claim and that the person uses as an expert source of information. In evaluating the reliability of an authority, make sure that (1) the authority is an expert in the field, (2) there is agreement among the experts, (3) the authority is in a position to know, and (4) you can in theory verify the claim for yourself. In the absence of any of these conditions, the appeal to authority is a false one, a fallacy.
8. Intuition is another secondary source of knowledge. Carefully defined as direct awareness that does not rely immediately on the senses or on reason, intuition may be a creative source of knowledge. Oriental thought in general and Buddhism in particular rely heavily on intuitive knowledge.

SECTION EXERCISES

Senses

1. Which of the following statements need public verification before you will accept them as true?

    a.   I think some evil spirit has possessed me.
    b.   Something tells me some evil spirit has possessed me.
    c.   I've got a feeling some evil spirit has possessed me.
    d.   Some evil spirit has possessed me.
    e.   It seems to me some evil spirit has possessed me.
    f.   Something has possessed me.
    g.   Whatever has possessed me is causing me to lose sleep.

Reason

1.   In deducing a conclusion, can you learn anything that you did not know from the evidence? Illustrate.
2.   Which, if any, of the following would you say are examples of inborn knowledge?
    a.   All squares have four sides.
    b.   Two plus two is four.
    c.   If X is smaller than Y and Y is smaller than Z, then X is smaller than Z.
    d.   Every even number is the sum of two prime numbers.
    e.   A statement is either true or not true.
3.   In which of the following instances would you accept "feeling" as proof of the truth of the statement of what is felt?
    a.   I feel sick.
    b.   I feel happy.
    c.   I feel my dead mother's presence.
    d.   I feel that Nixon has been unjustly treated.
    e.   I feel that Nixon has been justly treated.
    f.   I feel as if there are butterflies in my stomach.
4.   Illustrate how in a valid deductive argument the premises can be false and the conclusion false; the premises false and the conclusion true; the premises true and the conclusion *never* false.
5.   We have mentioned a few philosophers so far in one context or another: Plato, Descartes, Locke, Berkeley, Hume, Kant. In which school of thought would these philosophers probably find themselves, empirical or rational? Explain. We have also had reason to mention these terms: realism, idealism, rationalism, empiricism, deduction, induction. If you had to group them into groups of three, which would go together? Why?

Informal Fallacies

1.   Name the informal fallacies, if any, in the following statements:
    a.   "Of course he's against a national health-insurance program. He's a doctor, isn't he?"

b. "Right after he took out the big life-insurance policy on his wife, she died mysteriously. So he must have had something to do with her death."
c. "I'll tell you why I'm in favor of strip mining, and why you should be: I don't want this country dependent for its oil on the Arabs."
d. "What do you think of abortion?" "Why, it's nothing but killing!"
e. "If Congress had never passed the Gulf of Tonkin resolution, the Vietnam War would never have escalated."
f. "Of course the lower speed limits have saved lives. All the statistics show a decrease in traffic fatalities since the 55 speed limit went into effect."
g. "I would have done better on the exam if I hadn't been worried about losing my job."
h. "Candor requires that I tell you that such questionable behavior may have most unfortunate consequences."

2. Keep a list of the informal fallacies you find in this book. A good one to look for might be reification.

Authority

1. Leaf through a magazine or newspaper and find ten false appeals to authority. Find another ten in television ads.
2. Which of the following would you take on authority, and why?
    a. Light travels at 186,000 miles per second.
    b. It is impossible for a body to accelerate to the speed of light.
    c. A long time ago the earth was visited by astronaut gods.
    d. Prolonged and concentrated marijuana usage produces a loss of sexual desire.
    e. Fluoridated water is a health hazard.

Intuition

1. Evaluate the following claims to knowledge based on intuition.
    a. Don't drink that water; my intuition tells me it's poisoned.
    b. Let's go home; my intuition tells me something's wrong.
    c. My intuition tells me we're going the wrong way; let's turn around.
    d. My intuition tells me that the phone is about to ring.
    e. I'm going to stop thinking about this problem and follow my intuition.
2. In what sense do claims based on authority or intuition eventually stand or fall on primary sources? Demonstrate.
3. To what tests would you put claims based on faith and revelation before accepting them?

ADDITIONAL EXERCISES

1. Evaluate the following inductive arguments for probable truth.
   a. Since every President of the United States has been a male, the next one will be, too.
   b. On the only three occasions I've had dinner at her house, I've gotten sick. Every time I eat there I get food poisoning!
   c. Friday I got drunk on whiskey and water. Saturday I got drunk on Scotch and water. Sunday I got drunk on brandy and water. I'm sick of getting drunk. No more water for me!
   d. For the past 18,000 days, I've awakened. So I'll awaken tomorrow.

2. Are these arguments valid?
   a. All humans are mortal.
      Socrates is mortal.
      Socrates is human.
   b. If it's Tuesday, this must be Brussels.
      It is not Tuesday.
      This must not be Brussels.
   c. The speaker is either the President or the Vice President.
      He's definitely not the President.
      Then he must be the Vice President.
   d. No politicians are honest.
      Jones is honest.
      Jones is not a politician.

3. Which source or sources of knowledge would you rely on to support these claims?
   a. I feel sick just after I eat.
   b. The earth follows an elliptical orbit.
   c. God is good.
   d. Truth is a characteristic of a statement that corresponds to an actual state of affairs.
   e. A body will continue in a prescribed course until acted upon by some outside force.

4. State a belief that you hold on authority even though there is disagreement among the authorities. Why do you believe this? Do you act as if the belief were a truth? What theory of truth do you use to justify this belief?

5. It is frequently said that no generation in history knows as much as the present one. Do you agree? What do you think is the main source of this knowledge? Do you think the claim needs qualification? Or restriction to certain areas?

6. Do you believe in "woman's intuition"? Why or why not?

7. Today we are beset with numerous global problems. Many say that these problems have come as a result of our blind allegiance to science and the empirical method. Do you agree?

8. How reliable as sources of knowledge are the textbooks that you have studied? Have you found conflict among them? For example, perhaps you have discovered that many U.S. Presidents were hardly like the portraits elementary and junior high texts painted. Some have argued that young minds are not prepared for the unvarnished truth. Do you agree? Would you want your own children taught this way?

9. Do you see knowledge as worthwhile in itself, as a means to an end, or both?

10. How are you using education as a basis for self-discovery? Are you just "going along"? What are the dangers for the self implicit in "going along" with any source of knowledge?

PAPERBACKS FOR FURTHER READING

Aaron, Richard I. *Knowing and the Function of Reason.* Oxford: Clarendon Press, 1971. Aaron not only examines thought, knowing, and reason as parts of the reasoning process, but also demonstrates how intuition plays an integral role.

Castaneda, Carlos. *The Teachings of Don Juan: A Yaqui Way of Knowledge.* Berkeley: University of California Press, 1973. This is an anthropologist's provocative account of the claims of a Yaqui chief and his unconventional sources of knowledge.

Descartes, René. *Selections.* Ralph M. Eaton, Ed. New York: Charles Scribner's Sons, 1927. Especially appropriate in this volume, which has an excellent introduction, are selections from Descartes's *On Method* and "The Rules for the Direction of the Mind."

Pasch, Alan. *Experience and the Analytic: A Reconsideration of Empiricism.* Chicago: University of Chicago Press, 1958. An examination of empiricism and suggestions as to which directions it should take.

Siu, R. G. H. *The Tao of Science: An Essay on Western Knowledge and Eastern Wisdom.* Cambridge, Mass.: M.I.T. Press, 1957. This book offers a stimulating comparison of Western science and Eastern wisdom. Undogmatic and always open-minded, Siu tries to temper the frequently narrow tendencies of Western scientific method with Eastern humanism.

Reality

6

The true lover of knowledge is always striving after being. . . . He will not rest at those multitudinous phenomena whose existence is appearance only. —Plato

One of the best ways to throw light on the issue of self is to ask: what is ultimately real? Since we invariably view ourselves as unique in the scheme of reality, any description of reality is bound to reflect our view of human nature and, by implication, of the self. To understand this point, consider the following hypothetical situation.

You have fallen in love with a wonderful person. For the first time in your life you are giving serious thought to marriage.

You express your happiness and your plans to a very close professor friend at college. The professor couldn't be happier for you. Naturally, he asks if it is anyone he knows. You doubt it, but you mention the name.

Upon hearing the name, the professor gives a remarkably accurate description of your friend, even down to a birthmark on the inner right arm. You are astonished. Because you are sure the professor has never met your friend, you ask him how he did that.

"Because I manufactured your friend," says the professor. Manufactured! The professor insists that he's not fooling, that he's been doing it for years, that a number of his creations are around, living happy, constructive lives. In fact, one of his own is a very important person. Before you can catch yourself your mind riffles through a list of important people—Gerald Ford, Gloria Steinem, Joe Namath, Bella Abzug—could one of these be the professor's creation? Absurd!

"Sure, sure," you tell him, "but you didn't leave any loose wires dangling out anywhere, did you?"

Not only did he not, but he assures you that you will never be able to detect the slightest difference between your beloved and what we commonly call a human.

"You mean it isn't immortal?" you ask the professor.

"Of course not," he says. "As far as we know, all humans are mortal. So this creation is, too. It will age and be subject to the same physical laws that govern all organic life."

"What about having children?" you want to know.

He assures you that it is capable of reproducing. It functions sexually like any normal human. It will satisfy all your needs—physical, emotional, intellectual—and all your desires. His creation will be, in brief, the perfect mate—although admittedly a "mechanical" one.

Far-fetched? Probably. A mechanical creation that is identical to a human is still the brainchild more of fiction than of science. But unleash your imagination for a minute. What if the professor took you into his basement lab and demonstrated his craft before your disbelieving eyes? What if he showed you his creations and convinced you beyond a doubt that not only could he do what he claimed but that he was doing it, and that your intended mate was one of his products? Now ask yourself: would I still marry that individual?

In answering this question, you will probably reveal what you see as ultimately real—as the essence of all being, including yourself. In philosophy, the critical study of the nature of reality is called **metaphysics**, one of whose subdivisions is **ontology**, the theory of the nature of being and existence. Here we shall use the question of the mechanical mate to launch metaphysical inquiries. Is reality ultimately matter? Is it idea? Is it a combination? Is reality ultimately being or consciousness? Perhaps we can never say what reality ultimately is; perhaps the question and any subsequent theories are meaningless. In this chapter we investigate these issues to see what further light they throw on the question of what we are.

REALITY AS MATTER

Meet Ruth. Like the hypothetical "you" we just envisioned, she has met and fallen in love with someone very special, Max. Ruth also has a professor friend in whom she confides, only to hear the professor claim that he has produced Max in his basement lab.

Although Ruth does not believe the professor, ever since the conversation she has been restless. She finally decides to tell someone, her brother Brad.

Brad couldn't care less that the creature is mechanical. As far as he is concerned, if he cannot ever detect a difference between it and an ordinary human, then there is no difference. But Ruth points out that, because the creature was not born as we are, there really is a difference between us and it. But Brad thinks being born is not so special. After all, cats, rattlesnakes, and chimpanzees are born. Does that mean Ruth should marry one? No, but Ruth insists that it does mean she should marry a person, and this—this thing—just isn't a person. "But what's so sacred about being a person?" Ruth is astonished. Then Brad mentions a book about human behavior he has been reading that claims that much of what we do can be explained in terms of glands.

"I'll give you a for instance," Brad tells Ruth. "Let's say you're in the grocery store some night when a guy comes in and holds it up. He's got a gun and he's waving it around real crazy. Naturally, you're scared to death. Then all of a sudden, before you even know what you're doing, you spring at him."

"Me?"

"Yeah, you. Just like that! You leap through the air and clobber him. Smash! He's down. Then the cops come. They give you a medal. You're a real hero. The storekeeper even gives you a six-pack!"

"So?"

"So, do you know why you're a hero?"

"Why?"

"Glands."

"You're kidding."

"Nope. You reacted as you did largely because your glands pumped out adrenalin. It's that simple."

Ruth is not convinced. She asks how he would explain feelings like love or guilt or uncertainty, the impulse to believe in God, the urge to write a book or compose a song. Brad insists that those impulses, too, can be explained physiochemically. He mentions how brain surgeons have altered not only human behavior but feelings as well; how they have literally erased intense spiritual feelings people had; how they have turned psychopathic killers into placid, if unproductive, citizens.

"In the last analysis," Brad says, "everything is just matter, and all matter is subject to physiochemical explanation. It's that simple."

Is it that simple? Is matter the ultimate constituent of reality, including you and me? In replying to Ruth's inquiry, Brad reveals a whole concept of reality; it is this concept that inclines him to say without reservation that he would marry such a creature. We can call his metaphysical view *materialism*.

Reflection   Suppose the creature in question is a human clone—that is, an exact replica of a human produced from one of his or her cells. Would that fact alter your decision to marry the creature? Why or why not?

"Is matter the ultimate constituent
of reality, including you and me?"

The Development of Materialism

Materialism, the view that the ultimate constituent of reality is matter, is at least as old as the ancient Greeks. Democritus (460–360 B.C.) believed that reality could be explained in terms of matter. The smallest pieces of matter he called atoms; he described them as solid, indivisible, indestructible, eternal, and uncreated. These atoms were not qualitatively distinguishable from one another, and they constantly moved through space, where they combined to form the recognizable physical objects of the universe. According to Democritus, then, the universe consisted of atoms and empty space. He believed that even the soul, which he equated with reason, consisted of atoms. In this atomic universe "all things happen by virtue of necessity, the vortex being the cause of the creation of all things."[1]

The philosopher Epicurus (342–270 B.C.) espoused similar views, but a few centuries later the Roman poet Lucretius (96–55 B.C.) recorded the most complete statement of Democritus's atomic theory we have. In his poem *On the Nature of Things,* Lucretius provided additional principles of the atomic universe, including (1) nothing is created: "We must confess that nothing can be brought to being out of nothing, inasmuch as it needs a seed for things, from which each may be produced

---

[1]Quoted in Diogenes Laertes. *Lives and Opinions of Eminent Philosophers.* R. D. Hicks, trans. Cambridge, Mass.: Harvard University Press, 1925, Vol. 2, p. 455.

and brought forth into the gentle breezes of the air"; (2) nothing is destroyed: "Nor does [nature] destroy aught into nothing"; and (3) there is empty space: "There is a void in things."[2]

But the atomic theory never "caught on," for by Democritus's time people had become generally disenchanted with the many attempts to explain the cosmos. At various times, philosopher/scientists viewed water, fire, air, or earth as the fundamental reality. Others believed that reality could best be explained in terms of constant change. Eventually interest centered on more personal concerns, such as how one might lead a good and contented life. This interest was sparked by classical philosophy.

Although their interests reach much further than such questions, the Greek philosophers Socrates, Plato, and Aristotle did see the moral life as the road to knowledge and truth. The rise of Christianity fanned this interest in personal conduct, which predominated throughout the Middle Ages. Instrumental to this interest was the idea of a soul, which now assumed a religious dimension that included personal immortality. Such an emphasis gave the view of reality a distinctly nonmaterial bias that held sway into the seventeenth century, when growing interest in the world and the rise of the scientific method and scientific discovery turned minds once again to materialism.

Awakened by the discoveries of Copernicus, Kepler, Galileo, and Newton, the seventeenth century watched science cultivate a full-blown materialism. Committed to the belief that the world could be quantified, scientists fed the materialistic claim that all was just matter. In the systematic philosophy of Thomas Hobbes (1588–1679), for example, we see the Democritean belief that everything can be explained in terms of matter in motion. Claimed Hobbes:

Every object is either a part of the whole world, or an aggregate of parts. The greatest of all bodies, or sensible objects, is the world itself; which we behold when we look round about us from this point of the same which we call the earth. Concerning the world, as it is one aggregate of many parts, the things that fall under inquiry are but few; and those we can determine, none. Of the whole world we may inquire what is its magnitude, what its duration, and how many there be, but nothing else.[3]

Similarly, anticipating many contemporary psychological theories, Hobbes postulated that mental states were brain states, and that a "general inclination of all mankind" was "a perpetual and restless desire of power after power." In 1748, Julien Offray de La Mettrie carried Hobbesian psychology further when he published *Man a Machine.*

---

[2]Quoted in Diogenes Laertes, *Lives and Opinions*, p. 455.

[3]Thomas Hobbes. "Elements of Philosophy," in *The English Works of Thomas Hobbes,* Sir W. Molesworth, Ed. London: J. Bohn, 1839, Vol. 1, Ch. 1, Sec. 8.

You may wonder what had happened to the religious doctrine of the soul. What remained of the creature supposedly made in the image of God and possessed of an eternal destiny? So much medieval superstition, declared the materialists. Even Newton's mechanical universe was rapidly growing obsolete, because Newton had proposed a God who regulated things. In contrast, astronomer-mathematician Pierre Laplace proposed his theory of a self-regulating universe, which gained some respectability by the early nineteenth century. Naturally, such a universe needed not a God but a super computer as regulator. As Bertrand Russell pointed out:

When Laplace suggested that the same forces which are now operative (according to Newton's laws) might have caused the planets to grow out of the sun, God's share in the course of nature was pushed still further back. He might remain as Creator, but even that was doubtful, since it was not clear the world has a beginning in time.[4]

An interesting footnote to this historical development: it is said that when Napoleon asked Laplace why his theory omitted God, Laplace simply replied that God was an unnecessary hypothesis.

But these early materialists' optimistic faith that the human could eventually explain the universe and himself has tarnished over the last century, as we shall see. Nevertheless, just as a culture generally lags behind its science, so today we frequently find ourselves as enthusiastically materialistic as our nineteenth-century counterparts.

Today philosophical materialism takes many forms, but all have at least three characteristics in common that survive from the past. First, materialism seeks answers through objective methodology. Specifically, it is committed to the scientific method of observation, analysis, and tentative conclusions. What cannot be found out by this method cannot be known. Second, materialism is deterministic; that is, it believes that every event has a cause. Some materialists attribute these causes to physiochemical processes. Others would add biological causes. Still others wish to introduce psychological, sociological, and anthropological causes. We may not know the causes, they say, but they nevertheless exist. Finally, materialism denies any form of supernaturalistic belief, including belief in spirit, soul, mind, or any other nonmaterial substance. Reality is composed of matter and only of matter.

---

[4]Bertrand Russell. *A History of Western Philosophy.* New York: Simon & Schuster, 1945, p. 537.

Objections to Materialism

We said earlier that materialism, at least in twentieth-century scientific circles, has lost considerable ground. Let us rejoin Ruth and Brad and see why and how.

Ruth: I don't understand how you can deny what so many people have believed for so long.

Brad: What's that?

Ruth: The existence of a nonmaterial reality.

Brad: You mean a soul?

Ruth: A soul, a spirit, a mind—call it what you want.

Brad: Look, a lot of people once believed the earth was the center of the solar system; but that didn't make it so, did it?

Ruth: That was different. This is a belief that defies full scientific contradiction. What you seem to forget is that the very thing you're calling us—machines— we have created. *We* have invented them. If it weren't for people like the professor, these mechanical creations wouldn't exist to begin with. The creation isn't the creator, Brad. Machines aren't people. People love and hate, they dream, they hope, they strive. They write great books and compose beautiful music.

Brad: So what?

Ruth: So how can you explain all this in terms of physiochemical causes?

How can Brad deny what is fundamentally real to so many people? This is what Ruth is asking. She is also asking how he can reduce to material explanation those human qualities and behavior that are supposedly unique, such as consciousness. It does not seem to her that consciousness can be explained totally in terms of the physiochemical; neither can ideas or concepts.

Ruth: You say that everything in existence can be explained physiochemically. Then what about human consciousness?

Brad: What about it?

Ruth: How do you explain states of consciousness that we experience? How do you explain, for example, my experience of seeing something red, let alone the more complex experiences like being in love?

Brad: Look, what you're calling consciousness is no more than a brain state. When you're seeing red, your brain is merely functioning in a certain way. The same is true with love or any other experience.

Ruth: All right, suppose you're having a brain operation. In the operating room are mirrors placed so that you can observe what's happening. Now, the surgeon peels back the top of your skull and you observe your own brain.

Brad: So?

Ruth: So you can observe even the nerve pathways that are stimulated when you experience a color—red, for example. You can see precisely what ganglion reacts whenever you see red. Every time the surgeon shows you red, sure enough, that thing starts wiggling.

Brad: Okay. That's my brain state for the experience of red.

Ruth: Are you saying that the red you see and what's happening in your brain when you see it are the same thing?

Brad: Right.

Ruth: Then why isn't the surgeon seeing red?

Brad: What do you mean?

Ruth: Well, he's observing your brain state, too, isn't he? If your brain state equals the experience of red, why isn't the surgeon having the same experience when he observes your brain state?

Brad: Because he has his own experience of red, that's why.

Ruth: All right, let me ask you this. Can you have the surgeon's experience of red?

Brad: Of course not. But I could observe his brain state of red.

Ruth: So what you're saying is that the brain state and the experience are really two different things.

Brad: Okay, maybe they are. So what?

Ruth: Plenty. What makes them different is that one is publicly observable and the other is not. Everybody can observe the brain state. Why? Because it's physical. But only the individual can have the experience that accompanies the brain state. And that's because it's nonphysical; its *nonmaterial.*

Brad initially insists that Ruth's example portrays the brain observing itself. Yet consciousness, understanding, and experience seem to stand outside the particular brain state observed. Brad would seem to be having two experiences: one of the brain state itself, the other of the experience that the brain state signals. The experience does not seem to be physical, although it is undoubtedly accompanied by a brain and nerve state. How can the strict materialist account for this fact? Does it suggest the presence of a nonmaterial reality? Is there at the core of all being something that cannot be measured, pinpointed, or spatialized? Modern atomic physics suggests that the active agent in things is ultimately immaterial. This view has arisen in the wake of some startling modern discoveries.

For a long time we have known that all matter consists of molecules, of which there are a tremendous number. But even though there are many molecules, few different atoms—only about 100—make up each molecule. Before the twentieth century, no one believed these atoms could be split. Today we know that three particles make up the atom: electron, proton, and neutron. Yet everything in existence cannot be explained in terms of these three elementary particles.

Physicists have discovered that there are at least 30 so-called elementary particles, probably many more. As recently as 1974 another elementary particle, the J-psi, was discovered. Some believe that these elementary particles are themselves made up of still more elementary particles, called "quarks." The point is that modern science is showing reality to be more complex than has been thought.

But, even more important, it seems that these elementary particles are *not* matter. They are more likely energy forces. True, matter may depend on elementary-particle interaction, but the particles themselves seem to be energy, not matter. And what is energy? Nobody knows for sure. Whatever it is, it is in motion and it exerts force, but it does not appear to be matter.

The fact is that ever since the early 1930s, when Werner Heisenberg discovered that atomic activity is not uniform, materialism has been losing credibility. Heisenberg formulated his Principle of Indeterminacy on a startling premise: that there is no orderly causation. Because electrons change their positions in unpredictable ways, rational predictability is not possible. In his article "The Dematerialization of Matter," philosopher-scientist N. R. Hanson states the full implications of Heisenberg's discovery:

Matter has been dematerialized, not just as a concept of the philosophically real, but now as an idea of modern physics. Matter can be analyzed down to the level of fundamental particles. But at that depth the direction of the analysis changes, and this constitutes a major conceptual surprise in the history of science. The things which for Newton typified matter—e.g., an exactly determinable state, a point shape, absolute solidity—these are now the properties electrons do not, because theoretically they cannot, have. . . .

The dematerialization of matter . . . has rocked mechanics at its foundations. . . . The 20th century's dematerialization of matter has made it conceptually impossible to accept a Newtonian picture of the properties of matter and still do a consistent physics.[5]

---

[5]N. R. Hanson. "The Dematerialization of Matter," in Ernan McMillin (Ed.), *The Concept of Matter*. Notre Dame, Ind.: University of Notre Dame Press, 1963, pp. 556–557.

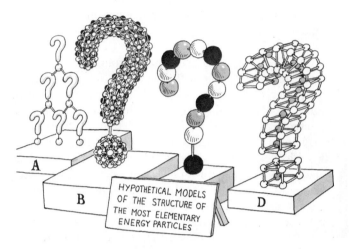

"And what is energy? Nobody
knows for sure."

As a result, many scientists, including Heisenberg, believe that we
are more likely to have an idealistic universe than a materialistic one.
To understand better what they mean, let us consider idealism as an
explanation of ultimate reality.

Reflection   Imagine a machine that can do things that we consider
uniquely human: love, hate, dream, hope, strive, create art, and so
forth. Would you consider it human?

REALITY AS NONMATTER

Modern atomic theory has led many to claim that reality consists of
more than matter. But this is not a denial of matter. It is an observation that if we push the question of reality far enough matter alone
does not seem to account for everything, that things really are not only
what they appear to be. What are they, then?

Today many would argue that ultimate reality resembles some
cosmic law, such as Einstein's relativity equation $E = mc^2$ (energy
equals mass times the speed of light squared). This law, they say, not
only describes how things work but, more importantly, implies a pattern,
a form, a principle that lies at the bottom of everything, that gives everything design and purpose, that provides our experiences with order.

The study of the theory that there is design or purpose working in the structure of the universe is called **teleology.** Can matter alone account for the general teleological tendencies in the operation of things? Can sheer coincidence? Can an accidental combination of electrons?

Critics think not. They argue that the survival-of-the-fittest theory does not fully explain evolution over millions and millions of years from very simple organisms to incredibly complex ones, from a mindless glob to human intelligence. In contrast, the nonmaterialists see *purpose* in the evolutionary trends we can empirically observe. They see *direction* in the operation of nature. They see Mind behind the way things interrelate and function. Purpose, direction, and mind are concepts foreign to materialism. Yet many say that when we push our investigation of physical phenomena far enough we end up in just such a mental world, a world of idea, not matter. This is why nonmaterialists are often called "idealists."

Idealists, as opposed to materialists, see a mental or spiritual force operating that accounts for what they perceive as the order and purpose in nature. Nature, they believe, is goal-directed; it evolves not by chance but by design. That humankind is coming to understand more and more the wonders of nature suggests an underlying law operating in the universe. This law or principle, they say, is not matter but idea. Like materialism, idealism has a long history.

The Development of Idealism

Although idealists differ, let us define **idealism** in general as the belief that reality is essentially idea, thought, or mind, and not essentially matter. Whether idealists believe that there is a single absolute Mind or many minds, they invariably emphasize the mental or spiritual, not the material, presenting it as the creative force or active agent behind all things.

The belief that reality is ultimately idea is at least as old as the ancient Greek Pythagoras (about 600 B.C.). It was Plato, however, who formalized it. He held that individual entities are merely shadows of reality, that behind each entity in our experience is a perfect Form or Idea. This Form or Idea is what makes the entity understandable to the human mind. Individual entities come and go but the Forms are immortal and indestructible. For Plato, there is the world of opinion, consisting of all sense objects. Then there is the knowable world, the world of Form or Idea. The world of opinion is one of illusion, impermanence, and perpetual ignorance, similar to what Buddhists call **maya.** But the knowable world, resembling what Hindus call **Brahman**, is real, permanent, and forever truthful.

Such thinking fit in well with Christian thought as it was developed by St. Augustine (354–430). In his work *The City of God,* Augustine warns us to beware the world and the flesh, for they are fleeting. What is real is the spiritual world, the world without matter. Although we are citizens of the physical world, we are ultimately intended to be citizens of the spiritual world of God. This is our divine destiny. For Augustine and fellow Christians, Jesus Christ is the embodiment of all perfection, of all "Forms"; he is the meaning of all that is. As St. John writes, "In the beginning was the Word and the Word was with God and the Word was God. He was in the beginning with all things." Notice that John says the *Word* was God—in Greek, the *logos*, the law, the word. In the nineteenth century the German romantic Goethe would express a similar idealistic notion through his immortal Faust: "In the beginning was the meaning."

We see the foundations of modern idealism in the epistemology of George Berkeley when, in the eighteenth century, he reacted against the growth of scientific materialism. Berkeley claimed that what exists is the conscious mind and its perceptions. For Berkeley, the world is Mind communicating with other minds. An abstract notion, but not so elusive when we understand that by "Mind" Berkeley meant God. Berkeley does not deny the physical world, only its independence from Mind. Since for Berkeley to be is to be perceived, a world separate from (independent from) Mind cannot exist, because it would be contradictory. Not everything perceived, however, is a human perception or idea. Phenomena that make for uniformity, consistency, continuity of entities are not known in any way by finite mind. They can be explained only in terms of ideas in the mind of God. For Berkeley, God is the ruling spirit of nature; God's will is nature's law. The orderly succession of events that Ruth perceives in everything, Berkeley would attribute to the will of God.

Like Berkeley, Immanuel Kant believed that all we know is how things appear to us. Unlike Berkeley, however, Kant held that we are not just passive receivers of sense experience. Once we receive sense impressions, our minds have the ability to do something with these impressions, to provide them with form. Our minds reveal relationships between sense experiences; they reveal law and principle at work. In short, our minds possess conceptual molds that order sense experience. These molds precede all sense data; they are nonmaterial, pure idea.

A nineteenth-century idealist, and one of the most complex—Georg Hegel (1770–1831)—disagreed with Kant. We do not impose order or form on nature, said Hegel, we discover it. Order, form, and shape are not made by humans; humans find them. They already exist in the nature of things, including the nature of self. Reality, for Hegel, expresses itself in our thinking. The essence of everything, including self, is purposive intelligence—Absolute Mind, God—whose essence is ultimately identical with the entirety of the world process. The entire world process is the actualizing of reality.

Obviously, there have been varieties of idealism. But they all appear to have several things in common. First, they all believe in mind, spirit, or thought as what is ultimately real. Second, they perceive purpose, order, and meaning in the workings of things. Third, they see some kind of purpose acting in our lives. As there are laws governing the operations of the physical universe, so there are laws governing the operations of our own lives: moral laws.

Reflection   Is there any public figure, living or dead, whom you would consider idealistic in the ordinary sense of the word, as one having ideals? Do you detect any connection between this ordinary usage of the word *idealism* and philosophical idealism?

Objections to Idealism

As we have seen, idealists rely heavily on one assumption: that there are order and purpose in the universe. Critics wonder whether the terms *order* and *purpose* are vague. They claim that in using them idealists are being evasive. They argue that experience exhibits such seemingly chaotic and purposeless events as natural disasters (the so-called acts of God), the human catastrophes of disease and war, and the personal and national tragedies of senseless deaths. The French writer Voltaire (1694–1778) perhaps best sums up this criticism in *Candide,* in which he uses ironic wit to question philosopher Leibnitz's (1648–1727) belief that everything happens for the best in this "best of all possible worlds." At one point in that philosophical tale, Candide points out to Martin the merits of a shipwreck: "You see that crime is sometimes punished; that scoundrel of a Dutch shipowner has had the fate he deserved." Martin's response: "Yes, but did the passengers who were on the ship have to perish too?"[6]

In addition, critics claim that idealists commit the fallacy of **anthropomorphism**; that is, they attribute human characteristics to the universe as a whole. It is one thing to speak of people as having minds but another to speak of the universe as having one. Similarly unwarranted, say critics, is the leap from ideas to Idea and from reasoning to Reason.

Finally, critics wonder who has ever experienced mind, idea, or spirit independent of a matter-energy system. They point out that in fact it is not even necessary to posit a nonmaterial reality to account for what we observe.

---

[6]Voltaire. *Candide.* Tobias George Smollett, trans. New York: Washington Square Press, 1962, p. 77.

Are we, in the last analysis, forced to choose between materialism or idealism? Is there some middle ground? For Voltaire's Candide, the answer is to reject both extremes: extreme materialism, which he sees leading to nothingness, and extreme idealism, leading to blind optimism. Yes, disorder, chaos, even evil exist. But Candide does not succumb to them. He feels that to cure evil we must first recognize its reality and its inevitability. He decides that within his own "garden" he can cultivate virtue and justice, although he probably will not find them in the universe. Thus Candide attempts to mediate between two extremes, to avoid what he considers the false dilemma of all or nothing. His attitude uses the practical consequences of a belief. In this sense, it is pragmatic. Pragmatism offers still another view of reality.

REALITY AS PRAGMATISM

As we noted earlier, pragmatism is a philosophical movement that has grown up in the last hundred years through the writings of Peirce, James, and Dewey. James defines pragmatism as "the attitude of looking away from first things, principles, 'categories,' supposed necessities; and of looking towards last things, fruits, consequences, facts."[7] Pragmatism is also a reaction to traditional systems of philosophy like materialism and idealism. These systems, claim the pragmatists, have erred in looking for absolutes, unchanging principles. Debates like those between Ruth and Brad are pointless, for reality is hardly a single thing, whether matter or idea. Nature is many things: it is **pluralistic.** And we are part of it. Using intelligence and reason, we can understand and exercise some control over nature; we can help create nature.

Pragmatism employs the method of scientific inquiry in order to learn the secrets of reality and of ourselves. But it does not look for any cosmic mind or reason; the fact that we have minds does not mean the universe does. Pragmatism asserts that mind is real, but only insofar as it is a function of behavior. We develop this function when we learn about the things around us. For pragmatists, thinking is coming to understand the connection between action and consequence.

Objections to Pragmatism

But its opponents do not consider pragmatism an acceptable middle ground between materialism and idealism. They claim it is muddled thinking, that it has no clear notion of what it understands to be real.

---

[7]William James. *Pragmatism.* New York: Longmans, Green, 1907, pp. 54–55.

Pragmatists claim to know only their experiences. But, claim critics, this is idealism. It is also inconsistent, because pragmatists also believe in an objective physical reality. Critics also disagree that mind is just a function of behavior, that it is only an instrument of biological survival. They point out that people meditate and contemplate and use the mind to compose great symphonies and to ask philosophical questions. Yet, these activities do not seem necessary for biological survival. Mind, say the pragmatists, exists to fulfil desires. Then why the commitment to scientific inquiry? Why such stress on impartiality when seeking truth, and not more reliance on the subjective impulses of the mind?

Reflection In your capacity as City Commissioner, you are offered a bribe. Assuming you are a pragmatist, how would you evaluate the ethics of what you will do: accept or reject it? Or would you not even consider it an ethical issue?

REALITY AS BEING

As for Ruth and her mechanical mate, it seems that pragmatism would not provide an acceptable compromise. Believing in the idealistic concepts of order and purpose, Ruth is not likely to be convinced by pragmatism, which shares more materialistic beliefs. She would also reject the pragmatic diagnosis that where no difference is detectable there is no difference. And she would hardly accept the contention that the mind is only a function of behavior. So let us see what happens when she takes the issue to Max, her fiancé, and is shown yet another alternative.

Ruth: You know, Max, the other day the professor said something really strange.

Max: What's that?

Ruth: He said he'd made you in his lab.

Max: That's funny. He told me the same thing about you.

Ruth: You're kidding.

Max: But he said you'd be like a human in every way.

Ruth: That you wouldn't be able to detect the slightest difference?

Max: That's what he said. And that you'd make the perfect mate . . .

Ruth: Even if I *was* mechanical, right?

Max: That's about it. Tell me something, Ruth. If I were a mechanical man, would you hesitate to marry me?

Ruth: Oh, Max, the whole question's so silly. I'm really tired of talking about it.

Max: Then give me a simple yes or no.

Ruth: Well . . . I guess yes, I would have some doubts.

Max: Why?

Ruth: Why? Isn't that obvious? I mean, you'd be more thing than man.

Max: More human *machine* than human *being*, is that what you mean?

Ruth: Yes, I guess so. I mean, if you came into the world the same as the rest of us, that would make you one of us, wouldn't it? You'd be fully human.

Max: Fully human? You make it sound as if my dues would be all paid up, that I'd be a member in good standing of the human race.

Ruth: Well, you'd be in better standing than if you had come by way of the professor's cellar, that's for sure.

Max: What would you like me to do—go back and come into the world again?

Ruth: Max, don't be so silly. You make it sound as if we're actually talking about you.

Max: I think you are.

Ruth: You're not going to tell me that the professor actually did create you?

Max: Look, you said you loved me, right?

Ruth: *Love*—not *loved*. I love you right now, this very minute. And I want to be with you as long as you want me to be.

Max: Why? Why do you love me?

Ruth: What a silly question! And I thought only females asked questions like that.

Max: Then humor me. Tell me why.

Ruth: Why? Because you're you.

Max: But what am I, Ruth—really?

Ruth: Well, who is Max, *really*? Max is kind and he's tender; he's loving and honest; he's handsome and intelligent . . . and he's going to be insufferably vain if I go on any more!

Max: My incredible humility will prevent that.

Ruth: Oh! You're hopeless!

Max: Seriously, is all that what you think I am? Is that your concept of me?

Ruth: I suppose that's part of it.

Max: Then the professor comes along and blows it. He says something that changes that concept. He says I'm not what you think I am, that I'm not like you or him or anybody else because I didn't come on the scene the way everyone else has. Suddenly this information overshadows everything else you know about me. Suddenly you don't know whether you want to marry me. Suddenly you don't know whether you can love me in the way you did before.

Ruth: But do you blame me?

Max: It's not a question of blame, Ruth. It's a question of *why* you loved me in the first place. You say it's because I am me. But I'm still me. I'm still the same being I was before the professor dropped his bomb. I haven't changed at all.

Ruth: But that's not true. Something about you has changed for me, something very important.

Max: Some *thing,* yes. But not me. I am the same. If I lost an arm, would you still love me?

Ruth: You know I would. But you're not comparing that to being a mechanical man, are you?

Max: In a way I am. Because it's clear that, for you, *what* or who I am is more important than *that* I am.

Ruth: Listen, do you think for a minute that I'd care if you were wealthy or had a fancy sports car or anything like that?

Max: Of course you wouldn't.

Ruth: Because if I did, I'd be treating you just like a thing.

Max: That's right. But you can treat people like things more subtly.

Ruth: How?

Max: Well, you can treat me like a thing when you insist that I be human. That's really no different from insisting that I be a Republican or a Democrat; that I be a Catholic, Protestant, or Jew; that I be a white American. Why must I be some *thing?* Why can't I just *be?* Why not be happy with my just plain old *being* and leave it at that?

Ruth: But I am.

Max: I really don't think so. Because if you were, it wouldn't matter whether or not I was human. It would only matter that I *was.*

Ruth: You mean I'd love you just for existing.

Max: Not *for* existing, just existing. You'd love my existing.

Ruth: I don't understand.

Max: Well, you wouldn't, you couldn't, love anything specific; you'd love the very core of me, my *being.*

Ruth: But I do love your soul.

Max: That's not what I mean. My being is not my soul or mind or body.

Ruth: Then what is it?

Max: It can't be described. It defies language because it's not a thing. It is my unique act of existing.

Ruth: You've got me confused with all this talk of being. I'm afraid I'm not following.

Max: That's because English doesn't help us very much. There's only one word for *being* in English, and that usually refers to some *thing*. But take German. In German there are two words for being—*das Seinde* and *das Sein. Das Seinde* means being as a thing, an object. You're a being, I'm a being, Brad's a being, the professor's a being.

Ruth: I see: being in the sense of someone *being* a student or a worker or a writer.

Max: Right. He'd be some thing; he'd be a being. But *das Sein* means being as an activity, not a thing. It refers to the *being* of the thing.

Ruth: You mean the student as *being* instead of the student as a being.

Max: Yes. In the same way you can speak of the lover as a being or simply as being. When you view the lover as a being, it seems to me that you view the lover as a thing. But when you view the lover as being, you don't.

Ruth: So you're saying that I shouldn't love you so much because you're you, but because you *are*.

Max: I think so.

Ruth: I never thought of that.

Max does not want to consider reality piecemeal. The trouble with traditional outlooks is that, in trying to simplify life, they reduce it to an abstraction. But there is nothing abstract about existing. Existence is what is ultimately real. And existence involves individuals who exist. We find this emphasis on existence and the individual in two twentieth-century movements: existentialism and phenomenology.

Existentialism and phenomenology share a number of outlooks on the human condition. First, both existentialists and phenomenologists observe suffering and pain as the overriding human experience. They point out that we suffer all kinds of pain: physical, emotional, psychological. We feel anxious, uncertain, indecisive. We know what it is to dread, to feel despair, to hurt. Daily we face the reality of death. True, we are not always conscious of death's imminence, but it is always with us.

Building on this basic insight into the human condition, existentialists and phenomenologists claim that we shall never understand the primacy of the individual so long as we explain life and people objectively, clinically, impersonally. In reducing individuals to scientific explanations, materialism makes things of people. In explaining reality in terms of cosmic mind, idealism submerges individual self in universal ego. Truth about life and ourselves is not something to be discovered, to be grasped and repeated in nice neat statements. We experience truth, like everything else, through living; the truth is within, not without.

Apart from these general similarities, various points of emphasis distinguish existentialism from phenomenology.

Existentialism

First, followers of existentialism are extremely diverse, including theists and atheists, philosophers, theologians, and artists. Specifically, it embraces the writings of the religious thinker Søren Kierkegaard (1813–1855), the Jewish scholar Martin Buber (1878–1965), the Protestant theologian Paul Tillich (1886–1965), the atheistic philosopher Jean-Paul Sartre (1905–), the novelist Albert Camus (1913–1960), and a long list of other thinkers, writers, and artists. Although their views often differ radically, they share the common bonds of concern for the individual, for subjective experience, for the importance of self, for the need for personal freedom, and for the reality of personal responsibility.

Kierkegaard may be considered the founder of modern existentialism. Two facts about his life will help us understand what he tried to do. First, Kierkegaard was a deeply religious thinker, a Lutheran; second, he despised Hegel's absolute idealism, so influential in nineteenth-century thinking. Hegel's thinking, Kierkegaard believed, impoverished the individual by submerging him in an abstract, absolute ego. More important, it evaded the central issue of life, which for Kierkegaard was what it means to be a Christian. How is an individual to bridge the gap between himself and his Maker, between creation and Creator? Kierkegaard observed that even ethical people, ones who recognize and accept the reality of universal moral laws, experience frustrating failure. These well-intentioned people experience the painful awareness that they are not what they ought to be. Kierkegaard wondered whether we should remain in this limbo of despair and anxiety, frustrated by our inability to be better than we are, or make a "leap of faith" to a recognition of God, to a genuine relationship between ourselves and our Creator. Kierkegaard saw this existential choice confronting all individuals.

Friedrich Nietzsche (1844–1900) disagreed. True, the individual is what matters; existence must be stressed above everything else; traditional thought is ultimately irrelevant to the human condition. But Christianity, held Nietzsche, is no different from traditional thinking. Its conventional values and morality inhibit rather than encourage individual freedom and growth, which can occur only in the absence of a traditional God. Thus Nietzsche's problem was how to live in a world in which "God is dead." His answer: unleash the individual's "will to power." Let the superior individuals be truly free—free from the bonds of traditional morality. Let their passions be subject only to the reins of a superior intellect. Let these "supermen" usher in a new age that elevates the individual to Olympian heights.

But the chief exponent of contemporary atheistic existentialism is Jean-Paul Sartre. For Sartre, the "death of God" is not good news. In his essay "Existentialism and Human Decision," he writes "The existentialist thinks it very distressing that God does not exist." Why? Since there is no God, there can be no one to conceive of a human nature. Without a human nature, we are free to be what we choose. There is nothing we *ought* to do, since there is nothing we *ought* to be. There are no absolutes, no norms of right behavior; we are on our own. We exist; what is uniquely ours, what makes each of us an individual— our essence—is ours for the making. We do not *discover* who we are so much as *make* it. Thus Sartre writes:

> A first glance at human reality informs us that for it being is reduced to doing. . . . Thus we find no *given* in human reality in the sense that temperament, character, passions, principles of reason would be acquired or innate *data* existing in the manner of things. . . . Thus human reality does not exist first in order to act later; but for human reality, to be is to act, and to cease to act is to cease to be.[8]

For Kierkegaard, we find ourselves in God; for Sartre, we are our own gods. For Kierkegaard, our uniqueness, our **essence**, takes precedence over our **existence**. For Sartre, our existence precedes our essence. Curiously, Max seems to argue that being precedes both existence and essence. In this sense he is closer to phenomenology than to existentialism.

Phenomenology

In his *Phenomenology of Perception*, Maurice Merleau-Ponty (1907–1961) says "The aim of phenomenology is described as the study of experiences with a view to bringing out their 'essences,' their underlying 'reason.'"[9] **Phenomenology** studies experience. It focuses on the individual and the individual consciousness. It attempts to describe the consciousness, to examine things as they appear to the consciousness. For the founder of phenomenology, Edmund Husserl (1859–1938), the overriding reality is the consciousness itself. You can think away everything, but you cannot think away thought. How things are is not so important as how they appear to be to the individual. What is ultimately real is pure consciousness, which we reach by removing attention from the specific experiences that occupy it.

Vital to an understanding of Husserl's method is his phenomenological stance, as opposed to what Husserl called "the natural stand-

[8]Jean-Paul Sartre. *Being and Nothingness*. H. E. Barnes, trans. New York: Philosophical Library, 1956, p. lxvi.

[9]Quoted in Edo Pivcevic. *Husserl and Phenomenology*. London: Hutchinson University Library, 1970, p. 11.

point." The natural standpoint is the stance toward the world that most people assume most of the time. This consists of being aware of a world that is "simply there," whether or not we pay any special attention to it. This "fact-world," as Husserl calls it, we find to be "out there," and we take it just as it gives itself to us. Despite all doubting and rejecting of the data of this natural world, he says that most of us most of the time would insist that the world as a fact-world is always present. Occasionally this fact-world differs from what we supposed: we experience illusions or hallucinations. But a world that has its being out there remains. In other words, although we may suspect or even reject parts of our experience, we most often unquestioningly accept the world as a whole. Indeed, this natural standpoint seems a most reasonable position. Yet Husserl asks us to question it—to doubt the world as a whole.

Husserl does not want us to abandon altogether the thesis of the natural standpoint—that the fact-world has its being out there—but to modify it. He asks us to *"set it as it were out of action . . . to disconnect it, bracket it."* Like the words within the bracket, the natural standpoint still remains; we simply make no use of it. We reserve judgments based on the thesis of the natural standpoint. Although we continue to be conscious of the entire natural world, which is continually there for us, we phenomenologically bracket it, an act that "completely bars us from using any judgment that concerns spatio-temporal existence."

To illustrate Husserl's meaning, suppose you are looking at a die in the palm of your hand. What do you experience? From the natural standpoint, the die is a cube of a certain color and size. On various sides of the die are dots, from one to six of them. What happens when we "bracket" this experience, as Husserl suggests?

When you bracket, you do not doubt the *experience* of having the die in hand. But you do doubt that you *actually* have a die in hand. After all, it may be that you are dreaming or hallucinating or imagining, and that your hand is actually empty. What Husserl is asking you to do, then, is to doubt that the die has being in the mode of existence. This is what he means by the phenomenological stance, which he would prescribe for all our experience.

Husserl is suggesting that we suspend the truth claims of our everyday cognitive processes. Because we assume the natural standpoint, this suspension seems unnatural for most of us. Why should I doubt that I actually have a die in my hand when I can feel and see it? Husserl insists that such bracketing, far from leaving us in a state of ignorance and skepticism, will actually leave us in the presence of important truths that would otherwise elude us. He believes that these truths experienced in the phenomenological stance are important because whatever remains after bracketing, after universal doubt, is absolutely certain. The obvious question is: what survives universal doubt? In general, Husserl believes that what survives universal doubt is consciousness—that ultimate reality consists of consciousness. As he puts it:

> For what can remain over when the whole world is bracketed, including ourselves and all our thinking? . . . Consciousness in itself has a being of its own which in its absolute uniqueness of nature remains unaffected by the phenomenologic disconnexion.[10]

By "consciousness" Husserl means that which involves both an act of intending and the intended object of this act. For example, what you see in the palm of your hand is a white die, on one of whose faces is a black dot. From the natural standpoint we hardly ever doubt this fact. But, says Husserl, we *can* doubt it. Yet it is not possible to doubt the *experience* of having seen and felt the die in the palm of your hand. Moreover, within this experience of a die in the palm of your hand, it is possible to distinguish the die (the intentional object) from your act of intending it. When you bracket, what you experience is both (1) your experiencing (that is, intending) of the die in the palm of your hand and (2) the die, as experienced (that is, intended) by you.

Further thought about the way in which objects are present to consciousness persuaded Husserl to devote more emphasis to acts of intending than to the objects themselves. Bracketing revealed to him deeper and deeper levels of ego activity that are impossible to understand without profound phenomenological training. It is enough here to repeat that, when all is bracketed, including ourselves, Husserl contends that consciousness remains. When we bracket our whole world, we tap our uniqueness, our essence, and realize that something precedes our experiences, namely being. "It therefore remains as a region of Being which is in principle unique and can become in fact the field of a new science—the science of phenomenology."[11]

For Husserl, phenomenology is a new science of being. It reveals a sphere of being that is ultimate, in the sense that it presents itself with certainty within our experience. Studying being is not, for Husserl, investigating another reality. It is delving deeper and deeper into the only reality—consciousness.

Another phenomenologist, Martin Heidegger (1889–), made this question of being his primary concern. The problem with traditional thinking, claimed Heidegger, is that it is confused over the question of Being. (Heidegger capitalized the word.) Being is not a thing; it is the very existing of the thing. Max tells Ruth that she is more interested in what he is than in *that* he is. Heidegger would make the same distinc-

---

[10]Edmund Husserl. *Ideas: General Introduction to Pure Phenomenology*. W. B. Boyce Gibson, trans. New York: Macmillan, 1931, Section 33.

[11]Quoted in Edo Pivcevic. *Husserl and Phenomenology*, p. 11.

tion. When we talk of being itself, we are talking about the very act of existing. Being does not consist of all the *things* a person is, all the characteristics the individual bears; for that is to speak of the individual ‑*as a being.* On the other hand, to speak of the individual's Being is to acknowledge that when all qualities and properties not necessary to being as being are stripped away, Being remains as *this* being, as individual. Where Sartre focuses on existence, Heidegger probes deeper, to the roots of existence itself: to Being.

But Being is a difficult concept to communicate, because it is not a thing. True, we may identify it with things. But this identification makes it all the more elusive, for we end up identifying the thing with Being. This is what Max says Ruth is doing. Equating him with a thing, a human thing. You may have heard someone say "Love me for what I am." Max is saying "Don't love me for what I am; love my *am!* Love my being, not what you may see as an expression of it: matter, mind, soul." If we are to understand reality, says Heidegger, we must abandon our mad commitment to the world of things. By becoming conscious of our own Being, we may better understand the Being that underlies everything. Then, in turn, we may establish a meaningful relationship with another person.

This emphasis on reality as being underlies the view of the human as an existential being. But it is also curious to note its connection with Buddhist thought, even though, as we have previously seen, Buddhism seems to share some outlooks with the view of the human as mechanical, especially in its denial of self and of personal freedom.

Although Heidegger is undoubtedly a Western thinker, there is enough Oriental flavor in his thought to lead Heidegger himself to remark, upon reading the work of Zen scholar D. T. Suzuki, "If I understand this man correctly, this is what I have been trying to say in all my writings."[12] The fact is that the Oriental thinker is generally more concerned, not with an objective, empirically verifiable reality, but with the inner nature of the "self." The world of the senses is short-lived and illusory. As a result, Eastern thought is preoccupied not with what is real but with *being* real. It distinguishes between the idea of ourselves and the immediate concrete feeling of ourselves. As Zen scholar Alan Watts puts it:

Zen points out that our precious "self" is just an idea. . . . When we are no longer identified with the idea of ourselves, the entire relationship between subject and object, knower and known undergoes a sudden and revolutionary change. It becomes a real relationship, a mutuality in which the subject creates the object just as much as the object creates the subject. The knower no longer

---

[12]D. T. Suzuki. *Zen Buddhism.* William Barrett, Ed. Garden City, N.Y.: Doubleday Anchor Books, 1956, pp. xi–xii.

feels himself to be independent of the known; the experiencer no longer feels himself to stand apart from the experience.[13]

If we are looking for a concrete reality, then, we shall find it *between* the individual and the world, "as the concrete coin is 'between' the abstract, Euclidean surfaces of its two sides."[14]

Obviously, Eastern thought eschews the bipolarities of knower and known, experiencer and experience, subject and object. These are artificial, and they preclude true knowledge of self and being. Heidegger, too, seems to consider this Western penchant for dividing a great error that began with Plato, who located truth in the intellect. Against the intellect Plato set nature—a realm of objects to be studied, manipulated, and quantified. Today we find ourselves inheritors of this tradition, technological "masters" of the planet. Along with this dubious distinction, we have suffered, as Heidegger and Eastern thinkers have also observed, an estrangement from being and from ourselves, which the will to power and dominance only intensifies.

Nevertheless, critics say that those espousing the position that reality is being or that it is consciousness worsen the very problem that they are trying to ease.

Reflection   Think of a person you care for very much. Precisely what qualities about the person do you care so much for? If the person lacked these qualities, could you care in the same way? Suppose you were the person in question. How would you react to your reply?

Objections to Existentialism and Phenomenology

Critics of both existentialism and phenomenology often argue that both of these movements have gone too far, that they really have lost the individual in a sea of being and consciousness. For example, Max insists that Ruth shouldn't love him for anything he may be, not even for being human. But after taking away all the things that make Max Max, what is left? His being. But after all Max's shape and form and definition have been removed, his being seems no different from anyone else's. What is left resembles a glob of wax that a flame has melted of all features. If everything is ultimately being or consciousness, then seemingly everything is nothing in particular.

[13]Alan Watts. *The Way of Zen*. New York: Pantheon Books, 1957, pp. 120–121.
[14]Watts. *The Way of Zen*, p. 122.

Arguing thus, opponents claim that these movements, in generally discarding objectivity and minimizing scientific knowledge, bog us down even further by fostering uncertainty and despair. The very problems that they have attempted to ease, say the critics, they actually have a tendency to create. True, we must be occupied with experience, but the sources of experience are worth investigating. Although neither school of thought actually takes this position, critics of existentialism and phenomenology detect a tendency to treat truth as if it were purely subjective. Accordingly, the insinuation is frequently made that no absolutes exist, that there is no right way to conduct our lives, that reason is a minimal avenue to knowledge. Even these suggestions, opponents argue, must leave us despairing of ever achieving interpersonal and world harmony, for no standards remain that we can apply to resolve disputes, other than will and might.

In addition, critics wonder if the statement "I exist" gives a complete picture of existence. Who, they ask, is this *I*? This self-conscious ego? If we are only conscious egos, we seem cut off from the world, from other *I*'s. But surely an objective *me* exists as well as the subjective *I*, for I am often a "thing," an object.

Despite these differences, existentialists, phenomenologists, and the critics of both are agreed at least on this point: statements about ultimate reality and being are meaningful. In fact, this element is shared by all the views we have discussed so far. Whether reality is matter, idea, a combination, being, or consciousness, all of these views agree that we can sensibly talk about metaphysical issues. Yet there is one school of twentieth-century philosophy that does not concede even this belief. Central to the movement known as linguistic analysis is the contention that statements about ultimate reality are nonsensical.

REALITY AS A MEANINGLESS QUESTION: LINGUISTIC ANALYSIS

Linguistic analysts believe that philosophical problems such as the ones we have been discussing are in large part language concerns. To deal with such problems, they say, it is first necessary to clarify the language being used. As Bertrand Russell puts it:

The most important part [of philosophy] . . . consists in criticizing and clarifying notions which are apt to be regarded as fundamental and accepted uncritically. As instances I might mention: mind, matter, consciousness, knowledge, experience, causality, will, time. I believe all these notions to be inexact and approximate, essentially infected with vagueness, incapable of forming part of any exact science.[15]

---

[15]Bertrand Russell. "Logical Atomism." In J. H. Muirhead (Ed.), *Contemporary British Philosophy*. New York: Macmillan, 1924, p. 380.

*". . . statements about ultimate reality
are nonsensical."*

Once we implement such analysis as Russell advocates, say analysts, we shall find that many problems actually dissolve. Philosophy, then, is a method—an activity—concerned with minimizing, if not eliminating, verbal confusion.

The analysts themselves disagree about precisely how to approach the job of dissolving problems. Some concentrate on the language and methods of sciences; others focus on ordinary language usage. The former are variously called logical positivists, logical empiricists, or scientific empiricists; the others are known as ordinary-language philosophers. Thus, **linguistic analysis** embraces a varied host of thinkers—Ludwig Wittgenstein, Alfred J. Ayer, Rudolf Carnap, John Wisom, Gilbert Ryle—all of whom agree on at least one point: that the clarification of symbols, especially linguistic symbols, is of primary importance.

Ruth's professor friend is a linguistic analyst, although Ruth does not know it until she confronts him with her frustration. Then she learns why he thinks that the debates she has had with Brad and Max are really futile. Ruth and the professor agree on this point, but for different reasons.

Ruth:	Max and I just had a fight. And do you know what it was over?
Professor:	What?
Ruth:	That stupid thing you said about our being your creations.
Professor:	Uh-oh. I'm sorry.

Ruth:	A lot of good that'll do.
Professor:	So you don't think it's possible to produce a mechanical mate, is that it?
Ruth:	That's not what we were arguing over. It was a lot heavier than that. It was about what's really real and things like that.
Professor:	Really real?
Ruth:	You know, whether everything is just matter or not matter. Or maybe being, as Max says.
Professor:	You really did get into it, didn't you?
Ruth:	And it's all because of you!
Professor:	Well, if it's any comfort, I agree with you that debating what is really real is a futile exercise.
Ruth:	You mean you think it's dumb, too?
Professor:	Yes, I do.
Ruth:	Well, I never expected to hear that from you.
Professor:	Why? Because you expect professors to serve as instigators and referees of intellectual games?
Ruth:	Something like that, I guess.
Professor:	Well, let me assure you I've thought considerably about those questions, Ruth. And do you know what I've decided?
Ruth:	What?
Professor:	That they defy verification.
Ruth:	What do you mean?
Professor:	Well, let me show you. Take the question that you were so hotly debating: what is reality? Now each of you had a different notion, I presume.
Ruth:	That's right. Personally, I think reality is nonmaterial, some kind of spirit or mind.
Professor:	Fine. Let's examine your belief: "Reality is nonmatter." Now, presumably, if you were arguing about this statement, you thought it was either true or false.
Ruth:	I think it's true, but Brad and Max don't.
Professor:	Let me ask you something, Ruth. How do you know when a statement, any statement, is true?
Ruth:	Well, you can tell some statements are true just by looking at them.
Professor:	Such as?
Ruth:	"My brother Brad is a male."
Professor:	How do you know that's true?

Ruth:	It's self-evident. If you're talking about a brother, you must be talking about a male.
Professor:	I see what you mean. Certainly, the truth of that statement is contained within the meaning of the words themselves. If you denied such a statement, the result would be an absurd self-contradiction: "My brother Brad is not a male."
Ruth:	That's silly.
Professor:	Right. But what about a statement like "The sun is between 90 and 95 million miles from the earth"? Is that statement self-evident?
Ruth:	No. You'd have to prove that.
Professor:	I agree. Somehow you'd have to measure the distance and determine if, in fact, the sun was between 90 and 95 million miles from earth.
Ruth:	Of course.
Professor:	What if you couldn't measure it? If you couldn't determine the precise distance? Would you call the statement false?
Ruth:	No; you just wouldn't know for sure, that's all. It could still be true. You'd just have to wait and see.
Professor:	So you'd say the statement is still either true or false.
Ruth:	Sure.
Professor:	What about a statement like "Unicorns like to eat fresh eggs"? Is that true or false?
Ruth:	That's just silly.
Professor:	But is it true or false?
Ruth:	It's neither.
Professor:	Neither?
Ruth:	Because unicorns don't exist.
Professor:	What difference does that make?
Ruth:	Well, if unicorns don't exist, how can you say anything about them that makes sense? How would you ever go about proving it? It's just ridiculous. Say whatever you want about unicorns; it doesn't make any difference, because you can't ever really find out.
Professor:	All right, then, what about this statement: "There's a Coke machine on the southern polar cap of Mars"? Is that true or false?
Ruth:	It's either one or the other.
Professor:	How come?
Ruth:	Because you can prove that. You can at least imagine what you'd have to do to prove it.
Professor:	So that's not like the unicorn statement?

Ruth:	No way. Coke machines, southern polar caps, Mars, all those things exist. So you know what you'd have to do to prove whether there really is a Coke machine up there. Go and see.
Professor:	You seem to be saying that, except for self-evident statements, a statement is true or false only if it lends itself to being proved. And that it lends itself to being proved only if the things that make it up really exist.
Ruth:	Yes, I guess I am.
Professor:	All right, then, let's see where that leaves us. What about your statement "Reality is nonmatter"? Is that statement self-evident?
Ruth:	If it were, Max and I wouldn't have fought.
Professor:	I agree. You could certainly deny that statement and still have something that makes sense.
Ruth:	Sure. Brad said reality was matter.
Professor:	It seems that leaves us with having to prove the statement true.
Ruth:	I suppose it does.
Professor:	Well, how do you propose to do that?

For the linguistic analyst, there are basically two kinds of meaningful statements: analytic propositions and synthetic propositions. Defining a **proposition** as a statement that is true or false, the analyst sees *analytic* propositions as true or false by definition, by their appearance alone. In an analytic statement, the predicate—the part that follows the verb *to be*—always repeats the subject in whole or in part. Thus, "The *red* bird is *red*." Sometimes the predicate is not the same term as the subject but carries part of the subject's meaning, as in "His *sister* is a *female*." *Female* is included in the meaning of *sister*. The professor calls such statements "self-evident"; that is, their negation always results in a self-contradiction. Thus, "The red bird is not red" or "His sister is not a female."

A nonanalytic proposition is said to be *synthetic*. Synthetic propositions are those that can, at least in theory, be proved true or false. This is possible only if their terms refer to actually existing objects or events. Apply scientific methods, say the analysts, to determine if the relationship between these objects or events is fact. "It's raining," "California is about 3000 miles from New York," and "A spirochete causes syphilis" are synthetic statements.

If a statement is neither analytic nor synthetic, say the analysts, it is epistemologically meaningless; it is nonsensical. Metaphysical statements appear to be neither analytic nor synthetic. Alfred J. Ayer puts it this way:

We may accordingly define a metaphysical sentence as a sentence which purports to express a genuine proposition but does, in fact, express neither a tautology (analytic statement) . . . nor an empirical hypothesis (synthetic statement). And as tautologies and empirical hypotheses form the entire class of significant propositions, we are justified in concuding that all metaphysical assertions are nonsensical.[16]

The analyst would view not only metaphysical statements as meaningless, but most ethical, esthetic, and theological ones as well, because most of them are neither analytic nor synthetic. Thus they would consider the following statements nonsensical: "God exists," "God doesn't exist," "Lying is wrong," "Lying is right," "A moral law operates in the universe," "The best form of government is the one that governs least." The fact that very few people can consider such statements meaningless has led to a major objection to the analytical school.

Reflection   Envision your home town 50 years from now, showing the influence of a heavy philosophically analytic bias. What changes do you observe to have taken place?

Objections to Linguistic Analysis

Ruth:	But you're saying that if something can't be verified it's not worth talking about.
Professor:	Can't be verified at least *in principle*.
Ruth:	As the Coke machine can, at least in principle?
Professor:	Exactly.
Ruth:	But that would make silly many of the very things that people have always taken seriously.
Professor:	Like what?
Ruth:	Like "Democracy is the best form of government," for example. Or "Honesty is the best policy" or "It's better to give than to receive."
Professor:	As well as "Man is the noblest work of God," "Admission of ignorance is the beginning of wisdom," "The unexamined life is not worth living," and all the rest. Yes, I couldn't agree more; they're meaningless statements in the sense that they're neither true nor false.
Ruth:	But people still make those statements.

---

[16]Alfred J. Ayer. *Language, Truth and Logic* (2nd ed.). New York: Dover, 1936, p. 41.

Professor:	Of course they do.
Ruth:	Then how can you deny their validity?
Professor:	Because there's no way they can be verified empirically, and they're certainly not linguistically self-evident.
Ruth:	But are those the only ways of measuring truth and knowledge?
Professor:	The only ones we have now.
Ruth:	But that doesn't mean they're necessarily the only ones.
Professor:	No, not necessarily.
Ruth:	Then isn't your belief based on an assumption? And isn't the assumption something that itself defies the empirical method? How would you ever verify the statement "True statements must be either linguistically self-evident or empirically verifiable"?

Ruth has not only questioned the analysts' definition of a meaningful utterance, she has also accused the professor of assuming the very thing he must prove: that with respect to knowledge and truth, only analytic and synthetic statements are meaningful. Critics claim that analysts are more deductive than they themselves think, that they are arguing this way:

All knowledge is either analytic or synthetic.

Religious, ethical, and esthetic statements are neither analytic nor synthetic.

Therefore, religious, ethical, and esthetic statements are not knowledge.

But, say critics, the first statement is an assumption; it can never be proved. Perhaps utterances other than analytic and synthetic ones may transmit knowledge and truth. In effect, they charge the analysts with assuming that the opening statement above is analytic.

Professor:	You're saying that my assumption is as meaningless as your statement that reality is nonmatter?
Ruth:	That's right, because there's no way you can prove your assumption.
Professor:	But it's necessary to start somewhere.
Ruth:	Why? Can you prove it's necessary to start somewhere? How would you verify that claim? It seems to me, professor, that you're a victim of your own classification.
Professor:	You mean that by reducing knowledge to what's linguistically self-evident or empirically verifiable, I haven't allowed for other possibilities?

Ruth:	Not only that. You've defined other possibilities right out of existence. . . . But you have convinced me of one thing.
Professor:	What's that?
Ruth:	That arguing about what's real isn't so silly after all. It's not so silly as pretending the problem doesn't even exist. True, believing the way you do, you have a lot less frustration. By simply eliminating the problems, you don't have to deal with them. But isn't that really playing ostrich? Aren't the problems still there? Don't people still think about them? Even *you* devise an answer to them. If the questions don't exist, then what are your answers answering? And in answering them, haven't you yourself taken a position on a question that you say can only lead to meaningless answers?

Ruth's criticism implies what is for many one of the most disappointing aspects of analysis: its attempt to reduce the idea of a person to sense data or to behavior. It seems that analysis oversimplifies and distorts human experience by disregarding whatever lies beyond the language of science, mathematics, or formal logic. Many contemporary analysts themselves are noticing this inadequacy, recognizing as legitimate not just one or two but many modes of meaning. Ultimately they may agree with their critics, who defend the philosopher's right and need to discuss questions not only of language, but of metaphysics, morality, religion, politics, and education as well. Certainly, any description of human nature and of self that ignores these aspects of human experience seems incomplete.

CONCLUSIONS

Despite the diversity of the metaphysical views we have examined, they really agree more often than they disagree. These points of agreement suggest insights into the self.

First, all views generally agree that something exists outside the individual self. Even the subjective idealism of Berkeley does not deny the physical world, only its independence from mind. And despite Sartre's stress on self and Husserl's emphasis on consciousness, they do recognize the distinction between things that lack consciousness— chairs, trees, books—and those that do not—humans. So there is agreement that "something is out there." Although the self may be insular, in that it is bound by the sea of its experiences, there are other human "islands," all joined by the similarity of their conditions and circumstances.

Second, all—whether materialist, idealist, pragmatist, existentialist, phenomenologist, or analyst—accept the senses and reason as primary sources of knowledge, as the tools by which the self comes to know things. True, some philosophers, such as the idealists, give reason a primacy that others do not; some, such as the pragmatists, emphasize more heavily the importance of experience. But these are differences of degree, not of substance. All agree that using both reason and senses we stand our best chance of knowing ourselves and our world.

Finally, all outlooks agree that there is an order or meaning in things that the senses and reason can discover. True, materialism may believe that the order is strictly mechanistic; idealism that it is spiritual, maybe even supernatural; pragmatism that it comes from personal experience; existentialism and phenomenology that it is being, or the purpose that each of us imposes on experience; and analysis that it is the symbolic form in which we express things. So even though all disagree on its nature, they seem to agree that there is some order. Most important, each of us is part of that order, whatever it is. To know the self is at least partially to know that order and how we fit into it.

At the same time, there are differences among these metaphysical outlooks that reflect and reinforce different views of human nature and of self. For the materialist, we are part of the matter that composes the universe and are subject to the same laws. As a result, the self is the product of its experiences, the sum total of everything that has ever happened to it. There is little point in speaking of individual responsibility or personal will, for we cannot help doing what we do. When we speak of "mind," we really mean "brain"; when we refer to mental states, we are really talking about brain states. The purpose of any life is to understand how the parts of the universe, including the self, fit together and work. With such knowledge we can control our environment to some degree and perhaps improve the human condition.

The linguistic analyst would generally agree and would add that the individual who tries to find personal meaning in religion, art, or politics or in seeking what is morally good wastes time on basically meaningless pursuits. We stand our best chance of understanding ourselves and the world by clarifying the linguistic symbols we use to speak about these things.

For the idealist, in contrast, the individual is part of cosmic mind, spirit, idea, or perhaps life force. In this sense, individuals are alike. But each finds a self-identity in personal understanding. Only the individual can be aware of his or her own experiences. In the last analysis, it is this personal awareness, these ideas, that make each of us unique. The purpose of each life is to understand the order at work in the universe. This order is not matter but pure idea; for some it is a divine dimension, God. In understanding this cosmic order or plan, we understand our position in it and, thus, the self.

The pragmatist views the self as neither primarily matter nor primarily idea. Since pragmatists avoid speaking of anything in absolutes, they choose to see the self as consisting of many dimensions, including materal and ideal. The self is a complex entity consisting of experiences, which include thoughts, feelings, sensations, concepts, attitudes, and goals. Although we are tremendously influenced by environment, we can and do play a formative role in determining the nature of the experiences we have. Using intelligence and reason, the individual can exercise control over nature. But we shall not find personal meaning and purpose in the cosmos, for the cosmos possesses none. For personal meaning we must turn to the consequences of our actions, judging them favorable or not according to the results they produce.

Existentialism shares pragmatism's skepticism of absolutistic doctrines. But more than any of the other outlooks it stresses the primacy of personal freedom. The self is essentially something in the making, something that is not "finished" until the individual dies. The self is whatever we choose to make it. We are ultimately free to think, choose, and act however we wish. Such freedom without guidelines is frightening, often leading to uncertainty, anxiety, and despair. But this, say the existentialists, is the human condition, and therefore the condition of each individual. For many phenomenologists, what we are is *that* we are. The fundamental self is not its characteristics, properties, or the other objective qualities that we observe, but being. The self is not our idea of what we are but the immediate concrete feeling of ourselves. We move furthest away from a knowledge of the self when we separate ourselves from the rest of reality, as we do when we view it as some object to be studied, quantified, and known. We are closest to the self when we strip from consciousness the specific experiences that occupy it. Then we realize that the self is what precedes its experiences — that is, pure being. Buddhist thinking generally agrees.

So, although these metaphysical outlooks do share much in common, in their emphases they tilt the issue of self one way or another. It is just such a tilt that may leave us affirming or denying the self, viewing it as essentially rational, divine, mechanical, existential, or nonexistent.

SUMMARY

We opened this chapter by noting that what we consider ultimately real reflects and influences how we see ourselves. We then discussed a number of metaphysical views, including materialism, idealism, pragmatism, existentialism, phenomenology, and linguistic analysis. We concluded that all positions seem to agree that something exists outside the individual, that they all accept the senses and reason as primary sources of knowledge, and that they perceive some order or purpose that individuals can discover. They disagree on their interpretations of these points. Out of their disagreement, different views of human nature and of self emerge.

MAIN POINTS

1. Metaphysics is a branch of philosophy that studies the nature of reality.
2. Ontology, a subdivision of metaphysics, is the study of the nature of being and existence.
3. Materialism is the position that reality is ultimately matter.
4. Idealism is the position that reality is ultimately nonmatter: idea, mind, spirit, or law, for example.
5. Pragmatism tries to mediate between idealism and materialism by rejecting all absolutistic assumptions. But it does seem committed to materialism's scientific method and empirical inquiry, although it admits the pluralistic nature of reality.
6. The concept of being plays an important part in existentialism and phenomenology. Both of these philosophies are founded on disillusionment with past philosophies and on a preoccupation with the individual.
7. Existentialism stresses individual freedom, the absence of an essential human nature, and the lack of behavioral guidelines.
8. Husserlian phenomenology emphasizes consciousness as the ultimate reality. Heidegger's phenomenology stresses being. What is ultimately real for the phenomenologist is pure consciousness, which itself has being.
9. Like phenomenology, Buddhism eschews the distinction between knower and known, between subject and object. We are one with our experiences. But Buddhism considers the question of personal freedom irrelevant.
10. Linguistic analysts believe that the question of ultimate reality is meaningless because no statement relating to it can be proved. There are only two kinds of epistemologically meaningful statements: analytic and synthetic.

SECTION EXERCISES

Materialism

1. Does being born the way humans are distinguish us from other forms of life? Would you agree that normal childbirth, including premature birth and Caesarean section, is a defining characteristic of being a person?
2. In his split-brain experiments, R. W. Sperry showed that either half of the brain can function efficiently independent of the other

half. If your brain were so severed, would there be two of you? What if you substituted a strange one-half brain in place of one-half of your own? Would you be two people?

3. Look up the meaning of *materialism* as it is ordinarily used. Do you detect any connection between its ordinary and its philosophical meanings?

Materialism Today

1. At one point, Ruth claims that the *persistence* of a belief in the soul removes this belief from the realm of superstition or ignorance. Do you agree? Can you think of any other beliefs that have so persisted? What about beliefs that lasted an extremely long time but are no longer widely held?

2. To explain things, would you introduce sciences in addition to the physical sciences that Brad advances? Which ones?

3. Do you think Ruth's example of the self-witnessing brain proves that states of consciousness are different from brain states?

4. Our discussion so far has focused almost exclusively on the problem of self. How is this question relevant to the question of what is real?

5. The seventeenth-century English poet Alexander Pope, exuding the enthusiasm of his age for scientific discovery, wrote an "Epitaph Intended for Sir Isaac Newton, in Westminster Abbey":

   > Nature and Nature's laws lay hid in night;
   > God said, *"Let* Newton *be!"* and all was Light.

   What view of human nature does Pope suggest? Do you think Heisenberg's Indeterminacy Principle advances, sets back, or has no effect on the belief that all can be explained in terms of discoverable cosmic laws?

6. Does research into the causes of human thought, consciousness, and behavior indicate a growing simplicity or a growing complexity of understanding?

7. Do you see the workings of the universe as orderly? Why or why not? (You might first define "orderliness" in terms of predictability.)

Idealism

1. Some argue for a principle that is at work in the universe. Perhaps such a universal law is at the bottom of everything, gives everything design and purpose, and provides our experiences with order. Do you see such a principle or law?

2. Can there be a principle or law at work without a purpose or goal? If there cannot, must the idealist account for the purpose of things?

3. In what sense is it true that the relationships among things are the only meaningful reality? Can you think of anything that you can understand without reference to something else?

4. It has often been said that idealism encourages a withdrawal from the world, a retreat from secular problems, and an immersion in otherworldly concerns. As a result, the idealist neglects real and pressing social concerns. Explain why you think this charge is justified or not justified.

5. Read Alexander Pope's "Essay on Man." What is his metaphysical position? What would be Candide's reaction to it?

Pragmatism

1. What are the assumptions of materialism and idealism that pragmatism looks away from?

2. In what respects does pragmatism incorporate materialism and idealism?

3. If you were a pragmatist, how would you reconcile your belief that you can know only your experiences with your belief that an objective reality exists?

4. Compare and contrast the everyday and philosophical meanings of *pragmatist.*

Existentialism and Phenomenology

1. What precisely does Max mean when he says "It's clear that for you *what* I am is more important than *that* I am"?

2. What is the difference between "being" and "being human"?

3. In what sense are you both "being" and "a being"?

4. Show how a failure to distinguish between "being as a thing" and "the being of a thing" leads to "thingifying" everything, including people.

5. Do existentialism, phenomenology, and pragmatism share any beliefs?

6. In what sense would you call Kierkegaard a rationalist?

7. Sartre claims that Kierkegaard's "leap of faith" to God is cowardly and not in the true existential spirit. Why would he say this? Do you agree?

8. What does Sartre mean when he says "existence precedes essence"?

9. How would you describe what Heidegger calls your "being"?

10. Would Ruth's supposed objections to Max's "being" argument bring her closer to materialism than she might think? Why?

11. If Ruth objected "If everything is being, then everything is nothing," what would she mean?

12. Is it possible to maintain a concept of individual difference if everything has "being" in common?

13. Sartre claims that in making a choice for self we are really making a choice for other. Is this statement consistent with a denial of any kind of universal human nature? If it is, what do you think led Sartre to such a claim?

Linguistic Analysis

1. In what sense do the analysts apply the adjective "meaningless" to nonsensical statements? Can something be intellectually meaningless but emotionally meaningful? Can you give an example?

2. What is your reaction to analyst Alfred J. Ayer's evaluation, below?

> It is impossible to find a criterion for determining the validity of ethical judgment . . . because they [ethical judgments] have no objective validity whatsoever. If a sentence makes no statement at all, there is obviously no sense in asking whether what it says is true or false. . . . They are pure expressions of feeling . . . unverifiable for the same reason as a cry of pain or a word of command is unverifiable—because they do not express genuine propositions.[17]

3. Which of the following statements would an analyst say are meaningful? Which meaningless?
    a. She wore a blue dress.
    b. Her blue dress was green.
    c. At the bottom of the ocean there's a shiny new penny lying in the belly of a dead carp.
    d. The zite dwart oilated twarily near an ach grul.
    e. The action in the preceding sentence takes place near an ach grul.
    f. Tooth fairies never appear to bad children.
    g. The good go to heaven, the bad to hell.
    h. Killing orphans without reason is an evil thing to do.
    i. Oxygen is necessary for combustion.
    j. Love makes the world go 'round.

4. How valid do you consider Ruth's criticism that the professor's definition of what is meaningful makes a sham of the things we take seriously?

5. Why is the professor's defense that "it's necessary to start somewhere" less convincing coming from an analyst than it would be coming from an idealist?

---

[17]Alfred J. Ayer. *Language, Truth and Logic* (2nd ed.). New York: Dover, 1946, pp. 107–109.

6. Ruth charges that the professor's position is inconsistent and self-contradictory. Why does she say this? Do you agree?
7. What would you say is linguistic analysis's primary contribution to philosophy?

ADDITIONAL EXERCISES

1. In what way does what you consider to be ultimately real affect what you think you can know and who you are?
2. Take an inventory of how you spend your leisure time. Presumably, you do what you do because it is a value to you. Do these pastimes tell you anything about how you view reality?
3. What is the most important factor to you in a relationship with a member of the opposite sex? Does your answer tell you anything about how you see reality? How you see self?
4. The assumptions of the eighteenth-century Enlightenment can be summarized as (1) a belief in a cosmic law or order, (2) a belief in the human's ability to discover this law or order, and (3) a belief in the human's ability to apply this discovery to his or her own life. Does the twentieth-century experience confirm or deny these assumptions?
5. Do events such as earthquakes, storms, and other so-called acts of God indicate a disorderliness in nature?
6. Is there a difference between "explanation" and "purpose"? What is important about making such a distinction? For instance, suppose someone objects: "If things always happen for the best, then how come that plane crashed and killed all those people?"
7. Point to one example from your own experience of the random, chance quality of life and living.
8. Is it contradictory, as Voltaire suggests, that in a universe governed by law and order and purpose there should be such evident absurdity?

PAPERBACKS FOR FURTHER READING

Coover, Robert. *The Universal Baseball Association, Inc., J. Henry Waugh, Prop.* New York: The New American Library, 1968. In this highly metaphysical novel, the main character, with the help of a deck of playing cards, creates a world of baseball players who ultimately dismiss their creator.

Du Nouy, Lecomte. *Human Destiny.* New York: The New American Library, 1949. A biologist argues against chance, accident, and physiochemical-biological mechanisms as complete explanations of reality. He argues that there is purpose in the universe, and that knowledge derived from intuition and religious faith is necessary to understand that purpose and, hence, reality itself.

Hesse, Hermann. *Siddhartha.* Hilda Rosner, trans. New York: New Directions, 1951. This is Hesse's beautiful story of the Buddha. Oriental mysticism, self-knowledge, and the unity that is change all figure prominently in this deceptively simple metaphysical tale.

Husserl, Edmund. *Phenomenology and the Crisis of Philosophy.* Quentin Lauer, trans. New York: Harper & Row, 1965. These two essays by the "father of phenomenology" present the framework, especially the method, of Husserlian phenomenology.

Krutch, Joseph Wood. *The Measure of Man: On Freedom, Human Values, Survival and the Modern Temper.* New York: Grosset & Dunlap, 1953. Krutch argues that the materialistic view of reality and humankind is fraudulent.

Pears, David. *Ludwig Wittgenstein.* New York: Viking Press, 1970. This is an introduction to the thought of perhaps the foremost linguistic analyst, Ludwig Wittgenstein.

Warnock, Mary. *Existentialism.* Oxford: Oxford University Press, 1970. One of the foremost writers on the subject, Warnock presents a succinct and trenchant analysis of the main concepts of existentialism.

Philosophy and Science

7

The highest wisdom has but one science, the science of the whole, the science explaining the creation and man's place in it. —Leo Tolstoy

In our own times, no field has had greater influence on how we view the world and ourselves than has science. What we know, believe, consider real, hold as religious values, and even view as morally right or wrong show the influence of science and its method. Unfortunately, it is often little-understood and ill-digested science that molds our outlook, frequently raising anxiety as well as hope. We seem to vacillate between indicting science for all our ills and praising it for all our benefits. But no one denies its influence on our lives. Therefore, no investigation of self would be complete without an examination of science.

At the outset, let us distinguish between basic and applied science. We frequently forget that all scientific knowledge takes root in basic science—that is, in hypothesis and theory. In other words, it begins as an explanation for something. That explanation is tested and perhaps verified. When it is finally put to use it becomes applied science. It is applied science whose effects we observe every day in various aspects of our lives: agriculture, manufacturing, communications, health.

Nevertheless, basic or pure science can be just as directly influential. The terms "basic" and "pure" refer to a quantitative and objective knowledge of nature. Basic or pure science is not primarily concerned with the practical applications of science, although what it investigates, discovers, and formulates almost always is applied. Its fundamental concern is to describe nature, and what we refer to as "nature's laws," as accurately and completely as it can. This description often takes the form of a *theory*—that is, an explanation for certain constant functions in nature containing a term that does not denote anything that can be directly observed. Thus, the proposition that protons and neutrons

181

exist is a theory, since these entities cannot be observed, although their presumed effects can be. Such theories frequently alter our self-concept by forcing us to consider new possibilities about ourselves.

For example, the Copernican theory of a sun-centered solar system not only revolutionized astronomy but ultimately challenged the assumption that humans were the center of creation. Likewise, the atomic theory describes not only the inanimate world but humans as well, for we are as much a molecular composition as is a pencil or a leaf. Since its formulation, people have wondered more seriously than ever before whether humans can ultimately be explained strictly in scientific terms. Similarly, Einstein's theory of relativity suggests as much about humans as it says about very swiftly moving objects. In establishing that time is not absolute, it implies that nothing is absolute—perhaps not even the moral prescriptions on which we base our conduct. Thus, a theoretical description of nature frequently affects how we view ourselves.

The point is that it is childishly simple to observe how applied science, in the form of the automobile, television, and the dialysis machine, influences our lives and self-concepts. It is a little harder, however, to see the influence of our knowledge of nature, which includes theories of matter, the universe and its origin, and time. In this chapter we shall try to examine this influence. We shall also see by what methods science arrives at its knowledge, the limitations of these methods, and whether scientific knowledge is certain. As we proceed, we shall be noting three important facts about the relationship between philosophy and science: (1) philosophy and science share much, although not all, of the same methodology; (2) philosophy generally reflects the science of its day; and (3) philosophy is in a unique position to integrate scientific findings and, consequently, various aspects of what we think we are.

SCIENTIFIC METHOD

Broadly speaking, we may define the scientific method as a way of investigation based on (1) collecting, (2) analyzing, and (3) interpreting evidence to determine the most probable explanation it suggests. To illustrate, suppose you wanted to find out why your car has failed to start one morning. First, you would investigate the problem by collecting evidence. In this case, you would probably check anything that could be part of the cause: distributor cap, spark plugs, points, battery cable, battery. Obviously, you would not check the tires, because their condition is not relevant to the fact that your car will not start. Having collected relevant sense information, you would then analyze and interpret it. These steps are the more complex parts of the procedure, often including such facets of the inductive method as reasoning by analogy, examining cause, and formulating hypotheses. Let us consider each of these aspects of scientific method.

ANALOGY

You might begin the analysis of your problem by reasoning that the last time your car did not start it was also a cold morning, like the present one. On that occasion, the battery was dead. Maybe that's what's wrong now. Notice how you reasoned: by recalling an instance similar to the present one, you formulated a conclusion about the present one. You reasoned by **analogy.**

Analogical reasoning is a common technique in analysis. It is based on the assumption that a group of events will show the same relationship in the future that they did in the past. You reason analogically when you conclude that because two or more entities share one aspect, they share another as well. Thus, in the past on a cold morning when your car would not start, the battery was dead. Another cold morning, another failure to start: another dead battery. But, of course, just because the battery was the problem the first time does not mean it must be the problem now. Remember that, as part of the inductive process, analogy never *proves* anything; it suggests **probability.** Yet there are ways to ensure the strength of any analogical conclusion.

Let us say that, not just last winter, but each of the past five winters, your car has failed to start, and that each time the battery was dead. This fact would strengthen your conclusion, for the more instances you can point to that are similar to the present one, the more probable your analogical conclusion.

Suppose further that each time your car would not start you had not driven it for about a week, you had not kept it in the garage, and you had not charged up the battery before winter set in. If the same holds true now, again your conclusion will be strengthened. The more similarities the instances share, the greater the probability of the additional similarity, in this case the dead battery.

Consider further the fact that you are not the only one who has ever had trouble with a car on a cold morning, and that frequently in such cases the problem is a dead battery. Here we are introducing *dissimilar* factors: other people, cars, and circumstances. Yet this fact strengthens your conclusion. Dissimilarities, or differences that strengthen an analogical conclusion, shouldn't be confused with disanalogies, differences that weaken them.

Suppose the previous times your car did not start you had left the lights on for many hours before. But this time you did not. The probability that you have a dead battery this time would be lessened by that fact because of a **disanalogy.** A disanalogy is a difference between the things compared that lessens the likelihood of an analogical conclusion. It does not preclude the conclusion; it lessens its likelihood.

What if the day the car wouldn't start the time before was a Thursday and this day is a Monday? This is neither a dissimilarity nor a disanalogy. It is simply irrelevant.

We can conclude, then, that an analogical conclusion is strengthened by the number of instances and their relevant similarities and dissimilarities, but weakened by their disanalogies.

Since reasoning is the spine of philosophizing, the analogy is a vital tool for the philosopher. Take, for example, the philosophical question of how we know that other people have minds, feelings, thoughts, and sensations. Philosopher Alfred J. Ayer (1910–1970) answers such questions analogically:

> Suppose that someone tells me that he has had a tooth extracted without an anesthetic, and I express my sympathy, and suppose that I am then asked, "How do you know that it hurt him?" I might reasonably reply, "Well, I know that it would hurt me. I have been to the dentist and know how painful it is to have a tooth stopped without an anesthetic, let alone taken out. And he has the same sort of nervous system as I have. I infer, therefore, that in these conditions he felt considerable pain, just as I should myself."[1]

Similarly, in discussing the possibility of God's existence, David Hume analogizes:

> Look round the world: contemplate the whole and every part of it: you will find it to be nothing but one great machine, subdivided into an infinite number of lesser machines, which again admit of subdivisions, to a degree beyond what human senses and faculties can trace and explain. . . . The curious adapting of means to ends, throughout all nature, resembles exactly, though it much exceeds, the productions of human contrivance; of human design, thought, wisdom and intelligence. Since therefore the effects resemble each other, we are led to infer, by all the rules of analogy, that the causes also resemble; and that the Author of Nature is somewhat similar to the mind of men; . . . by this argument alone, do we prove at once the existence of a Deity, and his similarity to human mind and intelligence.[2]

Or consider the theory of human evolution: that we are in a state of constant development from simple life forms to increasingly complex ones. Philosopher Herbert Spencer, among others, contended that our present condition must be explained in terms of millions and millions of years of gradual evolution.

> If a single cell, under the appropriate conditions, becomes a man in the space of a few years, there can surely be no difficulty in understanding how, under appropriate conditions, a cell may, in the course of untold millions of years, give origin to the human race.[3]

---

[1]Alfred J. Ayer. "One's Knowledge of Other Minds." *Theoria*, 1953, Vol. 19, p. 51.

[2]David Hume. *Dialogues Concerning Natural Religion.* N. Kemp Smith, Ed. Edinburgh: Nelson, 1947, Part V, p. 17.

[3]Herbert Spencer. *Principles of Biology.* Quoted in Irving M. Copi. *Introduction to Logic* (4th ed.). New York: Macmillan, 1972, p. 368.

From cars that will not start to evolution, analogical argument plays a crucial part in problem-solving. But never accept an analogical conclusion as certain, and always evaluate its probability by applying the criteria of (1) the number of instances involved, (2) the relevant similarities and dissimilarities among the instances, and (3) the disanalogies among the instances. In this way, you ensure reliability in analyzing and interpreting the relevant sense information you have collected. This reliability will be further increased by adding methodology for establishing cause.

Reflection   Suppose you are mulling over what you will be like in 20 years. Could you use analogical reasoning to forecast whether you will be married or not? What else would you predict about yourself, and on what basis?

CAUSE

Although daily we voice, point to, and demonstrate **cause**, it is hard to imagine a more complex philosophical question than "What is cause?" David Hume claimed that, when we say A causes B, we simply mean that A is regularly followed by B. After all, the only way we can say that a spirochete causes syphilis, friction causes heat, and lightning causes thunder is that these events occur in a sequence that we regularly observe. But, Hume insisted, this does not mean that we observe that they *must* occur that way—only that they *do*. As Hans Reichenbach, a modern Humean, puts it:

> Since repetition is all that distinguishes the causal law from a mere coincidence, the meaning of causal relation consists in the statement of an exceptionless repetition—it is unnecessary to assume that it means more. The idea that a cause is connected with its effect by a sort of hidden string, that the effect is forced to follow the cause, is anthropomorphic in its origin and is dispensable; *if-then-always* is all that is meant by a causal relation. If the theater would always shake when an explosion is visible on the screen, then there would be a causal relationship.[4]

Yet the explanation that cause is a statement of "exceptionless repetition" seems inadequate.

First, there are plenty of cases of sequential regularity that are not cases of **causality**. Night and day predictably follow each other,

---

[4]Hans Reichenbach. *The Rise of Scientific Philosophy*. Berkeley: University of California Press, 1951, p. 158.

but surely one is not the cause of the other. In a bright neon sign that blinks on and off, the "on" state does not cause the "off" state. And, although we wake up from sleep, sleep does not cause us to wake up.

There are also many instances of causality that are not cases of sequential regularity. We claim that striking a match causes it to light. But frequently the match does not light. It is argued that rich foods cause an adolescent's skin to break out. But frequently the skin does not break out. Although meeting a friend at an airport on one occasion might surprise you, meeting the same person there another time might not. So, it seems true that when we use the word *cause* we are referring to an event that regularly follows another, but at the same time we may be using the word in various ways. Perhaps the best way to understand cause is to determine how we speak about it.

One way to refer to cause is as a **necessary condition**. For example, we say that oxygen is necessary or needed for fire. This means that in the absence of oxygen there can be no fire. Obviously, we shall not have a fire every time oxygen is present. But in its absence we cannot have combustion.[5] When event B cannot occur in the absence of A, A is said to be a necessary condition of B.

We can use cause in another sense. Suppose you say "If a person is decapitated, he'll die." You are saying that decapitation is enough to cause death. Obviously, it is not necessary for death; death can occur in the absence of decapitation. But it is *sufficient* to produce death. A is said to be a **sufficient condition** of B if, without exception, whenever A occurs B occurs. So, in speaking of two causally related events that occur in the sequence A then B, we may state the relationship that holds between them in either or both of these ways:

If B, then A—necessary

If A, then B—sufficient

In addition to distinguishing between necessary and sufficient conditions, we should also differentiate *proximate* from *remote* conditions. Suppose, for example, that because a pyromaniac sets a building on fire the police must cordon off your normal route to school. The result: you are 20 minutes late for class and miss an important lecture. Two weeks later you take a test on the material you missed. You fail the test. Why did you fail? There are, of course, a whole chain of possible "causes": missing the lecture, being late for class, the detour, the fire, the pyromaniac. In such cases we are generally interested in the event closest in sequence to the event whose cause we are trying to establish; that is, we are interested in discovering the *proximate condition*. In

---

[5]Some recent studies indicate that this is no longer strictly true; certain chemicals will ignite in the absence of oxygen.

this instance, the proximate condition would probably be missing the lecture. The farther away the event is in sequence, the more remote the condition. In this case, a *remote condition* might be the psychology of the pyromaniac. In common usage, we frequently select the proximate condition out of an array of conditions and call it *the* cause.

Those using scientific method generally use *cause* in the sense of "sufficient condition." They are using it as John Stuart Mill did when he defined cause, philosophically, as "the sum total of the conditions, positive and negative, taken together; the whole of the contingencies of every description, which being realized, the consequent (event) invariably follows."[6] In short, in referring to cause, scientific methodologists are speaking of the sum total of conditions that are sufficient to produce an event. Having raised the question of cause, let us now see how cause is determined.

Reflection   What would you say *caused* you to study philosophy?

MILL'S METHODS OF ESTABLISHING PROBABLE CAUSE

John Stuart Mill is credited with formulating five methods of establishing probable cause. They are the methods of Agreement, Difference, Joint Agreement and Difference, Concomitant Variation, and Residue.

Method of Agreement

We can illustrate Mill's Method of Agreement using a case of food poisoning. Suppose that after eating in the school cafeteria five people become ill. Food poisoning is suspected. The problem: which is the bad food? The following chart indicates the foods that each of the sick people ate:

1.	salad	beef	potatoes	cauliflower	jello	coffee
2.	salad	chicken	rice	peas		tea
3.	salad	fish		string beans		milk
4.	salad	crab		spinach	cake	
5.	salad	cheese		carrots		buttermilk

Because the only food all five of the sick people ate is salad, salad is the *probable* cause of the food poisoning. To get even more specific, we

---

[6]John Stuart Mill. *A System of Logic*. London: Longmans, Green, 1959, p. 217.

could break down each salad and find out what ingredients each instance of food poisoning shares. This, then, is Mill's Method of Agreement: "If two or more instances of the phenomenon under investigation have only one circumstance in common, then that circumstance is the cause (or the effect) of that phenomenon."[7]

Consider the use of Mill's method in this discovery:

A few years ago a small number of people living in various sections of the United States were inflicted with an identical disease. At about the same time the eyes of these individuals developed what the physician calls cataracts—small, irregular, opaque spots in the tissue of the lens. Cataracts interfere with the clear passage of light through the transparent medium of the eye lens. In severe cases they may block vision. . . . It turned out that all the individuals who developed these cataracts were physicists and that all of them had been connected with nuclear-energy projects during the war. While they worked with cyclotrons in atomic-energy laboratories they had been the targets of stray neutron rays. They were under medical supervision all during their work, but the density of the neutrons was thought to be entirely harmless.

This case is one of the best examples of the insidiousness of nuclear radiation.[8]

Method of Difference

Let us return to the case of your car that refuses to start to illustrate Mill's Method of Difference. Suppose you have it towed to a nearby service station and it is inspected. You inform the attendant that you're particularly distressed because just three weeks before you had it tuned up.

On the chart below, (1) represents the condition of the car three weeks ago, after the tune-up, and (2) represents its present condition with respect to the items mentioned. "X" indicates adequate functioning.

	PLUGS	POINTS	BATTERY	BATTERY CABLE	CONDENSER
1.	X	X	X	X	X
2.	X	X		X	X

The two instances correspond in every way except under "battery." If we assume that the items listed are the only possible causes of the car's failing to start, then we can conclude that the battery is the probable cause of the problem. Notice how we have used the analogical

---

[7]Quoted by Irving M. Copi. *Introduction to Logic* (4th ed.). New York: Macmillan, 1972, p. 377.

[8]Heinz Haber. *Man in Space.* Quoted in Copi. *Introduction to Logic*, p. 379.

method combined with a method to establish cause—the Method of Difference. In describing the Method of Difference, Mill says:

If an instance in which the phenomenon under investigation [car won't start] and an instance in which it does not occur have every circumstance in common save one, that one occurring only in the former; the circumstance in which alone two instances differ, is the effect, or the cause, or an indispensable part of the cause of the phenomenon.[9]

In the example below, the Method of Difference advances dental science:

We have recently obtained conclusive experimental evidence that there can be no tooth decay without bacteria and a food supply for them. In germ-free laboratories at the University of Notre Dame and the University of Chicago, animals innocent of oral micro-organisms do not develop cavities. Where animals in normal circumstances average more than four cavities each, the germ-free rats show no signs of caries. At the Harvard School of Dental Medicine we have demonstrated the other side of the coin: the food debris also must be present. Rats that have plenty of bacteria in their mouths but are fed by the tube directly to the stomach do not develop cavities. In a pair of rats joined by surgery so that they share a common blood circulation, the one fed by mouth develops tooth decay, the one fed by tube does not.[10]

Joint Method of Agreement and Difference

When we combine the Methods of Agreement and Difference, we have a most potent tool for establishing probable causation. Mill terms this method the Joint Method of Agreement and Difference. Consider again the case of food poisoning. First, we can establish the probable cause through agreement:

1.	salad	beef	potatoes	cauliflower	jello	coffee
2.	salad	chicken	rice	peas		tea
3.	salad	fish		string beans		milk
4.	salad	crab		spinach	cake	
5.	salad	cheese		carrots		buttermilk

Using the Method of Difference gives us additional weight for the conclusion that the salad is the probable cause. In the chart below, the second instance in each pair represents someone who did not get sick after eating in the cafeteria.

---

[9]Quoted in Copi. *Introduction to Logic*, p. 380.

[10]Reidar F. Sognnaes. "Tooth Decay." *Scientific American*, December 1957. Quoted in Copi. *Introduction to Logic*, pp. 383–384. Reprinted by permission.

1.	salad	beef	potatoes	cauliflower	jello	coffee
2.		beef	potatoes	cauliflower	jello	coffee

1.	salad	chicken	rice	peas		tea
2.		chicken	rice	peas		tea

1.	salad	fish		string beans		milk
2.		fish		string beans		milk

1.	salad	crab		spinach	cake	
2.		crab		spinach	cake	

1.	salad	cheese		carrots		buttermilk
2.		cheese		carrots		buttermilk

Method of Concomitant Variation

Sometimes, however, none of these methods lends itself to a problem. Take the case of establishing a causal connection between air pollution and lung disease. To do this, you could discover whether the incidence of lung problems increases as air pollution does. If it does, and if you have controlled all other factors, then it is a safe bet that air pollution does increase the incidence of lung disease. Mill called this the Method of Concomitant Variation: "When a phenomenon varies in a particular way as another in a particular way, then a causal relation obtains between them."[11] This method was instrumental in establishing a causal connection between cigarette smoking and heart and lung disease.

Method of Residue

Finally, we sometimes need to use the fifth of Mill's methods, the Method of Residue. Suppose you were going on a trip and you wanted to determine the weight of the material your car was carrying. One way would be to weigh the car before it was loaded, then afterwards. The difference would be the weight of the materials it was carrying. As Mill formulated the Method of Residue: "Subduct from any phenomenon such part as is known by previous inductions to be the effect of certain antecedents [the weight of the unloaded car], and the residue of the phenomenon [the weight of the loaded car] is the effect of the remaining antecedents [the weight of the load]."[12] Consider the usefulness of the Method of Residue in the discovery of the planet Neptune:

---

[11]Mill. *A System of Logic*, p. 263.

[12]Mill. *A System of Logic*, p. 260.

In 1821, Bouvard of Paris published tables of the motions of a number of planets, including Uranus. In preparing the latter he had found great difficulty in making an orbit calculated on the basis of positions obtained in the years after 1800 agree with one calculated from observations taken in the years immediately following discovery. He finally disregarded the older observations entirely and based his tables on the newer observations. In a few years, however, the positions calculated from the tables disagreed with the observed positions of the planet and by 1844 the discrepancy amounted to 2 minutes of arc. Since all the other known planets agreed in their motions with those calculated for them, the discrepancy in the case of Uranus aroused much discussion.

In 1845, Leverrier, then a young man, attacked the problem. He checked Bouvard's calculations and found them essentially correct. Thereupon he felt that the only satisfactory explanation of the trouble lay in the presence of a planet somewhere beyond Uranus which was disturbing its motion. By the middle of 1846 he had finished his calculations. In September he wrote to Galle at Berlin and requested the latter to look for a new planet in a certain region of the sky for which some new star charts had just been prepared in Germany but of which Leverrier apparently had not as yet obtained copies. On the twenty-third of September Galle started the search and in less than an hour he found an object which was not on the chart. By the next night it had moved appreciably and the new planet, subsequently named Neptune, was discovered within 1° of the predicted place. This discovery ranks among the greatest achievements of mathematical astronomy.[13]

Although indispensable for determining the causal connections among things, Mill's methods have limitations. For example, they can never *discover* causal relationships. As an illustration, consider the case of the man who gets drunk every night. Realizing he is ruining his life, he sets out to establish scientifically the cause of his intoxication. He observes that he gets drunk after drinking Scotch and water, whiskey and water, gin and water, brandy and water, and rum and water. Using Mill's Method of Agreement, he vows never again to touch water! Of course, he failed to isolate the common ingredient in the liquors that accompanied the water: alcohol. In short, his analysis was faulty. But we see that Mill's method does not help us to make a correct analysis; it merely prescribes analysis of antecedent circumstances. This the man did. The second limitation of Mill's methods, of course, is that they do not *demonstrate conclusively* a causal connection. They provide probability.

Nevertheless, Mill's methods do provide a basis for arriving at probable explanation, which scientific method aims for. Without a need for such explanations, neither Mill's methods nor analogical reasoning would be necessary. Thus, if we never felt the need to know why the earth's position relative to the sun is constantly changing, why an apple falls from a tree rather than rises, why we contract diseases like dia-

---

[13]Edward Arthur Fath. *The Elements of Astronomy.* New York: McGraw-Hill, 1955. Quoted in Copi. *Introduction to Logic*, p. 389. Reprinted by permission.

"Using Mill's Method of Agreement, he
vows never again to touch water!"

betes, arteriosclerosis, and cancer, why the human body is apparently
influenced by the mind, and vice versa, or why matter in space is moving
away from us, we would have no need for analogies or causes. But we
do wonder. And that curiosity invariably reveals itself in explanations,
in what we call hypotheses—a vital part of the analysis and interpretation aspects of scientific method.

HYPOTHESIS

In general, a hypothesis is any working explanation for a phenomenon.
For example, in answer to the question "Why is the universe expanding?" some scientists hypothesize that, from originally being in a state
of extreme compaction, matter in the universe then exploded. Others
hypothesize that matter is being created out of nothing in interstellar
and intergalactic space. Like any hypothesis, these offer premises for
additional investigation and thus direct further research. Because they
are so instrumental in science, we often forget the common need and
use for hypotheses in everyday living, which we can illustrate with the
amusing case of Harry and Mildred Eagle.

Harry: Mildred, just out of curiosity, how important do you figure hair is?

Mildred: Well, just off the top of my head, Harry, I'd say hair is more important
than toenails and less important than a world war.

Harry: You think it's a joke, don't you?

Mildred: Harry, we're eating.

Harry: So we're eating! Tell me something: what would you say is the most important thing in this society today?

Mildred: Let me guess. Hair?

Harry: Hair! You said it! Hair is in.

Mildred: Hair should be in. If it were out we'd all be bald. So eat.

Harry: Why'd you bring that up?

Mildred: Because the meat balls are getting cold.

Harry: I mean "bald." How come you mentioned that all of a sudden?

Mildred: It just popped up, that's all.

Harry: "Bald" doesn't just pop up. So why'd you bring it up? No, I'll tell you why. Because I'm losing my hair!

Mildred: You are not.

Harry: That's all right, Mildred, you don't have to lie to me. I can see it happening. You know, I don't even want to comb it anymore!

Mildred: Harry, you're exaggerating. Sure, you may have a high forehead—

Harry: High forehead? If my forehead were any higher it'd be the back of my neck. No, there's no point in trying to kid ourselves. I'm losing my hair and that's that.

Mildred: Okay, let's eat.

Harry: So you admit I'm losing my hair.

Mildred: Harry, if you're losing your hair, you're losing your hair. That's that. *C'est la vie,* like the French say.

Harry: I don't care what the French say. And we're not eating until we figure out where my hair's going.

Mildred: Probably into the sauce.

Harry: Very funny! I mean *why*—why am I losing my hair?

Mildred: Look, if we can't eat before we figure out why you're losing your hair, we'll probably starve to death. Then think where you'd be: bald and dead.

Harry: Well, I say there's got to be a reason. A man like me, in the prime of life, full of all the vim and vigor of a kid half his age, I say a man like that just doesn't all of a sudden start shedding his golden locks.

Mildred: Nature, Harry. Blame it on Mother Nature.

Harry: Nature! That's a terrific reason. If they listened to you, men would still be in caves.

Mildred: Well, if they were, you'd still have your hair.

Harry: What do you mean?

Mildred: Have you ever seen a bald cave man?

Harry has a point. If humans persisted in attributing everything to "Nature" and leaving it at that, we probably would still be in caves— assuming we still existed. But history teaches that we are problem-formulating and problem-solving creatures. Without problems there are no hypotheses. The problems can be very complex, as in the search for a cure for cancer, or more simple, as in the question of the baldness of Harry Eagle. Having formulated a problem, we frequently develop a preliminary explanation and collect as many pertinent facts as possible. These facts may generate an additional hypothesis, which in turn directs further investigation and, perhaps, the formulation of still another hypothesis, and so on until the problem is solved. Occasionally, the preliminary hypothesis turns out to be the final explanation. But in most cases of problem-solving many hypotheses arise, and often simultaneously. How, then, do we recognize the best one? What makes a good hypothesis? A good hypothesis is relevant, compatible, testable, predictive, and simple. Let us examine each of these descriptive qualities.

Relevance

Mildred: All right, Harry. When did you first notice you were losing your hair?

Harry: About seven months ago. Now doesn't that ring a bell?

Mildred: Seven months ago—that'd make it September. The only bell I remember in September was the Avon lady ringing.

Harry: That's when I changed my image!

Mildred: Oh, of course, the youth kick! You threw out your old baggy suits and bought all those new outfits. How could I forget? But you don't think you're losing your hair because you're wearing bell-bottoms, do you?

Harry: Don't be ridiculous.

It would indeed be ridiculous to suggest that bell-bottoms cause baldness. Any good hypothesis must be relevant; that is, it should directly explain the problem under discussion. Suppose someone was late for an appointment with you. "Why are you late?" you ask her when she finally arrives. "Because Caesar was assassinated on the Ides of March," she replies. You would probably think she had lost her mind. On the other hand, suppose she replied "Because the President held

"Without problems there are
no hypotheses."

a news conference." Although this explanation alone does not account for her lateness, it might do so in combination with other relevant reasons. Perhaps she was watching the news conference on television and lost track of the time. Perhaps what the President said was so important that she had to wait for the conclusion. The point is that her explanation, although incomplete, is at least *relevant;* from it you can infer a possible explanation for her tardiness. But relevance alone does not provide a good hypothesis.

Compatibility

Harry: Do you remember what else was part and parcel of the new me?

Mildred: Let me see. . . . Well, eating granola in bed was.

Harry: Right!

Mildred: You think eating in bed's causing you to lose your hair?

Harry: No, but granola is!

Mildred: Granola?

Harry: Twice a day I've been eating that stuff—morning and night, as regular as clockwork.

Mildred: But, Harry, that's as silly as saying your bell-bottoms are affecting your hair. Granola wouldn't cause you to lose your hair. In fact, I'd think it would help you keep it.

Harry:	Well, it's awfully funny that as soon as I start eating that stuff my hair starts falling out.
Mildred:	That's just a coincidence.
Harry:	Some coincidence.
Mildred:	Look, you started dieting and jogging and weight-lifting as well, didn't you? Why don't you blame them?
Harry:	What do they have to do with hair?
Mildred:	Nothing, but becoming so worried about growing old before your time may have a lot to do with it. Harry, you're paranoid about growing old.

Mildred's explanation is certainly relevant. Moreover, it fits in with other hypotheses about hair loss, especially one that claims that nervousness can affect the condition of hair. When a hypothesis accords with a body of knowledge already accepted as true, it is said to be compatible with that information. Any hypothesis that is compatible with accepted knowledge is preferable to one that is not. For example, in his book *Chariots of the Gods?*, author Von Däniken's hypothesis—that signs of a developed culture in some "uncivilized" areas of earth can be attributed to the fact that "astronaut gods" visited this planet eons ago—hardly fits in with accepted thought on the matter. Likewise, author Immanuel Velikovsky's claim in *Worlds in Collision* that Biblical accounts of world calamities are actually reports of a collision between earth and a comet seems to contradict prevailing knowledge. This does not mean that these hypotheses are therefore incorrect, but only that they are *improbable*.

History, in fact, records several examples of incompatible hypotheses that proved accurate. The classic example is Copernicus's theory of a sun-centered solar system. His theory was not compatible with the prevailing Ptolemaic theory, which claimed an earth-centered system. Similarly, in our own century we have seen Newtonian concepts of mechanics modified in the light of Einstein's relativity theory. And in the field of physiological psychology we have witnessed a whittling away of the notion that individuals have almost complete control over their behavior. Generally, however, if a hypothesis is consistent with established thought, its reliability is thereby strengthened. Yet relevance and compatibility alone do not ensure a good hypothesis.

Testability

Harry:	You mean I'm going bald because I'm nervous?
Mildred:	Yes, I think so. But there's only one way to find out.

Harry: You know what this means, Mildred?

Mildred: Sure, you're going to have to relax.

Harry: No, it means I can still munch granola in bed!

In his relief, Harry ignores the test Mildred proposes to establish the soundness of her hypothesis. If nervousness is the only reason Harry is losing his hair, then if he calms down he should stop losing it. Like this one, any good hypothesis must be testable; it should permit observations that will confirm or disconfirm it. Unfortunately, not all hypotheses are directly testable. Darwin's theory of evolution, Einstein's theory of relativity, and the theory of a pulsating universe cannot be directly tested. But they can be tested *indirectly*. In other words, if these explanations are true, then other results should follow. And it is these other results that we can observe and test.

For example, if Newton's inertia hypothesis—that a moving body will maintain a line of direction unless disturbed by an external force—is true, then it follows that, when you fully apply the brakes to a car traveling at 50 miles per hour, the car should skid forward; the people in the car should be thrust forward; a parked car struck by the skidding car should move. We can test these phenomena directly, and, if they occur, the inertia hypothesis is strengthened. Testability is related to another characteristic of the good hypothesis: predictability.

Predictability

A hypothesis that leads to many observable phenomena is said to have predictive power; it is able to explain a great deal. Thus, Newton's law of gravitation allows for considerable deductive facts; it explains not only why apples fall from trees but why tides move as they do, why great booster rockets are needed in order to put an object into space, why an astronaut in space had better hold onto his glass of milk, and why the universe may have begun with a "big bang." What about Mildred's hypothesis? It helps explain how we can get dandruff and grey hair, as well as ulcers, migraine headaches, and a great many other nerve-related ailments. An explanation with even greater predictive power, however, would be that Harry inherited his baldness. Think of all the other phenomena we are able to predict from the principle of genetic inheritance. And, of course, that hypothesis would be relevant, compatible, and testable as well. Sometimes two or more hypotheses appear equal in all respects. Which one is preferable? Usually, the simpler one.

Simplicity

When the Copernican theory of a sun-centered solar system was accepted over Ptolemy's earth-centered explanation, it was done not on the basis of relevance, compatibility, testability, or predictability, but on the basis of simplicity. Copernicus's explanation was less complicated than the ancient Greek's. Similarly, it is often on grounds of simplicity that a jury decides between two persuasive opposing hypotheses. As you might imagine, the concept of simplicity is extremely vague and can, when used indiscriminately, lead to error. But when other factors are equal it does determine the more reliable of the explanations.

THE VALUE OF HYPOTHESIS

Since a hypothesis offers an explanation for a phenomenon, any speculative pursuit inevitably involves hypotheses. This is certainly true of philosophy. Consider the many hypotheses we have already related to the issue of self:

1. On views of human nature: the human as a rational, divine, mechanical, and existential being, and as no self.
2. On the question of language and perception: language affects the way we think and perceive; the way we think and perceive affects our language; peoples speaking different languages will perceive in significantly different ways.
3. On the question of the nature of knowledge: we know only what we experience; we have some innate ideas; we can know nothing but our ideas; our minds impose an order on sense experience.
4. On the question of truth: truth is a correspondence between what a statement says and the way things actually are; truth is a coherence between a statement and other statements; truth is what works.
5. On the question of reality: the ultimate constituent of reality is matter; the ultimate constituent of reality is nonmatter, idea; the ultimate constituent of reality is being; the ultimate constituent of reality is consciousness; there is no ultimate constituent of reality.

Philosophy is full of hypotheses. But few people are willing to live with such constant and intense speculation. As a result, they are sorely tempted to discard philosophy as a luxury or a waste of time. A couple of examples will show why this attitude is unfortunate and ultimately dangerous.

In ancient Greece, much speculation abounded concerning ultimate reality. Water, air, fire, and earth formed the core of many hypotheses. One of these, Democritus's atomic theory, although fairly respectable in the light of modern science, received comparatively little acceptance, partially because of the general disenchantment with such hypotheses. Although numerous other factors led to the submergence of Democritus's theory, including his inability to prove it, it is likely that the usefulness of his idea suffered as much from the growing disenchantment with such cosmic speculation as from the inadequacies of the theory itself.

Consider also the thinking of the ancient Greek astronomer Aristarchus of Samos. He believed that the earth and all the planets revolve around the sun. Elementary, we say. But the hypothesis was rejected for 2000 years, partly on the authority of Aristotle. In the fifteenth century, Copernicus had the boldness to revive Aristarchus's hypothesis. Kepler later discovered that the planets move in ellipses, not circles, with the sun at a focus, not at the center. Subsequently, Newton discovered that the planets do not even move in exact ellipses. But the usefulness of Aristarchus's hypothesis was lost for 2000 years primarily because of a bias—in this case the classical bias in favor of esthetics and ethics over science.

So we must be careful not to disregard any hypothesis too quickly. The temptation today is great, for we are bombarded with hypotheses of every sort. The result is a kind of hypothesis "overkill." We are rapidly reaching the point where we can no longer detect the good hypothesis among so many. But we must remember, as one philosopher has noted, "that any hypothesis, however absurd, *may* be useful in science, if it enables a discoverer to conceive things in a new way."[14]

We are in a sense all "discoverers," discoverers of ourselves and the world around us. No exploration gives us more freedom of self-discovery than philosophy, for no exploration makes more extensive use of the hypothesis. "If you have built castles in the air," wrote the American Henry David Thoreau, "your work need not be lost; this is where they should be. Now put foundations under them." Perhaps this advice catches the unique relationship between philosophy and science: science provides the foundations for the castles that philosophy erects. And these castles rise on the wings of hypothesis. At bottom, it is such hypotheses that constitute our knowledge of nature. We will consider this knowledge later in this chapter, but before leaving the subject of scientific method let us note some cautions in dealing with it.

LIMITATIONS OF THE METHODS OF SCIENCE

The first limitation of the methods of science is that *science and the scientific method grasp only as much as their tools allow them to reach.*

---

[14]Bertrand Russell. *A History of Western Philosophy.* New York: Simon & Schuster, 1945, p. 31.

The more limited the technique, the more speculative the theory. Thus, Galileo's law of falling bodies, although sound, could not be verified until 1654, when the air pump was invented. Then it could be shown that a feather and a stone actually do fall at the same speed.

Related to this is a second limitation: *we can learn only what the tools are designed to show.* For example, if you thought you had a fever, an accurate thermometer would confirm or disconfirm your belief. But no matter how accurate the thermometer, it would not tell you if you had pneumonia; other instruments must do this. Obviously, an instrument can measure only what it is designed to measure. Recall the first Russian cosmonaut, Yuri Gagarin. When he completed his suborbital flight of the earth, someone asked Gagarin if there was a God. Gagarin, an atheist, replied that he'd been up to the heavens and he hadn't seen any God. Facetious perhaps, but the point remains that the instruments Gagarin brought to his mission were not designed to detect the presence of a God. The fact that our tools do not (because they are not designed to) measure purpose, meaning, or freedom does not prove that these things do not exist. Simply to dismiss such concerns, along with similar phenomena such as thought and emotion, is to argue from ignorance— to claim that something does not exist because its existence cannot be proved.

A third limitation concerns classification, a vital part of the scientific process. As we noted previously, classification ignores individual differences. True, scientific classification frequently accounts for differences under subcategories, but the rule of classification is to group by similar defining characteristics. But, individually, entities bear many more traits than those that have provided the groupings. To ignore these differences is to ignore part of reality.

A fourth limitation concerns the scientific tendency not only to explain but to explain away. Thus, the "nothing but" attitude: color is nothing but light waves; heat is nothing but molecular motion; internal feelings are nothing but brain states. This tendency to reduce the whole to "nothing but" its parts encourages overlooking characteristics of the whole that the parts themselves may not possess. Taken by themselves, hydrogen and oxygen, two gases, do not show the characteristics they show when in the liquid state, water. Similarly, the heart, liver, and lungs taken alone do not show the characteristics of life they show when functioning together. The point is that, as **Gestalt** psychology argues, the whole is often greater than the sum of its parts. Missing this point, we might consider the parts more real than the unit. Philosophically, this attitude leaves us on the uncertain limb of trying to defend positions such as "My experience of green is less real than the color green's wave length," or "My experience of Beethoven's Fifth Symphony is less real than the sum of the measurement of alternating condensations of air that compose it."

The fifth limitation follows from recognizing that neither science nor the scientific method occurs in a vacuum. No matter how refined the instruments, no matter how advanced the computer, some *person* still must make the observations, formulate the problem, collect the relevant data, establish a hypothesis, draw deductions from that hypothesis, and, finally, verify the deductions. And where there is a person there is frequently a viewpoint and a bias that can color the investigations and findings—not necessarily invalidate them, but influence them.

One reason for the element of human prejudice is that, no matter how objective the investigators try to be, they are limited by their own physical and intellectual capabilities. Another reason is that, while the investigators shape a hypothesis, they are at the same time shaped by it; for it is this hypothesis that directs further research. A third reason is that the investigators function, even as scientists, within a cultural milieu that has to a degree influenced their perceptions. The fact that the individuals are engaged in such investigation is itself evidence of their Western cultural milieu; for other traditions, such as the Eastern, have put little store in science. Thus, the distinction between knower and known is not so sharp as John Locke would have it in distinguishing between knower-imposed secondary qualities of the object (color, taste, smell) and known primary qualities of the object (shape, size, solidity). At the very least, it would seem that scientific investigators assume an amount of "background" data. Therefore, in evaluating research, we must find out the assumptions of the investigators.

Keeping in mind these limitations helps us keep scientific knowledge in perspective. Specifically, it aids us in assessing our knowledge of nature, whose effects strongly influence how we view ourselves. Now let us turn to a discussion of this knowledge.

OUR KNOWLEDGE OF NATURE

Our knowledge of nature is of two kinds: empirical and rational. Empirical knowledge springs from sensory observations we make about things. Such empirical knowledge is hypothetical and therefore probable, not certain. For example, our experience indicates that humans need iodine to remain healthy and that plants need sunlight to grow. But we can imagine exceptions: a human that does not need iodine, a plant that does not need sunlight. We use the hypotheses that constitute empirical knowledge as long as they are compatible with our experiences, our observations. Those who believe that empirical knowledge is the only kind of knowledge are called empiricists.

But rationalists contend that there is another kind of knowledge of nature, rational knowledge, often called *a priori* knowledge. Rational or *a priori* knowledge is knowledge that does not seem to rely on obser-

"... while the investigators shape a
hypothesis, they are at the same time
shaped by it ..."

vation, knowledge to which we cannot imagine an exception. Such knowledge is termed "necessary."

Our knowledge that eight times seven is 56 is *a priori*. So is our knowledge that the circumference of a circle is determined by using the formula C = 2πr, and that a rectangle always has four sides. These seem to be **universal** truths; that is, they apply always and everywhere. From such rational knowledge rationalists have formulated the "exact sciences" of mathematics, geometry, and logic.

The ancient Greek philosopher-mathematician Pythagoras (about 500 B.C.) claimed that, when we fully understand a particular mathematical or geometric construct, we know a universal truth. His Pythagorean theorem is a good example: the sum of the squares of the sides of a right triangle always equals the square of the hypotenuse. But such an absolute truth is mental, not actual. It is not an empirical truth; it is not arrived at from observing, if it were possible, all right triangles. On the contrary, we need experience only one right triangle to realize that we are dealing with a logical truth, a mathematical principle. Once we understand the nature of a right triangle, we realize we are dealing with a universal truth.

It was this realization of the mental nature of absolute truths that led Pythagoras to claim that the nature of reality is nonmaterial. It has led subsequent thinkers to believe that nature is written in the language of mathematics, that all natural operations can be described mathematically. Thus, Plato held that God was a geometer, and, in the twentieth century, Sir James Jeans believes that God is "addicted" to arithmetic.

Both empirical knowledge and rational knowledge raise philosophical problems. The obvious problem with empirical knowledge is that it leaves us uncertain. We must continually wonder whether we collected and analyzed enough data to make a claim, whether our experiences are sufficient to warrant it. Even when we think we have enough information, we still must realize that we are dealing with probability, not certainty.

Rational knowledge, on the other hand, is mystifying. It bothers us philosophically. Granted that mathematics does accurately describe nature's operations, we are left wondering *why*. Consider this conversation between two students leaving a mathematics class.

Kevin: I wonder if everything really is as we say it is, or just because we say it is.

Fran: Funny, but I was thinking something like that.

Kevin: Well, what I'm wondering is why *does* eight times seven equal 56?

Fran: Exactly. You know, I've wondered that since I was a kid.

Kevin: Really? Didn't you ever ask anyone?

Fran: I thought it was a stupid question. That's what I was thinking just now in class when we were doing the Pythagorean theorem.

Kevin: I bet you were wondering why the sum of the squares of the sides of a right triangle always equals the square of the hypotenuse.

Fran: You too?

Kevin: You don't think we're cracking up, do you?

Fran: *Why* is the area of a circle always equal to pi r-squared?

Kevin: And its circumference equal to two pi r?

Fran: It's just the way things are, I suppose.

Kevin: You mean things work according to these mathematical principles?

Fran: I guess so.

Kevin: And we've simply discovered them?

Fran: You don't sound convinced.

Kevin: Do you think things *must* work that way?

Fran: What?

Kevin: Could nature operate differently from the way it does?

Fran: I don't follow.

Kevin: Well, do you think nature is operating in accordance with these laws out of necessity, or, say, out of coincidence?

Fran: You seem to be asking if things could be other than they are.

Kevin: I'm wondering if things must be the way our mathematics and science allow us to perceive them to be.

Fran: I suppose we'll never be able to say for sure.

Kevin: You know what that means?

Fran: What?

Kevin: That we really can't know what we're talking about.

Why does the sum of the squares of the sides of a right triangle *always* equal the square of the hypotenuse? Why does eight times seven *always* equal 56? Why is the area of a circle *always* equal to πr^2? We are led to more profound ponderings, such as whether nature actually operates according to perfect mathematical principles or whether the only reason we can be certain that there are perfect mathematical principles is that there cannot be exceptions to them. In short, we remain puzzled by the relationship between our mental constructs of nature and nature itself.

Another source of philosophical wonder is that perhaps one plus one equals two because we say so. Perhaps we are locked into our internally consistent system of logic, mistaking the coherence of our manufactured system for real operations in nature. Does one plus one equal two because it *must* be so or because it works? One mathematician once defined mathematics as the subject in which we never know what we are talking about or whether what we are claiming is true. When we say that one penny plus one penny equals two pennies, we are talking about observable things: pennies. But when we abstract and say simply that one plus one equals two, just what are we saying? We are speaking of nothing observable, nothing we can experience.

Finally, we must wonder whether our belief that there are two ways of knowing is not a false bipolarity. This belief assumes that humans are the knowers and that nature is what is known. In other words, it assumes a distinction between subject and object. Is this a true distinction? Perhaps our separateness from the object of our knowledge is only illusion. Perhaps we can only "know" nature by putting aside our quantification procedures and experiencing the process of nature through intuition. Zen Buddhists, for example, eschew any subject-object division, seeking instead a total awareness that finds us one with the world around us.

Despite these ponderings, our concept of how we know nature has led to many remarkable hypotheses. These hypotheses obviously influence the way we see the world around us and, consequently, the way we see ourselves. Although we cannot discuss them all here, we shall examine some of the more philosophically provocative. Let us consider three: one concerns matter, another concerns the cosmos, and another concerns time.

Reflection   Can you imagine a creature who possessed knowledge of nature that was neither empirical nor rational? What would this creature be like? How would it operate? How would such a creature be different from us?

MATTER

Take a look at a comb, or any other piece of matter. Suppose you were able to break it down into smaller and smaller pieces. What would you eventually find?

We know that all matter is made up of molecules. These molecules are specific in nature and arrangement for each material substance. Since there are an incredible number of material compositions, the number of kinds of molecules is staggeringly large.

We also know that every molecule is composed of atoms and that there are about 100 of these atoms, ranging from the simplest and lightest, hydrogen, to the most complex—some that have recently been synthesized. These atoms, in turn, are composed of what physicists call elementary particles. Three elementary particles make up all atoms, and thus all matter: electrons, protons, and neutrons.

In our age, a close study of these elementary particles has revealed that there are even more fundamental particles. These in turn are believed to consist of still more elementary particles, which physicists regard as energy. Although nobody knows precisely what energy is, it is suspected that energy is not matter.

Thus, in a real sense, when you wonder about the material composition of a comb or of matter generally, you could conclude that it is *nonmaterial*. The elemental particles of contemporary physics seem to be defined by the requirements of mathematical symmetry. Rather than thinking of them as "real," we would be more accurate to view them as expressions of basic mathematical constructions that we invariably come upon when, as with the comb, we try to break down matter into its ultimate constituents. But, in the last analysis, is the mathematical pattern not strictly a mental construct? If so, is matter not ultimately more mental than physical?

When we turn outward, away from the infinitesimally small to the incomprehensibly large universe of which we have only recently discovered ourselves to be a tiny part, the questions are no less philosophical.

Reflection   Pick up a blade of grass. Hold it in the palm of your hand and look at it. In what sense are you staring into the face of infinity?

THE COSMOS

We take the word *cosmos* to mean the universe considered as an orderly, harmonious whole. Our ancient ancestors understood their cosmos as closed and **finite.** What they could not understand they generally attributed to gods or spirits, who often interacted with earthlings. At various times they thought the sky was the lid of a box, a disc supported by mountains, or a "firmament" that separated heaven from earth. To the Egyptians the sun was a god, Amon-Ra; to the Mesopotamians it was a wheel of the chariot of the sun god Shamash. Although today we consider these beliefs primitive, we realize that they were formulated to explain the workings of the universe. This desire to explain things is no less urgent now; neither are the questions any simpler.

One of the things we have been trying to explain for almost half a century is why the universe is "expanding." In 1929, using sensitive photographic equipment, Dr. Edwin Hubble observed billions of galaxies that, as their color seemed to indicate, were moving away from earth at constant speeds. The galaxies nearer to us have since been shown to be moving more slowly than the ones farther away. At the outer edge of space as we can perceive it, galaxies appear to be moving at speeds approaching the speed of light (186,000 miles per second). In recent years a number of theories have been offered to explain what is occurring.

One of these is the "big bang" theory. This theory holds that gravity once pulled together all matter in the universe. The result was a massive molten ball. Intense gravitational forces so condensed the ball that pressure and temperature built up to incredible levels. The matter finally collapsed on itself—that is, imploded. In this implosion, the outermost layers of the molten ball fell inward until they reached a critical point. It was then that the molten ball exploded; thus, the big bang. Supposedly, the matter that we observe moving away from us is the condensed and clustered accumulative residue of that explosion, matter that continues to travel outward from the point of explosion. According to the big-bang theory, this cosmic journey will continue until all energy is dissipated, until there is no more heat or light—until the cosmos dies.

Astronomer Fred Hoyle of Cambridge University disagreed. He regarded the single-explosion theory of the big bang as too simple and accidental. Instead, he argued with his "steady-state" theory, that matter in intergalactic space was constantly being created out of nothing. Hoyle reasoned that, even if only one hydrogen atom was being created every century, that atom was enough to displace existing matter. It was just such a process of displacement, said Hoyle, that explained why the universe appeared to be expanding. The obvious problem with this theory is: How can something come from nothing? How can matter be created out of nothing? This consideration, along with additional evidence, has persuaded Hoyle himself to abandon his theory.

One of the explanations most widely accepted today is the theory of the "pulsating cosmos." It upholds the explosion feature of the big-bang theory but insists that the gravitational force of the universe's mass is greater than the force of the explosion itself. The result is that galaxies will eventually slow down and travel back to the scene of the explosion. Ultimately, they will again implode, explode, and travel outward. This process of cosmic pulsation is thought to be perpetual. Rather than being part of a "dying" universe, then, we are witnessing a dynamic, eternal process in which energy is built up, dissipated, and regenerated. How long does it take to complete one cycle? Scientists estimate 80 billion years. But there is little reason to panic, for we still have 60 billion to go.

All kinds of questions arise out of these theories. If we granted that a big bang did occur, what is the origin of the matter that went into it? What is the origin of the cosmos? If the pulsating-cosmos theory is accurate, could there not be other universes that are also pulsating? Could ours be just one of countless others? Is the completion of the cycle what various religions have called the Day of Doom, Armageddon, Doom of the Gods? Will there be creatures billions of years hence observing precisely what we are observing today? Have similar civilizations preceded us?

But one of the most fascinating things about observing intergalactic space is that we are looking back into the past. When we look up into the heavens, we are literally looking into the face of history. To understand this point better we should at least glance at the concept of time.

Reflection Imagine a person with strong fundamentalist beliefs. This person believes that the earth is of central importance in the cosmos, that humans represent the highest form of life, if not the only such life in the universe, and that God is personally involved in the affairs of humans. One night in a planetarium observatory, the person looks through a very powerful telescope into the starry sky. At the same time, an astronomer describes the view. What intellectual tugs and pulls might the person feel while listening to the astronomer?

TIME

We constantly deal with time as if it were absolute. Clocks, watches, calendars, heartbeats, all kinds of devices impress on us that we can so accurately measure when an event occurs that the event occurs for everyone everywhere at precisely the same time. This is not so.

It is impossible to appreciate this fact until we encounter incredibly fast speeds at great distances—that is, until we enter our **cosmological** reality.

To illustrate, imagine that someone on a fictitious planet in our galaxy—call it Alpha—wants to communicate with us. He sends out a radio message that takes eight years to reach earth. Ten years before astronomer Jones receives the message, she marries. To all observers everywhere, Jones married *before* the message was sent to earth.

Suppose further that, five minutes after she receives the message, Jones records the event. Again, for all observers everywhere, Jones recorded the event *after* the message was beamed from Planet Alpha.

Now, imagine that, five years after the message was sent, astronomer Jones has a baby. Although it appears that she has had the baby after the message was sent from Planet Alpha, Einstein's theory of relativity does not allow us to say this without qualification.

To see this, suppose that a traveler departs Alpha bound for earth at the time the message was sent. The traveler is moving at a speed that, by our standards, is relatively slow. According to the traveler's measurements of time, Jones will appear to have had the baby *after* the message was transmitted. On the other hand, suppose another traveler departs Alpha when the message is sent, but travels at speeds approaching the speed of light. Instead of taking the long time the first traveler took to complete the journey, the second will complete the trip in, say, a little more than eight years, as we would calculate it. But because of the speed at which he is traveling it will seem to him that he has completed the trip in just a few months. When he is told that Jones had a baby three years before, he will naturally conclude that the baby was born well before the message was sent, since by his calculations it was sent only a few months before.

This illustration makes us wonder about the nature of time. Philosophers, psychologists, and scientists are divided on the question of whether time really exists or whether it is simply experience. Many philosophers and psychologists regard time as being dependent on consciousness. Without consciousness there can be no time, since there can be no experience of it. But if this is so, was there no time before consciousness? Many physicists claim that time is real. Einstein did. Our timepieces, they say, measure not only conscious experience but time itself.

Relativity also leaves us wondering whether it is possible to move ahead in time. It is commonly thought that we move into the future at a constant speed over which we have no control. But what if we accelerate to speeds approaching the speed of light? Can we not, in theory, move millions of years ahead in time? This question provokes further speculation about the space through which we would travel—about the size of the universe. Einstein claims that our universe curves back on itself. If it is finite, then what lies "beyond" it? A source for further ponderings is the question of what life might exist "out there" in space. Astronomer Harlow Shapley says *"We are not alone* in the universe." He claims that there are "a hundred million planetary systems suitable for organic life." And he considers that a modest estimate.

Finally, we must also wonder whether something can exist outside time and, if so, whether we can be aware of it. Since apparently either we live within a time frame or a time frame "lives" within us, it seems that we can never have knowledge of what exists outside one of our essential dimensions. But, of course, we cannot be sure.

Reflection   Suppose that living beings in another planetary system contacted us. What do you think they might be like? What might our reaction be?

CONCLUSIONS

Theoretical science raises a number of issues with respect to self. First, what kind of universe do we inhabit? Is it orderly or capricious? Scientific evidence suggests that it is orderly. We seek to discover the nature of this order and our own place in it. Even more important, if the universe is orderly, we are more likely to see order in our own lives. At the same time, we must also account for the nature of this orderliness. Are the world and its inhabitants mechanistic or teleological (teleology being the claim that purpose, goal, or direction is part of the necessary nature of things)?

As we have noted, the twentieth century is witnessing the collapse of the Newtonian world view. More and more scientists view the universe as something unfixed and changing, as an evolutionary process. This outlook suggests that the individual may play an active, purposeful role in the shaping and direction of things. In brief, we are not bound by immutable mechanical laws to the degree we once thought. We are parts not of a fixed and stationary universe but of one in which novelty, creativity, and purpose play parts.

Other considerations pertaining to self arise. Previously, in discussing matter, scientists generally made the Lockean distinction between primary and secondary qualities. The primary qualities, like extension, solidity, and motion, were thought to be objective. The secondary qualities, like color, taste, and sound, were thought to be subjective. In other words, primary qualities existed in things themselves; secondary qualities existed in the minds of those who perceived and experienced them. This was the nature of physical things.

Today the distinction between primary and secondary is less clear. Instead, scientists talk about energy or force, which they do not consider matter at all. They do not deny the existence of matter or its properties, but they provide a fresh perspective for us to view our place in the world. The distinctions between knower and known, subject and object, self and other are no longer satisfactory. Rather than a division there seems to be a harmony, a complementary relationship, among all things, including people.

At the same time, perhaps never before has the role of the self as knower been more uncertain. In the past, the self was thought to know the world generally as it was. Now, because of the influence of relativity, we wonder if the self alters what it observes—if the standpoint of the observer affects the object of observation. We have always known that our minds interpret the world. Now we wonder if they play a role in creating it.

Finally, although we take up the question of values elsewhere, we should not ignore here the moral implications of the present technological capabilities of applied science. Earlier we pondered the question of the android, noting that it was still a problem more of fiction than of science. But genetic engineering—that is, the application of scientific principles to the design, construction, and operation of efficient human systems—has become a problem of science. Equally real is the capacity to produce a group of genetically identical cells descended asexually from a common ancestor—that is, a clone. Our options in using these capabilities, as well as psychological behaviorism, organ transplants, subliminal language, and so on, raise questions of values. So do the major problems that will confront us in the next 25 years: burgeoning populations, depletion of natural resources, maldistribution of goods, threats of nuclear war. Although we shall apply scientific knowledge to many of these problems, we should not forget the tendency of scientists to focus exclusively on quantitative, mathematical, and objective elements at the expense of the human element. As the problems worsen, the temptation to do this will increase. Consequently, the next quarter-century will probably see conflict between what we would like to do and what we must do, between our ideals and our obligations, between humanism and technocracy.

By **humanism** we mean the philosophical view that accepts humans as the primary source of meaning and value. A technocracy is a political and social system controlled by scientific technicians. Generally, technocracies put things before people. Much of our society is, perhaps necessarily, technocratic. But the question is: must we and are we prepared to abandon all humanistic values in favor of technocratic values? It is by keeping questions like these open that philosophy ensures that science does not overlook the human's place in the scheme of things, whatever that place may be.

SUMMARY

We opened the chapter by noting that science strongly influences how we see ourselves. To acquire knowledge, science uses a methodology that results in claims of probability. Many of these claims raise philosophical questions. Our knowledge of the microscopic world of subatomic particles, for example, leaves us wondering about the nature of reality, including self. Cosmological speculation raises questions about the nature and cause of the universe's origin, whether there are additional universes and whether the universe has purpose, and precisely what our position in the universe is. Theories about time cause speculation about its nature and reality—whether we are limited by a dimension we ourselves have created. These ponderings force us to reexamine ourselves and our place in the universe.

MAIN POINTS

1. "Pure" or "basic" science refers to a quantitative and objective knowledge of nature; "applied" science refers to the application of that knowledge.
2. Philosophy and science share much of the same methodology; philosophy reflects the science of its day and integrates scientific findings.
3. Scientific method is a way of investigation based on collecting, analyzing, and interpreting data to determine the most probable explanation they suggest.
4. Analogy, cause, and hypothesis are instrumental in the scientific method.
5. An analogy is strengthened by the number of similar instances, the number of likenesses the instances share, and by dissimilarities. It is weakened by disanalogies.
6. John Stuart Mill formulated five methods for establishing probable causation: Agreement, Difference, Joint Method of Agreement and Difference, Concomitant Variation, and Residue.
7. A good hypothesis should be relevant, compatible with accepted knowledge, testable, predictive, and simple.
8. Scientific method is limited by these facts: (1) we can learn only what the tools allow us to reach; (2) we can learn only what the tools are designed to show; (3) we may, through classification, ignore significant individual differences; (4) we may ignore the characteristics of the whole unit that the individual parts do not show; and (5) we are limited by our own physical and intellectual capabilities.
9. Our knowledge of nature is both empirical—dependent on sense observation and on experiences—and *a priori*, seeming not to

rely on observation. Empirical knowledge leaves us with probability, not certainty; *a priori* knowledge leaves us pondering the precise relationship between logical and mathematical explanations of nature and nature itself.

10. Evidence current today indicates that reality is nonmaterial.

11. Three theories have come forth to explain why matter in the cosmos appears to be moving away from us: the big-bang theory, Hoyle's steady-state theory, and the pulsating-cosmos theory (currently considered the most reputable).

12. Time is relative.

13. Philosophy can make a unique contribution to current civilization by bridging the widening gap between humanism and technocracy.

14. Theoretical scientific discoveries make us wonder whether there are order and purpose in our lives, whether we affect what we know, whether we are part of a complementary relationship that holds among all things, and whether we help create the world we know.

15. The technological capabilities of applied science in areas such as genetic engineering, psychological behaviorism, and organ transplants have serious implications for the individual.

SECTION EXERCISES

Scientific Method

1. Using the criteria by which you judge the worth of any hypothesis, evaluate Ayer's, Hume's, and Spencer's analogies.

2. Reread the dialogues in Chapters 1, 4, 5, and 7 and note any arguments by analogy. Are they good ones?

3. Can you legitimately draw analogies between the following?
   a. a timepiece and the universe
   b. football and politics
   c. love and war
   d. the human body and a machine

4. Although she has disliked the last couple of novels she read, Karen decides to read another, expecting again to be disappointed. For each of the following statements, decide whether its addition would strengthen, weaken, or have no effect on Karen's analogical argument (her expectation that she will be disappointed).
   a. The same author has written this novel.
   b. The last two novels were about war. This one is not.
   c. The last two novels were hardbacks. This one is a paperback.
   d. The last two novels had no female characters. This one has several.
   e. The last two novels were best-sellers. This one is not.

5. You have taken two philosophy courses and found them exciting. So you sign up for another, expecting the same excitement. For each of the following statements, decide whether its addition would strengthen, weaken, or have no effect on your positive feeling about philosophy courses.
    a. All three classes are taught by different professors.
    b. The first two classes were taught by Professor Brown; the third is taught by Professor Jones.
    c. The first two classes met at 8:30 A.M.; this one will meet at 2:30 P.M.
    d. While taking the first two philosophy courses, you had also taken and enjoyed literature, history, psychology, and physics.
    e. A close friend took the first two classes with you but will not be taking this one.

Mill's Methods of Establishing Probable Cause

Analyze the following in terms of Mill's methods:

1. Eight students ate lunch in the college cafeteria. Each then broke out in hives.
    a. Although they ate different foods, all drank milk. Therefore, milk was the cause of the hives.
    b. Since a ninth student did not eat the same food, drink milk, or break out in hives, these facts strengthen the conclusion that milk caused the problem.
    c. All eight students ate strawberries for breakfast. So perhaps strawberries caused the hives.
    d. Four of the eight students had two helpings of strawberries for breakfast, and their hives were more severe than those who had just one helping. So the strawberries must have caused the hives.
2. In an intensive-care unit at a local hospital, 15 out of 20 patients died during a 30-day period. Nurse Nightingale attended to all 15.
    a. Nurse Nightingale cared for the patients inadequately.
    b. Nurse Nightingale also attended to the five patients that did not die. Therefore, her care was not inadequate.
    c. The 15 who died all voiced strong desires to die in the weeks before their deaths. Therefore, their deaths were caused by an unwillingness to live.
    d. The five who lived also voiced desires to die. Therefore, an unwillingness to live was not the cause of death.
    e. The 15 who died were all on the same medication. That medication caused their deaths.

     f.   Those on the heaviest dosages of the medication were the first to die. The medication was clearly the cause of the deaths.

3.   In one week, five out of six planes crashed while flying over the ocean.

     a.   The five were testing a new Shell gasoline additive; the sole survivor was not. Shell gasoline caused the loss of the planes.

     b.   Hundreds of other planes use Shell. So Shell gasoline could not have been the cause.

     c.   But the five planes lost were testing a new Shell additive. So Shell could have been the cause.

     d.   All five planes had faulty fuel pumps. Therefore, the fuel pumps, not Shell, caused the crashes.

     e.   Each plane exploded only when soaring to 40,000 feet and exceeding the speed of sound. Therefore, altitude and speed caused the losses.

4.   Where you have established probable causation in the statements above, do you have a sufficient condition, a necessary condition, or both?

Hypothesis

1.   In terms of the criteria for a good hypothesis, which of the following are probable explanations for the Watergate affair? Is any one more probable than the others?

     a.   political axe-grinding

     b.   campaign funding

     c.   moral weakness

     d.   anti-Vietnam War dissent

     e.   increasing executive power

2.   In terms of the criteria for a good hypothesis, which of the following are probable explanations for the increase in crimes of violence? Is any one more probable than the others?

     a.   increasing unemployment

     b.   maldistribution of wealth

     c.   moral decay

     d.   the U.S. Supreme Court's "soft decisions"

     e.   overpopulation

3.   In terms of the criteria for a good hypothesis, which of the following are probable explanations for the origin of human knowledge?

     a.   the senses alone

     b.   reason alone

     c.   reason imposing order on sense data

     d.   a consciousness of which we are not fully aware

4. In terms of the criteria for a good hypothesis, which of the following are the probable constituents of reality?
   a. matter
   b. nonmatter
   c. being
   d. there is no single constituent
5. In terms of the criteria for a good hypothesis, which of the following best describes "self"?
   a. rational
   b. divine
   c. mechanical
   d. existential
   e. nonexistent

Our Knowledge of Nature

1. Which of the following statements are empirical? Which are *a priori?*
   a. Everything with size has shape.
   b. A thing cannot be in two places at the same time.
   c. Every particle of matter in the universe attracts every other particle with a force varying inversely with the square of the distance and directly with the product of the masses (Newton's Law of Universal Gravitation).
   d. It is proper to keep a promise.
   e. The sum of two prime numbers will always be an even number.
   f. If X occurs before Y and Y before Z, then X occurs before Z.
   g. December is the last month of the year.
   h. Two atoms of hydrogen combine with one atom of oxygen to form water.
   i. Hot air rises.
   j. Light travels at 186,000 miles per second.

ADDITIONAL EXERCISES

1. Philosophy invariably reflects the science of its age. As we noted earlier, two prevailing twentieth-century philosophies are existentialism/phenomenology and linguistic analysis. How do these philosophies reflect advances in modern science?
2. What trends do you detect in the physical sciences that will affect philosophy?
3. In what way is the problem of the "mechanical mate" illustrative of the relationship between science and philosophy? The problem of test-tube life? Of clones?

216 Chapter 7

4. Cryonics, the process of freezing a diseased body for thawing when a cure for its disease is available, has received some attention recently. What implications does this technique have for philosophy? For example, if a person were frozen for 50 years and then revived, would he or she still be the same person? Remember, the person has had no experiences in the interim.
5. The prospect of genetic engineering depresses as many people as it excites. What are its philosophical implications? For example, if your brain were so altered that you forgot the last five years of your life, or you lost an exceptional talent you once had and acquired one you did not have, would you be the same person?
6. Many people believe that if science has the capability of doing something, science should do it. For example, if it can fully produce test-tube life, it should; if it can alter genes to produce a superior race, it should. Do you agree?
7. What would you say is the main task facing philosophy in relation to science?
8. What aspects of contemporary society can you point to that illustrate the tension between humanism and technocracy?
9. What implications for philosophy does the area of extrasensory perception hold? Would it alter your idea of the nature of knowledge? Of reality? Which concept of reality among those discussed in this book do you think ESP would foster? How would it affect the way you perceive yourself and others?

PAPERBACKS FOR FURTHER READING

Anthony, Piers. *Macroscope.* New York: Avon, 1975. Suppose you could pass through a doorway that led beyond space and time. What would you find? That is the subject of this science fiction fantasy.

Barnett, Lincoln. *The Universe and Dr. Einstein.* New York: The New American Library (Mentor Books), 1957. This is a popular and valid sketch of philosophical concepts thrust upon us by twentieth-century science and a readable and informative account of Einstein's theory of relativity, including Einstein's views of God, religion, and mysticism.

Bronowski, Jacob. *Science and Human Values.* New York: Harper & Row, 1956. Bronowski contends that both science and art spring from human imagination, and that science cannot be divorced from its social and ethical implications.

Ellwood, Garcia Fay. *Psychic Visits to the Past.* New York: Signet, 1971. An investigation into the world of psychics who claim that they can move and have moved back and forth in time.

Gardner, Martin. *Relativity for the Million*. New York: Pocket Books, 1965. This is a lucid and entertaining account of twentieth-century science and its philosophical implications, full of fine examples and illustrations.

Kuhn, Thomas. *The Structure of Scientific Revolutions*. Chicago: University of Chicago Press, 1962. Not only does Kuhn clearly portray the nature of scientific changes and upheavals, but he places them within a social framework that makes for a readable and appealing work. A nice companion piece to this book is Arthur Koestler's *The Sleepwalkers* (New York: Grosset & Dunlap, 1963), in which the author traces the history of cosmology from the ancient Babylonians through the modern age.

Rosenfeld, Albert. *The Second Genesis*. New York: Vintage, 1975. Rosenfeld gives a detailed account of the implications of current brain research. Although some of his forecasts are optimistic, others are chilling in their promise to alter the human and the human condition.

Toulmin, Stephen. *Foresight and Understanding: An Enquiry into the Aims of Science*. New York: Harper & Row, 1963. This book offers a philosophically directed investigation into the nature of science. In a concise and uncomplicated way, philosopher-scientist Toulmin argues that the goal of science is not only to predict but also to make intelligible.

Whitehead, Alfred North. *Science and the Modern World*. New York: The New American Library (Mentor Books), 1948. This account of the historical development and impact of science and mathematics includes discussions on the nature of God and the relationship between science and religion. This work is challenging, but well worth the effort.

Philosophy and Religion

8

If "dead" matter has reared up this curious landscape of fiddling crickets, song sparrows and wondering men, it must be plain even to the most devoted materialist that the matter of which he speaks contains amazing if not dreadful power, and may not possibly be . . . [a] mask of many worn by the Great Face behind. —Loren Eiseley

Traditionally in the West there has been probably no greater influence on one's view of self than religion, which has fostered the view of the human as a divine being. The Judaic and the Christian religious traditions share the belief that what makes humans unique is that they share in a divine nature by possessing consciousness and the ability to love. We are creatures who stand midway between nature and spirit. We are on the one hand finite, bound to earth, and capable of sin. On the other, because we are partially spiritual, we are able to transcend nature and are capable of infinite possibilities. It is also primarily because of Western religion that we view ourselves as beings with a supernatural destiny, as possessing a life after death, as being immortal.

But religion has fostered beliefs, attitudes, and feelings not only about a supernatural dimension but also about this world. Thus, religious positions commonly circulate concerning various political, educational, and even economic questions. These positions are very influential in molding public opinion. In recent years, in fact, religions have become so socially directed that many traditionalists feel that religions are undergoing secularization—that is, becoming too worldly. Whether or not this charge is justified, the fact is that it is becoming increasingly difficult to define "religion," something we should attempt before examining precisely how religion relates to the issue of self.

219

RELIGION

When you hear the word *religion*, what do you think of? A church? A synagogue? Some belief? Indeed, religion includes many things: prayer, ritual, institutional organization, and so on. To define religion precisely is most difficult. Traditionally, the word has referred to a belief in God that is institutionalized and incorporated in the teachings of some religious body such as a church or synagogue. Some hold, however, that religion need not imply a belief in God. Buddhism, for example, although usually considered a religion, contains no belief in a personal God like the God of the Judaic and Christian traditions. Others claim that whatever anyone holds as the most important value in life is a religion, frequently finding expression outside religious institutions.

It is a little easier to note features of religion than to define it, although qualifications are still necessary. Religion continues to be one of humankind's dominant interests. Unlike science, it stresses personal commitment based on a meaningful relationship with that which is sacred, often a Supreme Being. Such commitment is generally founded on belief, although most religionists claim that belief divorced from reason is misguided. Feeling and emotion seem prominent in religion, although these too admittedly can mislead. Religion frequently finds expression through institutionalized ritual. Recent trends indicate, however, that many people feel that the emphasis on a symbolic object of devotion, ritualized through an organizational structure, has blurred religion's real import: a deep and personal experience with the object of one's chief loyalty.

In the last analysis, religion is not just an institution, a collection of doctrines, or a stylized ritual, although these have traditionally played an influential role in religion. Without exception religious leaders have spoken in terms of personal commitment, experience, and need. In so doing they have recognized the roots from which religion has sprung: our unending search for meaning and fulfillment. In this sense they have emphasized religious belief rather than religion.

In this chapter we shall have numerous occasions to speak of **religious belief.** We shall be using it in its most general sense, as the belief that there is an unseen order and that we can do no better than to be in harmony with this order. Likewise, when we use the term *religious experience*, we shall be referring to an experience of this unseen order and our individual place in it. When we do find this place, we feel an intense personal relationship with the rest of creation, perhaps even with a Creator. In this respect, we all seek a religious experience; we all search for an internal peace rooted in a harmonious personal relationship with all other living things. Religious belief and experience, then, are intimately bound up with the issue of self.

Just where do we find such experience today? Some find it in traditional religious concepts, such as the existence of a personal God who listens to and answers prayer, who rewards the faithful and punishes the unworthy. Others, finding such a belief irrational, relate to the divine without having to relate to a Supreme Being. They claim that religious experience is an intimately personal encounter with the ground of all being, with the source of all reality. Still others find a kind of religious experience in psychedelic drugs, through the expansion of consciousness—that is, the experience of reality as they are unaccustomed to normally. Finally, there are many who turn to Eastern thought—Hinduism and Buddhism, for example.

In this chapter we shall explore these and related concerns by thinking philosophically about religion. That is what the philosophy of religion is about. Although such a study ordinarily includes many aspects of religion, including God, immortality, salvation, creation, and all particular religions, we shall focus instead on the nature and varieties of religious experience, on the many ways in which individuals claim to discover their places in the cosmos.

THEISM

The most common way for people of a Judaeo-Christian culture to find their places in the scheme of things is in a relationship with a personal God—through theistic belief.

We may define **theism** as a belief in a personal God, **omnipotent, omnipresent,** and **omniscient,** who intervenes in the lives of His creation. This is probably the God most of us have been raised to accept, and the basis for our religious feelings and experiences. This God is the basis for the view of the human as divine, as having an immortal soul and a supernatural destiny. This concept has perhaps never been under such intense attack as today. Even theologians are asking whether the believer can any longer believe in this traditional God: a single all-powerful, all-knowing, and all-good God who, having created life, actively participates in the lives of His creatures by listening to and answering prayer. They are questioning an assumption that has centuries of tradition behind it, that is a cornerstone of the lives of many people today, and that has produced not only our religious beliefs but our ways of perceiving ourselves and the world around us.

Wilbur Daniel Steele, in his short story "The Man Who Saw through Heaven," portrays the dimensions of the problem facing the contemporary theistic believer. In it he depicts Herbert Diana, a self-educated man who, like many theists, had accepted a conventional amount of scientific facts as more proof of "what God can do when He puts His mind to it." Intellectually, Diana had accepted the fact of a spherical earth

"... deep down in his heart he knew 'that
the world lay flat from modern Illinois to
ancient Palestine ...'"

speeding through space, but deep down in his heart he knew "that the
world lay flat from modern Illinois to ancient Palestine, and that the sky
above it, blue by day and by night festooned with guiding stars for wise
men, was the nether side of a floor on which the resurrected trod."[1] How
would such a man of simple faith react to a vision of the heavens he has
never believed possible, to a look through an incredibly powerful telescope into an ink-black sky that he has always viewed as the floor of
heaven? To a vision of the enormity of the universe? How would his
simple belief in a personal God stand up and, with it, the sudden realization that his theistic God must also be personally and completely
involved in an infinity of galactic universes and lives? For the first time
in his life Herbert Diana's faith is tested. His well-ordered medieval
world concept has to deal with twentieth-century realities. His simple
idea of a heaven "up there" and a hell "down there," of a God who is
personally concerned with each person's immortal destiny, and of the
infinite importance of a single soul and of what that soul chooses to
do—all these staples of his belief suddenly shrink in the vastness of
what his eyes have seen and his mind cannot forget.

In a sense we are all Dianas, for we live in a period that pits traditional religious concepts against the growing weight of scientific fact.

---

[1]Wilbur Daniel Steele. "The Man Who Saw through Heaven," in *The Search for Personal
Freedom* (3rd ed.). Neal Cross, Leslie Lindou, and Robert Lamm, Eds. Dubuque, Iowa:
W. C. Brown, 1968, p. 27.

Can we, *should* we believe in the God of our ancestors, or must we modify this belief, perhaps abandon it? Consider, as Diana must, the millions of solar systems we view as stars. Imagine how many millions of satellites there must be that at some time have supported organic life. Imagine how many millions of untold populations of other creatures, perhaps grotesque by our standards, but creatures nonetheless. Then consider other clusters of universes apart from ours. And consider further that "all these, all the generations of these enormous and microscopic beings harvested through a time beside which the life span of our earth is as a second in a million centuries: all these brought to rest for an eternity to which the time in itself is a watch tick—all crowded to rest pellmell, thronged, serried, packed to suffocation in layers unnumbered light-years deep."[2] Do we know the God who rules over such universes?

Today science has brought many of us, like Herbert Diana, to ask not only if we believe in a traditional God but if there is any God at all. Many theories try to explain why people believe in God, but theologians have traditionally argued for God's existence on rational and empirical grounds. We shall briefly consider three of the more prominent arguments they have presented for God's existence: ontological, causal, and design.

Reflection   Put a drop of water in a spoon and study it for ten minutes. Let your mind roam. Afterward, record what feelings and thoughts you had.

The Ontological Argument

In the eleventh century, St. Anselm (1033–1109) offered the first known argument that attempted to prove the existence of God. It is unique because it relies on reason alone. Later proofs would use experience of the things of the world to argue for God's existence, but Anselm held that the mind by itself could arrive at such a realization.

God, he reasoned, is "that which none greater can be conceived." Now, what if God were just an idea? If he were, we could easily conceive of something greater: a God who actually existed. Therefore, Anselm concluded, if God is "that than which none greater can be conceived," then God must exist.

A number of theologians and philosophers since Anselm revived his argument, including St. Thomas Aquinas (1224–1274) and René Descartes. But more have attacked it. Immanuel Kant was one. He

---

[2]Steele. "The Man Who Saw through Heaven." p. 28.

claimed that the concept of an absolutely necessary being is not proved by the fact that reason apparently requires it.

To understand Kant's criticism, ask yourself this: under what conditions will a triangle have three sides? Obviously, when and where there is a triangle. In other words, *if* there is a triangle, it has three sides. But *if* is conditional; that is, what follows it may not be. "If there is a triangle" does not imply that there necessarily *is* a triangle. Likewise, if there is a perfect being, then a perfect being exists. But this does not mean a perfect being does exist. Kant claims that Anselm is defining God into existence—that he is asking us to form a concept of a thing in such a way as to include existence within the scope of its meaning. Undoubtedly, Anselm would object that it is contradictory to posit a triangle and yet reject its three angles. Kant would agree. But he would add that there is no contradiction in rejecting the triangle *along with* its three angles. "Likewise of the concept of an absolutely necessary being. If its existence is rejected, we reject the thing itself with all its predicates; and no question of contradiction can then arise."

But a perfect being is unique. Because Anselm thought nonexistence was an imperfection and therefore inconsistent with the nature of a perfect being, he argued that a perfect being must exist. And he was right, assuming that existence adds to a thing. But imagine a perfect companion. Attribute to it all the properties you wish that will make it perfect. Then ask yourself: does its existence add anything to the concept? The point is that to assert existence is not to add a property but to assert a relationship between the thing conceived and the world. In other words, you do not add anything to the creature of your fantasy by positing its existence; you merely establish its relationship to other things. It seems, then, that Kant is right: "When I think a being as the supreme reality, without any defect, the question still remains whether it exists or not."

Reflection

1. List all the attributes you would want in a perfect mate. Do it now, before reading further. Is *existence* among your mate's attributes? If not, why not?
2. Psychologists tell us that fantasy often plays a stronger role in our lives than reality. *Playboy* magazine offers a good example. Does the "playmate of the month" exist in the form in which *Playboy* portrays her? Many readers undoubtedly relate to her more actively than they would to living women. In what sense is the playmate's *nonexistence,* except as a fantasy, necessary to her being?

The Cause Argument

After Anselm's ontological argument for God's existence, the next important attempts to establish a proof are to be found in Thomas Aquinas's *Summa Theologica,* in which he offers five proofs. Unlike Anselm, Aquinas tried to rely not just on reason but on experience as well. His proofs move from observations about the world to the conclusion that the world cannot have such characteristics unless a God exists.

One of his best-known proofs is called the "first-cause argument," or the cosmological argument. Aquinas argues deductively that every event has a cause and that every cause, in turn, has a cause. This series must either continue infinitely or have a beginning, in which case it would have a first cause. Aquinas dismisses the possibility of an **infinite regress** and so concludes that there is a first cause, namely God. Why does he eliminate the possibility of an infinite regress of causes? Because in a series of causes, the first is the cause of the intermediate and the intermediate is the cause of the ultimate. Therefore, says Thomas, "to take away the cause is to take away the effect. Therefore, if there be no first cause among causes, there will be no ultimate, nor any intermediate cause. But if in cause it is possible to go on to infinity, there will be no first cause neither will there be an ultimate effect, nor any intermediate causes."[3] He concludes that such a case would be impossible; therefore there must be a first cause, God.

But why could a series of causes not regress infinitely, as the number system does? Thomas reasoned that an infinite regress might account for the individual links in the causal chain, but not for the chain itself. Is he right? Suppose a friend visits you at college. You wish to show her around the campus. You take her to the library, the humanities building, the science labs, the cafeteria, and so on until she sees the entire college. After this tour, she asks "But where is the college?" You might find that a silly question, since you had already shown her the college by showing her the parts that composed it. In a similar way David Hume questioned the cosmological argument: "Did I show you the particular causes of each individual in a collection of twenty particles of matter, I should think it very unreasonable, should you afterwards ask me, what was the cause of the whole twenty. For this is sufficiently explained in explaining the cause of the parts."[4] Hume is

[3]Thomas Aquinas. *Summa Theologica.* Quoted in *Philosophy of Religion.* William I. Rowe and William J. Wainwright, Eds. New York: Harcourt, Brace Jovanovich, 1973, p. 118.

[4]David Hume. *Dialogues Concerning Natural Religion.* N. Kemp Smith, Ed. Edinburgh: Nelson, 1947, Part V, p. 18.

arguing that the individual links in the causal chain find cause in their immediate predecessors. This fact is enough to account for the chain itself. He would further charge that the whole notion of cause is so fuzzy as to not allow any deductions based on the assumption that we do, in fact, observe causes.

But even if every event must have a cause, why stop with God? The notion of an "uncaused cause" seems to contradict the assumption that everything has a cause. And even if there is such an uncaused cause, why must it be God?

A number of contemporary Thomists (thinkers who generally agree with Thomas Aquinas) have modified this first-cause argument. For them, the endless series that the argument dismisses is not a regress of events in time but a regress of explanations. As John Hick interprets their position: "If fact A is made intelligible by its relation to facts B, C and D (which may be antecedent to or contemporary with A), and if each of these is in turn rendered intelligible by other facts, at the back of the complex there must be a reality which is self-explanatory, whose existence constitutes the ultimate explanation of the whole. If no such reality exists, the universe is a mere unintelligible brute fact."[5] But how do we know that the universe is not "a mere unintelligible brute fact"? The argument appears to present a false dilemma: *either* a first cause exists *or* the universe makes no sense. It also assumes that causal conditions make things intelligible—while failing to answer Hume's objection that causes are merely observed sequences, or Kant's objection that cause is a mental mold, something the mind imposes on reality.

Reflection   God is said to cause, in the sense of *create:* to make out of nothing. Let us presume that there is a God and that there is nothing. God says "Let there be life" and suddenly universes are born. How could you prove that God's utterance *caused* the universe—that is, created it?

The Design Argument

The most popular of the arguments for God's existence has been the proof from design, often called the teleological argument. Simply put, the proof from design argues that the order and purpose manifest in the working of things demands a God. Even when evolutionists offer an explanation for such apparent order, supporters of the design argument reply "Yes, but why did things evolve in *this* way and not in some

---

[5]John Hick. *Philosophy of Religion.* Englewood Cliffs, N.J.: Prentice-Hall, 1973, p. 21.

other?" Traditionally a prominent argument for God's existence, the design proof has currency even today among some biologists, such as Edmund W. Sinnott, and some theologians, such as Robert E. D. Clark. In 1802, theologian William Paley presented one of the best-known expositions of it.

As was the custom of religious thinkers of his day, Paley called on a long list of examples from the sciences to demonstrate his argument. The migration of birds, the instincts of other animals, the adaptability of species to various environments, and the human's ability to forecast based on probable causation all suggested a plan and a planner.

More recent writers often think similarly. How, they wonder, can we otherwise explain our continued safety from the two zones of high-intensity particulate radiation trapped in the earth's magnetic field and surrounding the planet (the Van Allen Belt)? As one writer says, "the ozone gas layer is mighty proof of the Creator's forethought. Could anyone attribute this device to a chance evolutionary process? A wall which prevents death to every living thing, just the right thickness, and exactly the correct defense, gives every evidence of plan."[6]

But critics have asked: does the appearance of order necessitate conscious design? The order in the universe, they say, could have occurred by chance, by accident, through an incredibly long period of evolution. Hume argues that in an infinite amount of time a finite number of particles in random motion must eventually effect a stable order. After all, it is impossible to imagine a universe without some design. In fact, by definition a universe must have design.

As Darwin later contended, the life we observe around us has won in the "struggle for survival"; the fit have survived, the unfit have perished. Through a process of natural selection, in which those that can adapt survive and the rest die, a stability in things comes to pass. Concerning our safety under an ozone umbrella, both Hume and Darwin would point out that it is not explained by a God who made things and then shielded them but by an evolutionary fact: that only life that adjusted to the precise level of ultraviolet radiation penetrating this ozone has survived. In other words, life has adjusted to the ozone; ozone has not sustained life.

Reflection Is it possible to imagine a universe without order? What would it be like? How would it be different from the one we know?

6Arthur I. Brown. *Footprints of God.* Findlay, Ohio: Fundamental Truth Publishers, 1943, p. 102.

Objections to Theism

The traditional proofs for God's existence, as we have seen, have obvious flaws. There are additional serious objections to the theistic position, of which the major one is the problem of evil.

We continue to be beset by all kinds of problems: sickness, poverty, suffering, death. Yet theism insists that there is an all-good, all-knowing God. Is this not at least paradoxical? In raising precisely this problem, Hume recalls the questions of the ancient Greek Epicurus:

Is he [God] willing to prevent evil, but not able? Then is he impotent? Is he able, but not willing? then is he malevolent? Is he both able and willing? whence then is evil?[7]

There have been a number of attempts to escape the horns of this dilemma. Augustine, for one, argues that evil is a negative thing—that is, the absence of good. To be real, said Augustine, is to be perfect. Since only God is perfect, only God is wholly real. God's creation, therefore, being finite and limited, must contain incomplete goodness—that is, evil. But this argument seems to dodge the issue. Call sickness lack of health, if you wish, and war lack of peace; the fact remains that people experience pain and suffering, which they commonly regard as evil. No amount of word play can ease their situation.

Others argue, on the other hand, that evil is necessary for good, that only through evil can good be achieved. It is true that in many instances good seems to depend on evil, as in the case of having to suffer surgical pain to rid one's body of disease. In such cases there seems no other way that good can be effected. But to say that God can bring about good in no other way than through inflicting or tolerating pain is to deny God's omnipotence.

But the most common and serious attempt to escape the problem of evil is to claim human freedom as the cause of evil. Since we are free, we are free to do evil as well as good. Even an omnipotent God could not make us free but not free to do evil, since this would be contradictory. Therefore, evil results from free human choice.

But there are several problems with this argument. First, it does not account for natural evils: earthquakes, droughts, tornadoes. Humans exercise no control over these. So the argument can pertain only to moral evils—that is, those perpetrated by humans on other creatures: war, murder, torture. Undoubtedly we are free to do this evil, but why did an all-powerful God enable us to do such terrible things? After all, if He is all-powerful, He could have made us differently. Already we are vulnerable, limited creatures. Why not make us unable

---

[7]Hume. *Dialogues Concerning Natural Religion.* Part X, p. 198.

to do evil? Perhaps we do not really understand the nature of evil; what we perceive as evil may in God's eyes be good. But if this is so, even more complex questions arise concerning the nature and morality of the Supreme Being. We are also left puzzled about what goodness itself really is.

Still other problems beset theism. One concerns God's all-knowing nature. If God is all-knowing, He is aware of what is going on. But can He be aware of our travail without suffering with us? Christians say that is precisely why God became man. But how can the timeless and unchanging become incarnate in our world of historical change? In addition, God's knowledge of our changing world is said to be itself unchanging. How is this possible? Traditional theism, furthermore, speaks of a God that transcends creation; God is said to be different from and superior to what He made. But isn't perfect knowledge contingent on knowing something "inside out"? A parent, for example, never completely knows its offspring, for it can never fully know what that offspring feels, thinks, desires; only the offspring can. If God has perfect knowledge, isn't He then a composite of the many things that make up reality? But if this is so, how can God at the same time be separate and distinct from His creation?

These objections are real and pressing. Today's thoughtful believer cannot write them off saying "Ours not to reason why." Such a traditional response is still adequate for some. But even many believers answer such a glib explanation with the question "Then why is it ours to reason at all?" Perhaps this is the most telling objection of all, for it wonders why God would endow us with reason and then restrict our use of it. As a result of these concerns, some reflective theists today often find pantheism and panentheism more comfortable than strict theism.

PANTHEISM AND PANENTHEISM

Pantheism means literally "all God." It is the belief that everything is God and God is everything. In brief, God and the universe are identical. Pantheists see God as an immense interconnected system of nature, in much the same way as did philosopher Baruch Spinoza (1632–1677). Spinoza reasoned that, if God is all-powerful, all-knowing, and all-present, as traditionalists claim, then God must be everything. If God is everything, He can't be separate from anything. If God is all-powerful, there can be no world outside him; hence all of nature, everything that is, must be God.

One version of pantheism sees God's nature as not possibly being anything other than what it is, since God is complete. But how can God be constituted of incomplete, changing parts, as we see manifest in nature? Spinoza's pantheism perceives things as necessary—that is, not able to be otherwise. If this is so, what happens to free choice? What happens to the human as an experience-confronting, choice-making entity?

Peculiar to the twentieth century is a brand of theism known as **panentheism,** which attempts to merge theism and pantheism. Rather than believing that all is God, panentheists hold that all is *in* God. God interpenetrates everything, as in pantheism; but God is also transcendent. Developed by G. T. Fechner, Friedrich von Schelling, and Charles Peirce, panentheism sees God as a Supreme Being whose original nature is fixed, unchanging, and inclusive of all possibilities. But at the same time God has a historical nature, one that exists in time as a growing, changing, expanding dimension. God, therefore, is a unity of diversity, Being and Becoming, the One and the Many. He contains all contrast with Himself.

Still, problems remain. How can such a fusion of opposites occur? Did God create His temporal nature? What precisely is the relationship between God's finite nature and His infinite nature? Was God "compelled" to exist in time? Panentheism may be more coherent than theism or pantheism, but it seems to raise further complexities that require an almost mystical grounding for acceptance.

The problems of establishing a panentheistic, pantheistic, or theistic God have led many to disbelieve God's existence. Such disbelief generally takes the form of atheism or agnosticism.

ATHEISM

Atheism denies the major claims of all varieties of theism. In the words of atheist Ernest Nagel, "Atheism denies the existence . . . of a self-consistent, omnipotent, omniscient, righteous and benevolent being who is distinct from and independent of what has been created."[8] Philosophical atheists generally share a number of characteristics. First, although they often differ on how claims to knowledge must be established, they agree that sense observation and public verification are instrumental and that scientific method is the measure of knowledge and truth. As Nagel states, "It is indeed this commitment to the use of an empirical method which is the final basis of the atheistic critique of theism." Thus, by means of respectable methodology, the atheist claims to explain what theists can account for only through introducing an unverifiable hypothesis about a deity.

Atheists reject **animism**—the assumptions that there exist supernatural creatures in the form of spirits and that these creatures exercise

---

[8]Ernest Nagel. Quoted in *Encounter: An Introduction to Philosophy*. Ramona Cormier, Ewing Chinn, and Richard Lineback, Eds. Glenview, Ill.: Scott, Foresman, 1970, p. 224.

control over the natural world. On the contrary, atheists deal exclusively with the natural, physical world. If we are to make any progress, they say, we must focus our attention on the properties and structures of identifiable objects located in space. The variety of things we experience in the universe can be accounted for in terms of the change things undergo when relating with other things. At the same time, there is no discernible unifying pattern of change. "Nature," says Nagel, "is ineradicably plural, both in respect to the individuals occurring in it as well as in respect to the processes in which things become involved." In short, "An atheistic view of things is a form of materialism."

With their emphasis on empiricism and the physical world, atheists generally accept a utilitarian code of ethics. Such a code, as we shall see in the next chapter, simply means that something is good if it produces good consequences and bad if it produces bad consequences. There is no code of morality apart from the results of human actions. The final standard of moral evaluation is no commandment, no divinely inspired code of conduct, but the satisfaction of the complex needs of the human creature.

As a result of these viewpoints, atheists focus directly on the world here and now, and they generally resist authoritarianism and stress individualism. Traditionally, they have opposed moral codes that try to repress human impulses in favor of some otherworldly ideal. At the same time, this stress on the individual has not made atheists forget the role that institutions can play in advancing human goals. Because atheists cannot fortify their moral positions with promises of immortality, threats of damnation, or guarantees of righteous recompense, they must rely on what Nagel calls "a vigorous call to intelligent activity —activity for the sake of realizing human potentialities and for eliminating whatever stands in the way of such realization." But there are objections to atheism.

Objections to Atheism

One obvious objection is that the atheistic claim that God does not exist can no more be proved than can the theistic claim that God exists. To prove their claim, atheists must empirically verify it. But this is not possible if God, by their own claim, does not exist to begin with, since it is not logically possible to claim anything about a nonexistent entity. To illustrate, try proving that unicorns, fairy godmothers, leprechauns, or gremlins do not exist. How would you do it? Obviously, the fact that you cannot does not imply that they do exist (an argument from ignorance). But if you claim they do not exist, you should be able to prove it.

But most people are not so analytical. Instead, they charge atheism with abandoning humankind to its own devices, of ignoring the persis-

"... try proving that unicorns, fairy
godmothers, leprechauns, or gremlins
do not exist."

tent belief in a force superior to humankind, a force that often leaves us with hope, confidence, faith, and love in the face of apparently insurmountable troubles. To strip us of these qualities is to leave us ill-equipped to cope with life and, more important, morally bankrupt.

Immanuel Kant, although arguing against many of the proofs for God's existence, maintained that there was no basis for morality in the absence of a God from whom all good emanates. Without such a figure, what is the point of trying to do good? Why not just act according to your own impulses, according to your own idea of what is good or bad, or according to what is fashionable? If there is no God, notions of right and wrong are inconclusive. This fact dooms us, in turn, to ignorance, uncertainty, and anxiety. In brief, without God we have no basis for evaluating our actions. Thus Kant argued for the existence of God.

AGNOSTICISM

Having studied the arguments for and against the existence of God, many thinkers claim that neither side is convincing. As a result, they say they just don't know. The position that claims not to know whether or not God exists is **agnosticism.** The nineteenth-century English scientist Thomas Huxley was one famous agnostic.

For Huxley, agnosticism expressed absolute faith in the validity of the principle "that it is wrong for a man to say that he is certain of the objective truth of any proposition unless he can produce evidence which logically justifies that certainty."[9] Huxley would find sympathy among contemporary linguistic analysts, who go further and assert that the propositions "God exists" and "God does not exist" are meaningless because there is no possible way of verifying these claims. Since we cannot even conceive of a way to verify these statements, both are meaningless. The linguistic analyst is much harsher than Huxley ever intended to be. For Huxley the statements were at least meaningful, if insoluble. So he suspended judgment.

Objections to Agnosticism

Agnosticism, unlike atheism, need not prove any claim, for it makes none that demands verification. But it is still open to all the other objections to atheism. In addition, one can validly wonder whether one can suspend judgment on the question of whether God exists.

It is one thing to suspend judgment on whether or not unicorns exist, but another, it seems, when God is in question. Whether or not unicorns exist makes no difference in our lives, but this cannot be said of God. Just imagine how much is tied up in our belief or disbelief in God's existence. For many, absolute proof for or against God's existence would mean a different life-style—a different way of thinking, seeing, and behaving. But whatever position we take, we are probably assuming it as if there were absolute evidence for it, even though we admit there is none. And in all likelihood we are trying to live accordingly. To suspend judgment on the question seems to be avoiding the issue, because the question evidently does not allow such a response. In short, critics of agnosticism argue that we are faced not with a false dilemma but with a genuine one: we must believe either that God exists or that He does not.

In the last analysis, the existence or nonexistence of a theistic God cannot yet be proved. But lack of certain evidence does not make the question any less important, any more than our knowing what to study in college makes the issue of an academic major unimportant. The point is that, lacking sufficient evidence, most of us still believe or disbelieve. And the position we take affects how we see ourselves. Whether we see ourselves as surviving after death—of being immortal, being reborn, or experiencing resurrection—is a good example.

LIFE AFTER DEATH

Any person who is conscious of death has wondered: will I continue to live after I die? This question has occupied humankind from earliest times and

---

[9]Thomas Huxley. Quoted in Cormier, Chinn, and Lineback, Eds. *Encounter*, p. 227.

perhaps penetrates the issue of self more deeply than any other. For if we continue to live after death we must wonder about the state, form, and condition in which we shall exist, whether our present life will affect those aspects of the next life; whether the departed currently live among us; and whether contact between this world and the next is possible. The belief in personal survival after death is closely connected with a belief in God: if we believe God exists, it is easier to accept the idea of a life after death.

When speaking of personal survival after death, the term **immortality** invariably comes up. We can speak of immortality in several ways. First, there is biological immortality, the continuance of germ plasm despite death. In this sense, we are immortal. We are also immortal in the sense that we leave behind us a social legacy or contribution by which we are remembered and thereby continue to "live." Some people also speak of an impersonal immortality in which, upon physical death, the self merges with the unity of all things, a world soul or an Absolute. Versions of this belief are popular in Oriental religions, in which the self may, upon physical death, assume a different form: another human, an animal, even an insect. Plato subscribed to the doctrine of transmigration of souls, or **metempsychosis,** the passing of the soul into another body after death. But these beliefs are not what people in the West generally mean by immortality. Rather, they view survival after death as the continuance of personal identity in some world or realm other than the present earthly one. The issue, then, is whether the conscious self persists after death.

Although they are generally agreed on the existence of some kind of personal survival after death, religious leaders are divided over its nature. The source of the division stems from two traditions: the Greek and the Judaeo-Christian.

The Greek influence stems primarily from Plato, who first attempted to prove the existence of the soul or reason. Plato argued that the body belongs to the world known to us through our physical senses, and shares the nature of this world: change, impermanence, death. On the other hand, the soul, or reason, is related to the permanent unchanging realities we are aware of when contemplating not particular things but universal, eternal Ideas. Being related to this higher and lasting realm, the soul, unlike the body, is immortal. Upon death, therefore, those who have contemplated the eternal realities will discover that although their bodies have turned to dust their soul, or reason, will gravitate to the world of eternal Ideas.

The Judaeo-Christian tradition, in contrast, has generally substituted resurrection for immortality. Whereas Plato considered the soul immortal, the Jewish and Christian view, as found occasionally in the Old Testament and more often in the New Testament, is that the complete human—soul and body—may be resurrected by God. This belief posits the direct intervention of a theistic God and a special divine act of re-creation. The human is utterly dependent on the love of God to survive the extinction that death brings. Christians argue that there is evidence for resurrection in the New Testament. But the belief arises as a necessary part of the purpose of God, which holds humans as beings beyond natural mortality. It is argued that God would be contradicting Himself to have created humans for fellowship with Himself, only to have them extinguished and this purpose unfulfilled.

Apart from its religious aspects, the question of life after death has recently received new attention with the growing interest in **extrasensory perception,** the phenomenon of having experiences without relying on the normal senses. Although there are many facets of ESP, the one relevant to this discussion is **telepathy,** the name given to the inexplicable fact that sometimes a thought in one person's mind evidently causes a similar thought in another's mind, even though there appear to be no normal means of communication between them, and sheer coincidence has been ruled out. For example, one person will draw a geometric pattern on paper and then transmit an impression of it to someone in another room, who then reproduces a similar pattern on paper. Experiments have been designed to rule out the likelihood of chance coincidence in instances of telepathy. Joseph B. Rhine, of Duke University, and S. G. Soal, for example, have reported experimental results demonstrating the probability of chance coincidence in such cases as ranging from 100,000 to one to billions to one.[10] In the light of these findings it is hard to deny that some positive factor, and not just chance, is operating.

Just how telepathic communication works is unknown. So far, only negative conclusions have been reached. Telepathy does not seem to consist of physical radiation, such as radio waves, for distance has no bearing on telepathic communication. Neither does the telepathized thought leave the sender's consciousness to enter the receiver's, for frequently the sender is not even aware of the thought until it is brought to his attention, and the receiver often receives just a fragment of it. As a result some believe that, although on the conscious level our minds are exclusive of one another's, on the unconscious level we are constantly influencing one another. It is at this level that telepathy is believed to occur, particularly through the link of emotion or common interest that may exist between two especially close people. Telepathy may also throw some light on the issue of survival after death.

The Proceedings of the Society for Psychical Research in London contain many documented cases of the appearances of people who had recently died to people who were still unaware of their deaths. In the

---

[10]Joseph B. Rhine. *New Frontiers of the Mind*. New York: Farrar and Rinehart, 1937, p. 66.
    S. G. Soal. *The Experimental Situation in Psychical Research*. London: The Society for Psychical Research, 1947.

case of "ghosts"—apparitions of the dead—it has been established that there can be "meaningful hallucinations" whose source is telepathic. The classic example is of the woman who, while sitting by a lake, witnessed the figure of a man running toward the lake and throwing himself in. A few days later a man killed himself by doing precisely this. Presumably, as the man contemplated his suicide, the man's thought was telepathically projected onto the scene by the woman's mind.[11]

The Society for Psychical Research also reports that minds that operate in mediumistic trances, alleging to be the spirits of the departed, frequently provide information that the medium could not possibly know. How is this possible? Again, one currently popular theory is that the communication really results from telepathic contact between medium and client. This theory is dramatized in the case of two women who decided to test the spirits by affecting the personality of a completely imaginary character in an unpublished novel written by one of the women. Having filled their minds with all the characteristics of this fictitious person, they went to a medium, who proceeded to describe accurately the fictitious character as a spirit from the beyond and to report appropriate messages from him.[12] Thus, although ESP is opening fascinating vistas on the mind, it is doing little to support the contention that there is an afterlife or other world. This, of course, does not mean that one does not exist.

The belief in one, inspired by religious conviction, will undoubtedly persist, and many people will continue to live their lives with one eye on this world and the other on the next. The point is that, although there is no conclusive evidence to resolve the question of God's existence, we live as if there is, incorporating along the way corollary beliefs and ways of viewing ourselves and the world. Do we have any real basis for such beliefs? Lacking certain evidence, are those who believe in God irrational, or are they justified in perhaps allowing their hearts to rule their heads? Since this question of religious belief is so influential in our lives, it seems appropriate now to examine it.

RELIGIOUS BELIEF

Whether or not the existence of God is an issue today, the question of whether or not to believe in a divine dimension remains. Is the cosmos far-flung matter that has originated in chance and is propelled by accident? Or is it, scientific explanations notwithstanding, something sacred, something divine? How we answer these questions will greatly affect

---

[11]John Hick. *Philosophy of Religion* (2nd ed.). New York: Prentice-Hall, 1973, p. 106.

[12]John Hick. *Philosophy of Religion*, p. 105.

our self-concepts and consequently our lives. In this case, the belief is as important a question as the fact.

A simple example will illustrate the influence of belief in our lives. Suppose at some point in college you begin to question whether or not you should actually be there. You are finding it neither interesting nor manageable. Besides, you have a pretty good job that you like and, if you work full time, you can make enough money to get married. On the other hand, limiting your education might restrict your personal and professional opportunities. What should you do: stay in school or quit? You must choose; there is no escaping the issue. Obviously, there is no certain answer. The best you can do is open-mindedly collect and weigh the data and decide. But whatever your choice, you will undoubtedly *believe* you are doing the right thing. In fact, that belief will help make the decision, which will have important consequences for your life. The decision might be reversible, but it will steer your life in a certain direction. That direction will be full of experiences that another direction would have lacked, experiences that will help shape you. So, in believing you should choose that direction, you have really decided to a degree what you will become.

Like the dilemma of whether or not to stay in school, the question of God's existence is inconclusive. But the question of *belief* in a divine dimension—call it theism, pantheism, or panentheism—is not. Although you cannot resolve the question of whether God exists, you can decide whether to believe in some kind of divine dimension. And that belief, if you are true to it, will affect your life, because through it you relate yourself to the world and everything in it. In effect, you fix your place in what you see as a cosmic order.

There are many responses to the question of believing or not believing. One is to become so overwhelmed by the question as to give up hope of ever believing anything. The unfortunate aspect of this reaction is that it is a decision; it is a decision to remain uncommitted. Another possibility is to avoid the anguish of decision-making by choosing whatever belief is conventional, popular, acceptable, or fashionable —in effect, to choose to become one of the statistics we allow to formulate our beliefs. On the other hand, we might face up to the anguish of decision-making, consider its implications, choose to believe or not believe, then live that decision. Any of these decisions is ours to make.

Aside from whether a theistic God exists, is there any basis for religious belief? Do we have any grounds for believing in a divine dimension of any sort? Perhaps religious belief ultimately is not based, and cannot be based, on any evidence. Perhaps it must be a personal decision made with the heart. In a classic address entitled "The Will to Believe," American philosopher William James addressed himself to this issue. Afterward, he wrote that he wished he had entitled it "The Right to Believe."

Reflection   Can you think of a belief you currently hold that cannot be proved but that is very influential in your life?

The Will to Believe

The thrust of James's address is captured in the following argument:

> Our passional nature not only lawfully may, but must, decide an option between propositions, whenever it is a genuine option that cannot by its nature be decided on intellectual grounds; for to say, under such circumstances, "Do not decide, but leave the question open," is itself a decision,—just like deciding yes or no,—and is attended with the same risk of losing the truth.[13]

Without understanding the terms James uses precisely as he understands them, we can easily misconstrue what he is saying.

Let us first consider the word *option*. By this James means a choice between two hypotheses, a hypothesis for him being anything that may be proposed to our belief. "There is a divine dimension to the universe" would be a hypothesis; so would "There is no divine dimension to the universe." Some hypotheses are *live;* a live hypothesis "appeals as a real possibility to him to whom it is proposed." For example, if someone proposed that you believe in the Mahdi (the Islamic messiah), the proposal would probably not appeal to you as a real possibility because of your Western acculturation and perhaps ignorance of Islam. The hypothesis would be a *dead* one. On the other hand, to an Arab it would probably be very much *live.* The deadness or liveness of any hypothesis, then, is a quality not inherent in the proposal but relative to the individual thinker. It is measured by our willingness to act; a hypothesis is most live when we are willing to act irrevocably—that is, to believe.

James further points out that an option, the choice between two hypotheses, may be of several kinds: (1) living or dead, (2) forced or avoidable, (3) momentous or trivial. A genuine option is one that is living, forced, and momentous.

By a *living* option James means one in which both hypotheses are live ones. For example, the proposal "Be a theosophist or be a Mohammedan" would probably be a *dead* option, because neither proposal is likely to be a live one for you. On the other hand, "Be a Christian or be an atheist" would probably be a living option, because both choices are probably live for you.

---

[13]William James. "The Will to Believe." In Cormier, Chinn, and Lineback, Eds. *Encounter,* p. 236.

With respect to *forced* or *avoidable* options, suppose someone proposed "Either love me or hate me." You could avoid a decision by remaining indifferent to the person. Likewise, if someone proposed "Either vote for me or vote for my opponent," again you could avoid the decision by not voting at all. Options like these are not forced; they are avoidable. On the other hand, if someone said "Either accept this proof or go without it," you would be forced to choose one of the options. When there is no way to avoid a decision, the option is forced.

Finally, an option is *momentous* when the opportunity is unique, when the stakes are significant, and when the decision is irreversible. For example, a friend comes by one night with some "sure-fire" stock. It is a once-in-a-lifetime opportunity to get in on this sort of investment, which, he promises, will yield incredible riches. To accept his offer or reject it would be a momentous option. On the other hand, whether to wear jeans or slacks to school would be a *trivial* option, because it is not unique, attended by high stakes, or irreversible.

Now, what does James mean by "our passional nature"? As an empiricist, one who believes that knowledge originates in sense experience, James forsakes an objective certainty. He claims that we can never be absolutely sure of anything except that consciousness itself exists. But—and this is a big but—he does not abandon the quest for truth itself; he still believes that truth exists. This belief springs more from desire and feeling than from reason; it is more passional than rational. It is this belief that provides the best chance of attaining truth, "by systematically continuing to roll up experiences and think." His point is that, since we can never know with certainty, there will invariably be a nonintellectual, nonrational element to what we choose to believe—a passional element. As James writes of such cases, "Instinct leads, intelligence only follows." The first two tasks of this passional element are knowing the truth and avoiding error.

Choosing between these two "commandments," we could end up coloring our lives in completely different ways. For example, suppose you regarded the avoidance of error as paramount and the search for truth as secondary. Since there is very little if anything for which there is absolutely sufficient evidence, you would probably draw no conclusions for fear of error. The result would be a lifelong intellectual suspense, in which you would hang in a mental limbo. Imagine a child who must choose one of 31 ice cream flavors and just cannot bring himself to the choice for fear that the one he chooses may not live up to his expectations, or that after he chooses it he will realize that he really should have chosen another. James is suggesting that in certain areas, when we are more committed to avoiding error than to chasing the truth, we necessarily lose the truth, since there will never be absolute evidence for it. But to make such a choice is to be "like a general informing his soldiers that it is better to keep out of battle forever than to risk a single wound. Not so are victories either over enemies or over nature found."[14] Or, we might add, over the self.

It is easy to misunderstand James. He is not saying that avoiding error should always be subordinate to attaining truth. On the contrary, in options that are not momentous, James claims that we can throw away the chance of gaining truth, and save ourselves from any chance of believing a falsehood, by not making up our minds until all the evidence is in. This approach would apply to most of the scientific questions and human issues we are ever likely to face. In other words, in most choices the need to act is seldom so urgent that it is better to act on a false belief than on no belief at all. But he also argues that there are forced and momentous choices that we cannot ("as men who may be interested at least as much in positively gaining truth as in merely escaping dupery") always wait to make. As he puts it, "In the great boarding-house of nature, the cakes and the butter and the syrup seldom come out so even and leave the plates so clean." The question of religious belief is similar.

Granted that, for some, religious belief is not a hypothesis that could possibly be true. But for most it is a live option. To these people, James says that religious belief is a momentous option. They stand to gain much by their belief and to lose much by their nonbelief. It is also a forced option. If they choose to wait in order to avoid error, they risk losing the chance of attaining the good that religious belief promises. "It is as if a man should hesitate indefinitely to ask a certain woman to marry him because he was not perfectly sure that she would prove an angel after he brought her home. Would he not cut himself off from that particular angel-possibility as decisively as if he went and married someone else?" Or, more simply, should the ice cream shop close while the child is debating his choice, the result for him would be the same as if he had chosen to have no ice cream. On such a question that cannot be answered on intellectual grounds, James argues that we not only can but *should* allow our "passional nature" to decide it. We must choose to chase truth, not to avoid possible error; for in fearing to be duped, we exclude the possibility of being right.

James's argument has relevance not only for those who believe in a personal God but also for those whose innermost feelings detect a divine dimension at work in the cosmos, but not necessarily a Supreme Being such as the one of traditional theism. Because he relies on the importance of personal experience in religious belief, James is providing a philosophical basis for a personal encounter with the sacred, whatever we may experience that to be. Just what constitutes a personal

---

[14]William James. *The Varieties of Religious Experience.* New York: Longmans, Green, 1929, p. 74.

experience of the divine is a complex question, but today, perhaps more than ever, individuals are using it as their source of or justification for religious belief.

Reflection Describe a living option currently facing you, perhaps a career choice.

Personal Experience of the Divine

We said earlier that religious belief, in its most general terms, is the belief that there is an unseen order and that we can do no better than to be in harmony with this order. It is from this belief that our religious attitudes spring. But this belief need not be rooted in objects present to our senses. On the contrary, the *belief* in a thing's existence can evoke in us a reaction as powerful as sensible objects can evoke. As an example, consider this encounter between a man and a woman who meet in a park.

Young Man:	Do you come here often?
Young Woman:	Whenever I need to feel the presence.
Young Man:	The presence?
Young Woman:	Haven't you ever felt a void, an emptiness?
Young Man:	A quiet desperation?
Young Woman:	That, too.
Young Man:	It's not something one can easily speak of.
Young Woman:	No, it's not.
Young Man:	And coming here helps?
Young Woman:	It stills the loneliness.
Young Man:	But there's no one here.
Young Woman:	There's the sunshine and sometimes the rain. And almost always the breeze.
Young Man:	I guess nature *can* be therapeutic.
Young Woman:	No, it's the presence that brings me here.
Young Man:	The presence of what?
Young Woman:	Of something greater than myself.

Young Man:	God?
Young Woman:	If you want. I'd rather not name it, for words are so misleading. But I know there's something there. . . . Why are you looking around? You won't see it, you know. But it's there, all the same.

This young woman has felt a sense of reality, a feeling of actual presence, that is deeper and more real than her sense experiences. She cannot fully communicate what she seems to be experiencing. It cannot be defined, does not consist of facts of sensation, does not consist of specific hypotheses based on such facts, and does not allow definite inferences to be logically drawn. Yet what she feels is more convincing than those truths arrived at through rational methods.

The fact is that, if we turn to the nonspecific, nonlearned parts of our mental lives, we see that rationalism has given a small and sketchy account of it. True, reason and logic are prestigious: they can argue, point out flaws, and refute. But in the presence of what James calls "dumb intuitions" rationalism invariably loses the fight. It seems that this woman's whole subconscious life—her impulses, faith, needs, divinations—has prepared the premises of which her consciousness now feels the weight of the result; and something in her absolutely *knows* that the result must be "truer" than any rationalistic talk, however clever, that may contradict it.

The weakness of the rationalistic level of our thinking shows up dramatically in discussions of religious belief, particularly in the proofs for God's existence. Probably very few of us today believe in God because we have been convinced by any of those proofs. Even fewer of us first came to believe in God because of any of those proofs. Similarly, few do not believe, or have stopped believing, because the beliefs are flawed. The point is that many people, perhaps most, do not need any rational proof for their religious belief, any more than they would need proof that they felt joyful or loving. Others might point out innumerable reasons that these people should not feel joyful or loving, but to those experiencing these feelings such arguments bend like straws in the wind. It is this kind of personal, direct, nonrational experience that frequently characterizes the sense of a divine presence that is not the personal God of traditional theism. This experience often takes the form of mysticism.

MYSTICISM

Young Man:	Can you describe what you feel when you experience the presence?
Young Woman:	Not really. Words are really inadequate, and I think it all sounds very foolish to someone who thinks more than feels.

Young Man:	But I'd like for you to try. You see, what you say may touch my life. And it would be terrible to lose that possibility because you thought I'd ridicule what you say.
Young Woman:	All right. I'll try to describe what happened last week on this very spot. At first I was frightened. I was losing myself, I thought, perhaps losing my mind. Then suddenly I had a vivid impression of something indescribable—call it God if you wish. At that moment when I felt most abandoned, I became one with this infinite power, this spirit of infinite peace. Through my attachment to this prodigious power, I sensed myself as I'd never done before. I felt one with everything: trees, birds, insects. I gloried in my existence, of being part of it all—part of the blades of grass, the bark of trees, the drops of rain. It was as if my thoughts were piercing the great veil of confusion and ignorance that I had always looked through. Suddenly I saw why we suffer, why it's necessary to suffer, why there will always be suffering. I also saw the thread of love that weaves through nature and makes it all one. I saw all the terrible hatred as love and the love as potential hatred, the one serving as counterpoint to the other, the two together producing the song of the universe, a cosmic harmony that left me in a divine ecstasy. There was more, much more; but even now I feel the inadequacy of words, and I'd rather not reduce my experiences any further.

The young woman appears to have had a mystical experience. One problem in trying to speak of such experiences is that, by nature, they defy verbalization. Religious belief often finds its origins in mystical states of consciousness.

In his *Varieties of Religious Experience*, William James proposes two characteristics by which an experience may rightly be termed "mystical." First is *ineffability*; that is, the person experiencing the state feels that it defies expression. Like the young woman, the experiencer feels that no adequate report of the mystical experience's content can be given. Second, there is a *noetic quality* about these experiences: to the individual they appear to be knowledge. They are states of insight into the depths of human experience that no amount of intellectualizing can reach. They are revelations and illuminations that are full of meaning, truth, and importance.

Mysticism, then, is the experience of a reality more inclusive than that we are generally conscious of. It is that aspect of religion or philosophy that claims we can truly know only when we surrender our individual selves and sense a union with the divine ground of all existence. Certainly, mystical experiences vary in content, but like the young woman's they often involve an acute awareness of a divine presence and of a direct communion with divinity, although this divinity is more likely to be an incomprehensible One than a theistic deity.

Like most people, mystics have sensed within themselves a desire or longing that goes beyond the imperfect world of which they are a part. They may feel an urge for something permanent and free, something that transcends sorrow and is of everlasting value. They may feel airborne looking for a place to land. Most of us in the Western world deal with such feelings and desires by seeking outside ourselves to quell the insecurity and discontent we feel within. But mystics believe that the outward search is a race on a treadmill.

Mystics turn instead to the self to still uneasy inner feelings, to grasp the reality behind the endless parade of entities and changes in experience. What occurs is impossible to describe; it must be experienced. But from the writings of mystics we are led to believe that, above everything else, the inner way leads to an understanding that all is one and one is all; that the self is one continuous process with God, the Cosmos, the Ground of Being, or whatever term a particular culture or individual chooses to designate an ultimate and eternal reality. Such an inner experience has been termed variously "religious experience," "mystical experience," and "cosmic consciousness." But none of these terms captures the nature of such experiences, any more than the phrase "in love" describes what we experience in that state.

Today, especially among youth, there is intense and unprecedented interest in what we can call the transformation of consciousness. Much of it springs from a growing sense of personal estrangement from the world. Many feel out of touch with things, cut off from reality. This feeling has resulted in an effort to locate themselves in the scheme of things. More and more, people are rejecting the traditional institutional prescriptions for inner peace and contentment and pursuing their own vague but pressing sense of what is good for them. This pursuit takes many forms: "self-healing," "consciousness expansion," "positive growth potential," "survival experiments." But they all seem to have one thing in common: the search for a "religious experience." Moreover, they all appear to have nonrational, mystical overtones. It is impossible to treat them all, but we can introduce three activities that, although quite different in their content and methodologies, do seem similar in their attempt to gain religious experience through a kind of mystical transformation of consciousness. These are radical theology, the use of psychedelic drugs, and the study of Eastern religious thought.

Reflection   Recall a night on the beach, a day in the mountains, a walk in the woods, or a like experience which evoked feelings in you that perhaps lay too deep for words. In what sense was the experience different from an "ordinary" one? Would you call it "mystical"?

"Today, especially among youth, there is
intense and unprecedented interest in . . . the
transformation of consciousness."

RADICAL THEOLOGY

The nagging questions about the existence and nature of a Supreme
Being have spawned in our time a school of theology that moves away
from traditional theism more radically than do pantheism and panentheism. Such "radical theologians," as these thinkers are often termed,
perceive God not as a being among other beings but as an aspect of reality. As a result, they feel that our relationship with God is more experiential than rational.

The chief exponent of radical theology has been Protestant theologian Paul Tillich (1886–1965). Tillich, an existentialist, contends that
traditional theism has erred in viewing God as *a* being and not *being
itself,* an error that he believes the proofs for God's existence, discussed
earlier, have fostered. As a result, we have bound God to our subject-object structure of reality. *He*—notice the sexualization—is an object
for us as subjects, becoming the target for our prayers, worship, and supplications. He becomes almost some *thing* to which we direct our lives.
At other times we make ourselves object for Him as subject, because
theism posits an all-knowing, all-powerful God. Since we are neither,
the relationship must therefore be one of superior (God) to inferior (us),
controller to controlled, subject to object. An antagonistic tension results. As Tillich says, "He deprives me of my subjectivity because he
is all-powerful and all-knowing. I revolt and try to make him into an

object, but the revolt fails and becomes desperate. God appears as an invincible tyrant, the being in contrast with whom all other things are without freedom and subjectivity."[15] This image of God as "invincible tyrant," he feels, is a much more telling blow to theological theism than all the objections to the traditional proofs for God's existence. Tillich believes that his blow is justified, for God as tyrant is "the deepest root of the Existentialist despair and the widespread anxiety of meaninglessness in our period." Notice that Tillich rejects traditional theism not on empirical but on theological grounds. For Tillich, theism is just bad theology.

If Tillich and other radical theologians reject the theistic concept of God, just what do they substitute? What kind of God do they believe in?

Tillich's God is a "God above God," "the ground of being." This God transcends the God of theism and so dissipates the anxiety of doubt and meaninglessness it has created. This "ground of being" is not "proved," because it cannot be proved. It is neither an object nor a subject. It is present, although hidden, in every divine-human encounter. Tillich grants that this notion is paradoxical. But he notes that Biblical religion and Protestant theology are already studded with paradoxes. Consider the "paradoxical character of every prayer of speaking to somebody to whom you cannot ask anything because he gives or gives not before you ask, of saying 'thou' to somebody who is nearer to the I than the I is to itself." Indeed, it is paradoxes like these, says Tillich, that "drive the religious consciousness toward a God above the God of theism, a God that is the Ground of our very being."

The "ground of being" is only one of Tillich's many slippery concepts. "Depth" is another. "Depth is what the word God means," he writes; but still we ask what "depth" is. The word seems to have no meaning. "If the word has not much meaning for you, translate it," advises Tillich, "and speak of the depths of your life, of the source of your being, of your ultimate concern, of what you take seriously without any reservation." Atheists might reply "That there is no God; now *that* I take seriously, without any reservation." But Tillich would say that this is impossible, for to call themselves atheists they would have to forget everything traditional they ever learned about God, maybe even the word itself. The only people who can rightly call themselves atheists are those who can say "Life has no depth. Life is shallow. Being itself is surface only. If you could say this in complete seriousness, you would be an atheist; but otherwise you are not. He who knows the depth knows about God."

Like many existentialists, Tillich is not easy to understand. But clearly he believes that traditional theism has erred in making God an

---

[15]This and all other Tillich quotes are from: Paul Tillich. *The Courage to Be.* New Haven, Conn.: Yale University Press, 1952.

object. It does so in defining Him the way it has and in presenting proofs for His existence. God cannot be "proved," as if He were an equation or a specimen you could drag into a lab and examine. Such "objectivation" not only limits the deity but, worse, raises the very kinds of inconsistencies that are leading to a loss of faith. Tillich's God, therefore, defies traditional definitions and proofs. His God is closer to the concept attained by the mystic, but significantly different. Where the mystic would eschew sense experience and reason and through intuition alone move to a knowledge of God, Tillich confronts the world of experience and the nagging questions it raises. He is no escapist, no dodger of doubt. On the contrary, he faces the concrete world of finite values and meanings and uses all its imperfections, skepticism, and meaninglessness to come to grips with what is ultimately real: being. And in this "ground of all being," he experiences God. Everyone does, everyone "who knows the depth."

Reflection   Take any relationship that you are part of—perhaps that between you and your parents, you and the person you are dating, or you and a teacher—and test it as an object-subject experience.

Objections to Radical Theology

Besides having many elusive concepts, Tillich's theology provokes other objections. He seemingly says that those who do not recognize his God, the "ground of all being," are not "ultimately concerned." Suppose you tell an unaccomplished violinist that the reason he failed to become a virtuoso is that he never practiced long enough. "Long enough!" he protests. "Are you kidding? Why, I have practiced every day of my life!" Obviously, it wasn't long enough, you reply, because he never became a virtuoso. Clearly, by "long enough" you mean "until one becomes a virtuoso." Your directive to the would-be virtuoso, then, was nothing more than "Practice until you become a virtuoso (that is, long enough), and you will become a virtuoso." In logic, a statement whose predicate repeats its subject, as this one does, is called a **tautology**. Is Tillich's argument tautological? Has he, as Anselm evidently did, defined something into existence? When Tillich says "He who knows about the depth knows about God," he seems to be saying "He who knows about God knows about God." When he argues "If one is ultimately concerned or has the courage to be, then one knows God," he appears to say "If one knows God or knows God, then one knows God"!

Tillich also claims to have an experience of divine presence, of a merging with some fundamental reality. No one may question his experience; it is as personal as a headache or a hunger pang. But his

"God cannot be 'proved,' as if He were an
equation or a specimen you could drag
into a lab and examine."

interpretation of his experience can be questioned. We can and should, it seems, ask for verification when he interprets that experience as resulting from contact with the "ground of all being." Tillich must (1) verify the reality of the "ground of all being" and (2) establish it as the cause of his transcendent experiences.

Tillich would probably reply that the knowledge of his God is a completely different kind of knowledge from that which we customarily speak of. Taking his departure from psychology or from religious or mystical experience, areas open to all, he would argue that his knowledge transcends empirical data and defies scientific verification. It is knowledge whose source is much closer to mystical intuition than to senses or reason, although the latter are instrumental in generating the intuitive response. This knowledge is similar to the mystical knowledge of the young woman in the dialogue, who knows in her heart what she feels and that what she feels plumbs the depths of reality. Both are rooted in a personal experience, traditionally induced through prayer and meditation. Today, however, some seek a similar experience in less traditional ways.

PSYCHEDELICS AND
RELIGIOUS EXPERIENCE

If you look up the word *psychedelic* you will see it defined as "of or pertaining to or generating hallucinations, distortions of perception, and, occasionally, psychotic-like states." It is true that the five principal psychedelic drugs—LSD-25, mescaline, psilocybin, dimethyl-tryptamine (DMT), and cannabis—when used indiscriminately have produced these characteristics in certain people. But the same characteristics frequently accompany the so-called mystical or religious experience.

Raynor Johnson, in his excellent collection of accounts of mystical experiences *Watcher on the Hills*,[16] lists some principal states of consciousness that mystical experiences invariably involve, all of which also characterize psychedelic experiences. First, common to both experiences is a sense of timelessness. Mystics as well as psychedelic-drug users frequently describe a loss of the sense of time. A minute may seem like an hour, an hour like a minute. Both seem to lose a normal awareness of time sequence; they fall into a state of such utter relaxation that they become oblivious to the temporal affairs that occupy us. Accompanying these feelings is often an acute realization that the whole point of life is to live and experience every moment as richly as possible.

It is because of such similarities that the young man in our dialogue, who once used cannabis, can understand the woman's seemingly unintelligible mystical experience.

Young Man: Funny, but as I've been listening to you describe your experience I've had a feeling of *déjà vu,* a sense of having been there myself.

Young Woman: Then you know what I'm trying to describe.

Young Man: I think I do. But let me ask you something. Did you have the feeling that time slowed down?

Young Woman: Not only did it slow down, but it was as if I were anchored in the present. Every pore seemed to open to what was occurring *now.*

Young Man: The past didn't exist.

Young Woman: Nor the future.

Young Man: You had none of the normal concerns about the future?

Young Woman: I had neither anxiety about it nor anticipation of it. It simply didn't exist.

Young Man: I once felt that way—that I had crossed the time barrier between the finite and the infinite, that time was just an illusion. And then I experienced something strangely wonderful, something very difficult to explain, and that was that everything was somehow integrated. Somehow, having broken through the bubble of time, I experienced the oneness of everything, things that before had somehow been distinguished by time relationships.

---

[16]Raynor Johnson. *Watcher on the Hills.* London: Hodder and Stoughton, 1959.

Young Woman:	And spatial relationships.
Young Man:	Yes, time and space—they both struck me as illusions.
Young Woman:	And so long as we're committed to those illusions, we persist in perceiving reality in terms of opposing forces: good and bad, love and hate, right and wrong.
Young Man:	But there are no opposites. I felt this more strongly than I've ever felt anything. That all things are interconnected and intertwined with everything else.

Here is another principal feature of the mystical and psychedelic experience: the loss of a sense of bipolarity. What we commonly view as opposites are seen as different sides of the same coin. There is an interdependence in all things, such as between heads and tails or between up and down. Self necessitates other; good, bad; solid, space; saints, sinners. In this state the mystic, and often the drug user, realize that each thing in existence can have meaning and definition only in terms of something else. There is, then, just One.

Such a loss of conventional classification labels can produce a heightened sense of the interdependence of all parts of creation.

Young Woman:	I recall becoming engrossed in watching a tiny ant that was moving across my foot.
Young Man:	Did you wonder at the ant's universe?
Young Woman:	Really! I thought that the ant must think of itself as I think of myself, although it sounds silly to speak of an ant thinking. But then I recognized that I couldn't even begin to speak of myself thinking if it weren't for the ant, if it weren't for the apparent difference between us.
Young Man:	Without the ant you would lack self-definition.
Young Woman:	In a sense I would. And without everything else I stand in relation to, I would melt away, evaporate.
Young Man:	I'd be terrified by the thought.
Young Woman:	I was, but then I was filled with marvel at this cosmic order that finds a place for everything and somehow ordains a role for each.

The young woman seems to be describing an experience of the relativity of all things, an experience similar to one the young man experienced under the influence of cannabis. Such an experience frequently reveals a sense of the self as one link of an infinite chain linking each life to all other lives. This hierarchy of processes and beings ranges from subatomic particles through bacteria and insects to human beings and, perhaps, to supernatural beings. And in this hierarchy each link is in the same wondrous and perplexing situation of taking its own meaning from its position relative to the others in the gradation and giving meaning to them at the same time.

There is a final feature that frequently accompanies both experiences. Some describe it as the awareness of eternal energy.

Young Man:	I think the most marvelous part of my experience was the sense of incredible strength or power I had.
Young Woman:	A kind of energy.
Young Man:	Yes, you could call it that.
Young Woman:	I remember seeing an almost blinding light.
Young Man:	Did you feel that this light was the source of all life, of all being?
Young Woman:	More than that. I felt that the light was me.
Young Man:	Yes, that the concentrated energy was your own being.
Young Woman:	That I was the source of all life, that it all flowed from me, that I was . . .
Young Man:	Divine?

Accompanying such experiences is the profound recognition that the totality of existence is a single energy. But even more often this energy is one's own being, which, like pulsations of energy, rises and falls but is never lost. It is a realization that the individual is the divinity and the divinity is all that is.

Obviously, not everyone under the influence of psychedelic drugs can or will experience these states of consciousness, but some do. Neither should everyone seeking a religious experience try psychedelic drugs. In too many cases, excessive and indiscriminate use can end tragically. But, that fact notwithstanding, the similarity between the mystical and psychedelic experiences in altering states of consciousness raises philosophical curiosity about why society disapproves of drug usage.

First, it is obvious that society disapproves of psychedelics because of their effects. But if their effects are strikingly similar to those of a religious or mystical experience, are we, in effect, disapproving of those as well? Alan Watts, in his fascinating essay "Psychedelics and Religious Experience,"[17] says we are. He gives a number of reasons, two of which are noteworthy here.

Like the psychedelic experience, the mystical experience is not logical. Because it defies "common sense," it runs counter to empirical and rational knowledge, the bases of Western epistemology. Such experiences are inconsistent with the way we relate ourselves to the universe —that is, as separate, individual egos confronting an external and often alien world. Religious, mystical, and psychedelic experiences, then, are truly revolutionary. They suggest ways of seeing and knowing that contradict most of what we have grown up to accept.

Even more important, when we claim consciousness of oneness with God or with the universe we fly in the face of our society's concept of religion. Our Jewish and Christian origins do not sanction the individual's claim to identity with the Godhead, even though this identity may have been peculiarly true of Jesus Christ. For any of us to claim that we, individually, are the all-powerful and all-knowing ruler of the world has traditionally been considered blasphemy.

Watts is suggesting, then, that the prohibition against such drugs, even in controlled scientific studies, is really a prohibition against questioning traditional secular and religious values. As evidence, he records how suspicious institutional religion has always been of mystical claims and how persecutive of those like Johannes "Meister" Eckhart, whose claims of equality with God resulted in his condemnation as a heretic. When such mystics as St. Teresa of Avila and St. John of the Cross received church acceptance, it has always been when they have acknowledged the difference and distinction between themselves and their God.

The Eastern philosophical and religious traditions, on the other hand, have always been sympathetic to mystical claims and experiences. It may be for this reason that many today are seeking the source of their religious experiences not in drugs or in radical theology but in these traditions.

EASTERN RELIGIOUS TRADITIONS

When we speak of Eastern or Oriental philosophy, we refer to those systems of thought, belief, and action espoused by many non-European peoples of the Near and Far East. It is neither our intention nor within our capabilities here even to mention all of these, let alone adequately discuss them. But we should mention at least two of the principal religions to which many Westerners are turning for meaningful religious

---

[17] Alan Watts. "Psychedelic and Religious Experience," *California Law Review*, 1968, Vol. 56, No. 100, p. 74.

experience: Hinduism and Buddhism. The nuances of these philosophy/
religions are so intricate that we shall not even try to detail them.
Rather, we shall focus on the possible reasons that these beliefs are
becoming progressively more attractive to many Western minds.

Hinduism

One of the oldest of Eastern traditions is Hinduism, which has been
practiced by hundreds of millions of people for about 5000 years. There
are many divisions and subdivisions of Hinduism, and no one Hindu
sect acknowledges the same leader or belief that all the others accept.
In fact, so diversified is Hinduism that it is very difficult to describe
it as a whole. Like this one, any attempt at a sketchy description is
bound to be an unfortunate oversimplification. A further complication
is the fact that our language provides no precise equivalents for certain
Indian terms and concepts.

Aware of these limitations, let us begin with the literary source of
Hindu teaching. Although many texts form the body of Hindu scripture,
one has influenced Hindu thought more than any other: the *Bhagavad-
Gita,* the Song of the Lord. Reading the Gita will introduce you to the
principal concepts of Hinduism, as well as to beautiful poetry.

One concept common to all expressions of Hinduism is the oneness
of reality. This oneness is the Absolute, or **Brahman,** which the mind
can never fully grasp or words express. Only *Brahman* is real; everything else is an illusory manifestation of *Brahman.* A correlative belief
is the concept of **atman,** or No Self. What we commonly call "I" or the
self is an illusion, for each true self is one with *Brahman.* When we
realize this unity with the Absolute, we realize our true destiny.

Also common to all Hindu thought are four primary values. In their
order of increasing importance, they may be roughly translated as
wealth, pleasure, duty, and enlightenment. The first two are the less
important worldly values, which when kept in perspective are good
and desirable values. Duty, or righteousness, refers to patience, sincerity, fairness, love, honesty, and similar virtues. The highest spiritual
value is enlightenment, in which one is illuminated and liberated and,
most importantly, finds release from the wheel of existence. Repeated
existence is the destiny of those who do not achieve enlightenment.

To understand enlightenment you must understand the law of
karma, the law of sowing and reaping. All of us, through what we do
or do not do, supposedly determine our destiny. If we are particularly
evil, we may find ourselves reborn as subhumans. If we are noble, we
may be reborn as especially favored humans. This wheel of existence
turns until we achieve enlightenment, after which we are released from
this series of rebirths.

Sri Sarvepalli Radhakrishnan in *A Source Book in Indian Philosophy*[18] lists those characteristics common to all Indian thought. First is an emphasis on the spiritual. It is the spiritual that endures and is ultimately real. Second is the realization that our philosophy and our life are inextricably wed. What we believe is how we live; if our beliefs are in error, our lives will be unhappy. Third is a preoccupation with the inner life. The road to enlightenment stretches not outward but inward. To understand nature and the universe we must turn within. Fourth is an emphasis on the nonmaterial oneness of creation. There are no bipolarities; a unity of spirit provides cosmic harmony. Fifth is the acceptance of direct awareness as the only way to understand what is real. Unlike the user of psychedelic drugs, the Indian believer finds this direct perception through spiritual exercises, perhaps through the practice of yoga. Reason is of some use, but in the last analysis we know only through an inner experience of oneness with all of creation. Sixth is a healthy respect for tradition, but never a slavish commitment to it. The past can teach but never rule. Finally, Indian thought recognizes the complementary nature of all systems of belief. Hinduism is not rooted in any uniform doctrine; neither does it claim monopoly on truth or wisdom. It preaches tolerance of all sincere viewpoints and includes many of these within its own spiritual teachings.

Buddhism

Another major Eastern tradition is Buddhism, contained in the teachings of Siddhartha Gautama (563 B.C.–?), its founder. Since Gautama found no evidence for a belief in a personal God, his teachings are a diagnosis of and a prescription for the "disease" of living.

He preached the Four Noble Truths. The First Noble Truth is concerned with the suffering we experience in living as we are accustomed to. Paul Tillich might call this suffering "existential despair," although attributing it to theism. The Second Noble Truth identifies the cause of this suffering, or, more accurately, this frustration: clinging or grasping based on **avidya,** ignorance and/or unawareness. This unawareness is characterized by commitment to the world of things and illusion, **maya,** and not to the concrete world of reality. This unawareness is also characterized by a doomed attempt to control oneself and the environment, which can lead only to a futile grasping that results in self-frustration and the viciously circular pattern of life called **samsara,** the round of birth and death. The Third Noble Truth concerns ending *samsara*. This ending is called **nirvana,** release or liberation. It is the way of

[18]Sarvepalli Radhakrishnan and Charles A. Moore, Eds. *A Source Book in Indian Philosophy*. Princeton, N.J.: Princeton University Press, 1957, pp. xx–xxvi.

life that results when we stop grasping and clinging. Tillich would call it experiencing the "depth," the "ground of all being"; in the *nirvana* state we are released from the round of incarnations into an immeasurable and infinite state that defies definition. The Fourth Noble Truth describes the Eightfold Path of the Buddha's **dharma**—that is, the doctrine whereby self-frustration is ended.

The Eightfold Path consists of:

1. Right understanding: we must realize that suffering ends only when ignorance disappears and physical desires cease. Failing to see this, we will remain in a state of discontent.
2. Right purpose or intention: we must aspire to transcend our state of ignorance and craving.
3. Right speech: we must be honest and humble, speaking kindly of others.
4. Right conduct: we must avoid harming other life, killing, and polluting ourselves and the environment.
5. Right mode of livelihood: we must adopt a way of providing for ourselves that is consistent with our spiritual goals.
6. Right effort: we must have proper self-discipline to make our way along the path of enlightenment.
7. Right frame of mind: we must recognize the necessity of entertaining healthful thoughts directed toward our purpose. Allowing our thoughts to wander and dwell upon cravings is spiritually obstructive.
8. Right concentration: we must exercise proper concentration and meditation to experience enlightenment, which is the recognition of our oneness with truth. When we reach this state, we are released from the physical and intellectual entanglements of *maya* and enter *nirvana*, the state in which the finite, craving self is extinguished and we experience freedom, serenity, illumination, and oneness with all of creation.

Obviously, there is much more to Buddhism and Hinduism than we have outlined. But, scanty as they are, these sketches do illustrate major points of difference that generally distinguish Eastern thought from Western.

DIFFERENCES BETWEEN EAST AND WEST

First, the East rejects the West's "objectified" God. There is no claim of a personal, all-knowing, all-good, all-powerful, and all-loving God, as there is in the Western tradition. As a result, Eastern thinkers have never sat around debating the arguments for God's existence. As a corollary to this, Buddhism does not share the Western view that there is a moral law, enjoined by God or by nature, which it is our duty to obey. In contrast, Western religions frequently, if not always, include behavioral proscriptions that if violated may lead to eternal damnation. In short, our tradition is one that presents a God who expects us to behave in a certain way. In contrast:

The Buddha's precepts of conduct—abstinence from taking life, taking what is not given, exploitation of the passions, lying, and intoxication—are voluntarily assumed rules of expedience, the intent of which is to remove the hindrances to clarity of awareness. Failure to observe the precepts produces bad *"karma"* not because *karma* is a law or moral retribution, but because all motivated and purposeful actions, whether conventionally good or bad, are *karma* in so far as they are directed to the grasping of life. Generally speaking, the conventionally "bad" actions are rather more grasping than the "good."[19]

Finally, whereas the thrust of Western religion traditionally has been to align us with our divine Creator, Eastern thought, like Tillich's emphasis on being, aims to ground us in what is real. To do so, Eastern thought generally prescribes discipline, self-control, moderation, and detachment. Although these values are frequently observed in Western religious practice, they are just as frequently seen as means to an end: salvation and reward. They are ways not so much of attaining wisdom and truth as of avoiding damnation, of saving our souls, of "going to heaven."

Perhaps these differences explain why, since the middle 1960s, there has been a growing interest in the United States in Eastern thinking and religions. Many are turning away from their traditional faiths in favor of Zen Buddhism, Yoga, transcendental meditation, the Hare Krishna Society, Vedanta, and so on. Obviously, converts to Eastern religions have not stopped asking about their places in the scheme of things. On the contrary, they are asking perhaps more intensely than ever. Apparently, the answers they have traditionally received no longer work. The traditional concepts of self, subject-object distinction, Judaeo-Christian dogma, the egocentric emphasis on one's personal relationship with a theistic God, the dismissal of nonhuman natural objects as essentially inferior and alien—perhaps all have conspired to guide these seekers in other directions. Many features characterize these new directions: the emphasis on the workings of the mind and inner growth; the importance of discipline, practice, and method; a distrust of doctrines and dogmas; and hope for integrating body and intellect, feelings, and reason through a personal philosophy. But central to these features seem to be a reevaluation and a redefinition of one's traditional concept of the divine and one's relationship to it.

---

[19]Alan Watts. *The Way of Zen*. New York: Pantheon Books, 1957, p. 61.

CONCLUSIONS

The concept of religious experience is inextricably linked with a psychology of self, for religious experience is one way that we can integrate the facets of our personalities and lives and thereby achieve wholeness. This wholeness seems to be what psychologist Abraham Maslow means when he speaks of "peak experiences," vivid moments in our lives when everything seems to fall into place, when our vision is clear, our lives meaningful, our place in the order of things certain.[20]

Up until very recently, it was thought that the experiences Maslow describes happened only to saints or mystics, artists or poets, but certainly not to "average people." Maslow's "new psychology" suggests the contrary and offers a constructive insight into religious experience that might provide common ground for divergent viewpoints.

The moments that Maslow describes seem linked to feelings of self-fulfillment, achievement, and creativity—to a one-with-the-universe feeling. As such, they can happen to anyone. But we must allow them to happen; we must open ourselves to them. This element of personal receptivity has always been an integral part of religious teaching, but it is often buried under pomp and ceremony. Now, growing interest in what can be called humanistic psychology is suggesting ways of getting in touch with the self and thereby with religious impulses.

This humanistic psychology has spurred interest in expanding our awareness of self by increasing our creativity, improving our health, enhancing our learning and problem-solving, and, most importantly, providing intrinsically satisfying ecstatic experiences. As a result, there is a burgeoning network of mind and brain investigations that attempts to see the human from all sides. These are leading to new concepts of self that originate in a kind of religious experience, in which we experience self and reality in a way different from our "normal" way.

Where once we viewed humans as a bundle of responses to stimuli, we now accept the richness and complexity of the human and the importance of each individual. Central to this emphasis on the individual is a recognition of wholeness. The centuries-old split between mind and body has been abandoned for the *holistic* approach, which recognizes the inseparability of mind and body and the influence of each upon the other. Appropriately, there is more recognition of the roles that emotions and spiritual feelings play in our lives and that logic and rationality do not. As a result, subjective experience is gaining a more respectable place in scientific circles, a place heretofore reserved for objective experience. The realization that science and individual experience are not incompatible is growing. In addition, whereas we once had presumed ourselves to be objects of Freud's subconscious forces, we have found

---

[20]See Abraham Maslow. *Toward a Psychology of Being.* New York: Van Nostrand, 1968.

a new belief in our own capacity for growth, self-transcendence, or what Maslow calls "self-actualization." Related to this belief is the idea that we are not static or fixed systems but can more accurately be described in terms of "energy flow" and "energy fields." Finally, where purpose and meaning were once seen strictly as religious, they are now coming back to psychology, which is beginning to recognize a spiritual dimension.

The potential for what we have been calling religious experience is staggering. The next 25 years will perhaps open areas of conscious awareness that we hardly dream possible today. And, wherever that awareness takes us, it will no doubt be accompanied by a deep and reverent sensitivity to the profound mystery of life and our wondrous part in it.

SUMMARY

We opened this chapter by noting that all religions speak in terms of personal commitment and experience and our need to find our place in the cosmic scheme of things. Traditionally in the West, these phenomena have been sought through a relationship to a personal, theistic God. Seeing weaknesses in the theistic position, many have adopted pantheism or panentheism, others atheism or agnosticism. Whether or not God exists, the question of religious belief persists and makes a difference in our lives. For many, this decision involves a relationship not to a personal God but to a divine dimension to the universe, which they sense through personal experience. There is a growing emphasis on this kind of personal experience as the basis of religious belief. In this connection we examined mysticism and contemporary movements with mystical overtones such as radical theology, psychedelic drug usage, and Eastern religious thought. We concluded by noting the role that the new humanistic psychology may play in providing direction for the future potential of religious experience.

MAIN POINTS

1. Traditionally, religion refers to a belief in God that is institutionalized and incorporated in the teachings of some religious body such as a church or synagogue. Today, emphasis is on deep personal experience with the object of one's chief loyalty.

2. Theism is the belief in a personal God who intervenes in the lives of His creation.

3. Three traditional arguments for a theistic God are ontological, cause, and design. None offers conclusive proof.

4. Besides the flaws in these arguments, theism has other problems:
   a. How can so much apparent evil emanate from an all-good and all-powerful God?
   b. How can God be all-knowing and yet not suffer along with us?
   c. How can God be unchanging and yet have perfect knowledge of our changing world?
5. Pantheism argues that everything is God and God is everything.
6. Panentheism argues that God is both fixed and changing, unity and diversity, inclusive of all possibilities.
7. William James called the acquisition of religious belief a live, forced, and momentous option.
8. Many people, unable to find religious belief or experience in a theistic God, find both in a deep personal encounter with a divine dimension.
9. Mysticism claims direct and immediate awareness that is not dependent on direct sense experience or on reason. The mystical experience is inexpressible and noetic.
10. Radical theology, as presented by Paul Tillich, has mystical overtones. It appeals to deep personal experience as justification for belief. Tillich's God is being itself, the "God above God," the "ground of all being."
11. The psychedelic experience curiously resembles mystical states of consciousness.
12. Eastern religious views, such as Hinduism and Buddhism, are much more sympathetic to claims of personal religious experience than are Western religious views.

SECTION EXERCISES

The Ontological Argument

1. Anselm argues that a perfect being *must* exist because the lack of existence is an imperfection. Could you argue that, on the contrary, a perfect being must *not* exist because existence is an imperfection? Explain.
2. If you believe in God, do you believe on the basis of Anselm's ontological argument? If you do not believe in God, do you disbelieve because you consider the ontological argument inadequate?
3. Explain the difference between these two statements: "If there is a perfect being, then a perfect being exists"; "If there can be a perfect being, then a perfect being must exist." Which represents the ontological argument? Which the objection to it? With which do you agree, and why?

The Cause Argument

1. Evaluate these statements:
   a. God was the first event.
   b. God caused the first event.
   c. God is an uncaused cause.
   d. First there was a mind without a body, God, who then created matter, including bodies.
2. Do you agree that if there is no first cause, the universe makes no sense? Is an infinite regress nonsensical?
3. If you believe in God, do you believe because of the argument from cause? If you do not believe in God, do you disbelieve because of the inadequacy of the argument from cause?
4. Aquinas's proofs are based on analogical reasoning, in which he compares what we have experienced directly with what we have not. What is the source of his analogy in the cause argument? Is the analogy a good one?

The Design Argument

1. Explain what Hume means when he says "A universe by definition must appear designed, for it shows design."
2. In what ways would you say organic evolution is compatible with the account of creation given in *Genesis*? In what ways is it incompatible with it?
3. If you believe in God, do you believe because of the argument from design? If you do not believe in God, do you disbelieve because of the inadequacies in the argument from design?

Radical Theology

1. In your own words, what is Tillich's objection to traditional or theological theism?
2. Are you sympathetic to Tillich's objections? If so, cite instances to illustrate that your sympathy is grounded in experience.
3. Anglican Bishop John Robinson has said "The traditional material is all true, no doubt, and one recognizes it as something one ought to be able to respond to, but somehow it seems to be going on around one rather than within. Yet to question it openly is to appear to let down the side, to be branded as hopelessly unspiritual, and to cause others to stumble." First interpret this statement, then explain it from the viewpoint of a church leader. Finally, ask yourself if it has any meaning for you, for the religious feelings you may or may not have.

4. Remember how Anselm's ontological argument claimed that existence was a necessary part of the meaning of a perfect being. Is Tillich similarly claiming that God is a necessary part of the meaning of "ultimately concerned"? Is he defining God into existence?

5. Some claim that the mere fact that Tillich interprets his own knowledge of the "depth" as an experience of God does not make it so. Neither does it guarantee the existence of God. Are such critics distinguishing between belief and knowledge? How?

6. Some compare Tillich's claim that experience of the ground of all being is an experience of God to someone's claiming "I have a toothache because some mad genius has possessed my body and is causing the pain." Evaluate this analogy.

7. Do you think that Tillich's claims need public verification, as critics say they do? Is Tillich talking about a completely different kind of knowledge, a knowledge that transcends empirical data? In what ways is this a mystical knowledge?

Psychedelics and Religious Experience

1. Would you say that the two characteristics of a mystical experience James gives would also apply to a psychedelic-induced state of consciousness?

2. If through fasting, meditation, and prayer someone induced in himself a conscious state similar to a psychedelic-induced one, do you think society would react as it does to the user of psychedelics? If not, why not?

3. A common objection to the use of psychedelics is that the user loses touch with reality. What does such an objection assume? Do you think that the validity of this objection depends on the circumstances under which the drug is used?

Eastern Religious Traditions

1. What would you say are the main sources of attraction for Westerners in Eastern thought?

2. What obstacles would you note that many Westerners might face in adjusting to Eastern thought?

ADDITIONAL EXERCISES

1. People often argue for the existence of God by saying that, since there is obvious injustice in this life, there must be a God to right things in an afterlife. Is this argument sound?

2. In *Religion and the Modern Mind*, philosopher Walter T. Stace states "No scientific argument—by which I mean an argument drawn from the phenomena of nature—can ever have the slightest tendency either to prove or to disprove the existence of God."[21] Do you agree?

3. **Anthropomorphism** is the attribution of human characteristics to nonhumans. Show how we anthropomorphize God. In what sense have we created God in our image?

4. What role would you assign to contemporary religion in today's world?

5. What concrete difference would a religious experience make in the way you see things?

6. If you believe in a divine dimension, show how this belief is affecting your concept of knowledge and reality.

7. What is the most compelling reason for your belief in the divine? Is this reason sufficient to compel others to believe?

8. Can you speculate on what "religious experience" might mean in the future?

PAPERBACKS FOR FURTHER READING

Camus, Albert. *The Plague.* New York: Vintage, 1972. The theme of evil permeates this novel by a leading existentialist. Ultimately, Camus's is a humanistic posture, based on compassion for the meaningless plight that all people suffer.

Dostoyevsky, Fyodor. *The Brothers Karamazov.* New York: Signet Classics, 1971. Especially relevant in this classic is Book V, Chapter IV, in which Ivan's philosophical crisis over the presence of evil in the world crystallizes.

Huxley, Julian. *Religion Without Revelation.* New York: The New American Library (Mentor Books), 1957. Huxley argues for agnosticism and for religion as a way of life independent of revelation and theistic belief. The evidence Huxley finds for his own belief is established in science.

Needleman, Jacob. *The New Religions.* New York: Doubleday, 1970. This is a clear and inclusive study of the burgeoning interest in new forms of religious expression. Especially well-covered are the reasons behind the growing enthusiasm for Eastern thought.

---

[21]Walter T. Stace. *Religion and the Modern Mind.* Philadelphia: J. B. Lippincott, 1952, p. 76.

Robinson, John. *Honest to God.* Philadelphia: Westminster Press, 1963. Anglican Bishop Robinson is a leading spokesperson for radical theology. In this work, he argues that theism is untenable in modern times. He rejects any absolute moral values and posits a new morality centered around the love principle.

Russell, Bertrand. *Religion and Science.* New York: Oxford University Press (Galaxy Books), 1961. Russell reviews the historical conflict between religion and science. He argues that the ascendency of science has had positive intellectual and humanistic influences on religion.

Stace, Walter T. *Religion and the Modern Mind.* Philadelphia: J. B. Lippincott (Keystone Books), 1952. Stace argues for a divine principle, declaring that our lives are rooted in the mystical as well as the natural. He contends that religious values are necessary to correct the distortions of science's own subjective relativism.

Watts, Alan. *The Way of Zen.* New York: Random House, 1957. This is a very popular and readable presentation of Zen Buddhism, including its nature, history, and value. A more simplified version of the same material is found in Watts's *The Spirit of Zen* (New York: Grove Press, Evergreen Edition, 1960).

Ethics

9

Man is the only animal that blushes, or needs to. —Mark Twain

Even a cursory look at contemporary religious ritual reveals that traditional concepts are undergoing dramatic changes. The "God is dead" philosophy of Nietzsche has become part of the theology of respectable Christian thinkers who view traditional theism as a hindrance to enriching faith. We can also observe surface changes in religious ritual. Today, guitars commonly find a place once reserved for the organ; laymen help conduct services, a task once restricted to clergymen; couples compose and perform marriage ceremonies, once the province of the anointed. Women are ordained to the priesthood, once an unquestioned male prerogative.

Occurring also are changes in our life-style, our way of living. Our fashions, diet, and language are changing; so are our attitudes toward sex, the family, society, and ourselves. No one knows where these changes will lead, but one thing is certain: they are steeping in the pot of affluence and leisure time, a pot of unprecedented size.

It is true that no people in history have had so much of the world's bounty and so much time in which to use it as we have. It is no wonder that we keep hearing the phrase "quality of life." After all, many of us are now in a position to seek, if not share, the "good life." But just what is this good life? Various interests will gladly tell us, from the latest brand of beer to transcendental meditation. All pretend to offer a value worth our time and money, if not our devotion. The number of interests vying for our loyalties boggles the imagination. To which drummer should we march? What values should we pursue?

Much of how we see ourselves is determined by what we **value,** for our values shape our thoughts, feelings, actions, and perceptions. Our

265

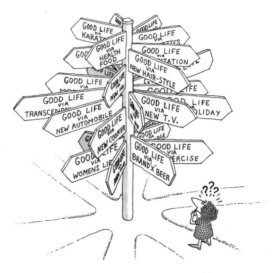

"But just what is this good life?"

values also express who and what we are. In the past, perhaps because of strong family ties, values were in a sense served up at the dinner table. We frequently attended a particular church, voted for a certain party, read select magazines, and behaved in a prescribed way because our parents did. But for many today the family is little more than a holiday house, checking account, and mailing address. Familial bonds, once so strong and far-reaching, often extend no farther than the nearest freeway; loyalty stretches no farther than the next meal. The affinity for family that many once felt is now often felt for a friend, a cause, or a commune. In most instances, however, these experiences with family substitutes are not long-lived or profound enough to instill lasting values. The result is frequently short, although often intense, romances with various values that can leave us intellectually dizzy.

Just what values should we hold and pursue? What values should we nourish in our own lives, in the running of our country, in our artistic tastes? So important are these questions in expressing and shaping us that we shall spend the next three chapters investigating them. We do this not to provide easy, simple-minded answers but to provide a framework in which to develop our own value systems. But first we should say something about the nature of values.

THE NATURE OF VALUES

A look at history reveals that no society has ever been without some value system. We can add that every individual, as well, has some code of values. The issue, therefore, is not whether individually or collectively we are to have values but what those values will be—whether they will advance or retard life, whether they will be consistent or not. In philosophy such questions about values fall under the heading of **axiology,** a term derived from the Greek word *axios* meaning "worthy." Axiology is the study of the general theory of values, including their origin, nature, and classification, as well as their place in our lives. Axiology is too broad a study to consider fully here. But it will be helpful before examining one field of axiology, ethics, to introduce some general axiological ideas.

First, philosophers distinguish between a fact and a value. A factual judgment is one that describes an empirical relationship or quality. For example, "Washington, D.C., is the nation's capital" and "Water boils at 212 degrees Fahrenheit at sea level" are factual statements. A value judgment, on the other hand, is one that assesses the worth of objects, acts, feelings, attitudes, even people. For example, "Beethoven was a good composer," "I should visit my sick brother," and "You were wrong in lying" are value judgments.

Throughout our discussion of axiological issues, specifically in ethics and esthetics, one question will recur: do value judgments express knowledge or feelings? When I say "Beethoven was a good composer" or "You were wrong in lying," am I expressing a truth or a personal preference? The answer is uncertain, and this uncertainty underscores the fact that there is little agreement on how the term *value* should be defined. Perhaps the best definition we can give is that a value is an assessment of worth.

Another axiological concern is whether values are subjective or objective. When I say, for example, that the "Mona Lisa" is beautiful, does the value I express originate in me or in the painting? Some say that a value is the subjective satisfaction of a human want, desire, or need. Others claim that a value is a quality within an object that satisfies the individual, and therefore is objective. Still others contend that a value has both subjective and objective elements.

Our Greek and Judaeo-Christian traditions provide us with the idea that there are certain absolute, unchanging values that are rooted in the nature of the universe or given by God. Because these traditions posit a moral order, we believe that we can call things good or evil regardless of what anyone thinks. Likewise, because an esthetic order is part of the nature of the universe, we think that we can call some things beautiful, others ugly, regardless of what anyone thinks.

In modern times another view of the nature of values has arisen that appeals to those of a less rigid and dogmatic bent. In this view, the basis of all values is found in the human. Since the human is a growing entity in a changing, dynamic universe, values reflect this developmental process. There are, consequently, no fixed or immutable values. Rather, with changing human conditions and ever-expanding knowledge, values change. In this view, what is ultimately of value is what advances human and community development.

Finally, the selection of values is an important axiological concern. Just what should we value? There is general agreement that certain groups of values, such as moral, political, esthetic, religious, and intellectual, exist, and that genetic, biological, and cultural influences produce many of these values. But there is little agreement about the nature of these values, their relative importance, or their relationship to one another. Nevertheless, most philosophers use the following principles in discussing axiological issues:

1. We should prefer what is of intrinsic value over what is of extrinsic value. A thing has intrinsic value when it is valued for its own sake. For example, some believe that pleasure has intrinsic value—that is, it is worthwhile in itself, not because it can yield something else. On the other hand, a thing has extrinsic value when it is a means to something else. A film could be said to have extrinsic value; that is, it is not a value in itself but can yield a value, perhaps pleasure. But intrinsic and extrinsic values are not necessarily mutually exclusive. What is valued in itself may also be a means to something else, as in the case of knowledge. Knowledge is worthwhile in itself, but also because it may lead to a job, affluence, or prestige.

2. We should prefer values that are productive and lasting to ones that are not. Physical and material values are generally less productive and long-lived than social, artistic, intellectual, and religious values. Long after a new car has worn out or a fortune has been spent, a genuine friendship or one's personal integrity persists.

3. We should choose our own values based on our own goals and ideals. When we allow values to be thrust upon us, we live others' lives, not our own. The values we hold should be consistent with one another and responsive to our own circumstances and experiences.

4. Finally, in choosing between two values, we should prefer the greater. What constitutes the "greater" will be determined largely by the previous three criteria. On the occasion of having to choose between two evils, we should prefer the "lesser," again allowing these criteria to influence our choice.

Admittedly, the theory of the nature of values is extremely general and frequently vague. But the theoretical skeleton takes on flesh when we examine specific branches of axiology, the first of which will be ethics.

ETHICS

In this chapter we focus on values that govern what is called good and bad conduct, **ethics.** Ethics is occasionally used synonymously with

"Long after a new car has worn out . . . a
genuine friendship persists."

morals. We would be more accurate, however, to use the terms *morals*
and *morality* to refer to the conduct itself, and the terms *ethics* and
ethical to mean the study of moral conduct or the code one follows. In
ethics we are concerned with questions of right and wrong, of duty and
obligation, of moral responsibility. When ethicists use words like *good*
or **right** to describe a person or action, they generally mean that the
person or action conforms to some standard. A good person or action
possesses qualities desirable for humans.

One branch of ethics, normative ethics, tries to determine precisely
what standards to follow so that our actions may be morally right or
good. Normative ethicists have presented principles by which to judge
the morality of an action. We shall examine these. In recent years, other
ethicists have relegated ethical questions primarily to language clarification. They are students of metaethics, and we shall examine their
positions, too. We are examining ethics not to conclude that one way
to behave is necessarily "better" than another but to develop our resources for ethical self-introspection, formulation, and analysis that
will provide us with a personally enriching moral life-style.

NORMATIVE ETHICS

Where do most of our moral beliefs come from? In the realm of ethics,
how do we come to act the way we do? For most of us, ethical action
springs from some principle. "Do unto others as you would have them
do unto you"; "Act in such a way that you bring about the greatest good

for the greatest number"; "Always act in your own best interests"; "Act however you choose, but don't hurt anyone else." When we think about why we choose to act the way we do, we can usually discover some principle with which we agree. **Normative ethics** is the reasoned search for such principles.

What makes the question of right and wrong so tough is that moral rules frequently differ from place to place, from time to time, and from people to people. John Hospers, in his *Introduction to Philosophical Analysis*, mentions what different people at various times have thought it morally necessary to do:

Never take a human life; never take a human life outside one's own tribe; never cause needless pain and suffering; do not gamble or wager; do not engage in sexual activity outside marriage; do not eat pork or shellfish; always turn the other cheek when you have been injured; always take revenge upon the party that has injured you; do not steal from others; do not get caught stealing from others; kill your parents when they are too old to travel with the caravan; honor your father and your mother; never tell a lie; never tell a lie except to an enemy (or a stranger).[1]

We must wonder how we can know what is the right way to behave, what is the good thing to do.

At the outset, we should concede that we shall never know for certain. But that does not mean that all ways are equal. To say that it does not matter what we choose, since we can never know for certain whether lying, for instance, is morally right or wrong, is to ignore many factors. First, we must take into account the effect on self. Such indifference invites into our lives an intolerable moral inconsistency that leaves us moral reeds in the winds of fashion. Operating thus according to whim undermines the integrated personality, which marks the contented and fulfilled person. Second, callous indifference to moral issues translates into disregard for the feelings and welfare of others. Consequently, the social contacts we need to be complete beings suffer. Third is the effect on universal moral law, if such a law exists. Simply put: if we are morally indifferent, we should allow everyone else to be. The picture of a world so populated is not attractive.

These three concerns traditionally have provided the basis for most ethical beliefs. In the normative positions we shall discuss, we shall notice an emphasis on self, other, or rule. The stress on ·self or other is generally found in normative positions that consider the consequences of actions; stress on rule is generally found in positions that consider factors other than consequences. We shall consider the consequentialist positions first.

---

[1] John Hospers. *Introduction to Philosophical Analysis*. Englewood Cliffs, N.J.: Prentice-Hall, 1967, p. 596.

CONSEQUENTIALIST THEORIES

To begin, let us join two city policemen, Obie and The Kid, as they do their tour of duty. Obie is the veteran, the "hair-bag," as the experienced officer is termed in police slang. The Kid is new, fresh out of the police academy, with ideas gathered more from school than from the street.

Obie: I see where B. B. McGeester was sprung this morning.

Kid: McGeester?

Obie: Maybe you don't know him. I busted him three times. Fourth last month. The third time he served a total of 18 months for pushing snow. Then he was out —"rehabilitation," they call it. Last month I nailed him for second-degree murder.

Kid: I take it you don't think they should have released him.

Obie: Ask the storekeeper he killed if B. B. should have been released. Civil rights. They said this morning his civil rights had been violated. Well, I say if you're not civil you don't deserve civil rights.

Kid: You don't think a criminal has any civil rights?

Obie: He loses them the day he breaks the law, that's what I think. But don't worry about it, Kid, he gets them back. The minute we bust him some judge who's never been in the street says, "Mister McGeester, sir, we apologize for violating your civil rights. We hope we haven't inconvenienced you." "Oh no, Your Honor, not in the least. But don't let it happen again. Because if you do I'm going to sue the pants off you. How's a guy supposed to make a dishonest living if you keep violating his civil rights?"

Kid: But what if his civil rights *were* violated, Obie? What if he was being held illegally?

Obie: What if, what if, what if . . . what if an hour after he's released he breaks some storekeeper's head; what if tomorrow he rapes some woman in the park; what if next week he swipes a car and runs over a child? The trouble with you, Kid, is the same trouble with those judges and lawyers: you haven't been on the street yet. You see only the criminals, never the victims. Those judges are never on the streets; they never have to pick up the pieces. They can make their decisions, then go hide in their chambers. They don't have to witness what their decisions lead to. I tell you, Kid, it's not right. It's downright immoral! And it won't be long before you see what I mean.

What Obie means is that an action is wrong if its consequences are undesirable. And since releasing criminals often leads to additional crime, releasing them on the basis of a civil-rights violation is immoral.

What would you rather have, Obie would ask, a civil right violated or a known felon walking the streets? Just consider the consequences and that should tell you. In considering the consequences of an action, we must distinguish between consequences for self and consequences for others, two subdivisions of **consequentialist theory.**

Egoism

Some ethicists believe that in deciding the morality of an action we should consider only the consequences to ourselves. These ethicists are called egoists. **Egoism** is the position that contends that we should always act in a way that promotes our own best long-term interests. Although egoists argue about precisely what actions these are, they agree that, once we know which action will promote our best long-term interests, we should embark on it. This notion does not imply, however, that we should do whatever we want; for often our best immediate interests are not our best long-term ones. Many a Watergate conspirator lied, presumably in the hope that his lie would cover up his own and others' corruption. And it did, for a while. But eventually much of the corruption came out and the liar then faced an additional problem: perjury. Thus, although his immediate interests might have been served, his long-term interests were not.

But a problem still nags: just what *are* our long-term interests? We are notorious for changing our minds. For example, we begin college with a particular major, confident that it is what we want to study. Shortly thereafter we change our minds, and we may do this several times before finally deciding on a field. Likewise, we marry, confident our marriage will last. Frequently it does not; we get divorced and perhaps try again. Sometimes we start a job believing that this work is what we want to do with our lives. A few years later we scrap the whole thing for something "more interesting."

Another problem: are we always the best judges of our best long-term interests? Suppose you like sweets. As far as you are concerned, eating cakes and candies and ice cream is just fine; you like them, they seem to agree with you, and they give mealtime a pleasure it would lack without them. During a physical exam, your physician notes that you have a high blood-sugar level. If you continue to eat sweets, he says, you will contract diabetes. That is important information. The physician is telling you your best long-term interests: to cut out sweets. You might not have discovered that on your own. Physicians, teachers, lawyers, psychologists, and clergymen frequently seem to know our best long-term interests better than we do. Should we listen to them? Perhaps we should, *if it is in our best long-term interests.* But, again, we do not really know whether their advice is in our best long-term interests. For example, if a trusted confidante is herself an egoist, she is advising us in her own best interests, not necessarily ours.

Then there are conflicting interests. Suppose that by telling a lie you will save yourself much trouble and heartache but will cause much for others. What should you do? There are those who argue that you should always act in the best interests of others. This position represents another consequentialist viewpoint, utilitarianism.

Reflection Try to recall an ethical decision you have made strictly on an egoistic basis. How desirable were the long-term consequences?

Utilitarianism: Act and Rule

Some ethicists claim that we must evaluate the consequences of an action in the light of how much good the action will produce for *everyone*, not just ourselves. This school of thought that emphasizes the other instead of the self is generally called **utilitarianism**. Utilitarians often find themselves in one of two schools: act or rule. **Act utilitarianism** is the ethical position that contends we should act in such a way that our action produces the greatest happiness for the most people. In other words, before acting, ask yourself: what will be the consequences of my action, not only for myself but for everyone else involved? If the consequences are good, so is the action; if they are bad, the action is bad as well. In effect, for the act utilitarian, the end justifies the means. This raises problems.

Kid: Obie, you remember that big drug bust on the East Side last month?

Obie: Sure, I remember it. That's another example of what I'm talking about. "Entrapment" they called it, and threw it right out of court.

Kid: But it *was* entrapment.

Obie: Look, Kid, when you're trying to catch a criminal you're interested in what works. Am I right?

Kid: Do you really believe it doesn't matter how you accomplish something just so long as you accomplish it?

Obie: When it comes to incorrigibles, that's exactly what I believe.

Kid: But how can you break the law to keep it?

Obie: Look, Kid, just because something's the law doesn't make it right. A lot of laws are lousy ones. That's the whole point. The system's gone soft. Take capital punishment, for instance. I say if a man murders in cold blood he loses his right to live.

Kid: What if he's innocent?

Obie: What're you talking about, *innocent?* Didn't I just say he murdered in cold blood?

Kid: But suppose he's innocent this particular time. Suppose he's guilty of a lot of other things, maybe even murders, but on this particular occasion he's innocent.

Obie: How can he be innocent if he's guilty of so much to begin with?

Kid: He's innocent in this one instance. That's what I'm saying.

Obie: And guilty all the rest of the time?

Kid: Right.

Obie: And he's gotten away with it all?

Kid: Suppose he has.

Obie: Then I say, when you get the chance, nail him.

Kid: You know what you're saying? You're saying it's okay to railroad somebody, to send him up for something he didn't do.

Obie: He did plenty. You said so yourself.

Kid: But not this particular thing.

Obie: A technicality!

Kid: A technicality?

Obie: Look, you got a choice: you either get this guy off the streets or you don't. Now are you going to tell me we should leave him out there on some technicality? Use your head, Kid, this is a public menace we're talking about, not some Boy Scout. You're removing a public menace from the streets! Who cares how you do it?

Kid: Then why not just shoot him and save us all a lot of time and money?

Obie: Because we're a law-abiding country.

What if an action that promises the greatest good for the greatest number, such as imprisoning an innocent person, appears to be patently wrong? The consequences of removing a chronic public threat, although never certain, appear to provide safety and happiness for the vast majority of people. Yet suppose that in this particular case the individual is innocent.

A number of ethicists point out that we get into such dilemmas when we apply the "greatest-happiness" principle to a particular act and not to the rule that the act implements. For example, in this case the ethical rule that the Kid is defending seems to be "People should never be imprisoned for something they didn't do." To determine whether this is a good rule we must evaluate the consequences of breaking it. How much fear and anxiety would arise if all of us knew we could be imprisoned for something we did not do? Would these feelings make us happy or not? Would breaking such a rule leave us feeling secure? Would it perhaps encourage us to break the law when we could, since abiding by it would be as perilous as breaking it? The consequences, it seems, are not good. Therefore, say the rule utilitarians, acting in a way that violates this rule would be bad, whereas acting in a way that promotes the rule would be good. In short, **rule utilitarianism** maintains that we should act in such a way that the rule governing our actions produces the greatest happiness for the most people.

But is it that simple? What about this rule: "When people are chronic and deliberate violators of the law, and they are found by reasonable criteria to be public menaces, it is good and desirable to imprison them, even for something they did not do"? The consequences of violating this rule appear to be similar to the ones we saw of violating the preceding rule. It would seem bad, then, not to promote this rule, and good to promote it. In brief, it is not easy to say what constitutes a "good rule." It is especially difficult to assess the rule on the basis of its consequences. But is any other basis possible? Some think so—that we must consider criteria other than consequences in evaluating morality. These **nonconsequentialists** are generally divided into those who emphasize nonconsequentialist duties and those who emphasize nonconsequentialist rules.

Reflection At the end of the semester a student appeals to a professor: "I know that I deserve a B in this philosophy course. But this B is going to spoil my 4.0 grade point average. And, competition being what it is, that B might stand between me and a scholarship to law school. If I don't receive a scholarship, I won't be able to go. That means I'll probably spend my life doing something I'd rather not be doing. If you gave me an A, it really wouldn't make any difference to you at all. Besides, no one would know it but you and me. What do you say?" The professor refuses the student's request. Explain the possible ethical bases of the student's argument and the professor's. With which would you be inclined to side? Why?

NONCONSEQUENTIALIST THEORIES

Duties

Rather than looking ahead to consequences, some ethicists look back to the past, where they find duties that have accrued, **obligations** we have assumed. These duties, they believe, should determine the morality of an action. This is the **duty theory** of ethics. The Kid holds this position.

Obie:	You're not telling me you'd turn a guy like that loose, are you?
Kid:	That's exactly what I'm telling you.
Obie:	But you said yourself he was one of those incorrigibles.
Kid:	But he's innocent in this particular case.
Obie:	What's that got to do with it?
Kid:	Everything.
Obie:	You realize that he's going to go out and do the same thing again?
Kid:	Maybe so.
Obie:	And that he may even kill somebody?
Kid:	That's possible, too.
Obie:	And despite that you'd release him?
Kid:	I would.
Obie:	How come?
Kid:	Because, no matter what the results, I don't believe it's right to imprison somebody for something he didn't do. It's just not fair.
Obie:	You know, Kid, I can see you've got a long and brilliant career ahead of you —as a judge!

"It's not fair," says The Kid. Notice that he does not call the action or rule wrong because of its consequences. No matter what the consequences, it's just not fair. A lot of ethicists would agree with him. They would argue that utilitarians are being too narrow when they evaluate only the consequences of an action. What we need to do is examine the past, not just the future. When we look at the past, we invariably detect duties of justice, gratitude, or fidelity that should guide our conduct.

In this case, the past provides a legacy of honesty and fair play, a sense of *justice.* Philosopher Sir David Ross tells us that justice is the distribution of good and evil in accordance with what is deserved. There is a certain code of equity that we have inherited and have implicitly agreed to live by. Part of this code says that people are to be considered innocent until proved guilty; that people should not be punished for something they did not do, even if they have done other things. It is argued that we are duty bound to follow this principle.

Other ethicists see duties of gratitude that arise from peculiar relationships with people—with parents, say, or other relatives. Suppose a father is out sailing with his small son and his son's friends. The boat capsizes. In the terror that follows, the son becomes separated from the others, who themselves are struggling to survive. The father is closest to the other boys and knows that he can rescue them, but only at his own son's peril. If he saves his son, the others will probably drown. If he rescues them, surely his son will perish. Whom should he save? The duty-bound ethicists would probably oblige the father to save his son, because of the unique relationship that exists between them.

Still others who would oblige us on the basis of duty weigh the importance of fidelity to agreements we may have entered into in the past. Suppose that you promise your best friend, a widow, on her deathbed, that you will make sure her young children are properly cared for. You are the only one who knows of this agreement. Some wealthy distant relatives subsequently try to adopt the children. You know that your friend distrusted and despised these people, and are reasonably sure that the widow would not want her children entrusted to them; yet they seem to be able to provide the children with all the material things they will need. Should you seek other arrangements, even at great personal inconvenience to yourself, and even though your ability to alter things is remote? Yes, say the duty-bound ethicists, who stress the importance of maintaining fidelity to past agreements.

The trouble with duties is that they are not always clear and mutually exclusive. Consider the case of a soldier who has sworn to obey the orders of his superiors. They order him to kill an innocent civilian. Is he obliged to carry out the order? Suppose the soldier refuses. Since the military pledges to court-martial those who disobey commands, is it obliged to court-martial the soldier who appeals to a "higher law of conscience"?

In the play *The Victors*, Jean-Paul Sartre portrays six French Resistance fighters captured and tortured by the Nazis, who wish to extract vital group-movement information from them. When it comes time for his painful interrogation, fifteen-year-old François informs his fellow cellmates that he'll reveal all rather than be tortured as they have been. His cellmates have a choice: silence him, or let him speak and thus imperil the lives of 60 soldiers. Lucy, the boy's sister, is among the prisoners. Seeing herself bound by fidelity to the other troops, she votes to kill François. Is she wrong? Does she have a conflicting duty because she is the boy's sister? One of the prisoners does strangle François. Some might argue that this prisoner "deserves" to be tried and found guilty of murder, and that the others "deserve" to be charged as accomplices. Thus, not only are duties often hard to spell out, but they also frequently seem to conflict.

Reflection   Take the situation you described in the Reflection section on page 273 and view it in terms of duty to justice, gratitude, or fidelity. What possible duties do you perceive?

Rules

Not all ethical viewpoints that wish to introduce factors other than consequences are based on some idea of duty. On the contrary, some look neither to the past nor to the future. According to these viewpoints, there operates a universal rule of moral behavior that obligates everyone, everywhere, at all times, to behave in a prescribed way. Two very influential rules have been the Golden Rule and the Categorical Imperative.

THE GOLDEN RULE

Obie: So it's wrong to put somebody in the slam for something he didn't do, is that it?

Kid: Yes, I think it is.

Obie: Well, if you know so much, tell me something—how come it's wrong?

Kid: How come? I'd think that would be pretty obvious, Obie.

Obie: Well, I guess I'm just dense, Kid, but it's not obvious to me. In fact, I'll tell you what it is to me: unbelievable!

Kid: Why? Because I'm putting myself in that guy's position and asking how it would feel? Is that so unbelievable?

The Kid wants to treat others as he would want to be treated. This is the **Golden Rule,** "Do unto others as you would have them do unto you." If you want to be fairly treated, treat others fairly; if you want to be loved, love others. The core of this principle is that you should never make an exception of yourself. Don't do to others what you are unwilling to have done to you. Given our Judaeo-Christian backgrounds, this ethical rule is perhaps the one that is most familiar to us. Yet the Golden Rule has a history that precedes Judaism. Sixth-century B.C. Confucianism admonished "What you don't want done to yourself, don't do to others." Fifth-century B.C. Buddhism warned "Hurt not others with that which pains yourself," and Zoroastrianism preached "Do not do unto others all that which is not well for oneself." Plato, in the fourth century B.C., hoped that "I do to others as I would that they should do unto me," and the teachings of Hinduism, third century B.C., include "Do naught to others which if done to thee would cause thee pain." The Golden Rule as formulated in Judaism states "What is hateful to yourself, don't do to your fellow man." Jesus preached "Whatsoever ye would that men should do to you, do ye even so to them." Notice that in abiding by the Golden Rule you consider neither consequences nor duties owing to the past. You simply apply the rule to ethical situations and choose the path it directs.

Obie:	Oh, so that's how you did it.
Kid:	Did what?
Obie:	Figured out it was wrong.
Kid:	You make it sound like a trick or something.
Obie:	Well it is, kind of. I mean here you are, an innocent guy, a cop even, but you know how it would feel to be charged with a crime you haven't committed. I mean that's quite a trick, Kid. You should go on TV.
Kid:	What are you talking about? I don't have to know how that guy would feel. I just have to know how *I'd* feel.
Obie:	But how do you know he feels the same way?
Kid:	What difference does that make?
Obie:	All the difference in the world. I mean what if he figures "I don't mind if somebody goes around ripping me off, so I guess it's all right for me to rip them off."
Kid:	He wouldn't think that way.
Obie:	Listen, Kid, you don't know those guys. They live by jungle rules. You think they mind if somebody beats them to the punch? They're only mad because they've been outsmarted, that's all. You think they're worried about whether the thing's right or wrong? Don't kid yourself. What you're doing is playing the game by a rule they couldn't care less about. When you say you know what it would feel like, you're speaking only for yourself. That guy may not even mind going in for something he didn't do because he beat the rap for so many things he did do. Win some, lose some, that's how he's thinking. Do unto others as they would do unto you—only do it first! That's their law.

One problem with the Golden Rule is that it does not seem specific enough. It does not account for different desires. Suppose a car thief reasons "I can steal as many cars as I want, since I allow anyone to steal my beat-up car who wants to." Surely the Golden Rule cannot sanction such behavior. But perhaps this example is too narrow an application of it. More precisely, in such a case it prescribes that, if we have something of value that we would not want taken, then we should not take something that someone else values, whatever it is. Still, problems persist.

Suppose the same thief is perfectly willing to "do as he would be done by." Because he has no reservations about stealing, he is perfectly willing to help others steal in return for their helping him. Certainly the Golden Rule cannot condone their conduct, yet by itself it seems powerless to discriminate the good action from the bad. It seems to be saying that, if something is good for you to do, it is good for everyone else;

if bad for you, bad for everyone else. But the Rule is not telling what is good or bad.

Another problem with the Golden Rule is that what's good or bad for someone else is not always good or bad for you. Suppose you decide that it is wrong for the couple next door to get divorced. Are you then committed to believe that it is wrong for you? Your circumstances may be quite different from theirs. Perhaps they have children, but you do not; perhaps they've had trial separations, but you have not; perhaps they are involved in extramarital affairs, but you are not. It seems, then, that to be useful the Golden Rule must imply that what is wrong for others is wrong for you, providing the circumstances are sufficiently similar. But then we must decide when circumstances are sufficiently similar.

Philosophers have not been indifferent to those objections to the Golden Rule. In the eighteenth century Immanuel Kant attempted to remedy the weaknesses of the Golden Rule by formulating his Categorical Imperative.

KANT'S CATEGORICAL IMPERATIVE

To understand Kant's thought, it helps to note the emphasis he placed on the idea of good intentions. Kant believed that nothing was good in itself except a "good will." Intelligence, judgment, and all other facets of the human personality are perhaps good and desirable, but only if the will that makes use of them is good. By "will" Kant meant the uniquely human capacity to act according to the concepts behind laws —that is, principles. Kant saw these laws or principles operating in nature. A good will, therefore, is one that acts in accordance with nature's laws.

In estimating the total worth of our actions, Kant believed that a good will takes precedence over all else. Contained in a good will is the concept of duty. Only when we act from duty does our action have moral worth. When we act out of feelings or inclination, our action, although otherwise identical with the one that springs from a sense of duty, has no moral worth. For example, merchants have a duty not to shortchange their customers. But the simple fact that they do not shortchange their customers does not mean that they are acting from a good will. They may be acting from an inclination to keep business or to avoid legal entanglements. Likewise, the fact that we practice kindness does not mean that our kind actions have moral worth. We may be acting to produce a sense of inner satisfaction, to be well thought of, or to advance ourselves. Thus, actions have true moral worth only when they spring from a recognition of a duty and a choice to implement it.

To illustrate an act of true moral worth, assume that you were deeply troubled, your mind so clouded with sorrow that you in no way felt like

". . . the fact that we practice kindness does not mean that our kind actions have moral worth."

being kind or loving to anyone. Suppose you tore yourself out of this numbness and performed an act of kindness, without inclination and only from duty. This action would have true moral worth. In effect, when you act in such a way you act out of love. As Kant put it, "The beneficence from duty, when no inclination impels it and even when it is opposed by a natural and unconquerable aversion, is practical love." This love resides in the will.

But what duties should we follow, and how do we know them? Kant believed that there was just one command or imperative that was categorical—that is, one that presented an action as necessary of itself, without regard to any other end. He believed that from this one **Categorical Imperative,** this universal command, all commands of duty could be derived. Kant's Categorical Imperative states that we should act in such a way that the maxim, or general rule, governing our action could become a universal law.

Suppose you make a promise but are willing to break it if it suits your purposes. Your maxim can be expressed thus: when it suits my purposes, I'll make promises that I'll break when keeping them no longer suits my purposes. This maxim could not be universally acted upon, because it involves a contradiction of will. On the one hand, you are willing to make promises and have them honored; on the other, you are willing to break the same promises. Notice that Kant is not a utilitarian; he is not arguing that the consequences of a universal law condoning promise-breaking would be bad, and that therefore the rule is bad.

Instead, he is claiming that the rule is self-contradictory, that it is self-defeating, that the institution of promise-making would dissolve if such a maxim were universalized.

But Kant is not always so persuasive as he is regarding promise-keeping. First, it is highly doubtful that all acts falling under a categorical rule are always wrong. For example, one of Kant's maxims is "Don't lie." But is lying *always* wrong? Is it wrong to lie to save your life? To save someone from serious pain or injury? Second, duties frequently conflict. If, as Kant argues, it is always wrong to tell a lie and always wrong to break a promise, then which do I choose when these duties conflict? Finally, there is no compelling reason that the prohibition against certain actions should hold without exception. In other words, there seems some doubt that the prohibition against actions like lying, promise-breaking, and killing must function without exception. Apparently Kant failed to distinguish between saying that *persons should make no exceptions to rules* and *a rule itself has no exceptions*. The statement that a person should make no exceptions to rules means that one should never except oneself from being bound by a rule. But because one may never make an exception of oneself, it does not follow that the rule has no exceptions and can never be qualified.

Having discussed the major normative positions, we can draw one obvious conclusion: it is difficult to choose among imperfect and frequently contradictory theories. What do we do? We may, on the one hand, base our ethical choices on consequences to self or on consequences to others. On the other hand, we may base them not on consequences but primarily on duties we have accrued by being a mother or father, son or daughter, husband or wife, lover or loved one, employer or employee. Still another possibility is to base ethical choice on a code of justice that we have inherited or some rule that we respect.

The apparent insolubility of ethical problems has inspired in the twentieth century an ethical movement concerned almost exclusively with clarifying ethical language. It is called metaethics.

Reflection If you had the power to universalize one moral rule, what would it be?

METAETHICS

Metaethics is the study of the meaning of terms and language used in ethical discourse and the kinds of reasoning used to justify ethical statements. The metaethicist is concerned not with discovering and defending a principle of good conduct but with determining the meanings of ethical words and sentences.

Take as an example the issue that Obie and The Kid were debating: "It's wrong to imprison a person for something he didn't do." Meta-ethicists do not debate which principle—act-utilitarian, rule-utilitarian, Golden Rule, or some other—is the one upon which a decision should be based. Instead, they attempt to discover what is meant by the ethical word *wrong*. They contend that once you define the ethical term being used you can then evaluate the truth of the ethical statement. These metaethicists generally fall into one of three schools: naturalism, non-naturalism, and emotivism.

Naturalism

Naturalism is the metaethical position that contends that ethical statements can be translated into nonethical or empirical ones. Naturalists frequently find themselves in one of three schools: autobiographical, sociological, or theological.

To illustrate, *autobiographical* naturalism considers one possible meaning of *wrong* to be "I disapprove of something." Thus, when The Kid says "It's wrong to imprison a person for something he didn't do," he means "I don't approve of it." He uses himself as the standard of right or wrong. He takes what is called an autobiographical position. If something is *wrong*, that means "I disapprove of it"; if something is *right*, that means "I approve of it." Such an interpretation is consistent with egoism. An ethical statement with an autobiographical meaning is easy to verify, for it is little different from one that reports internal states: "I feel sick," "I have a toothache," "I'm tired." Defining ethical words this way has the effect of dissolving moral questions by viewing them as expressions of personal preference.

For other naturalists, however, ethical words imply more than just our own approval. We might argue, for example, that it is wrong to kill infant twins because most people in our society disapprove of it. Here we appeal not to the self but to the group. This is the *sociological* position, which contends that the meaning of the ethical word hinges on societal approval or disapproval. Thus, "It's wrong to imprison a person for something he didn't do" may mean "Society disapproves of imprisoning a person for something he didn't do." This view is consistent with the utilitarian position. We can verify such a statement easily enough. Conduct a poll, find out what society really thinks about that issue; until we do that, there's little point in getting heated over the question. Thus once again the ethical problem is dissolved, if not resolved.

There is still another way to interpret ethical words and statements. Many people would argue that killing infant twins is wrong, but not because any person or group disapproves of it. It is wrong because God Himself, as He made Himself known through sacred writings, disapproves of it. This *theological* interpretation of ethical words would render the statement "It's wrong to imprison a person for something he didn't do" as "God disapproves of imprisoning a person for something he didn't do." To verify this statement you must point to the Scriptures, the Koran, the Ten Commandments, or some other religious text. The question then becomes: does such verification exist? If it does, the ethical statement is true; if it does not, the statement is false. Once again the effect is to dissolve the dispute.

No doubt these possible interpretations of ethical words go far toward clarifying ethical disputes. Any time we can agree on terms, we are closer to understanding content. But what if two people disagree on the interpretations? Surely atheists would not accept the theological interpretation of ethical words. If they did, they would be contradicting themselves: "Killing infant twins is wrong because God, who doesn't exist, disapproves of it." For the subscriber to the theological interpretation, it would seem that an atheist cannot be moral. In addition, adherents to the autobiographical position frequently disagree: "I approve of killing infant twins" versus "I disapprove of killing infant twins." Who is *right?* Or what about statements like "I approve of living together before marriage but choose not to"? According to an autobiographical definition, this statement is contradictory: "I approve of living together before marriage, but I disapprove of it." We can also raise objections to the position that holds society as the standard of ethical meaning. What if one society approves of killing infants and the other does not? There are, moreover, cases in which society clashes with individuals. "Because I disapprove of this war," many argued during the Vietnam War, "I will not serve in the army." At the same time, their society was approving of the same war. There is an additional problem with naturalist positions, which has led many to espouse nonnaturalism.

Nonnaturalism

Notice how the three interpretations of the sentence "It's wrong to imprison a person for something he didn't do" use the word *disapprove*. But *disapprove* itself seems to be an ethical word. *I disapprove* apparently means "I think it's wrong"; *society disapproves* apparently means "society thinks it's wrong"; and *God disapproves* apparently means "God thinks it's wrong." It would seem, then, that to define *right* or *wrong* in terms of *approve* or *disapprove* is merely to define those words in terms of themselves. But isn't this circular reasoning? Many metaethicists believe it is. Therefore, they support **nonnaturalism,** the metaethical position that ethical statements defy translation into nonethical language. As George E. Moore, a leading exponent of this position, says:

There is no empirical observation and no mathematical, logical calculation which would enable us to discover the truth of ethical propositions. All we can do is to distinguish them carefully from all other propositions (especially some empirical ones with which they are apt to be confused), and then reflect upon them and see whether, after this reflection, we believe that they are true.[2]

One problem here is reliance on "reflection" as a source of knowledge. Just precisely what does that mean? After "reflection," two people could formulate opposite and contradictory ethical positions. Which, if either, would be correct? Nonnaturalism appears to provide no answer. This suggests to some that perhaps ethical statements present no ethical positions at all but are, rather, emotive expressions.

Emotivism

Emotivism is the metaethical position that ethical statements express surprise, shock, or some other emotion. To say "It's wrong to imprison a person for something he didn't do," according to emotivists, does not necessarily voice moral indignation. Rather, the speaker is simply voicing amazement: "What! You've imprisoned an innocent man!" Sometimes we may use so-called ethical statements to get someone to behave in a certain way. "Lying is wrong," we tell a child, not necessarily because we believe lying is wrong but because we don't want the child to lie. But still there are problems.

How do we know that ethical statements are used only in this way? Even if they are, when we tell the child not to lie rather than to lie we seem to be implying a moral stand in which the expression of emotion is rooted. If we say "How terrible!" at the news of someone's death, it is true that we are expressing feeling. But feeling in turn expresses something else: that we deplore this occurrence, that we deplore the death of anyone, that we deplore the consequence of that event, that we deplore how this makes us feel. If "It's wrong to imprison a person for something he didn't do" means "You've imprisoned an innocent man!" we should ask: Why this reaction? Why this shock or surprise? Thus, at the very least, it seems that the speaker is voicing disapproval of something—taking a position we have already discussed: autobiographical naturalism.

For most of us, metaethics is probably not of vital concern. Day in and day out we are faced with moral choices that seem unavoidable. As a result, the great majority of us act or try to act from some normative position. Nevertheless, knowing these metaethical positions can help locate our or someone else's ethical whereabouts and further clarify normative positions. It can also reveal inconsistencies and underscore complexities of moral decision-making that we may be unaware of.

---

[2]George E. Moore. *Principia Ethica.* London: Cambridge University Press, 1903, p. 7.

Reflection   Do you believe that something can be morally wrong for you to do but right for someone else? Right for you but wrong for someone else?

THE COMPLEXITY OF MORAL DECISIONS

To understand the complexity of moral decisions, and how an understanding of normative and metaethical positions can at least help elucidate them, imagine a convalescent home, one of those havens for the elderly infirm and in general for those aged who no longer seem to "fit into" society. Janet, a 22-year-old nurse, works at Sunnyview. Janet likes her work very much and hopes some day to be a physician. She particularly enjoys the elderly people she attends and considers herself more a friend than a nurse. For the most part, they feel the same about her.

Janet is particularly fond of one old gentleman at Sunnyview, Mr. Pitman; he reminds her of her grandfather, who died only a year before after a long and painful illness. In his prime Mr. Pitman was vigorous, but now his 80 years have hobbled and enfeebled him. He has no family and depends on welfare to pay his bills. He despises Sunnyview so much that he has tried to take his life twice. Although alert and rational, he sees no further point in living. He simply wants to die. Sunnyview officials have told him that if he persists in his suicide attempts he will be transferred to a state psychiatric hospital for the remainder of his life.

The long shadows of a winter's afternoon have just fallen across Mr. Pitman's room when we join him and Janet.

Mr. Pitman:	Janet, you once said you'd do anything for me.
Janet:	I would, Mr. Pitman, you know that.
Mr. Pitman:	Anything?
Janet:	Anything in the world.
Mr. Pitman:	You wouldn't fool an old man, would you?
Janet:	You know better than that.
Mr. Pitman:	Yes, I suppose I do. . . . Tomorrow when you come in, would you bring me a bottle of . . . sleeping pills?
Janet:	Sleeping pills? You know you don't have to send out for those, Mr. Pitman. The doctor will prescribe them if you can't sleep.
Mr. Pitman:	You don't understand. I have no trouble sleeping. It's waking up that's the bother.

Janet:	You mean . . .
Mr. Pitman:	I mean I wish a quick and painless death. But at the same time, I don't want you to get into any trouble on my account. So here, take this money.
Janet:	I'm sorry, Mr. Pitman, I can't do that.
Mr. Pitman:	You can't do it? But, Janet, I thought you were my friend.
Janet:	But you can't ask me to help you . . .
Mr. Pitman:	Die? Janet, I'm old and I'm sick, so very sick. And tomorrow I'll be even older and sicker. It will never be different. Only worse. You don't wish that for me, do you?
Janet:	No, of course I don't. But it'd be wrong for me to do what you ask.
Mr. Pitman:	Why would it be wrong?
Janet:	Because it goes against everything people believe is right and decent. You know that, Mr. Pitman.
Mr. Pitman:	No, I don't. I don't know that. All I know is there's no one in this bed suffering but me. Where are all those right and decent people? Out there, out in the streets and in the film shows and in front of television sets. They're not feeling all the pain and hurt, Janet. I am—Robert Pitman—I'm feeling it all. And the loneliness—the agony of having nobody, no family, no friends, just people like you who come to work here and poke me and prop me up. Those good and decent people you speak of—what right do they have to tell me what to do? Let them lie here awhile and then tell me that. In the meantime I say it's right, Janet, and I want you to help me.

Janet has been asked to help someone kill himself. On what basis will she decide what to do? "It goes against everything people believe is right and decent," she replies, giving us the best clue to her position. Metaethically, she seems to be relying on what society approves and disapproves of to guide her—on a sociological definition of what is good and bad. In her view, society disapproves of suicide; therefore she opposes it. She may ultimately see that her disapproval is based on something else, but initially this is her stance.

Mr. Pitman objects. Society is not sharing his experience. He suffers alone. Whether he would argue from this autobiographical position on all ethical questions is uncertain; but on this one he believes that, since he approves of Janet's helping him, her helping him is right. Notice that the issue here is not whether suicide is moral or immoral, although it no doubt enters the question. The real issue is whether a person under these circumstances should help another person end his life. It would be entirely consistent for Janet to see nothing wrong with suicide but still insist that it is wrong for her to assist a potential suicide.

Janet:	But I can't help you, Mr. Pitman.
Mr. Pitman:	Do you think it's wrong for me to take my life?
Janet:	I'm not sure. But I think almost everybody would say it's wrong for me to help you.
Mr. Pitman:	Now listen. If I had a family, if people were depending on me, if there were loved ones who would be deeply hurt by my action—
Janet:	But I will be, Mr. Pitman.
Mr. Pitman:	That's kind of you, my dear. But can you honestly say that your hurt will be greater than what I'm going through? What I *will* go through?
Janet:	No, probably not.

The element of utilitarianism is clear in this exchange. True, suicide is not the moral issue here, but Mr. Pitman believes that the consequences of his suicide are relevant to whether it is right or wrong for Janet to help him commit suicide. He is not, however, egoistic, as one might expect from his previous autobiographical position. He does not assume that only consequences to himself are at stake. In effect he asks Janet to compare the consequences of his proposal for all concerned.

Mr. Pitman:	Then why not help me?
Janet:	But what if I helped everyone who asked me to do that?
Mr. Pitman:	But not everyone is asking you.
Janet:	Would you believe that Mrs. Kandinsky asked me the same thing last month?
Mr. Pitman:	Mrs. Kandinsky. The poor soul . . . But Mrs. Kandinsky has a family to consider.
Janet:	You think that makes her suffering any the less? Am I supposed to just help people without families, Mr. Pitman? Or those with families that don't love or visit them? Or maybe those with families who only visit them on Christmas and Thanksgiving?
Mr. Pitman:	Why not just help those who are desperate and who beg you, like me? Is that so hard, Janet? Wouldn't that be the right thing to do?
Janet:	I don't know. Do you know what Mrs. Kandinsky said to me yesterday? That she's looking forward to the spring and the birth of her grandchild. So you tell me, Mr. Pitman, what's desperation? How do you measure it?

How do you make up a rule to cover situations like these? This is what Janet is asking Mr. Pitman. She does not wish to consider the consequences of his isolated act. She wants to look at the rule that the act is following. Assuming the role of the rule utilitarian, Mr. Pitman says simply that she should aid anyone who asks and who is desperate. But precisely what does "desperate" mean? How many of us have not felt at some time desperate enough to want not to live, only to have that feeling pass like a nightmare?

Mr. Pitman: Janet, I thought you were my friend.

Janet: But I am, Mr. Pitman. And I'll continue to be.

Mr. Pitman: Well, don't friends generally do things for each other?

Janet: Yes, but—

Mr. Pitman: Didn't you tell me just a minute ago that there wasn't anything you'd not do for me?

Janet: But that didn't include helping you hurt yourself.

Mr. Pitman: *Anything,* Janet, You said you'd do *anything* for me.

The conversation has turned; the consequences of the action are no longer the issue. Now the issue is duties that have accrued in the past, especially the duty to fidelity. Janet has made a promise to Mr. Pitman, and he is trying to hold her to it. In his eyes she is duty bound. But, she says, the promise didn't include helping him commit suicide. This raises the question of just how far promises go. Are all promises contingent on mental reservations, conscious or otherwise? When people promise to love and honor "from this day forward till death us do part," does that promise exclude "incompatibility," "irreconcilable differences," and the like, which excuse from their marriage vows more than half the people who take them? It is one thing to argue normatively that we are bound to be faithful to the promises we make; it is another to specify the nature, conditions, and limitations of a promise.

Janet: But I've made another promise, Mr. Pitman.

Mr. Pitman: What other promise?

Janet: To help you stay well and healthy. I've sworn to help you stay alive, not to help you die.

As we have previously seen, duties often conflict. Perhaps Janet does have a personal obligation to Mr. Pitman stemming from promises she has made to him. But she also has a professional obligation to him that stems from an oath she swore when becoming a nurse.

Mr. Pitman:	All right, Janet. Just tell me one thing and I'll not bother you anymore. If you were me, would you want this request refused?
Janet:	I don't know, Mr. Pitman, I honestly don't. But let me ask you something.
Mr. Pitman:	Go on.
Janet:	If you were me, what would *you* do?
Mr. Pitman:	I'd like to think I'd help an old man die with dignity. . . . But I guess I don't know, either.

As a last resort to enlist Janet's aid in his death, Mr. Pitman endorses a variation of the Golden Rule. If she were in his position, he assumes she would want to be treated as he wishes to be. But Janet confounds his ploy by asking him to stand in her shoes. After all, turnabout is fair play. What would he do?

What would *you* do? That is the real question. Forget Janet and Mr. Pitman, Obie and The Kid. Focus on yourself. *You* must decide—perhaps not whether it is right to imprison an innocent person or whether to help an old man end his life—but other issues, pressing ones for you. On what basis are you making the moral decisions that are shaping who and what you are and will be?

CONCLUSIONS

Having seen the complexity of moral decision-making, we may be tempted to throw up our hands in exasperation and wonder what difference it all makes. Since we cannot know for sure, why bother?

The fact is that it does make a difference, and we must bother, for the moral values we hold are an expression of who we are, how we see things, and how we wish to be seen by others. In choosing a moral life-style, we are really defining a large part of self. Yet the complexity of moral decision-making persists; the choices remain murky. The question each of us must ask is: what moral life-style should I adopt to live the fullest, most rewarding life I can?

Obviously, there is no certain answer. But it seems that we can garner factors from our discussion that are appropriate ingredients for a personal morality. First, any moral code you follow must be your own. Granted, we cannot fully escape our social, cultural, and religious backgrounds; neither would we want to. Nevertheless, if our morality is to be an expression of self, we must carefully reflect on the values we have inherited, weighing their merits and liabilities in the light of our own lives, times, and circumstances. Such reflection places heavy emphasis on self-growth, especially on increasing our knowledge and awareness of self and the world, and on being willing to adjust our moral views as relevant new discoveries arise. It also recognizes the dynamic, experimental value of morality.

The second factor appropriate to a personal morality is related to the first. It stems from Immanuel Kant's concept of a good will. As just suggested, to make moral decisions primarily on the basis of social or institutional influence is to surrender what most consider a uniquely human quality: the individual capacity to make moral decisions. These outside forces should not be our primary reasons for acting morally. For the mature and thoughtful person, right intention or good will is a necessary ingredient of the true moral act. This ingredient introduces the elements of motive, sincerity, and love. It is true that these are hazy concepts, but in context they frequently clear up. For example, the motives of the person who gives to charity primarily for the sake of a tax write-off are different from those of the person who gives to improve the conditions of the less fortunate; the intention of the person who flatters to ingratiate is different from that of the person who speaks the truth for its own sake. Invariably the teachings of ethicists and great moral leaders have stated or implied the importance of right intention, good will, or love in the moral act.

But these two subjective elements of a personal moral code, moral self-determination and right intention, are insufficient to ensure right action. After all, we may be morally self-determining and well-intentioned but do something heinous. The third element, therefore, is an objective one, involving a consideration of the results or consequences of our actions. It seems that consequences must be a factor in any moral stance, for to be indifferent to the consequences of our actions is itself to act irresponsibly—that is, without moral regard. As we have seen, however, determining the consequences of an action is often difficult. It requires much evidence, analysis, and reflection. Even then we cannot be certain. But without such an examination our action will not be in the highest sense moral.

No doubt there are other factors that you might wish to introduce. But these three—self-determination, right intention, and consideration of consequences—are the building blocks of a personal moral code.

SUMMARY

We opened this chapter by observing that values, like so many other things today, are changing. Axiology, the study of the nature of values, includes debates about whether value judgments express knowledge or feeling, whether values are subjective or objective, and precisely what is of value. One important value area is ethics. Normative ethics is the search for principles of good conduct. Broadly speaking, it can be divided into consequentialist and nonconsequentialist schools. The consequentialist school, in turn, is subdivided into egoism, act utilitarianism, and rule utilitarianism; the nonconsequentialist school is subdivided into duty nonconsequentialism and rule nonconsequentialism. Metaethics is the study of ethical words and the sentences in which they appear. Metaethicists generally fall into the schools of naturalism, nonnaturalism, and emotivism. Although moral questions are complex, we must formulate a personal moral code that includes self-determination, right intention, and consideration of consequences.

MAIN POINTS

1. Axiology is the study of the nature of values.
2. Ethics is concerned with questions of right and wrong, of duty and obligation, and of moral responsibility.
3. Normative ethics is the reasoned search for principles of moral behavior.
4. Consequentialist theories are those that claim that the morality of an action depends only on its consequences.
5. Egoism is the consequentialist position that states: always act in such a way that your actions promote your own best long-term interests.
6. Act utilitarianism is the consequentialist position that states: act in such a way that your actions produce the greatest happiness for the most people.
7. Rule utilitarianism is the consequentialist position that states: act in such a way that the rule of your actions produces the greatest happiness for the most people.
8. Duty-directed normative ethicists claim that we are bound by obligations we have accrued in the past, such as gratitude, fidelity, and justice.
9. The Golden Rule is the normative position that charges: Do unto others as you would have them do unto you.
10. Kant's Categorical Imperative is the normative position that recommends: Act in such a way that you could wish the rule of your action to become a universal law.
11. Metaethics is the study of the meaning of ethical words and the sentences in which they appear. It attempts to clarify the meaning of moral statements.
12. In general, metaethicists fall into three groups: naturalists, nonnaturalists, and emotivists.

SECTION EXERCISES

Egoism

1. Some people argue that everyone is ultimately an ethical egoist. What do they mean by this? Do you agree? Would this prove that egoism is the base of all ethics?
2. What are the connotations of the word *egoism?* Are these connotations compatible with what you know about ethical egoism?
3. With which concepts of knowledge and of reality do you think ethical egoism is compatible?
4. How prevalent do you think ethical egoism is in contemporary society?

Utilitarianism

Below are four ethical problems. How would an act-utilitarian solution differ from a rule-utilitarian solution in each case?

1. An aide is conferring with the President of the United States. "Mr. President, it's imperative that you win the upcoming election. If you don't, subversives will take over the government. This could spell the end of our government as we know it. We could present the public with all the facts and let them decide, but that would only alarm and panic them. There's another way, and that is to use the enormous financial connections of this administration to manipulate and mold public opinion. This, it's true, will necessitate illegal election contributions, misrepresentation of facts, and considerable fancy footwork in the campaign. But it's an immediate, practical, and judicious solution in the best interests of the nation."
2. The daughter of a very rich and important public figure has been kidnapped. The kidnappers threaten to murder the young woman unless her father delivers a quarter of a million dollars in ransom money. Authorities have told him that if he does so he'll only be encouraging future terrorist activities that will invariably involve more people, more suffering, and more deaths. He must decide.
3. Taxpayer Smith decides there are plenty of things he dislikes about the way the U.S. government is run: exorbitant defense spending, collusion between business and government, mismanaged funds, and so on. As a result he is contemplating ceasing to pay income taxes.
4. Jones and Brown are debating whether a person has a moral obligation to obey all laws. Jones claims that deliberately breaking a law is immoral. Brown denies this.

Duties

1. Reconsider the four preceding situations in terms of duties. What duties are possibly involved? Would the duty ethicist's solutions differ from the act utilitarian's? The rule utilitarian's?

Rules

1. Can you reasonably apply the Golden Rule or the Categorical Imperative to any of the four situations of the previous exercise?
2. Would it be possible or desirable to universalize the following maxims?
   a. Never work unless you absolutely must.
   b. Do your own thing, unless it hurts somebody else.
   c. Give nothing, and expect nothing in return.
   d. Sell all you have and give to the poor.
   e. Let your conscience be your guide.
3. Do you approve of any of the following rules? Would you want to qualify any of them? How?
   a. Always stick by your friends.
   b. Never discriminate against someone on the basis of race, religion, color, or sex.
   c. Never punish a child physically.
   d. Without prior approval, you should never take something that doesn't belong to you.
4. Evaluate the Ten Commandments. How and why have they been qualified? What has been the effect of the qualifications? Would you qualify them further?

Metaethics

1. What would be the probable metaethical base of each of the normative positions we discussed?
2. With which school of philosophy discussed in previous chapters would metaethical theories in general find the most sympathy? Why?
3. If you believed that ethical statements were translatable into nonethical terms, what would be your probable position on questions of knowledge and reality? On the existence of God?

ADDITIONAL EXERCISES

How would you resolve the following ethical questions, and why?

1. You are a personnel director. Two equally qualified people are applying for a job. You are physically attracted to one but not to the

other. It enters your mind that, in giving the job to the one you are attracted to, you might be striking up a friendship that could prove very satisfying for you personally. You realize, of course, that their looks will have no bearing on their job performances. What do you do?

2. Two young people away at college wish to live together, primarily to enjoy a sexual relationship. If their parents knew, they would disapprove and be greatly distressed. The young woman can and intends to take the pill. Both agree to be honest and open with one another and to dissolve the relationship when either one wants out. Should they enter into this relationship or not?

3. You are part of an advertising firm that has been asked to write promotions for an oil company. Because you have "inside information," you know that what you have been asked to write is false and misleading. If you do not write it you will lose your job and will, at least temporarily, jeopardize the economic well-being of your spouse and two young children. What do you do?

4. Late one night you are driving along a lonely road in a strange town. For a moment your eyes wander from the road, and you scrape a parked car. You stop and assess the situation: the parked car is brand new, the damage is about $250 worth and absolutely no one has seen you (not even a house light has turned on). You know that another claim might cost you your insurance, and you need your car to make a living. You believe that the owner has probably insured his brand new car, that the neighborhood is an affluent one, and that the damage is minimal. You wonder if you should drive off. Should you?

5. During an especially important final exam, panic seizes you. You can't think; you start to sweat. If you fail this test, you may have to drop out of school. You will certainly lose the financial support of your family, as well as all the privileges they have extended to you as long as you stay in school. The person next to you has carelessly placed his answer sheet so that only a blind person couldn't see it. Under normal circumstances it would be difficult to resist the temptation to look. But with this kind of pressure you find it virtually impossible. What should you do?

6. Two people are in love. Both are physicians. She is white; he is black. Both have been raised by their families to eschew interracial marriages. Both realize that their marriage will not only deeply offend their families, but will probably sever all relations with them as well. What should they do? Would it make any difference if one of them ensured surgically that it would be impossible for them to procreate?

7. A young man and woman take to displaying their mutual affection in public, not in any particularly offensive way, but mostly through

hand-holding and affectionate kissing. People have complained to them, especially in public parks where there are young, inquisitive children. The couple realize they are making a lot of people anxious, but at the same time they feel they have certain rights and privileges of their own. What should they do? Would your opinion differ if they were two gay young men?

8. You are a newspaper reporter who has been arrested for not divulging the news source of a sensational story. You believe you are safeguarded by the First Amendment, and you also feel a moral obligation to shield your source. You know also that the only way your source could have obtained the information he has provided was to break the law himself. In fact, he is a known Mafia leader, who apparently confided in you more with the intention of revenge than out of a sense of civic responsibility. The public would only be served by getting rid of him as well as the individual that his information has indicted. If you do not reveal your source, you will go to jail. True, you may appeal the case, but that will be a drawn-out and expensive affair that you don't welcome. Besides, your spouse and children are already being harassed by neighbors who, curiously enough, view you as a self-righteous crusader rather than a person of high principle. What should you do?

PAPERBACKS FOR FURTHER READING

Brand, Stewart. *Updated Last Whole Earth Catalog.* New York: Random House, 1974. This work has become as popular for the code of values it embodies as for the "set of tools" it recommends.

Burgess, Anthony. *A Clockwork Orange.* New York: Norton, 1963. The central question in this disturbing novel is: who is less moral, an individual with no moral sense or the society that attempts to "rehabilitate" him?

Mill, John Stuart. *Utilitarianism: With Critical Essays.* Samuel Gorovity, Ed. Indianapolis: Bobbs-Merrill, 1971. This book is a collection of 28 critical essays on Mill's philosophy, as well as the text of Mill's *Utilitarianism* and a chapter from *A System of Logic.*

Muller, Herbert J. *The Children of Frankenstein.* Bloomington: Indiana University Press, 1970. This is an interesting and informative analysis of the decline of values in the face of increasing technology.

Nietzsche, Friedrich. *On the Genealogy of Morals.* Walter Kaufman, Ed. New York: Vintage, 1967. While attacking the ethics of humility and self-denial in this classic, Nietzsche provides deep insight into the subsurface motives for adhering to such ethics.

Social Philosophy

10

Freedom and bread enough for all are inconceivable together.
—Fyodor Dostoyevsky

One undeniable fact about human beings is that we are social animals. We work with, depend on, and relate to one another for our survival and prosperity. The totality of the relationships among people is known as society. A specific society consists of a group of human beings broadly distinguished from other groups by similar interests, shared institutions, and common culture. Because society so strongly influences our attitudes, values, loyalties, and outlooks, we should examine the relationship between the individual and society in order to shed more light on the issue of self.

Fundamental to this relationship will be the question: just what are the limits to society's influence and authority over the individual? There are many facets to this issue. One of them is law, which traditionally has drawn a line of demarcation between individual and society. But often laws seem to violate human freedom, which is another facet of the individual-group relationship. Just what freedoms, if any, are individuals entitled to? There are those who say very few—that the state has sovereign rights over the individual (**totalitarianism**). Others preach the elimination of the power of the state and the elevation of the individual. Both positions have their immediate roots in classical conservatism and liberalism, two more subjects we shall examine.

Additional concerns govern our exploration of the proper relationship between individual and society. One of them is justice. Social and political philosophers from Plato onward have spoken of the need for a just society and have offered their concepts of it. Our political and social structures seek to attain justice through a contract between the individual and the "state," by which we mean municipal, state, and federal

299

"One undeniable fact about human beings
is that we are social animals."

governments. The nature of this contract, as we shall see, bears directly not only on the social and political aspects of self but on the economic aspects as well.

The concepts and issues we shall examine in this chapter have one characteristic in common: they arise out of the social milieu. Although they have ethical and political implications, they do not directly involve either ethics or politics. They are not directly ethical because they are not primarily concerned with establishing a norm of good conduct; they are not specifically political because they are not concerned with evaluating political power and the institutions that exercise it.

Rather, these concerns fall into the category of **social philosophy,** which is the application of moral principles to the problems that fall within its sphere: freedom, justice, equality. We shall not consider all aspects of social philosophy, but we shall focus on those that today seem to carry the most important implications for our search for self-identity, for helping us draw the proper line of demarcation between individual and society. One issue in particular promises to become even more important than it already appears to be: the issue of who is entitled to what in a society and world in which the few have much and the many have little.

LAW

Traditionally the line of demarcation between individual and society has been the *law*, by which we mean a rule or a body of rules governing the activities of individuals within the state. These rules or laws tell us what we may and may not do.

Our Western legal system, which we inherit from the Judaeo-Christian tradition, is a hierarchy of laws with a definite order of priority. For example, provincial or local laws are subject to higher laws. When there is a conflict between, say, a town law and a state law, the state law takes precedence. Likewise, federal laws take precedence over state laws. Does anything take precedence over federal law, over the so-called law of the land? Both the Jewish and the Christian traditions maintain allegiance to a law that transcends any state, what they have historically referred to as the "law of God." We find a similar concept in ancient Greek philosophy.

The Stoics, members of a school of thought founded by Zeno around 300 B.C., believed that the world did not operate by blind chance but involved divine providence. The universe, they believed, was rational, in the sense that it operates according to laws. The human mind can discover these laws. This orderliness or world reason the Stoics variously termed "Zeus," "nature," or *logos* ("word"). Since people are happy when they act in accordance with nature—with the order of the universe—the purpose of institutions, according to the Stoics, was to enact laws that reflected this single universal law. Thus what we today call "civic laws" have their basis in **natural law,** in the law of the universe.

This idea was more fully developed during the Middle Ages by St. Thomas Aquinas, who distinguished among several kinds of law. First, there is divine or eternal law—that is, God's decrees for the governance of the universe. According to Thomas, all things obey eternal law, for the way they behave simply reflects this law. Thus, a flame rises, a stone falls. God, then, is the lawmaker of the universe; things behave the way they do because He so decrees it. They cannot behave otherwise. But Thomas also applied this concept to the affairs of states. For Thomas, laws applying to the universe—what we today call physical laws—found their counterpart in the lesser communities called states.

Thomas defined natural law as divine law applied to human situations. The most basic precept of natural law, he claimed, is to promote good and avoid evil. Since he believed that all being is good and that all being seeks and preserves what fulfills itself, this first precept is one of self-preservation, but always within a context of promoting the common good. Thus, a politician should take this first precept as justification not for advancing only his own interests, but for promoting the good of all. Thomas believed that for humans this first precept of natural law took shape in the rules governing human behavior.

Although these rules do not vary, the way they are enforced does. Since we live in societies with diverse geographies, climates, cultures, and social customs, Thomas believed that different codes of justice were needed to fulfill the general requirements of natural law. These specific codes of justice he called human law. It is the function of human rulers to formulate human law by informing themselves of the specific needs of their communities and then passing decrees to guide those living under these conditions. So, whereas natural law is general enough to govern the community of all humans, human law is specific enough to meet the requirements of a particular society.

For Thomas, then, there are two points of difference between human law and natural or divine law. First, human laws apply to a specific group, society, or community; second, they are the expressed decrees of some human agent, and not laws operating in the universe at large. Nevertheless, what makes a human law *law* is its being an articulation of divine law. Put another way, human law is not law because it emanates from a legislator or ruler but because it implements divine law.

From Thomas's theory of law we can draw one conclusion that is particularly relevant to our discussion: subjects have the right to rebel. This conclusion follows from his idea that human law must be obeyed only when it expresses divine law. Since humans are capable of poor judgment, rulers can pass unjust laws, laws that are not "an ordinance or reason for the common good." In Thomas's view an unjust law is not a law at all, and therefore it cannot bind.

In his famous "Letter from Birmingham Jail," civil-rights leader Martin Luther King, Jr. relied in part on this point to defend his civil disobedience of segregation laws.[1]

A just law is a man-made code that squares with the moral law or the Law of God. An unjust law is a code that is out of harmony with the moral law. To put it in the terms of St. Thomas Aquinas: An unjust law is a human law that is not rooted in eternal law and natural law. Any law that uplifts human personality is just. Any law that degrades human personality is unjust. All segregation statutes are unjust because segregation distorts the soul and damages the personality. It gives the segregator a false sense of superiority and the segregated a false sense of inferiority.

But when people refer to a "higher law" they do not always mean a religious or God-given law. Many men who refused to fight in the Vietnam war, for example, were no doubt atheists, but they felt that to fight would violate their personal code of behavior. By "higher law," then, we mean any law that an individual considers to take precedence over the body of rules that governs the activities within the state.

So the belief that human law is subject to error and must be viewed in terms of some higher law, be it natural or divine, has a long and con-

---

[1]Martin Luther King, Jr. "Letter from Birmingham Jail." In *The Norton Reader*, 3rd ed. (Arthur M. Eastman, Ed.). New York: W. W. Norton, 1973, p. 665.

tinuing history. Moreover, it suggests an important question in establishing the proper relationship between self and state: precisely when is it moral to break a law? Under what conditions may we disobey the state? Since law essentially restricts freedom, to answer this question requires an examination of personal freedom.

Reflection   Describe a situation in which you would feel obliged to break a law of the state.

FREEDOM

The kind of freedom we shall talk about can be called political and social freedom, under which fall the freedoms of speech, religion, and governance. History records many heroic battles fought to secure these freedoms, as well as to win *equality*—that is, the same kind of treatment for all citizens in the state. All of these noble struggles were and are for political and social freedom. But the term finds its classic description in John Stuart Mill's essay "On Liberty."

One of Mill's chief concerns is the freedom of the individual. He is specifically concerned with what actions individuals in society should be allowed to perform. In essence, Mill claims that, in matters that involve other people, society may interfere with the individual. But in matters that involve only the individual, society may not interfere. He distinguishes between two spheres of interest: the outer and the inner. A matter belongs to the outer sphere if it involves more than just a few other individuals; it belongs to the inner if it involves only the self or a few others.

Although Mill appears to have drawn some line of demarcation between society and individual, it does seem fuzzy. After all, just how many constitute "a few others"? Furthermore, Mill argues that since, within the inner sphere, the individual and not society is the best judge of what advances self-interest, within such areas the individual should be free from interference. But it seems that we do not always know our best interests; freedom from interference actually may not be in our best interests. Suppose a man who enjoys heroin "shoots up" every day. This matter might fall within the inner sphere, and therefore he should be free from interference. Yet his behavior is probably not in his best interests. Therefore, it could easily be argued that he should be interfered with.

The problem with Mill's concept of freedom is that it guarantees noninterference, but not much else. What kind of freedom is it that can guarantee a drug addict freedom from interference while he "shoots" himself into oblivion? Although this kind of freedom is necessary, it is nonetheless a negative freedom, a freedom *from*. These are the freedoms guaranteed us by the Bill of Rights, freedom from outside influence. But perhaps something more positive is needed, a freedom *to*.

"Freedoms to" are positive statements that guarantee people more than noninterference. They guarantee people certain choices: the right to an education, the right to medical care, the right to a decent neighborhood, the right to equal opportunity regardless of race, national origin, or sex, and the right to equal pay for equal work. When the "freedoms to" are combined with the "freedoms from," we seem to have a more adequate description of political and social freedom and a climate favorable to personal security and growth.

Without understanding the distinction between negative and positive freedoms, we are hard pressed to understand the intense social unrest in the United States. Seeing freedom only as "freedom from," we would probably say that all Americans are equally free. But introducing the concept of "freedom to" clearly shows that some of us are more free than others. So, although individuals are guaranteed all of the "freedoms from," without certain "freedoms to" they will have, in reality, very little freedom.

A currently divisive issue is how much the government should interfere to guarantee "freedoms to." Some contend that there is already too much interference; that the executive, legislative, and particularly the judicial branches of government are poking their collective noses into areas where they do not belong. In short, there are too many bad laws. Others claim that what is really needed is more, not less, governmental interference; that society has grown too unwieldy for individuals to fight their own battles for freedom. In brief, there are too few good laws. Both views share a deep concern for the individual, a concern difficult to grasp without an understanding of at least the immediate roots of individualism.

Reflection   How many "freedoms to" have you enjoyed? How have these affected your life-style?

THE GROWTH OF INDIVIDUALISM

With the rise of philosophical materialism, the belief that reality is ultimately matter, we can note a couple of trends evident as early as the seventeenth century: (1) the desire to break away from established patterns of thinking and (2) the belief in law at work in the universe. These tendencies show up in the social, political, and economic developments of the eighteenth and nineteenth centuries.

For example, the tendency toward free and independent ways was fostered by an economic theory that accompanied the industrial revolution. This theory was known as **laissez-faire** individualism—the belief that business and commerce should be free from governmental control, thus enabling the entrepreneur to pursue free enterprise. Adam Smith (1723–1790), the leading spokesman for *laissez-faire* economics, insisted that government interference in private enterprise must be reduced, free competition encouraged, and enlightened self-interest made the rule of the day. Where obvious inequities might arise, thinkers like Thomas Malthus (1766–1834) and David Ricardo (1772–1823) argued that these would resolve themselves, for in such affairs natural law or order operated as surely as Newton's laws of gravitation and motion operated in the universe. Therefore, natural law would regulate prices and wages; natural law would correct inequities. Such thinking was bolstered by the nineteenth-century utilitarianism of John Stuart Mill.

Like Smith, Mill feared government interference in the economy. A government should interfere, said Mill, only in those matters for which society itself cannot find solutions. Such matters should be resolved according to the principle of utility. The principle of utility is that what is good is that which produces the greatest happiness for the greatest number of people. Under no circumstances should the government unnecessarily restrict individual freedom, including the individual's right to realize as much pleasure and progress for himself as possible.

There are at least three beliefs that characterize the philosophy of individualism as it appeared in the eighteenth and nineteenth centuries: (1) individuals should be free to pursue their own interests without interference, providing they do not impinge on the rights and interests of others; (2) individuals should be allowed to earn as much money as they can and to spend it however they choose; and (3) individuals should not expect the government to aid or inhibit their economic growth, for such interference only destroys individual incentive and creates indolence. So, in order to combat the antiquated laws and regulations that fettered humans, to keep pace with the scientific discoveries of natural law, and to bury the last vestiges of feudalism, eighteenth-century thinkers elevated the importance of individualism.

Much has happened between then and now. The individual has lost control of the means of production. For one thing—as Karl Marx observed as early as the middle of the nineteenth century—exorbitant costs, complex machinery, increasing demands, and intense competition have all worked against individual productiveness. Specialization in the textile and steel industries has tended to depersonalize the worker. Whereas the earlier economy of the Industrial Revolution was characterized by relatively free and open competition, the later economy of the twentieth century is made up of a relatively few enormous holding companies that can secretly fix prices, eliminate smaller competition, and monopolize an industry. Occasionally, the government steps in to regulate industry, as the Justice Department did in 1974 when it attempted to sever Western Electric from IT&T. But most efforts are token and ineffective. Today's corporation apparently wishes government to stay out of its business only when things are going well. Frequently, however, when a company is about to "go under," it expects to be subsidized as a "vital industry," as did Pennsylvania Railroad and Pan American Airlines. And it is no secret that businesses openly solicit governmental favors in return for political support. Favorable tariffs, franchises, and laws have become the plums many politicians offer in return for whopping sums of money before, during, and after campaigns. It is little wonder, therefore, that today we find ourselves largely trying to undo the solutions of the nineteenth century. In so doing, often yesterday's liberals find themselves today's conservatives. Because so many of us view ourselves socially and politically in these unstable terms of conservatism and liberalism, it would be wise to attempt to clarify them.

LIBERALISM AND CONSERVATISM

The words *liberal* and *conservative* have been so bandied about that they have lost precise meaning. Perhaps the best we can do to understand them as they are currently used is to contrast their present meanings with their past meanings.

Liberalism

We have already stressed the importance that classical liberalism placed on individual rights, especially in economic matters. The government, these liberals felt, should interfere only as a last resort. John Locke, for example, believed that since we are by nature free, any social arrangements we enter into in the form of government are an encroachment on that freedom. For Locke, state power was inherently at odds with individual liberty. The best government was the one that governed least.

Although in this area generalizations can be dangerously misleading, we might risk saying that today's liberal frequently feels that in many areas the best government is the one that governs *most*. Although they would agree with Locke that individuals are perhaps by nature free, they would add that individuals are *in fact* unfree. Therefore, it is the job of government to free individuals, especially to provide the "freedoms to." People's only hope of gaining freedom and equality, they claim, is through government action. Furthermore, they probably would not agree with Locke that state power is inherently at odds with individual liberty. Without governmental interference, they would point out, we'd still have sweatshops, rampant segregation, subminimal wages, inadequate roads and transportation, and insufficient schools, colleges, hospitals, and waterworks; and we would be without many other kinds of services that government now provides. Whereas Locke viewed the adequately structured government as the one that promotes individual liberties and rights and leaves individuals free to earn their own livings as they see fit, contemporary liberals view that kind of government as the reason we have monopolies, ruthless competition, slums, unemployment, and social inequalities. It is that very "rugged individualism" preached by classical liberals that their contemporary counterparts like Philip Slater[2] say underlies many of our social ills. In brief, today's liberals generally believe that desirable changes in the human condition can be brought about through an intelligent application of collective human effort realized in an adequately structured government.

It is clear that liberalism today is significantly different from the classical liberalism espoused by John Locke and later by Jeremy Bentham and John Stuart Mill. True, there are similarities: both types believe that humans are social animals on whom environment wields great influence; both claim that the job of government is to promote the general welfare; both uphold the sacredness of life, liberty, and the pursuit of happiness. But the differences are major. Whereas classical liberals minimized government interference, contemporary liberals often maximize it. Whereas classical liberals paid only token attention to the state's active role in promoting individualism, today's liberals think that strong communal bonds are necessary to preserve individual life, liberty, and the pursuit of happiness, and that government must play a vital role in strengthening these bonds. Finally, whereas classical liberals held individuals ultimately responsible for their own liberty and prosperity, contemporary liberals generally charge political authority with this responsibility.

Conservatism

The same contrasts we detected between classical and contemporary liberalism also apply if we examine conservatism. Consider as an example of classical conservatism the thought of Edmund Burke (1729–1797).

Central to Burke's political ideology is a distrust of the individual. Emphasis on individualism, he felt, led to the anarchy of the French Revolution. Certainly, individualism was incompatible with social and

---

[2]See Philip Slater. *The Pursuit of Loneliness.* Boston: Beacon Press, 1971.

political stability, Burke's primary concern. For Burke, society represented an organic and mystic link binding together the past, present,
and future. The state, therefore, was not an artificial but an organic
structure, nourished by religious fervor, patriotism, and faith. This
concept of the state as an organism persuaded Burke to conserve tradition, to nurture respect for established institutions such as religion and
private property, and to honor whatever had proved its worth by surviving generation after generation. As a result, Burke considered radical changes signs of disaster, contending that all change must evolve
naturally and should never represent a rupture with the past.

Obviously, Burke's political ideas emphasize institutions over individuals. The survival of the state is by far more important than individual interests, which always must be consistent with established or
evolving tradition. Individual rights exist only side by side with duties,
which, along with faith and loyalty, provide the mortar of a solid society.
In contrast with liberals, Burke believed that individuals are not by
nature equal. This belief, along with his observations of political unrest
in Europe, led him to distrust the masses, democracy, and any form of
popular rule. As a result, Burke's ideal state is ruled by a landed aris-
tocracy—sovereigns whose circumstances of birth, breeding, and education mark them as natural rulers. Only such aristocrats are capable
of enforcing the law and inspiring respect for traditions and institutions.

Today's conservatives, while sharing much Burkean thought, differ
significantly from him. Modern conservatives still support traditional
institutions, placing high premium on time-proven ethical and religious
values, loyalty to state and country, and fidelity to duty. In addition,
today's conservatives generally emphasize respect for property and law.

It is perhaps on the issue of individualism that we detect the biggest
difference between classical and contemporary conservatism. Many of
today's conservatives are pessimistic about people's capacities to manage their personal and public lives. As a result, they frequently support
political systems that attempt to control human shortcomings. Where
they do emphasize individualism, they do so frequently in terms of
moral values, personal integrity, responsibility, and worth of character,
all of which are measured against time-tested standards. But it is in
the economic sphere that today's conservative places greatest emphasis
on individualism, as in the *laissez-faire* tradition of classical liberalism.

Contemporary conservatives frequently argue that it is governmental interference that is strangling society. If the government would
only allow individual states, communities, and people more powers of
self-determination, things would straighten themselves out. Instead,
they say, the federal government more and more regulates commerce,
education, transportation, and utilities. Rather than liberating individuals, it watches over them from cradle to grave, and in so doing it destroys initiative and self-respect. As a result, many conservatives today

agree with David Riesman's judgment that "no ideology . . . can justify the sacrifice of an individual to the needs of the group."[3]

Thus, conservatism has maintained its emphasis on order, continuity, traditional institutions, and personal discipline. But, with economic problems increasing, the disparity between the haves and the have-nots more evident than ever, and growing pressure on government to redress these and other inequalities, contemporary conservatives seem inclined to define individualism in terms of economic rather than political freedom. Since contemporary liberals argue for more government involvement to redress economic and social inequities, ideological tension is bound to arise. At the root of this tension is a fundamental difference between liberals, who espouse the greatest possible equality among individuals, and conservatives, who espouse the greatest possible respect for individual rights. At the core of this issue is the question of justice—what it is and what constitutes the just society.

Reflection   Name one area of your life that you feel is interfered with by government more than you consider necessary. How do you deal with this interference?

THE JUST SOCIETY

In evaluating a state we invariably wonder how fairly it treats its citizens. We probably think that the just state is one that tries to treat its citizens fairly; the unjust state, one that does not. But what are "justice" and "fair" treatment?

To draw out the issue of justice, consider the phenomenon of the graduated income tax. In theory, Americans pay taxes proportional to their incomes: the more they make the more they are supposed to pay. Many feel this is fair. But, with demands for and costs of goods and services rising, a sizable number think that it is unfair, especially those who disagree with the programs for which taxes are spent. Take, for example, the case of a childless couple whom we shall call the Millers.

Bruce Miller, a chemical engineer, and his wife Marge, a dental hygienist, have no dependents and can claim very few deductions. As a result, they pay a hefty income tax every year. Although they like to consider themselves loyal Americans who are willing to bear their economic share of the nation's expenses, in recent years they have grown resentful of the tax system.

---

[3]David Riesman. *Individualism Reconsidered.* Garden City, N.Y.: Doubleday, 1954, p. 27.

Bruce: You know, I really think it's unfair that the government takes such a big bite of our income.

Marge: What bothers me even more than the amount is the way it's spent.

Bruce: Well, there's a lot of waste. There's no question about that.

Marge: I don't even mean the waste. Do you realize that our money is being used to support things we don't even directly benefit from? Take that swimming pool they put in the high school last year. We're never going to use that. And we don't have any children who ever will. But our property tax has gone up this year to help pay for it, so we wind up paying for it whether we like it or not.

Bruce: I see what you mean. But I'll tell you what really galls me even more than being forced to pay for something we're not going to use.

Marge: What's that?

Bruce: Being forced to pay for something I think is wrong.

Marge: Like what?

Bruce: Well, I know that you disagree with me on this, but I don't think abortion is right. And yet I'm helping finance the abortion clinics that the state's set up.

Marge: You know, I never thought of that. Even though I do support abortion, I think you're right. You shouldn't be forced to violate your conscience. That's what you're saying, isn't it?

Bruce: You bet it is.

Notice that the Millers are resentful not of paying taxes but of how their tax money is being spent. They are questioning the fairness of a system that, in some instances, compels them under penalty of law to pay for programs they cannot in good conscience support. Is this just?

The question of justice is bound up with the question of **rights.** If someone forbade you to express yourself, you would probably feel you were being treated unjustly. Why? Because one of your rights was violated—in this instance the right of freedom of expression. When we speak of someone's being treated unjustly we usually mean that the person's rights are being violated. Likewise, when we speak of the "just state" we commonly mean the one that ensures a person's rights.

There is very little controversy over what we may call general rights. Almost all agree that the just state must ensure the individual's rights of freedom of expression, including speech, religion, and press. Similarly, there is little dispute that the state must ensure certain human or natural rights, such as the right to life, as well as respect the individual's right to be treated equally with other citizens regardless of his religion, race, or sex. But in order to ensure these individual rights, the state must have certain rights or powers of its own. We tend to think that the state derives these rights as a kind of "regulatory agency" with which individuals have entered into a contract whereby they forsake certain individual freedoms in return for the protection of certain rights. The theory behind this contractual relationship is complex, but it is necessary to understand it in order to perceive the dimensions of the justice issue.

THE CONTRACT THEORY

The so-called **contract theory** is one explanation of the origin of the state, and one defense of its authority, that philosophers have frequently given. We see evidence of this contract theory as far back as Plato. But its most noteworthy proponents were Thomas Hobbes (1588–1679) and John Locke.

Hobbes developed his political philosophy based on the principles of scientific materialism as it was interpreted in the seventeenth century. According to this doctrine, the world is a mechanical system that can be explained in terms of the laws of motion. Even the behavior of humans or complex societies, it was argued, allowed for geometric and physical explanations. Hobbes accepted this view of reality and from it deduced the way things must of necessity occur.

In his most famous work, *Leviathan*, Hobbes portrays humans as selfish, unsocial creatures driven by two needs: survival and personal pleasure. Therefore, human life is characterized by constant struggle, strife, and war, in which individual is pitted against individual in a battle for self-preservation and gain.

To this, war of every man against every man, this also is consequent: that nothing can be unjust. . . . It is consequent also to the same conditions, that there be no propriety, no dominion, no mine and thine distinct; but only that to be every man's, that he can get; and for so long, as he can keep it.

Although Hobbes believed that the instinct for self-preservation was the basic drive behind human behavior, he also held that humans had the capacity to reason.

Although Hobbes never viewed reason to be so energizing a force as self-preservation, he believed that reason could regulate human actions and anticipate their results. Thus Hobbes pictured humans as self-centered but rational. This rationality enabled them to evaluate the long-term results of behavior originally motivated by self-interest.

Rational concern for their own survival and best long-term interests impels humans to enter into a contract with one another that brings society into being. Because they recognize that their lives are destined to be "solitary, poor, nasty, brutish, and short," humans agree to accept an authority outside themselves that has the power to force all to act in the best interests of the majority. For Hobbes this authority is irrevocable. Once set up, the political body wielding this power exercises complete authority over its subjects and remains in power as long as it is able to compel them to do what they otherwise would not do.

So, although individuals contract for society, the society that is thus formed becomes superior to the individuals, who owe complete allegiance to it. For Hobbes, the state cannot bear any resistance to its rule. If such resistance becomes effective, the state has proven itself unable to govern—in which case the established officials no longer rule and the people are no longer their subjects. At that point the people revert to their natural state of struggle for self-preservation and gain, where they remain until they form another contract.

Hobbes is really a modern echo of Plato. Although Plato's classical Greece was characterized by great art and philosophy, it was nevertheless undergoing institutional change that constantly threatened war and civil unrest. Against this background, Plato wove, as Hobbes would weave later, a totalitarian political fabric in which the basic purpose of the state was to produce order. As he presents this utopia in *The Republic*, the basis of its order is the eternal values that exist apart from personal preference or practical need and that reason can discover. When human nature is not informed with this reason, humans are as beastly as Hobbes subsequently describes. And, like Hobbes, Plato believed in an elitist ruling class composed of those who could reason about the eternal truths. To these rulers the citizens owed absolute allegiance and retained no right to question, reject, or rebel against their prescriptions.

In contrast with Plato's and Hobbes's rather pessimistic view of humans in the state of nature, John Locke viewed them as essentially moral beings who ought to obey natural moral rules. Whereas Hobbes saw the human's natural state as characterized by warfare, Locke saw it as characterized at least partially by a system of natural moral laws. As a result, Locke viewed humans as by nature free and equal, regardless of the existence of any government. It is not any government, he argued, that decrees mutual respect for the freedom and liberties of all, but nature itself. The law of nature decrees freedom and self-determination for all individuals.

Nevertheless, like Hobbes, Locke saw a need for a contract. Although he maintained that humans are by nature free, rational, and social creatures, he said that they establish governments because three things are missing in the state of nature: (1) a firm, clearly understood interpretation of natural law, (2) unbiased judges to resolve disputes, and (3) personal recourse in the face of injustices. So, in order to maintain their natural rights, individuals enter into a social contract whereby they create a political entity capable of preserving the inherent rights of "life, liberty, and estate." This contract is based on the consent of the majority, and all willingly agree to obey the decisions of the majority. The state's authority is limited by the terms of the contract, which is continually reviewed by the citizenry. So, unlike Hobbes's absolutistic state, Locke's is specific and limited. Most important, one of the fundamental moral rights that humans retain in Locke's political state is the right to resist and to challenge authority. Where Hobbes believed that resistance to authority was never justified, Locke regarded the right to rebel as an inherent human right.

Although the contrast between Hobbes and Locke is sharp, they do agree that humans are rational and that this rationality enables them to perceive the necessity for forming a social contract. This contract theory, especially as enunciated by Locke, has heavily influenced our own concept of government, as these lines from the Declaration of Independence suggest:

... to secure these rights (life, liberty and the pursuit of happiness), governments are instituted among Men, deriving their just powers from the consent of the governed. That whenever any Form of Government becomes destructive of these ends, it is the Right of the People to alter or to abolish it, and to institute a new Government, laying its foundation on such principles and organizing its powers in such form, as to them shall seem most likely to effect their safety and Happiness.

The Declaration and the contract theory agree that, when a government becomes destructive of the individual rights of life, liberty, and the pursuit of happiness (or property, for Locke), the people have the right to dismiss it.

But precisely when is a government destructive of those rights? Perhaps it would not be hard to designate when a government is depriving us of our rights to life, but what about liberty and the pursuit of happiness? It could be argued that the liberties referred to are political and civil in nature and thus can be spelled out constitutionally. Still, it is one thing for a constitution to guarantee the right of assembly, but quite another for a mayor of a city to interpret an assembly as a mob, and for a court to uphold this interpretation. In other words, the U.S. Constitution, like the contract theory on which it is based, provides a general framework to ensure liberties but leaves great latitude for the interpretation and possible restriction of those liberties. It is even more difficult to determine when a government has become destructive of the pursuit of happiness. Some might argue that a graduated income tax inhibits the pursuit of happiness. When a wealthy person's earnings and holdings are taxed considerably more than an average income-earning person's, is the government by this action destructive of the wealthy person's pursuit of happiness? On the other hand, perhaps the government has the right and duty, in the interests of the lowliest of the parties to the social contract, to levy such taxes even against a majority. This is really the basis for the Millers' discontent.

Marge: You know, when you actually sit down and start adding up all the things you don't morally support and subtract from your taxes how much is going to each, you come up with quite a sum.

Bruce: You can say that again. I'd like to have every penny of my tax money that went to that Vietnam War.

Marge: We both thought that was wrong.

Bruce: But we helped finance it.

Marge: And the maddening thing about it is that we end up depriving ourselves of things that will make us happy in order to support many things we don't think are right.

Bruce: That sure is a switch, isn't it? I thought the job of government was to help in our pursuit of happiness, not to hinder it.

Under the social contract, then, we give up certain rights to gain others. Specifically, under our political system we are guaranteed the rights to life, liberty, and the pursuit of happiness. The problem for today is: Is the government acting in such a way as to secure these rights? Or is the government acting in such a way that it is actually depriving us of these rights?

There are no simple answers to these questions, and perhaps any answer depends on the particular issue you examine and your particular interests. But there is one issue that not only cuts across all others but bears directly on the question of justice and our concept of it. This issue is the distribution of goods.

Currently circulating are two very important theories of justice that speak directly to this problem and already have had great impact on contract theory. They are called the maximin-principle view of justice and the entitlement view.

Reflection   Recall the classic case of Henry David Thoreau's going to jail rather than pay taxes that would have gone to help support what he considered the morally indefensible Mexican War. Can you imagine circumstances under which you would go to jail before paying all or part of your taxes?

THE MAXIMIN-PRINCIPLE VIEW VERSUS
THE ENTITLEMENT VIEW

There are a lot of poor people in America. There are even more people who, although not legally designated poor, are struggling to "make ends meet." In contrast, there are some incredibly wealthy people, people in whose hands a large portion of the nation's wealth is concentrated. Question: Is it fair that so few have so much and that so many have so little?

If you think it is not fair, you may believe that the state has the right and the obligation to redistribute the wealth. One current view of political justice says that the state does have this right; another does not view this inequality as unfair at all and therefore denies the state any right of redistribution. Both views are proposed by Harvard professors of philosophy, both chart quite different political courses, and both offer contrasting concepts of the individual in relation to the group.

Bearing directly on these views of justice is the question of whether an individual has rights that no person or state may violate. In raising this issue, we return to a fundamental question dividing today's moral and political philosophers.

For a long time there were two basic views on this question and on justice generally. One was the utilitarian view, according to which principles of justice are rules that work for the common good. In effect, there are no individual rights that are inviolate. If in violating an individual right we bring about more general good than individual suffering, then we may so violate that right.

The other view, associated with Locke and Kant, prohibits the use of one person to advance another's end. We have previously seen evidence of this tradition in the fabric of American political theory, which holds that there are some "unalienable rights" that, no matter how much collective good will result from violating them, may never be violated.

The Maximin-Principle View of Justice

In 1971, professor of philosophy John Rawls in *A Theory of Justice* presented a modern alternative to utilitarianism, which at the same time was compatible with his belief that justice requires us to improve the lives of the poorest members of society. In proposing his theory, Rawls speaks of people's "original position." Like the contract theorists who would have us imagine a "natural state," Rawls asks us to visualize a hypothetical state of nature in which people are ignorant of their talents and socioeconomic conditions. Rawls claims that, when asked in this original position to choose a fundamental principle of justice to be followed in a newly created society, people would choose the principle that inequalities are allowable only insofar as they improve the position of the lowliest group in the society. This principle has been termed the **maximin rule** because it tries to maximize the lot of the worst off in a society.

Rawls claims that those favored by nature with advantages of talent and wealth should gain from their good fortune only in terms that improve the situation of those who have lost out. This he considers a principle of a just social contract.

Now let us see how Rawls's theory might work in practice by relating it to the graduated income tax. Some economists argue that a sharply graduated income tax reduces work incentive—that the most productive and talented members of a society are discouraged from working and so cut back on their effort. Physicians would be a good example. If physicians lost their incentive to work, everyone would probably end up worse off than they were originally, including the worst off. Under Rawls's maximin rule, therefore, it seems defensible not to tax physicians so much as, say, artists of equal income, since the loss of the physicians' work would probably reduce the state of the worst off, but the loss of the artists' probably would not. It is conceivable, on the other hand, that the artists might be heavily taxed as long as such taxation reduced the economic gap between them and the poorest group in society. But wouldn't the artists, like the physicians, ultimately lose incentive? And, with that loss, wouldn't their tax dollars be lost to the poor? Presumably, at this point, Rawls would favor the unequal economic status of the groups, since such inequality would actually serve to improve the position of the lowliest group in the society. It is clear that Rawls's maximin rule is compatible with considerable inequality, but only if it improves the status of the poorest members of society.

In his argument, Rawls relies on a traditional "patterned" distribution of goods. A patterned distribution is one that can be summed up in some formula like: "To each according to his _____," in which the blank may be filled in with "need," "work," "intelligence," or "effort," for example. It is highly unlikely that in any society the distribution of wealth will already reflect the formula. Therefore, to achieve a just society, the goods must be redistributed until people's holdings correspond with what is thought to be the just pattern. Rawls believes the just pattern to be his maximin rule.

Objections to the Maximin Principle

In 1975, Rawls's Harvard colleague Robert Nozick published *Anarchy, State and Utopia*. In it he charges that any theory of justice relying on a patterned distribution of wealth is inherently unjust, because it coerces individuals and thus violates their basic rights. It does so, says

Nozick, by depriving citizens of the free exercise of their preferences even in cases in which they are not hurting anyone else. To illustrate, Nozick provides an ingenious example.

He asks us to imagine a society in which the goods are distributed in accordance with some patterned concept of justice such as equality, whereby everyone has precisely the same holdings. Suppose that basketball star Wilt Chamberlain signs a contract with a team under which he receives twenty-five cents from the price of each game ticket. Excited by the prospect of seeing Chamberlain play, fans gladly pay the surcharge on their tickets. In the course of the season, 1 million people attend Chamberlain games. As a result, Chamberlain ends up with $250,000—much more money than anyone else has in the society. The transaction has obviously altered the patterned distribution of wealth, but is the new distribution unjust? If it is, why? Nozick argues that the source of the injustice cannot be that a million people freely chose to spend their money in this way and not some other. Since they knew where their money was going, they have no just claim against Chamberlain. As for those who did not see him play, their holdings are unaffected. And, Nozick points out, if they had no claim against the goods of the transacting parties before this alteration took place, they shouldn't have any now.

Nozick is raising several objections to Rawls's maximin rule. One is that Rawls is using the better-off people in society to assure the welfare of the worst off. Nozick regards this utilitarian ethic as fundamentally unjust. As a corollary, he claims Rawls is not impartial, for he is seeing things only through the eyes of the worst off. Finally, he objects to Rawls's apparent contention that under certain circumstances individuals are not entitled to what they create. A person's "entitlement" is very much a part of Nozick's thinking, and his book is largely devoted to spelling out this concept.

Reflection   If you were establishing a pattern for a just society according to the maxim "To each according to his _____," with what word would you fill in the blank?

The Entitlement View of Justice

In Part I of his book, Nozick argues for the existence of a minimal type of state, the "night watchman" state of classical liberal theory that is limited to the protection of individuals from assault, theft, fraud, breach of contract, and so on. In Nozick's view the modern state has exceeded this social contract. Nozick's minimal state is not so different from the one envisioned by contract theorist Locke. It is a kind of protection agency to which we all contribute for protection of our life and property. But that is all. We have not contracted to be victims of paternalistic laws such as those forbidding drug use, laws that, in Nozick's view, are primarily designed to coerce "bad" citizens into becoming "good" ones. Neither, according to Nozick, have we contracted to be taxed nor to have private business regulated by governmental agencies.

In Part II of his book, Nozick offers his **entitlement theory** of justice. This theory departs radically from traditional patterned concepts of justice, especially ones claiming, like Rawls's, that a more extensive state is justified in order to redistribute wealth.

In defining his entitlement theory, Nozick uses the word *holdings* to describe goods, money, and property. According to the entitlement theory, people are entitled to their holdings so long as they have acquired them fairly and squarely. Paraphrasing John Locke, Nozick argues that, so long as you acquired your holdings without making anyone else worse off, you are morally entitled to them.

For example, suppose you obtained a vast fortune without injuring anyone else. You are, according to Nozick, entitled to do with that fortune as you see fit. Whether you choose to bequeath it to a relative, endow it to a university, squander it on uranium mines in downtown Los Angeles, or pour it into a river, you are morally justified; you are entitled to do with it as you wish. In short, so long as citizens acquire their original holdings justly, without recourse to deceit, fraud, force, or injury to someone else, then the resulting distribution of wealth will be just no matter what inequalities it may contain. Like duty-directed ethics, the entitlement theory of justice evaluates the justice of our holdings on the basis of the past—on how they were acquired—and not on the basis of their conformity to a given pattern.

Appropriately enough, Nozick is not committed to the graduated-income-tax system. In a time when the government seems to be taking an even bigger bite of each dollar we earn, this aspect of Nozick's view appeals even to those who otherwise are willing to pay their fair share. The Millers are a good example. Like many people around April 15th every year, they suddenly become conscious of what they believe they are entitled to.

Bruce: Here's another one. "Inheritance tax."

Marge: Uh-oh. Uncle Henry.

Bruce: Right, my good old Uncle Henry, who spent a lifetime working hard on the railroad and saved probably every nickel he ever made. Henry dies and leaves his considerable legacy to his favorite and only nephew: yours truly. And look what happens.

Marge: Your other uncle expects his inheritance.

Bruce: Right. Good old Uncle Sam. Now, I ask you: is that right? What fair claim does the government have to any part of Henry's bequest to me? He earned that money fair and square and paid plenty of taxes on it. His final wish was that I have it—all of it. Isn't he entitled to say where every last penny of his estate goes?

Under Nozick's entitlement theory, Uncle Henry certainly does have the right to decide. And the state that violates that right acts immorally.

Reflection   Suppose you believe in a minimal state. How would you justify the raising of an army to fight an aggressor?

Objections to the Entitlement View

On the one hand, Nozick's theory has the advantage of justifying what is a widely accepted principle of distributive justice: we are entitled to what we create. If you choose to will your vast fortune to your child, you have the right to do that, or to spend it however you choose. On the other hand, his theory seems patently unfair; for is it really just that one baby should, at birth, inherit a vast fortune, the best schooling, and social, political, and business connections that will ensure its future, while another inherits indigence, inferior schooling, and connections with the "big house"? At birth neither baby *deserves* anything —a fact that suggests that an equal division of holdings and opportunities is the only fair one. But Nozick points out that deserving has no bearing on the justice of inherited wealth; people are simply entitled to it, if it was not ill-gotten.

But who will determine what has been "fairly" acquired? How can you know that the wealth you have inherited from your great-grandfather is not the result of unfair play? There seem to be no procedures for working out past injustices that may account for the advantages many of us enjoy today. Indeed, what procedures are there for determining the injustices themselves?

But there is still another objection that seems valid and pertinent, if rather philosophical. It underlies Nozick's theory and is at the heart of the battle between the patterned-distribution theorists and the entitlement theorists. It involves free choice.

Nozick's theory evidently provides considerable free choice. With the state exercising only minimal control, the individual is left with an apparently large measure of self-direction. But this state of affairs presumes that we are capable of making free choices. Granted, we make choices, but we do so under historical circumstances that greatly influence those choices. This is the basic Marxist objection to classical liberalism: we do not allow people to govern their lives freely when we ignore the conditions under which they must choose. For example, it is naïve to think that we are allowing children to choose freely what they will do with their lives when we do nothing about the poverty, filth, squalor, and moral decadence in which they may be growing up. Almost as naïve is to ignore the flow of information that is necessary for us to make so-called free choices. Do we really believe that our information is uncluttered and complete, in the light of the billions of advertising dollars spent to propagate a life-style based on conspicuous consumption and the suppression of bad breath?

In his fascinating and frightening book on the use of subliminal language in our society, psychologist Wilson Bryan Key says:

> It is virtually impossible to pick up a newspaper or magazine, turn on a radio or television set, read a promotional pamphlet or the telephone book, or shop through a supermarket without having your subconscious purposely massaged by some monstrously clever artist, photographer, writer or technician.[4]

Similarly, political philosopher Herbert Marcuse, in his widely read *One-Dimensional Man*, argues that our society is caught up in such a network of self-contradictions that our ability to choose freely is an illusion.

> Free choice among a wide variety of goods and services does not signify freedom if these goods and services sustain social controls over a life of toil and fear—that is, they sustain alienation. . . . "Totalitarian" is not only a terroristic political coordination of society, but also a non-terroristic economic-technical coordination which operates the manipulation of needs by vested interests.[5]

For all its analytical rigor, then, it seems that Nozick's entitlement theory not only must tie up the apparent loose ends noted, but must also justify the implicit assumption that the context of decision-making does not materially affect the individual's ability to choose.

CONCLUSIONS

It seems that from time immemorial men and women have valued individualism, as experienced through personal freedom and liberties. Everyone seems agreed on this. Specifically, there is consensus about

---

[4]Wilson Bryan Key. *Subliminal Seduction*. Englewood Cliffs, N.J.: Prentice-Hall, 1973, p. 11.

[5]Herbert Marcuse. *One-Dimensional Man*. Boston: Beacon Press, 1964, p. 3.

"Do we really believe that our information
is uncluttered and complete . . . ?"

the worth of political and moral freedom—that is, the right to do something without having to bend or break a law to do it. There is also apparent agreement that the state bears responsibility for protecting its citizens from ills against which, as individuals, they are helpless; and for fostering an atmosphere in which individuals can enrich their own lives within a social context. Disagreement arises, however, when we try to spell out precisely which freedoms, liberties, and rights the individual and the state shall possess.

Obviously, where the line of demarcation between individual and society is drawn will help determine who we are. Although we recognize its influential nature, we cannot be sure where that line should be drawn. Some, like psychological behaviorist B. F. Skinner, would use principles of behavioral control to produce a more efficient state. Others, like psychoanalyst Erich Fromm, argue that efficiency and individualism are incompatible, that we stand little chance of self-discovery when we subordinate the individual to the machine.

The social machine works more efficiently, so it is believed, if individuals are cut down to purely quantifiable units whose personalities can be expressed on punched cards. These units can be administered more easily by bureaucratic rules because they do not make trouble or create friction. In order to reach this result, men must be de-individualized and taught to find their identity in the corporation rather than in themselves.[6]

---

[6]Erich Fromm. "The Present Technological Society," in *The Revolution of Hope.* New York: Harper & Row, 1968, p. 32.

"The social machine works more efficiently,
so it is believed, if individuals are cut down
to purely quantifiable units . . ."

For us who are trying to discover ourselves by asking who and what society says we are, perhaps it is best to remember that the line between individual and state is one that must be drawn ever anew. Although we glibly profess to live in an age of relativity, our beliefs, attitudes, and actions frequently betray allegiance to a bygone era of immutable truths, especially as they apply to social institutions. Thus, even today we are shocked to think that what we regard as absolute rights and freedoms are, in fact, tentative and tenuous propositions in the ever-changing line of demarcation between individual rights and collective rights. Such shock bodes ill for society. As an illustration, consider how difficult it is for us to realize that the seemingly fundamental right to procreate is *not* a basic and inviolate individual right.

In a now famous essay entitled "The Tragedy of the Commons," biologist Garrett Hardin demonstrates the danger of considering the procreation right "untouchable." Hardin asks us to imagine a pasture open to all. Presumably, every herdsman will keep as many cattle as possible on the pasture. For centuries such an arrangement works beautifully "because tribal wars, poaching, and disease keep the numbers of both man and beast well below the carrying capacity of the land."[7] But times change; conditions improve; more people and cattle begin to exhaust the pasture. The long-desired goal of social stability is threat-

---

[7]Garrett Hardin. "The Tragedy of the Commons," *Science*, December 13, 1968, Vol. 162, pp. 1243–1248.

ened. Each herdsman seeks to maximize his profit; each wonders about the utility to himself of adding one more animal to his herd. As Hardin points out, the utility has one negative and one positive feature:

1. The positive component is a function of the increment of one animal. Since the herdsman receives all the proceeds from the sale of the additional animal, the positive utility is nearly +1.
2. The negative component is a function of the additional overgrazing created by one more animal. Since, however, the effects of overgrazing are shared by all the herdsmen, the negative utility for any particular decision-making herdsman is only a fraction of −1.[8]

Being a rational man, the herdsman concludes that it makes sense for him to add another animal to his herd. And why not another? And another? But naturally every other herdsman reasons likewise. "Therein is the tragedy. Each man is locked into a system that compels him to increase his herd without limit—in a world that is limited. Ruin is the destination toward which all men rush, each pursuing his own best interest in a society that believes in the freedom of the commons. Freedom in a commons brings ruin to all." In brief, when we persist in regarding any individual right as absolute and inviolate, then we invite conditions that make no individual right possible. When we ignore the social aspect of our nature, we create an atmosphere that stifles self-discovery.

Obviously Hardin advocates not the abolition of individual rights, but rather an appraisal of them within a context of social responsibility. The proper line of demarcation between self and society, it seems, must be one that, while not ignoring the historic circumstances in which people make choices, does not so ignore individual rights that the individual loses the incentive, opportunity, and capability for self-definition.

SUMMARY

We opened this chapter by noting that a continuing problem in self-definition is clarifying the line of demarcation between the individual and society. Law traditionally has done this, but some laws seem unjust. The question of whether and when it is moral to break a law involves the problem of freedom, which in turn demands a concept of rights. Today, as always, there are those who wish to emphasize individual rights over the rights of the state; others believe the rights of the state need more emphasis. In general, today's conservatives, unlike their counterparts in the past, emphasize individual rights, especially in the economic sphere; today's liberals, unlike their historic counterparts,

---

[8]Hardin. "The Tragedy of the Commons," p. 1245.

stress the rights of the state. Central to this debate is the question of the just state. Our social institutions are founded on a contract theory, which supposedly provides for justice through a contractual arrangement between individual and state. Two current views of social justice are embodied in John Rawls's maximin-rule theory of justice and Robert Nozick's entitlement theory. Finally, the proper line of demarcation between self and society seems to be one that recognizes individual rights within a historic context of social responsibility.

Obviously, where the line of demarcation between individual and society is drawn will help determine who we are.

MAIN POINTS

1. Social philosophy is the application of moral principles to the problems that fall within its sphere, such as freedom, equality, and justice.

2. Thomas Aquinas distinguished among divine (eternal), natural, and human law. He believed that you could break a human law if it was not consistent with a divine law.

3. We enjoy "freedoms from"—that is, guarantees against state interference in such spheres as those spelled out in the Bill of Rights.

4. An adequate and complete definition of freedom requires "freedoms to" as well, such as the rights to education, medical care, and housing.

5. It is in the "freedoms to" area that the question of individualism arises.

6. The classical conservative, unlike today's, generally emphasized the role and rights of the state over those of the individual; classical liberalism generally emphasized the role and rights of the individual over those of the state. This is especially true in the economic sphere.

7. In general, the just society is one that tries to ensure the rights of the individual; the unjust one does not. Although differing in many ways, Hobbes's and Locke's contract theories both play a formative role in establishing the just society.

8. The question of just how far the state can or must go in ensuring individual rights is hotly debated today, especially in the area of distributive justice: who is entitled to what.

9. One theory of social justice is John Rawls's maximin rule. It contends that inequality is allowable only insofar as it improves the lot of the worst off in society.

10. Another theory of social justice today is Robert Nozick's entitlement theory. It contends that individuals are entitled to the hold-

ings they have acquired if they have not harmed anyone in the process.

11. The proper line of demarcation between self and society seems to be one that, while not ignoring the historic circumstances in which we must make decisions, leaves individuals the ability to define themselves.

SECTION EXERCISES

Law

1. What laws, if any, do you regard as unjust? Why?
2. Does the state have the right to make laws concerning homosexuality, pornography, and consumption of marijuana?
3. To what extent, if any, do you feel that your own ability to live as you believe you should is cramped by laws?

Freedom

1. Do you think that every American has a right to a college education?
2. Do you think that every American has a right to good-quality medical care?
3. Do you believe that all peoples have the right to determine the political system under which they live? If you do, does one state have a moral obligation to assist another that is fighting to exercise that right? Is there any point at which the obligation ends?

The Growth of Individualism

1. In *The Pursuit of Loneliness*, Philip Slater contends that our cultural emphasis on individualism is frustrating the spirit of community we need to solve many of our social problems. This love for individualism is warring against "the wish to live in trust and fraternal cooperation with one's fellows in a total and visible collective entity."[9] Do you agree that the United States is experiencing this cultural emphasis, and that it is having the consequences that Slater sees?
2. Slater also argues:

   Our approach to social problems is to decrease their visibility: out of sight, out of mind. This is the real foundation of racial segregation, especially its most extreme case, the Indian "reservation." The result of our social effort

---

[9]Philip Slater. *The Pursuit of Loneliness*. Boston: Beacon Press, 1971, p. 27.

has been to remove the underlying problems of our society farther and farther from daily experience and daily consciousness, and hence to decrease, in the mass of the population, the knowledge, skill, resources and motivation necessary to deal with them.[10]

Do you agree?

3.   Do you agree with Riesman's statement: "No ideology, however noble, can justify the sacrifice of an individual to the needs of the group"?

4.   In what ways can excessive concern with individualism actually undermine individualism?

Liberalism and Conservatism

1.   How true to the *laissez-faire* ideal is our present economy?

2.   Is Mill's political philosophy consistent with his ethical philosophy, which argues that the moral action is one that produces the greatest happiness for the most people?

3.   How realizable today is Mill's belief that "the only freedom which deserves the name, is that of pursuing our own good in our own way, so long as we do not attempt to deprive others of theirs, or impede their efforts to obtain it"?

4.   Burke believed that the state has the right to compel the individual to conform to its ideas of social and personal excellence. Do you agree that in certain areas the state has this right? In what areas? Are there areas today in which the state is exercising a right you believe it does not have?

5.   "Democrats are generally liberal and Republicans are generally conservative." Do you agree with this generalization? Would you prefer to qualify the statement by specifying an area (economics, for example)? What are the connotations of *liberal* and *conservative?* Cite particular politicians you would misrepresent by putting them into one or the other of these categories.

The Just Society

1.   Is it just to be taxed for something you do not morally subscribe to?

2.   Can you think of a situation in which it is more just to treat people differently than to treat them equally?

3.   Is the law requiring young people to remain in school to a certain age just? Is the one that requires parents or guardians to enroll their children or charges in a school just?

---

[10]Philip Slater. *The Pursuit of Loneliness*, p. 15.

The Contract Theory

1. What is the fundamental difference between Hobbes's and Locke's contract-theory concepts?
2. The contract theory contends that we should obey the state because we have contractually promised to do so. How, if at all, have you contracted to obey the state?
3. The Declaration of Independence contends that "whenever any Form of Government becomes destructive" of individual life, liberty, and the pursuit of happiness, "it is the Right of the People to alter or to abolish it." Under what circumstances, if any, would you personally exercise this right? Specifically, what conditions, if any, must prevail for you to act to alter or abolish your form of government?

The Maximin-Principle View of Justice

1. Rawls argues for a view of justice as seen from the position of the worst off in society. Would it be unrealistic to argue a case for a view from the position of the best off in the society? How might you do this?
2. Applying Rawls's maximin-principle view to your society, which groups do you think would stand to receive preferential economic treatment? Why?
3. What evidence would you point to that indicates Rawls's theory is already operative in your society?

The Entitlement View of Justice

1. What areas would you point to that indicate the state is not acting as a "night watchman"?
2. Suppose a very wealthy man, in the midst of desperate poverty, sickness, and human suffering, chose to ignore those conditions and to hoard his wealth. Do you think he is morally entitled to do that, assuming he earned his wealth fairly?
3. What contradictions and inconsistencies would you point to in our society to support the conclusion that our ability to choose freely is more illusory than actual? (A good place to begin might be with advertising and television programming.)

ADDITIONAL EXERCISES

1. Just where would you draw the line of demarcation between individual and state in the area of population growth? The use of drugs? Students' rights?

2. For a long time it has been assumed that law protects the moral fiber of a nation. In England in 1957, however, the Wolfenden Committee recommended that homosexual activity between consenting adults no longer be considered a crime. An eminent British jurist, Lord Patrick Devlin, disagreed and insisted that the law must enforce morals. Do you agree? Are there areas of individual morals over which the law should exercise control? What are they?

3. Under what circumstances, if any, would you say an individual has the right and obligation to break the law?

4. Does the government have the right of censorship? If so, under what circumstances?

5. Frequently we hear of people who, from deep religious or moral convictions, refuse desperately needed medical care for their helpless children. As a result, these children often die. Do people have the right to refuse life-saving medical attention for their children? Should they be prosecuted if they do? Should they have the right to refuse it for themselves? What if, by refusing a vaccination for themselves, they became a disease-bearing threat to the community?

6. Would you say that the growth of democracy in this country has contributed to the growth of political freedom?

7. To whom (the individual, private enterprise, state or local government, federal government) would you leave the responsibility for solving the following problems:
    a. constructing bridges, roads, and freeways
    b. operating a postal service
    c. operating schools and colleges
    d. handling trade and commerce
    e. ensuring equal employment
    f. determining which elementary and high school your children will attend
    g. choosing where to locate your home and what kind of home it will be
    h. regulating the sale of marijuana
    i. handling divorces

8. What problems did the Watergate scandal reveal concerning the following:
    a. the two-party system
    b. governmental invasion of privacy
    c. governmental manipulation of public opinion
    d. money and politics
    e. big business and government
    f. individual and collective repression

9. What do you intend to do to inform yourself of the impact of subliminal perception on how you perceive yourself and the world around you?

PAPERBACKS FOR FURTHER READING

Golding, William. *Lord of the Flies.* New York: Capricorn Books, 1959. Golding creates a "state of nature," then portrays the attitudes and behavior of a handful of "innocents" who find themselves a part of it. A disturbing portrayal of the darker side of human nature.

Hoffer, Eric. *The True Believer.* New York: Harper & Row, 1966. This is longshoreman-philosopher Hoffer's study of those who lose their identities in throwing themselves into social causes and mass movements.

Kaufman, Arnold S. *The Radical Liberal: The New Politics in Theory and Practice.* New York: Simon & Schuster, 1968. Kaufman, a professional philosopher, argues for fundamental liberal values while advocating active engagement in bringing about radical social change. He argues for the "politics of radical pressure" with respect to black power, education, and foreign affairs.

Marcuse, Herbert. *One-Dimensional Man: Studies in the Ideology of Advanced Industrial Society.* Boston: Beacon Press, 1964. This is an attack on the alienation and dehumanization of mankind in "advanced" technological societies. Marcuse argues that, rather than being used to enslave humans technologically, the capabilities of science and technology could be used to liberate human capacities.

Plato. *The Republic.* F. M. Cornford, trans. Oxford: Oxford University Press, 1945. This book portrays Plato's classical utopia.

Slater, Philip. *The Pursuit of Loneliness: American Culture at the Breaking Point.* Boston: Beacon Press, 1971. Standing on the side of social activism, Slater argues against intense individualism, which he sees as precluding solutions to social problems.

Esthetics

11

Art is, indeed, the spearhead of human development, social and individual.
—Susanne K. Langer

What if you had just five minutes to live? What thoughts would run through your mind? What regrets might you entertain? Would you think about how you might have done things differently? In his novel *The Idiot*, Fyodor Dostoyevsky pictures just such a man.

He had only five minutes more to live . . . those five minutes seemed to him an infinite time, a vast wealth; he felt that he had so many lives left in those five minutes that there was no need yet to think of the last moment, so much so that he divided his time up. He set aside time to take leave of his comrades, two minutes for that; then he kept another two minutes to think for the last time; and then a minute to look about him for the last time. He remembered very well having divided his time like that. He was dying at twenty-seven, strong and healthy. As he took leave of his comrades, he remembered asking one of them a somewhat irrelevant question and being particularly interested in the answer. Then when he had said good-bye, the two minutes came that he had set apart for *thinking* to himself. He knew beforehand what he would think about. He wanted to realize as quickly and clearly as possible how it could be that now he existed and was living and in three minutes he would be *something*—someone or something. But what? Where? He meant to decide all that in those two minutes! Not far off there was a church, and the gilt roof was glittering in the bright sunshine. He remembered that he stared very persistently at that roof and the light flashing from it; he could not tear himself away from the light. It seemed to him that those rays were his new nature and that in three minutes he would somehow melt into them. . . . The uncertainty and feeling of aversion for that new thing which would be and was just coming was awful. But he said that nothing was so dreadful at that time as the continual thought, "What if I were not to die! What if I could go back to life—what eternity! And it would all be mine! I would turn

331

every minute into an age; I would lose nothing, I would count every minute as it passed, I would not waste one!" He said that this idea turned to such a fury at last that he longed to be shot quickly.

Dying must be a sobering experience. Too bad it is so final. Most of us could probably benefit from a dry run or two. We could benefit from seeing a profile of the basics, from touching the cutting edge of "what really matters," from hearing again, or perhaps for the first time, the drummer we meant to march to. As a result, many, like Dostoyevsky's prisoner, would lust to turn every minute into an age.

Dostoyevsky's character responds to the scent of his own mortality: he perceives what he did not fully perceive before. Call it what you will: blowing away the cobwebs, putting things in perspective, knowing which side is up, getting his house in order or his head together. In short, he knows who he is. He is in touch with himself. A scrape with death often has this effect, perhaps because imminent death causes us to experience what Aristotle called **catharsis,** a purging or cleansing of the emotions. Every drama, said Aristotle, must result in catharsis—a purifying of the audience through their complete emotional involvement in the play. Anything less is bad tragedy. Today, of course, we have empirical evidence of the healthful value of catharsis. In medicine, the word usually describes a cleansing of the digestive system; in psychoanalysis, it is a technique of cleansing the emotions to relieve tension and anxiety by bringing repressions to consciousness. For many of us, a brush with death would cleanse us of the irrelevant, the extraneous, the superficial. It would purify us of false needs—needs to seek artificial success, to have fun, to be accepted, to want what others want, to dislike what others dislike, to seek society's values in pursuing job, position, and reward. A scrape with death often acquaints us with the essentials of our lives, whatever they may be—our true needs. And what are these? Outside the physical needs of food, shelter, and clothing and the psychological needs of loving and being loved, each of us decides. That is the point. If a false need is one that is imposed on us, a true need is one that springs from within, from the core of our being. It can be defined no more easily than can "religious experience." But we are unable to determine true needs as long as we are controlled, indoctrinated, and manipulated to pursue false needs, just as we are probably cut off from true religious experience as long as we seek it outside rather than within ourselves.

Although a brush with death frequently frees us of artificial bonds, obviously we cannot wait for such an experience. Neither can we assume that such a showdown will liberate us. On the contrary, it might send us on a lemming-like rush to experience "all" before dying. Ignorant of what we need, then, we pursue false needs because these are the only ones presented to us. We adopt societal values and needs because, as psychoanalyst Erik Erikson puts it, "We deal with a process located in *the core of the individual* and yet also *in the core of his communal culture*, a process which establishes, in fact, the identity of those two identities."[1] As a result, if society fails to perceive true cultural needs, rest assured that our perception of true individual needs will become increasingly obscured.

Perhaps your own needs are already fogbound. Perhaps you already feel the more than sneaking suspicion that you are drowning in a sea of plastics and pre-fabs, that the TV dinners have grown moldy, and that the talk shows are all talked out. If you do sense a perception gap between how your society sees things and how you see them, just what do you do about it? Do you become, in Camus's words, a "living reproach"? Perhaps withdraw into the cocoon of transcendental meditation or hawk "Jesus Saves" pamphlets? If you do, can you remain impervious to polluted air, befouled water, burgeoning populations, imminent war, mushrooming crime, unstable economies, racial unrest, and sexual tensions? The problem is: what experience as cathartic as facing our own death will purge us of false and artificial needs and return us to our true and real ones? In brief, we wish to know what experience will get us in touch with the self.

It might seem odd and frivolous to answer "esthetic experience." For most of us, the word *esthetics* probably calls up images of cool, marbled museums peopled by snobs gawking and snorting at inscrutable paintings whose only possible value could be in the frames that hold them. This is inaccurate. Actually, **esthetics** is that branch of philosophy that studies beauty, especially in art. By "art" we mean not only painting but also music, literature, sculpture, drama, and architecture. The study of esthetics examines the natures of beauty, taste, and standards of artistic judgment. But above all, the study of esthetics brightens perception. In fact, *esthetics* derives from a Greek word meaning "perception." Just as a brush with death often heightens our perception and puts us in touch with our true needs, so does esthetics. It raises our level of consciousness and self-awareness and makes us more responsive to the world around us and to ourselves.

It is hard to imagine, then, a study more fitting than esthetics to answer the question: who or what am I? First, we shall consider the "esthetic experience," its meaning and content. In doing so, we must talk about various theories of art as well as investigate the purpose of art: whether art should teach morality or exist only for its own sake, or perhaps do both. In addition, we shall ask: what is "good" art? We shall see whether there are objective standards to judge art or whether all esthetic judgments are subjective. This chapter concerns artistic values, but more specifically the *value of these values*. It assumes that

---

[1]Erik Erikson. *Identity, Youth and Crisis*. New York: W. W. Norton, 1968, p. 18.

self-discovery is bound up with an awareness of our needs, and it tries to show why a discovery of our needs must begin with the discovery that we need esthetics.

Reflection   Recall a personal experience that heightened your perceptions of life, of yourself, and of your own needs.

THE ESTHETIC EXPERIENCE

Suppose you are viewing *Guernica*, a painting by Picasso that portrays the horrors of war. As a result of the visual stimuli—color, shape, form, and so forth—you receive a sensation. You sense the colors and the shape. At first you may do nothing more than sense them. But then, as you look longer, you begin to organize your sensations in such a way that you recognize objects: a bull, a soldier, a woman, a light bulb, a horse. These organized sensations are called perceptions or percepts. Thus, you *sense* the color grey but you *perceive* the bull; you sense the color white but you perceive the light bulb. You might then perceive the state of these objects: the shrieking horse with a spear in its back; the screaming woman with her dead child; the crying victims engulfed in flames. You perceive the terror in the painting, and with it the terror of war. You may perceive other things: Picasso's opposition to the Spanish Civil War, his expressionistic and cubistic skills, his imitation of photographic techniques using stroboscopic light. There are many levels of perception.

Esthetics relates to these many perceptual levels of human experience. With *Guernica* one of the perceptual levels involves the agony of war. War is a frightful thing. Picasso is telling us that even a so-called just war is full of deprivation and agony. People suffer and die as much in a "good" war as in a bad one. It is terrible that people must experience such suffering. We should strive to ensure that they do not have to, that we do not have to. What is happening when we experience these feelings?

Through an esthetic experience, we have cut through what we might term a societally imposed need: that we must have wars. What are the reasons often given for the necessity of war? There are many: to end all wars, to make the world safe for democracy, to ensure the self-determination of people, to bolster the economy, to protect our vital and national interests, to guarantee that our children won't have to fight, to perfect weaponry, to unify a country, to divert public attention from divisive issues, to fulfill a cycle of history, to return us to a fear and respect for God, to rid the world of Satan and his heathen followers,

Pablo Picasso, *Guernica*. (1937, May–early June). Oil on canvas, 11′5½″ x 25′5¾″. On extended loan to The Museum of Modern Art, New York, from the artist.

to bury capitalist pigs, to destroy godless communists, and so on. But what is our *true* need? Peace. Without peace, both external and internal, there is little else we can do but attend to the unrest of war. When there is no peace we must consciously be striving to survive, having no time or energy for anything else. The point is that *Guernica* puts us back in touch with this basic and real need by presenting the shocking, terrifying, and perhaps disgusting side of war. The effect is similar to the one philosopher-scientist Jacob Bronowski wished to impart after World War II when he proposed that Nagasaki be preserved intact as an appropriate meeting ground for diplomats and governments who perhaps had forgotten the horrors of war. Bronowski was saying that we need this perceptual experience, this esthetic contact, to remind us of our desperate need for peace. We can forget. We do.

Neither Bronowski nor Picasso was denying the reality of war, or even its necessity. They were simply saying that there are other necessities—that the reasons for war constitute one slice of human needs, but that there is another slice, the reasons for peace. The esthetic experience asks us to perceive the part in order to understand the whole. As James Ogilvy puts it:[2]

Esthetic education not only educates the student to the man-made products of his cultural tradition; it also quickens his sensitivity to his own felt needs for a balanced and whole human existence. Wholeness is an elusive standard when the parts of human existence keep changing with the flux of history. A fixed inventory of human capacities no more functions as a checklist for wholeness than a list of colors tells a painter when he has completed a picture. The point is not to use each of the colors or human capacities. We need an esthetic sensibility to tell us whether man's most recent creations of himself cohere in a healthy pattern of wholeness or fall apart into schizoid decadence.

In this sense, then, esthetic sensibility helps us sort out the true needs from the false ones. It blows away the cobwebs, orders our universe, puts things in perspective. It expresses for us the inexpressible. As the nineteenth-century English essayist and critic Walter Pater put it: "Art comes to you proposing frankly to give nothing but the highest quality to your moments as they pass." Surely this is a gift of inestimable worth.

What we have described through the example of *Guernica* suggests a most useful concept of esthetic experience for a practical philosophy. It stems from the belief that the function of art is primarily to point to human feelings, clarify our inner lives, brighten our vision. But this is only one theory of the function of art. There are many others. Since the ancient Greeks, individuals have held as many beliefs about the nature of esthetics as they have about the natures of knowledge,

---

[2]James Ogilvy. *Self and World*. Harcourt, Brace, Jovanovich, 1973, p. 461.

reality, and goodness. These theories give birth to various concepts about the functions of art. It would be worthwhile to note at least the major theories of the nature of art, for each has validity. Moreover, each is compatible with the view that the esthetic experience reveals true needs. So let us look at these esthetic theories of the nature and function of art before returning to our own preference.

Reflection   Art has always been an integral part of most religions. Why do you think this is so?

THEORIES OF ART

Have you ever been part of a museum tour? Sometimes you can learn as much from other tour members as you can from the guide—perhaps not about art but about attitudes toward art.

To explore some of the main traditional and popular esthetic theories, we are going to join a tour. With us, in addition to our guide, are Jerry and Betty, a married couple who are taking the tour as part of a "vacation package" they bought. After this tour, they will visit a botanical garden, a zoo, and a discotheque. Then there is Smitty, a man of little formal artistic training but who has read some and enjoyed an esthetic experience or two. He secretly believes that if things had been different, he himself could have been a great artist. But a long time ago he bought a taxi instead. Finally, there is Nellie, a retired schoolteacher from Anaheim, California, not far from Disneyland. Her conscience has never permitted her to miss any tour that purported to be a "cultural must." Her last tour: Dachau. As with all the other tours she has taken, she found it "interesting" if "excessively long."

As we join the tour, the group is reacting to "action painter" Jackson Pollock's *Convergence* (1952). As with many of his works, in painting this one Pollock laid the canvas on the floor in order to move in the orbit of his creation. Then, using commercial paints, he flung, splattered, dribbled, smeared, and smudged his way to what some consider an expression of artistic genius. Others see little more than a well-soiled smock.

Jerry: Well, if you ask me, it looks like a chicken with the runs ran across that canvas.

Betty: Shhh, it's a Pollock.

Jerry: It's appalling!

Guide: Do you have a question, sir?

Betty:	No.
Jerry:	Yes, I do have a question.
Betty:	Jerry.
Jerry:	Relax, I'll take care of this. Not meaning any disrespect, Miss, but for the last half-hour you've paraded us through a collection of so-called paintings that I wouldn't line my canary's cage with, let alone hang on my wall. What gives?
Betty:	He doesn't mean that. We don't even own a canary.
Guide:	Apparently you don't appreciate modern art.
Jerry:	Appreciate it? What's there to appreciate?
Betty:	The frame, Jerry, look at the frame. It's beautiful!
Guide:	The line, the form, the color, the motion, the rhythm . . .
Nellie:	That's all well and good, young lady, but what the gentleman's asking is "what is there to see?"
Jerry:	The lady's right. What's there to see?
Nellie:	What does it all mean? The trouble today is there's no pleasure in looking at art.
Guide:	Must it mean something?
Jerry:	What!
Smitty:	I can see that.
Jerry:	What do you mean, you can see that?
Smitty:	Well, like she says: why must it mean something? If you ask me, I see a painter who's having a lot of fun.
Jerry:	Where?
Betty:	Stand back, Jerry, you're always supposed to look at a painting from afar.
Jerry:	Oh yeah? Well I couldn't look at this one from too far afar. If there's a guy in there that's having fun, then I'm the monkey's uncle who painted this.
Guide:	Perhaps the artist felt as you do.
Jerry:	Frustrated?
Guide:	Perhaps. And he's expressed this.
Jerry:	You mean that's why he's made this mess? To frustrate me?
Smitty:	I see what you're saying, Miss, but as I said before, I think Pollock was playing.
Jerry:	You make this Pollock sound like a quarterback.
Smitty:	Yes, in a way. Like a football player, an artist releases excess energy through play. His play is his art: painting, music, sculpture, literature, whatever. You could say art is a kind of spiritual play.

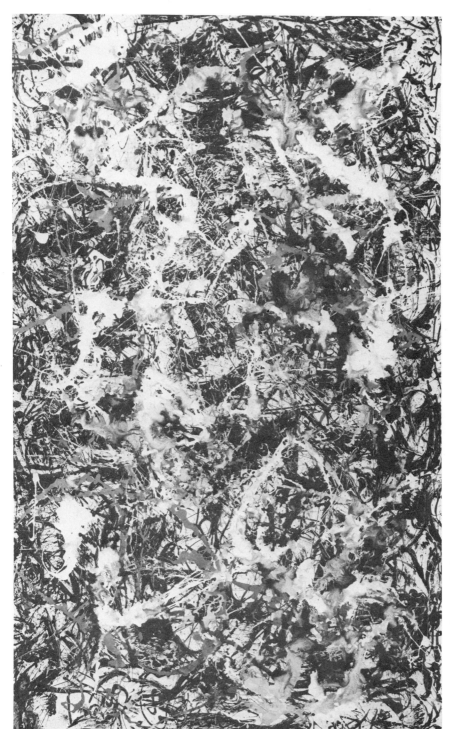

Jackson Pollock, *Convergence*. Albright-Knox Art Gallery, Buffalo, New York. Gift of Seymour H. Knox.

Jerry: But, what's play got to do with life?

Smitty: It's an escape from life.

Jerry: So anybody who escapes from life is an artist, is that what you're saying?

Nellie: Of course he's not. He's saying that an artist escapes from life.

Jerry: Well, what's an escapist got to tell me about life? That he's escaping? That he's playing? That he's having fun?

Smitty: Well, you allow the athlete to. Why not the artist?

Jerry: Because the athlete is entertaining me, that's why. He helps me pass my idle hours, fills my spare time. He even lets me grow old gracefully. What artist ever did that for me?

Smitty: What artist have you ever given the chance?

Jerry: I'll tell you who. What's his name? The guy that drew all those magazine covers for the *Saturday Evening Post*.

Betty: Norman Rockwell.

Jerry: Yeah, that's the guy.

Nellie: Now there's a man who brought years and years of pleasure into my life.

Jerry: A better painter never lived! Vermont in the winter; a kid's first haircut; Presidents; old people with gnarled hands—stuff like that. The thing about this guy is, his stuff is real, you know what I mean? If he does a winter scene, you feel cold; if he does a pot-bellied stove, you feel warm. Now, when a guy can make you feel that way, that's what I call an artist.

Smitty: Well, if you want something real, why don't you just photograph it?

Jerry: What do you mean?

Smitty: If you want a tree to look precisely like a tree, perhaps you should photograph it and not paint it at all.

Jerry: Well, by the same token, why don't I just stare at it, then? And not even photograph it?

Smitty: Why not? The tree itself is more real than a representation of it, and if you really must have what's *real*—

Jerry: Look, all I'm saying is that if I'm going to look at a painting I want to see something, that's all. What's wrong with that?

Guide: Nothing, absolutely nothing.

Let us halt the tour for a minute to find out what is causing all the heat. Obviously, there is disagreement about just what art is. Jerry believes that art is a representation of reality, that it should imitate the way things are in life. Nellie doesn't quite agree. For her, art should give pleasure. When it does, it's good; when it does not, it's bad. Smitty has still another viewpoint: for him art is primarily the artist's own experience, which is one of escape or play. The artist does not necessarily owe his audience anything, for the esthetic experience is essentially the artist's. The guide, also, seems to focus on the artist's experience, but for her the artist is expressing something that finds its completion in the viewer who shares the artist's experience. Betty has her hands full refereeing. Let us try to capsulize each of these theories.

Art as Imitation

Jerry's view of art as imitation has a respectable history. It is as old as Plato and Aristotle. Plato, a lover as well as critic of the arts, held that all art should imitate something in the physical world. To the degree it does it is good art. Since Plato saw the physical world as an imperfect reflection of his ideal world of Forms, he was especially critical of art that was not strictly imitative, for such art was just a reflection of a reflection. Plato, and Aristotle as well, believed that through imitation we portray the universal—that which many things share. The greatness of Oedipus's tragedy, for example, lies in that he represents the self-undoing pride of all humans. The magnificence of the Parthenon lies in that it imitates the harmony and balance that promise peace and fulfillment.

Art as Pleasure

But neither Plato nor Aristotle ignored the role pleasure plays in art. On the contrary, both believed that, in being imitative, in representing the physical world, art gave pleasure. Consider, for example, the pleasure we experience when we watch a good impressionist at work—Rich Little or David Frye, say. Their impressions of famous people often give more pleasure than would the experience of the people themselves talking. In his short story, "The Real Thing," Henry James (brother of William) portrays the inability of a duke and a duchess to find employment modeling as a royal couple because they just are not "believable" enough. Thus, frequently the imitative and pleasurable qualities go together. For example, Nellie indicates fondness for Norman Rockwell; it is likely that she derives this pleasure from the imitative quality of his art. This fact does not mean, however, that what is not imitative will not give her pleasure.

Art as Play

The Pollock painting is not imitative. Clearly, it does not give Jerry or Nellie pleasure. But it seems to give pleasure to Smitty and the guide.

Smitty's pleasure seems to derive from his recognition of the "fun" Pollock is having. We might compare this kind of pleasure to witnessing a child in a playpen having fun with a cardboard box. (Jerry would probably liken it to a visit to the monkey house!) For Smitty the pleasure is primarily the artist's, not the audience's. Nevertheless, through the art the audience can find release from the tension and stress that attend their lives. Like artists, we too need a break from drudgery; we need an outlet for an uncontrolled expression of energy. The artists find this in art; we find it indirectly through their expression. In his *Critique of Judgment*, Kant developed this idea by pointing out that art is in itself fun, that it is closer to play than to work.

Art as Expression

The guide agrees with Smitty that art is a form of expression. But for her it is not so much an expression of play as an expression of an internal feeling. Perhaps Pollock was frustrated, she says, and he expressed his anger in *Convergence*. For her, artists seek the most reflective forms and techniques for what they are trying to "say." The Italian philosopher Benedetto Croce, accordingly, saw art as "intuitive knowledge" of mental states. Freud later viewed such an expression as a revelation of the artist's sexual impulses. Jung considered it an expression of basic and universal images. In these forms of the expressionistic theory, the emphasis is on the artist's need to express a particular insight. Whether we grasp the insight is secondary, although obviously desirable.

Art as Empathy and as Experience

There are, in addition, other theories of art. A common reaction to a Eugene O'Neill play, for example, is one of physical and mental exhaustion—shades of Aristotle's catharsis. The reason is that we become so involved in the lives and relationships of O'Neill's characters that we experience much of the physical and mental anguish they experience. William Gibson's *The Miracle Worker* is an especially good example of this. By the end of this play we are "wrung out." Art makes us feel **empathy.** The empathetic theory of art contends that art functions to make us feel what we would if we were actually experiencing the artistic depiction that we perceive.

For John Dewey, on the other hand, art is a process of doing or making. In *Art as Experience* he argues that art has become separated from experience. The impulse of art is to elevate common experience by recognizing the quality of it; it should idealize qualities found in common experience. It accomplishes this by serving up to the mind unified, ordered experience. The esthetic experience, for Dewey, resides in our recognizing the wholeness in the interrelationships among the things depicted. The artist's intention is not the art's meaning but the unified quality of the experience that the work elicits. And the more pervasive the experience depicted, the more expressive the art.

As we noted before, all of these theories have validity, and none is mutually exclusive of the others. The appropriateness of one or another frequently relies on a particular social, historical, or artistic context. Emphasis on one theory does not necessarily mar the esthetic experience, unless the emphasis biases us against other interpretive possibilities. This is essentially the problem with our tour members. Jerry refuses to consider any approach to art other than a representative one, while Smitty professes almost a scorn for this view. It is likely that these biases will also turn up in what they believe the purpose or function of art is to be.

Reflection   Consider any great work of art—painting, novel, film, music. Can you see in its effect on you elements of all of these theories?

THE FUNCTION OF ART

One of the esthetic questions that invariably arises in discussing the function of art is whether art should impart moral teaching or exist only for its own sake. Jerry, for example, believes that art should serve a moral function; Smitty does not.

Guide: But often there's more to art than meets the eye.

Smitty: You said it.

Jerry: Sure there is. But lots of times these guys don't even know themselves what they mean.

Nellie: I must agree with him, you know. I knew a painter once who said he was always amazed by what the critics wrote about his work. He never understood any of it. I think much of this modern art is—how do you say it—a put-on?

Smitty: But what is play but a put-on? A pretense? A sham?

Nellie: Like that young man a few years back who was painting Coca-Cola bottles and Brillo boxes.

Guide: Andy Warhol.

Jerry: You call that stuff art?

Smitty: Well, *you* should. Or isn't it realistic enough for you?

Jerry: What do you mean?

Smitty: If you so admire Rockwell for his believability, why not Warhol?

Betty: But how can you relate to a Coke bottle or a Brillo box?

Jerry: There's your answer. You can't *relate* to those things. But a cozy living room in winter with a big fire burning and a mother teaching a child how to read and a father buried in the daily paper and a big woolly dog half asleep at his feet—now that's telling about something, something worth listening to.

Smitty: What?

Jerry: Are you kidding? The *family,* that's what. The family as a value in society.

Nellie: He has a point.

Guide: Are you saying, sir, that art, to be art, should encourage a value, an ethic?

Jerry: Call it values or morals or ethics, whatever you want. I say that good art always teaches a moral. In fact, you could say that's the function of art.

Smitty: Nonsense! *Ars gratia artis:* art for the sake of art! Art is its own purpose.

Jerry: I couldn't agree less.

Smitty: Then tell me something. Whose values will you use to measure art?

Jerry: What are you talking about, *whose* values?

Guide: Whose morality? Whose ethics? The Russian writer Solzhenitzyn was condemned in Russia but praised in the United States. Why? Because in Russia his art was politically heretical, but in America it was not.

Nellie: She has a point.

Jerry: But what are you going to do, make moral and practical concerns take a back seat to art? Okay, go ahead, but don't come yelling to me about all the hard-core pornography that's polluting our kids' minds, and all the blood and guts on the tube and in the movies, and all the language that's not fit for a locker room, let alone a living room.

Nellie: Well now *you've* got a point.

Smitty: Sure he has. And you can see it in the scissors of the censor.

Jerry: What're you talking about? I'm no blue-nose.

Smitty: Of course you're not. Except when it comes to something that offends you personally. As long as art is confirming your own narrow preconceptions and predispositions, you're quite open-minded and tolerant. But let something run against the grain of your moral, religious, or political biases and you react with all the self-righteous indignation of the bluest of the blue-noses.

The contention that art should contain a moral function is at least as old as Plato, who believed that when art does not advance the interests of social harmony and stability, it should be censored. For Plato, art that did not bring the audience closer to knowledge of the eternal Forms had no place in his republic. That same attitude is evident under Communistic and Fascistic regimes. Recall the many depictions of the Russian or Chinese worker who, through dedication and obedience to the state, advances the cause of social revolution. It is easy for us to sneer at this obvious propaganda, because we disagree with the doctrine. But consider the propagandistic value of classical Greek art, which as much fostered a way of life as it was an artistic expression. Or the obvious and intended religious propaganda of great Renaissance art, or the early twentieth-century movement called "naturalism," whose purpose was to shock the public into action. Upton Sinclair's *The Jungle*, a work whose primary purpose was to so outrage the public conscience that people would demand social reform, is a good example of the propagandistic use of art. We can hardly be consistent and make a distinction between the "good" ethic and the "bad" one. It seems that, if we argue for the inseparability of art from values, we must entertain a great variety of ethics—even those that contradict our own. Should we not, we must be prepared to defend the unquestionable righteousness of our own position. As we saw in our discussion of ethics and social/political philosophy, this is most difficult.

If, like Smitty, we argue for the separation of art from moral judgment, we seem to restrict ourselves to *estheticism*, the view that art must be ultimately judged in terms of esthetic enjoyment. For this outlook, art exists for art's sake. But this belief is not trouble free. Jerry asks about pornography. It seems irresponsible to sit by indifferently as children's and adults' minds are poisoned by the lewd and obscene, whose only evident purpose is to make a "fast buck." Likewise, when evidence indicates a causal connection between cinematic and social violence, can we ignore celluloid horrors "for the sake of art"? We seem to be on the horns of a dilemma. Let us see if we can escape them by proposing that art functions to reveal personal alternatives and deepen sensitivity.

Reflection Explain why you feel a particular film you have seen is good.

Guide: But why must art exist either for art's sake or for morality's? Why must one exclude the other?

Smitty: How can art that advances a moral standard exist for its own sake?

Jerry: And how can art for its own sake teach morals?

Guide: By offering new possibilities, by expanding human sympathies and imagination, by revealing to us our common bonds.

Betty: I think I know what she means. It reminds me of that film *That Certain Summer.* It was a TV drama about two gay men and how one had to reveal to his son that he was gay.

Nellie: Oh, I do remember that. You know, I didn't think I'd like it when I came across it in *TV Guide,* but then as I started to watch it I began to feel compassion for them, and after a while I saw them as just two human beings suffering, if you know what I mean. For whatever reason, all I know is my attitude changed.

Jerry: So what does all this mean? That you're now out campaigning for gay liberation?

Nellie: Of course not. It simply means that now I understand better. How would you say it—I had my eyes opened to a different viewpoint. Well, I suppose you could say that with respect to the human condition I had my horizons broadened.

In this third view of the function of art, art serves morality not by promoting a particular viewpoint but by quickening our imaginations and sensibilities to the common bonds of the human condition. For Nellie, the import of *That Certain Summer* was not that she did or did not become gay, did or did not agree with that preference. Neither was it the film's intention to "convert" anyone. Rather, it was to heighten our consciousness of the agony of decision-making and value-selecting that all humans suffer. In this context, the moral purpose of art is not to confirm us in our own preconceptions but to elevate us to new possibilities, new values. It is to humanize us for tomorrow by sensitizing us today.

But even if we agree that art can and should serve morality, not by promoting the *status quo* but by expanding the imagination to conceive new possibilities, we are still left with the question: who decides how well the art has executed these possibilities? Notice that we are not asking who decides the worth of the possibilities. That would merely pitch us back into the ethical juggernaut. We are asking who should be the judge of good art. Who decides what is great, good, fair, poor, terrible? Are there objective criteria that apply? Or, in the last analysis, must the individual decide?

We Americans are notorious for reserving judgment on art because our esthetic training is so shallow. We frequently wait to see what the "experts" tell us: the critics, the reviewers, the professors, the ones who supposedly know what art is all about. Then we ritualistically read and listen to their dictates, mouth their pithy witticisms, and, in general, ensure that we remain robots in our approach to esthetics. To a degree, these tendencies may explain why the advertiser can sell us virtually anything. In many cases we simply do not trust our abilities to distinguish the substantive from the decorative, the tasteful from the gawdy; we simply do not know good art from bad. With this underdeveloped esthetic sense often travels a whole bizarre value system.

ESTHETIC JUDGMENT

Jerry: Well, what does this Pollock picture do for your horizons?

Nellie: I must admit, not very much.

Jerry: Now you're talking.

Betty: You know, I don't see too much in it either. I can see your getting something out of *That Certain Summer*. After all, it did deal with real people in a real situation. But what does this deal with?

Guide: For one thing, it deals with the medium of painting. I think that's important to see here. Within that medium it combines technique, form, and content . . .

Jerry: Technique? What technique?

Smitty: Expressionism.

Guide: That's right. Abstract expressionism, to be precise—an explosive artistic movement that erupted in New York right after World War II. It's quite complex to explain without first going into cubism, nonobjectivism, and surrealism.

Jerry: Why do I get the impression the tour's just resumed?

Guide: One point I do think you should grasp is that in abstract expressionism the act of painting is frequently considered more meaningful and important than the content itself.

Jerry: But I thought you said this had content.

Guide: I did. But for Pollock, unlike your Rockwell, representing the familiar things in life isn't as important as portraying impressions, emotions, and insights in symbolic form. Believe it or not, sir, *Convergence does* have unity, coherence, rhythm, balance, and all the other formal ingredients that make any creative piece—in music, literature, sculpture, architecture, as well as painting—a work of art. But these formal features may elude you because your esthetic sense, if you'll pardon the expression, may be underdeveloped.

Jerry: Underdeveloped?

Smitty: Frankly, Miss, I think I detect a hint of elitism in your remarks.

Guide: Really?

Jerry: Right!

Smitty: Well, you make it sound as if only a qualified observer can appreciate good art. That you need an understanding of cubism, nonobjectivism, and surrealism to understand *Convergence*.

Guide: Well, it would certainly help.

Smitty: Help, perhaps. Yet surely you don't believe that judgment of beauty should be left only to those who are trained in esthetics and in the art they're evaluating?

Guide: But where are standards to come from if not from those who have refined their esthetic faculties so that they can separate the quality from the trash?

Jerry: I'll tell you. From the average Joe who experiences it, that's where from. From you and me. We decide what's good and what's bad, just as we do in life. Like lying. For you lying may be okay, for me it's not. Who's to say? Each person decides for himself. You take this painting here by Pollock. Okay, you say it's terrific. I say it stinks. This lady, she's straddling the fence—

Nellie: I just can't make up my mind, you know.

Jerry: Okay, so who's right? Is the painting great, lousy, or somewhere in between? The answer, folks, is none-of-the-above. Nobody can tell for sure. It all comes down to a matter of personal taste. And arguing about it is as smart as arguing about which is better, steak or chops.

Smitty: Up to a point, I agree with you. But I also think that, although there are no clear-cut guidelines for assessing esthetic worth, we can decide on some general properties that will determine it.

Jerry: What general properties?

Smitty: Structure, for example. Without structure or form, as our guide calls it, there can be no object of art to begin with.

Guide: Certainly we all agree on that point.

Jerry: But what's form? Answer me that.

Smitty: It's internal relationships. Form is how the parts of the object fit in with one another. I think good form is present in a piece of art when the piece has many different parts so interrelated that they form a complete unit, a whole. It's this, it seems to me, that gives art its glow, its intensity, its impact. The better the form, the greater chance the work has to provoke an esthetic response. And that, I think, is the test of any piece of art: its capacity to bring out an esthetic response. And I don't believe the experts are the best or the only judges of that capacity.

For simplicity, we can boil down the debate about esthetic judgment to this question: is esthetic judgment a matter of personal taste, or are there objective standards that you can apply to evaluate a work of art? Notice that the question is reminiscent of the one we faced in ethics: is the good act strictly subjective, or are there objective criteria we can apply to determine it? Similarly, in discussing knowledge, we asked: can we know an objective world or are we confined to our own experience? Obviously, Jerry insists on the subjective position. What he likes is artistically good; what he dislikes is not good. This, in effect, makes each of us our own esthetic judge, in much the same way as egoism makes each of us an ethical judge. Furthermore, this view consigns esthetic debates to the realm of the meaningless. But perhaps they should be. After all, we can point to societies whose artistic tastes differ markedly from our own. We all know individuals who regard hard rock as the ultimate musical "trip" and others who hear nothing but loud cacophony. As Jerry puts it, "Who's to say?"

Yet people have been "saying" for some time. Virtually all who "know" regard Sylvia Plath as a better poet than Rod McKuen and Joan Didion a better writer than Jacqueline Susann. They hold that there are certain standards we can apply to evaluate art. Some, like the guide, believe that a qualified judge should determine what is good and what is bad art. And who is qualified? David Hume believed it was one who has spent a lifetime cultivating the esthetic attitude of detachment, disinterest, and distance. Others, like Immanuel Kant, claimed that we could judge the worth of art objects by comparing them with an absolute standard or idea that we know. Recall how Kant believed that the mind imposes harmony and order; these two qualities serve as a universal basis for esthetic evaluation. Still others, like Smitty, would deny these absolute standards and the experts' preferred status in esthetic determinations; but they would admit the existence of certain esthetic properties such as structure. These **objective relativists,** as they are termed, evaluate art in terms of its capacity to inspire an esthetic response.

As in most philosophical debates, there seems to be merit in all positions. As on the question of subjective versus objective knowledge (rationalism and idealism versus empiricism and materialism), we discerned elements of both positions in the process of knowing. So it is here. Undoubtedly we exercise subjective choice in voicing an artistic preference. The question is: do we when we voice artistic judgment?

Although it is possible to consider Beethoven a great composer and at the same time to not *like* him, more often in the arts a judgment of worth is also an expression of preference. But the converse is less frequently true. When people say they like John Wayne's acting, they would not necessarily claim that John Wayne is a great actor. In fact, they may readily admit that John Wayne is probably not a great actor, but nevertheless they like his acting and go to see every movie Wayne makes. On the other hand, it would be unusual for someone to say "Richard Burton is a great actor, but I don't like his acting." This would be comparable to saying "Lying is wrong, but I don't disapprove of it." In general, then, it seems true that an esthetic judgment involves some measure of subjective preference.

But the fact that we frequently say "I like John Wayne's acting, but he's not a great actor" should tell us that more goes into an esthetic judgment than personal preference. In this case, we might claim that Wayne doesn't have depth, he hasn't established his versatility, he hasn't demonstrated an acting ability outside the Western genre, he's never done any "serious" theatre, or whatever criteria may separate the "good" actor from the "bad" one. Although we may not be mindful of them, we frequently apply objective criteria in value judgments. Consider the heated discussions otherwise "non-arty" people get embroiled in over the relative merits of two athletes: Who is the greater baseball player, Henry Aaron or Babe Ruth? Which is the better motorcycle, the Harley Davidson or the BMW? Who was the wiser general, Grant or Lee? The person who insists that Lee was the wiser general because he "feels he was" would not be taken seriously, and for a good reason. You would want to know *why* he believes that. If he then spoke of Lee's handsome grey beard and beautiful white horse, you would still laugh at him, because the criteria are irrelevant to Lee's status as a general. But if the person discussed strategy, tactics, imagination, and daring, you would listen. These are relevant criteria in assessing a general's worth.

So it is with art. Frequently we discuss technique, content, form, and so on as measures of artistic worth, as objective criteria. And just as frequently we call on the experts to fortify our opinions, as readily as we would call on Civil War expert Bruce Catton to lend believability to our recognition of Lee. The trouble, of course, is that many of us are so ignorant of the arts and so lacking in an understanding of esthetic experience that we vacillate between never judging for ourselves and insisting there are no standards. But ignorance of standards is not absence of standards. There *are* standards, and we can and do learn them by studying the arts.

Of course, an art object is not an athlete, a motorcycle, or a general. And an esthetic judgment is neither a simple "I like that" nor a "Based on these criteria, that's good." Moreover, if it is only a combination of the two, then it is a sterile exercise that warrants no more than the little time most give to it. Ultimately, esthetic judgment must be rooted in the esthetic experience that we spoke of earlier. It must be rooted in feeling as well as thinking, imagining as well as reasoning. Without the subjective element of feelings and imagination, it is doubtful that we would ever experience an esthetic impulse, although our esthetic learning may be impressively broad and refined. As the writer Stendhal put it, "The people who passionately love bad music are much closer to good taste than the wise men who love with good sense and moderation the most perfect music ever made."

We live in times in which the phrases "man's inhumanity to man" and "hell is other people" have the ring of painful truth. Perhaps the root cause is our inability to "feel." But what is an inability to feel if not a dysfunctional imagination? It seems that we lack the imagination not only to see our way out of our problems but to feel fully their gravity. Just as physiologically our most necessary sense is the tactile one, emotionally and psychologically our most necessary sense is the ability to feel. True, without feeling we experience no pain, but also no danger. Without feeling we cannot distinguish the harmful from the harmless or the wise from the foolish. Without feeling we run a perilous, though admittedly painless, course to destruction. Therefore, however we judge art or determine its nature and function, we must return to the esthetic experience, whose chief value seems to be that it puts us in touch with ourselves and others by first putting us in touch. This idea deserves development.

Reflection   Have you ever had the experience of reading something and thinking "Now that's exactly how I feel"? Yet, if you had to recount to someone what you had read, it would come out all wrong. Since you couldn't express these feelings before the reading or afterward, what was the value in the reading?

ART AS TRANSMISSION OF INNER EXPERIENCE

In her essay "The Cultural Importance of Art," philosopher Susanne K. Langer gives a definition of art that seems relevant for a practical philosophy. "Art," she says, "may be defined as the practice of creating perceptible forms expressive of human feeling." By "feeling" she means everything that may be felt, and not just pleasure or displeasure, sensibility, or emotion. By "form" she means "an apparition given to our perception," as

. . . when you say, on a foggy night, that you see dimly moving forms in the mist; one of them emerges clearly, and is the form of a man. It is in this sense of an apparition given to our perception that a work of art is a form. It may be a permanent form like a building or a vase or a picture, or a transient dynamic form like a melody or a dance, or even a form given to imagination, like the passage of purely imaginary, apparent events that constitute a literary work. But it is always a perceptible, self-identical whole; like a natural being, it has a character of organic unity, self-sufficiency, individual reality. And it is thus, as an appearance, that a work of art is good or bad or perhaps only rather poor —as an appearance, not as a comment on things beyond it in the world, or as a reminder of them.[3]

---

[3]Susanne K. Langer. "The Cultural Importance of Art," in *Philosophical Sketches*. Baltimore: The Johns Hopkins Press, 1967, p. 86. Reprinted by permission.

But for our purposes the operative part of the definition is that these perceptible forms are "expressive of human feeling." By this she means that art transmits inner experience.

Early in our study of philosophy we discussed language. At that time we saw how language expresses the world around us and, on occasion, the world within us. It expresses self. We noted how we often have feelings that defy language, that "lie too deep for words." Frequently, when we do seem to find the right words, they belie our real feelings. This is so, some say, because feelings are irrational. "On the contrary," writes Langer, "they seem irrational because language does not help to make them conceivable, and most people cannot conceive anything without the logical scaffolding of words." When we learned how language affects our perception, classifies things, orders the world, and makes sense of reality, we saw that language can thus misrepresent and distort; for its classifications, order, and relationships are not precise. Now, if language manifests this unfitness to express the world around us, how much more unfit is it to describe the elusive world within us? At least we can detect a resemblance between the form of our language and the world around us (whether or not we have imposed that form on things is not relevant here). But how does language form reflect the natural form of feeling?

As an illustration, recall how our language inclines us to see in terms of things. But feeling is no thing. Furthermore, our language allows expression primarily in terms of actor and action: "I am feeling angry." But what does this mean to someone else? Not much, for that person has no way of knowing what "feeling angry" means for you. Only you know what "feeling angry" means for you, and no amount of words can convey that feeling. The word *anger* simply refers to a very general inner experience, as do *fear, love, excitement,* and *resentment.* Thus, whereas language gives outward experience a form and makes it sensible, it is really unfit to shape and define inner experience. As Langer puts it:

Human feeling . . . has an intricate dynamic pattern, possible combinations and new emergent phenomena. It is a pattern of organically interdependent and interdetermined tensions and resolutions, a pattern of almost infinitely complex activation and cadence. To it belongs the whole gamut of our sensibility —the sense of straining thought, all mental attitude and motor set. Those are the deeper reaches that underlie the surface waves of our emotion, and make human life a life of feeling instead of an unconscious metabolic existence interrupted by feelings.[4]

It is this dynamic pattern, according to Langer, to which art gives expression. A work of art is a "symbol of feeling," for it formulates our

---

[4]Susanne K. Langer. "The Cultural Importance of Art," in *Philosophical Sketches*, p. 88.

inward experience as language formulates outward experience. "Art objectifies the sentience and desire, self-consciousness and world-consciousness, emotions and moods, that are generally regarded as irrational because words cannot give us clear ideas of them."

Yet, we may ask: so what? What is the cash value of art? After all, it's not practical; it's not religion or morality, business or science. Just what is it? What does it offer to society and to its members? The answer may be: imagination.

Imagination is perhaps our oldest mental capacity. It is probably "the common source of dream, reason, religion, and all true general observation." Even language stems from imagination. Remember how language breaks up reality, organizes it, and makes it manageable for us. But by what other process but imagination could this occur? True, imagination gives rise to the arts, but the arts in turn inspire imagination. By representing in an objective way what we subjectively feel, art permits us, says Langer, to "imagine feeling and understand its nature." It is for this reason that Nellie and Betty are able to sympathize with the characters of *That Certain Summer*, why Jerry is moved by the Rockwell illustrations, why Smitty is able to see Pollock at play, why the guide is able to sense Pollock's art in his execution of it. It is why you, at a rock concert, perhaps, "really envisage vital movement, the stirring and growth and passage of emotion, and ultimately the whole direct sense of human life." And since only *you* are having *your* feeling, the esthetic experience is opening you up to yourself, revealing dimensions you did not know were yours, offering you possibilities heretofore hidden from rational scrutiny. In this way it is showing you at least part of what you need to be complete. In effect, the "arts we live with—our picture books and stories and the music we hear—actually form our emotive experience." In their absence, we lack certain ways of feeling, and thus our impulses are less than human, and so are the society's that we compose. For "a society that neglects [esthetic education] gives itself up to formless emotion."

CONCLUSIONS

In Dostoyevsky's novel, the prisoner who must die in five minutes received a last-minute reprieve. You might wonder what he did with his "eternity of life." Did he live counting each moment? "Oh no. . . . He didn't live like that at all; we're told he wasted many, many minutes. Life goes on. We forget. It seems impossible to live 'counting each moment.'" And yet this is what the esthetic experience allows us to do.

What would allow the prisoner's experience to live on—to constitute again and again the basic wellspring of values that he touched in himself that gloomy afternoon before the guillotine? Perhaps a painting.

"One thought came into my mind just now," Dostoyevsky has Myshkin say to Adelaida, ". . . to suggest that you should paint the face of the condemned man the moment before the blade falls, when he is still standing on the scaffold before he lies down on the plank."

"The face? The face alone?" asks Adelaida. "That would be a strange subject. And what sort of picture would it make?"

Myshkin doesn't know; he simply saw a painting like that once, and it struck him. But Myshkin intuits that it is important for us to be struck more often than once in a while, for the experience enables us better to understand what is important in our lives. And knowing what is of real value and need to us provides deep self-insights.

Today we have little time for these experiences. In the words of the poet Wordsworth:

The world is too much with us; late and soon,
Getting and spending, we lay waste our powers:
Little we see in Nature that is ours.
We have given our hearts away a sordid boon.

As incredible as it may sound, we seem to be without time to feel and, as a result, without time to cultivate an aspect of self that we need to be happy as individuals and to survive as a species. Worse, we seem to have lost the ability.

As an example, recall two stunning moments from the court-martial of Lieutenant William Calley, accused and convicted of engineering the My Lai massacre of civilians in Vietnam. At one point, Calley's corporal is explaining why he shot civilians even though he did not think the original orders to "waste" them still applied. Said the corporal: "Some of my men had already opened fire. I figured these people were wounded anyway, so I might as well go ahead and shoot." The second astonishing moment is when Calley was asked to explain why he thought he was being sent home after the My Lai massacre. "I thought I was coming home to be decorated and promoted, sir." There is in these words a chilling, if understandable, logic that suggests an unconcern for or ignorance of personal and societal needs apart from the ones imprinted in boot camp or Officer's Candidate School. An effective way, and some believe the only way, to make reasonable beings of sensuous ones is to teach them a sense of the esthetic. We seem to be paying a high price for having forgotten this sense.

SUMMARY

We opened this chapter by noting that the esthetic experience heightens perception. It allows us to perceive personal needs more clearly than we could otherwise. In fact, we may describe the esthetic experience as, in large measure, getting in touch with profound personal needs and values through artistic media. We examined various theories of the nature and function of art, all of which are compatible with esthetic experience. In the last analysis, the great value of art is that it seems to express the inexpressible, to give form and shape to feelings that frequently lie too deep for words. In discovering these dimensions of the self through art, we can actually discover who we are by discovering what we need.

MAIN POINTS

1. *Esthetics* derives from a Greek word meaning "perspective." Esthetics is the branch of philosophy that studies beauty, especially in art. The study of esthetics heightens perception and puts us in touch with our true personal needs.
2. There are a number of esthetic theories. First, art is imitative; second, art gives pleasure; third, art is a form of play; fourth, art is expressive of the artist's internal state; fifth, art produces empathy; and sixth, art unifies and orders experience.
3. There are a number of theories concerning the function of art. One contends that art should instill morality; a second holds that art should exist for its own sake; a third contends that art should reveal new possibilities and alternatives to conventional ways of seeing things.
4. Some believe that the final judge of good art is the individual; others hold that there are objective standards to measure art; others, like the objective relativists, admit that there are some general standards but believe that art ultimately must be evaluated according to its ability to inspire esthetic response.
5. Susanne Langer believes that the function of art is to transmit inner experience. Art expresses what is inexpressible; it gives shape, form, and meaning to our feelings. It puts us in touch with ourselves and the world around us.
6. Esthetic education can help clarify and define inner needs.

SECTION EXERCISES

The Esthetic Experience

1. It is possible that the total effect of *Guernica* might be to marshal sentiment for peace and against war. Is this effect the esthetic experience, or is the esthetic experience something different?
2. The phrase "true needs" or "real needs" was not clearly defined. Why not? Can it be?

3. What does Ogilvy mean when he says "We need an esthetic sensibility to tell us whether man's most recent creations of himself cohere in a healthy pattern of wholeness or fall apart into schizoid decadence"?
4. Although Nazi concentration camps were the epitome of horrifying inhumanity, in what sense does their preservation enable us to have an "esthetic experience"?
5. For many, "esthetic" is synonymous with "beautiful." Thus, esthetics is the study of beauty and what constitutes the beautiful. In what sense is this definition accurate? Do "beautiful" and "beauty" need definition? Might their definition include that which is "ugly"? How?

Theories of Art

1. How is Plato's theory of art consistent with the totalitarian society he constructs in his *Republic?*
2. Which theory of art would an epistemological idealist probably adopt? Why?
3. Is it possible to generalize about the theory of art most Americans probably hold? If so, what evidence would you point to? Is William James's pragmatism consistent with this esthetic theory?

The Function of Art

1. Some have argued that, as long as there are serious social ills, people should spend neither their time nor their money on art. In other words, art is frivolous compared with the demands of life. How would you respond to this criticism?
2. Under what circumstances, if any, would you approve of government censorship of art?
3. Jerry believes that art should be representative and morally instructive; Smitty sees art as play and believes it should exist for its own sake. Do you think there is some general correlation between an esthetic theory and the function of art? What kind of art do you enjoy most? What you like probably betrays your theory of art and what you hold to be its function. Do you find such a correlation?
4. Some say that any work of art that has strictly moral or political value tends to be consumed in the very fires of passion that inspired it. Why would they say this? Is it valid?

Esthetic Judgment

1. Pollock's *Convergence*, like much of modern art, is abstract. Therefore, it is more difficult to perceive how such art works to expand our

imagination to conceive of new personal, moral, and social possibilities. But it can and frequently does. How? (Perhaps select an example of your own from painting, music, literature, architecture, or other artistic field.)

2. Why does an underdeveloped esthetic sense invite a self-defeating value system?

3. Describe the three positions on esthetic judgment voiced in the dialogue on page 347.

4. In what sense is Smitty's position a compromise between subjectivism and objectivism?

5. Do you see any connection between these esthetic-judgment positions and the various beliefs about knowledge, truth, and being that we have examined?

6. Do you think it would be inconsistent for someone with Jerry's belief about esthetic judgment to dislike a work of art but admit that it has esthetic worth?

7. Why is imagination necessary to "feel" fully?

ADDITIONAL EXERCISES

1. Is Myshkin's desire for a picture of the condemned man consistent with Langer's thinking about the value of esthetic experience?

2. State precisely how you believe art can help us distinguish true needs from false ones.

3. There is perhaps no branch of learning more neglected than esthetics. If you were in charge, what would you do to ensure that the elementary and secondary schools developed in students an esthetic sense and appreciation?

4. Thinking of what Langer says about esthetics, how would you describe the process by which art affects how you perceive self, others, and the world?

5. Some people believe that although art may formulate and define feelings and sentiments, these feelings and sentiments are not long-lasting. They believe this because they hold that art makes of us passive spectators who watch, listen, think about, and often appreciate objects, but always on a detached, uninvolved level. As a result, art's total effect is one of withdrawal, not engagement, and contemplation rather than action. Do you agree?

6. Do you think that, in general, television advances or sets back esthetic sensibilities? Why?

PAPERBACKS FOR FURTHER READING

Asimov, Isaac. *The Foundation Trilogy.* New York: Avon, 1975. Asimov's three-part epic is about galactic conflict and the establishment of a galactic empire, the Foundation, dedicated to art, science, and technology. This trilogy spans 1000 years and ends with an effort to combat a mutant that challenges the survival of the Foundation. Especially relevant is the role that art plays within the Foundation.

Edman, Irwin. *Arts and the Man: A Short Introduction to Aesthetics.* New York: W. W. Norton, 1939. This simple and readable introduction to esthetics examines the relationship of art to human experience, the origins and function of art, and the ways that art can elucidate and unify personal experience.

Fallico, Arturo B. *Art and Existentialism.* Englewood Cliffs, N.J.: Prentice-Hall, 1962. Painter, sculptor, and philosophy professor Fallico argues, very literately, that art springs from spontaneity, feeling, imagination, and authenticity.

Gaddis, William. *The Recognitions.* New York: Bard, 1975. The central character of this novel rejects inclinations to be a priest in order to become an artist. Then he abandons the ideal of originality to imitate the masters. In his search for a new reality, he faces every kind of bogus knowledge: religious, social, esthetic, and political.

Tolstoy, Leo. *What Is Art?* Aylmer Maude, trans. Indianapolis: Bobbs-Merrill, 1960. Chapters 5, 15, 16. Tolstoy argues that for art to be good it must transmit a kind of religious experience that will unite people in a brotherhood under God.

Wieman, Henry. *Man's Ultimate Commitment.* Carbondale, Ill.: Southern Illinois Press, 1958. Wieman argues that creativity is vital to a full, rich personal life and to the quality of our social institutions. Only through creativity can we experience and enlarge the quality of life.

Philosophy and Autonomy

12

Nobody is almighty and knows everything. Your knowledge and your power will always be limited. Still you can decide about your own life, and you need not accept what you have been told. —Walter Kaufman

Just what have we learned from our study of self through philosophy? We have learned one thing for sure: whatever the definition of human nature and the perception of self, these are influenced by the social, political, and ethical conventions within which they grow. We may deny our social/political milieu, for example, and our Judaeo-Christian ethical values, but we cannot fully escape their influences. Likewise, definitions of human nature and self undoubtedly function within a framework of linguistic and intellectual learnings, and they express themselves religiously and esthetically in a given time and place.

But there is more. Being "influenced" is not being molded. The future is never exactly like the past, because we learn from the past. Thoughtful, sensitive individuals make neither too little nor too much of their personal and historical legacies; they are simply aware of them and use them to build their futures. This we have also learned from our study of self through philosophy.

Also, a great deal of who we are and what we are is determined by how well we integrate and transcend our individual legacies. By integration is meant unity, wholeness, harmony. We are integrated when our beliefs are unified and our actions work in harmony with them. For example, people who claim they are thoroughgoing materialists but insist on the existence of a supernatural world are not integrated. They are "out of kilter" because they are maintaining incompatible beliefs. Similarly, people are not integrated who praise the virtues of the simple life, frugality, and thoughtful contemplation while living a frenzy of materialistic acquisition. What is so important about integration? In

361

its absence, thoughtful, sensitive people frequently feel intellectually short-circuited.

But integration alone is not the measure of self. Transcendence is also necessary. We rise above our individual legacies. Rather than falling under their weight, we overcome them to see deeper and farther than those influences seemingly would allow. The tragedy of never cultivating esthetic appreciation, for example, is not that art is necessarily more desirable than other pursuits. The tragedy is that frequently these people's families, friends, and immediate circle of influence lack esthetic sensibilities as well. So, rather than transcending their legacies, such people choose to be slaves to them. As a result, they are condemned to relive their pasts. A simple illustration involves a famous star of a popular television comedy. When asked how he rose out of poverty into the public limelight, and what advice he would offer young actors, he replied that he determined his life by what he did between 3 P.M. and 10 P.M. What he meant was that it was not his social, educational, and family influences that determined his life but what he allowed them to do. What he allowed them to do *he* determined during the time he was not directly under their spell. In short, he rose above his legacy; he transcended it.

Philosophy plays an important role in personal integration and transcendence by helping us discover who we are. It helps us gain control over our lives. In this final chapter we shall focus on the issue of self-governance—why it is worth pursuing, the obstacles to it. We shall particularly establish the connection between self-governance and philosophy and what is perhaps the most important thing a student can gain from an introductory philosophy class: a philosophical attitude.

PHILOSOPHY AND SELF-DISCOVERY

By now it should be clear that philosophy does not tell us who we are. It helps us discover that for ourselves. Likewise, philosophers do not pretend to know the answer. If philosophy pretends to know any certainty, it is that it doesn't know with certainty. And it is neither ashamed nor embarrassed by such an admission. Rather, it is proud of it and thrives on it, because uncertainty leads to questing, and questing is what philosophy is about—especially the quest for self.

Philosophy contends that questing for wisdom is one of our highest pursuits. Certainly, wisdom is difficult to define; perhaps it consists of understanding what is true, right, and lasting. And if the quest reveals that these values are illusory, philosophy says: let that be your wisdom, and let it set you free.

Furthermore, philosophy believes that the quest for wisdom is liberating. Conversely, the absence of such a quest is enslaving. If we do not seek, we do not find. We may stumble upon or bump into, but we do not find in the sense of *discover*. To discover, we must be looking for, searching out, questing after. No discovery is truly accidental, in the sense that it happens in the absence of a quest. We speak of the "accidental" discovery of penicillin only because Fleming was not searching for it. But he *was* searching for something. You cannot find something if you are looking for nothing; it is also highly unlikely that you will *recognize* the importance and consequence of something you stumble across. No doubt what we recognize and cherish in that beloved bungler Don Quixote is the undying quest without which there can be no discovery. And if there is no discovery, there is little chance of change. There is only a never-ending present so firmly rooted in the past as to be indistinguishable from it, victim of it, and slave to it.

The most profound discovery we can make in our quest is the discovery of self. In the last analysis, this is the wisdom that all questers seek. Notice that we did not say all *creatures* seek, for many of us do not. Many of us are content to be told who we are, to ignore who we are, or to pretend who we are. To the extent we do, we are slaves to myth, ignorance, and illusion. On the other hand, to seek is to find; for the discovery lies in the questing itself. And the questing is liberating, because it frees us from those forces that work against autonomy. Autonomy is vital to self-discovery.

AUTONOMY

In his book *From Decidophobia to Autonomy Without Guilt and Justice*, Princeton University professor of philosophy Walter Kaufman defines autonomy as "making with open eyes the decisions that give shape to one's life."[1] You might think that in this sense everyone wishes to be autonomous. But, as Kaufman points out, "The fear of autonomy is a nameless dread, which leaves me free to coin a name for it: *decidophobia*."[2] By **decidophobia** Kaufman means the fear of choosing fateful alternatives with one's eyes wide open, fully aware of the risks. In short, decidophobia is the fear of **autonomy**—the fear of making an important decision that will give form to your life.

Philosophy tries to get us over our decidophobia. This statement seems at least paradoxical. After all, philosophy examines so many alternatives that a resolution seems impossible, that there seem to be no answers, that we seem to be stranded on an island of uncertainty and inconclusiveness. But such thinking is one of the many bromides

---

[1]Walter Kaufman. *From Decidophobia to Autonomy Without Guilt and Justice*. New York: Delta, 1975, p. 2.

[2]Walter Kaufman. *From Decidophobia to Autonomy*, p. 3.

available to us for avoiding the dizziness of decidophobia—in this case an absorption in microscopic distinctions to such a point that we avoid facing fateful decisions.

A good example of a victim of this type of decidophobia is the character Grand from Albert Camus's novel *The Plague*. Grand is a writer who is composing a novel. But the first sentence of his novel is so bothersome that he keeps rewriting it and spending weeks on a single word. True, the proper choice of words is obviously crucial to a good novel. But Grand is so bogged down on his first sentence that the novel goes begging. Likewise, we can become so immersed in microscopic philosophical distinctions that we avoid making the major philosophical decisions with any sense of perspective, or close our eyes to the major philosophical alternatives.

Philosophy, then, is an avenue to autonomy—to the state in which we make with open eyes decisions that give shape to our lives. In such an autonomous state we stand our best, perhaps our only, chance for self-discovery. Perhaps we can best see how philosophy helps us achieve autonomy by seeing how it breaks down obstacles to autonomy.

Reflection   Are you tending to be decidophobic in your career choice? How are you making the decision?

OBSTACLES TO AUTONOMY

Kaufman cites what he believes are common strategies by which we avoid autonomy:

A.   Avoiding fateful decisions.
    1.   Strategies involving recourse to authority.
    2.   Strategies that do not involve recourse to authority and are compatible with going it alone.
B.   Stacking the cards to make one alternative clearly right and remove all risk.
C.   Declining responsibility.[3]

Avoiding Fateful Decisions

One clear way to avoid self-discovery by avoiding decisions that give shape to our lives is to rely on authority to decide for us. Authority can take many forms: religious, political, philosophical, and educational, to name a few. Let us take educational authority as an example.

---

[3]Kaufman. *From Decidophobia to Autonomy*, p. 30.

Right now you find yourself in college. How did you get there? Primarily by accidents of geography and financial conditions. It is possible that you never considered the alternatives of going elsewhere, and you probably never considered who composed the faculty. And it is almost certain that you never knew what particular books and ideas you would be exposed to. Yet, for the next several years, all these factors will wield an authoritative influence over your life. In some instances this influence will last a lifetime.

For example, let us imagine that the only psychology course you ever take is taught by a behaviorist. There is a good chance that your subsequent psychological perceptions, including how you see yourself, will betray a strong behavioristic bias. Again, suppose a history course you find particularly stimulating is taught by a Spenglerian. In 1917 Oswald Spengler wrote a very influential book called *The Decline of the West,* in which he argued that Western culture is in a state of decay. Having sat through a term of Spenglerian history, it would not be unusual for you subsequently to identify with that school of thought. If you doubt this, ask yourself how seriously you have ever thought about socialism, Communism, Fascism, libertarianism, or anarchism as alternative political life-styles. Probably not much, because the authoritative influences in your life have not carried these biases. As a result, you probably don't either. But *don't* does not mean *can't.* This is the point: in locking into authorities, we equate don't with can't. The result is often an evasion of autonomy, an avoidance of deciding with open eyes, an escape from self-discovery.

On the other hand, some of us reject authority and attempt to "go it alone." The result can be drifting.[4] We all know people who would rather go along with the way things are than choose their own life-styles, their own places to live, their own pastimes. Do you know people who watch a lot of television? Commercial television is currently glutted with two kinds of programs: police dramas and situation comedies. When was the last time any of these people you know wrote to a network and asked for different programming? Perhaps they are happy with what they get. They are content with the *status quo,* with what somebody is giving them. They are so immersed in the way commercial television is that they do not consider the alternatives. They drift until next season, or the season thereafter, when something else becomes fashionable.

But there is another way to drift. Some turn their backs on the *status quo,* on tradition, on conventionality. They accept no values, no codes, no purpose, no plan. They simply "drop out." They become society's flotsam. In living by chance and whim, they avoid the dizziness of making decisions with open eyes.

---

[4]Kaufman. *From Decidophobia to Autonomy,* p. 9.

"There is a good chance that your subsequent
psychological perceptions, including how
you see yourself, will betray a strong
behavioristic bias."

As an example of avoiding fateful decisions, consider Susan and Bob, a young couple whose life together has gradually grown stale and tedious. On the particular evening we join them, they are watching television—their primary pastime.

Susan: Bob, I'm bored.

Bob: Well, this certainly isn't one of the best shows I've ever seen, either.

Susan: I don't mean that. Bob, do you realize that every Wednesday night we watch this?

Bob: You want to see what else is on?

Susan: No, I know what else is on—more of the same. And tomorrow night and the night after that.

Bob: What about a movie?

Susan: No, no movies.

Bob: Then what is it?

Susan: I don't know. Yes, yes, I do know. Things have become so predictable.

Bob: Predictable?

Susan: You know, the same old stuff. Even you and me; we've become predictable. Do you realize I knew you were going to suggest we see a movie?

Bob: How did you know that?

Susan: Because whenever anything vaguely unsettling comes up, you always suggest that.

Bob: I'm sorry, I didn't realize that.

Susan: Oh, Bob, I'm not trying to put you down. Gosh, you probably feel the same way about me. Tell me the truth: can't you almost anticipate how I'm going to react to things?

Bob: Sure, a lot of times I can. But is that so bad?

Susan: No, but it could mean we're stagnating, couldn't it? That we've pretty much discovered all there is to discover about each other and ourselves? Now we just sit back and look forward to growing old together, secure and bored.

Susan feels that she and Bob are drifting, that their life has become routine. Sure, it is comfortable and secure, but it is also dull and boring. And another movie will only intensify the boredom, because movies and television apparently have become the way that Susan and Bob avoid important questions. Whenever something unsettling arises, Bob suggests they see a movie. This strategy has become one of escape, not confrontation. It is a way of avoiding fateful questions and decisions, such as those concerning the quality of their relationship, which has grown stagnant and tedious, at the same time restricting Susan and Bob's individual and mutual possibilities. But there are other ways to avoid governing our lives besides resorting to authority or drifting.

Reflection Cite an example or two of the roles that authority and drifting have played in your life.

Stacking the Cards

Many people insist on making decisions, but they load the choices so as to avoid the pain of choosing between live options. Let us say you are offered two plates of food. One is tasty and healthful; the other is distasteful and poisonous. The choice is obvious: the first dish. That decision was not hard because the deck was stacked on the side of the first dish. In a similar way, many of us stack the choices that profoundly affect our self-discovery.

One way we stack the deck is to ignore unsettling facts. Let us say that every afternoon a man has a can of beer just to "relax." After a while, he begins to have a couple of beers. Pretty soon he finds that something stronger, maybe a martini, really does the trick. Then he feels he just must have a drink to unwind. A friend suggests he has a drinking problem. That's absurd, the man insists. After all, he doesn't get drunk; he can do his work, discharge his responsibilities, remain pleasant and altogether unabusive. Although he concludes he has no drinking problem, he may be stacking the deck—selecting only those facts that support how he wants to see himself and ignoring the overriding fact that he *needs* a drink to unwind. Even admitting that he might have a problem would mean, among other things, a painful self-examination that could reveal many personal flaws, inadequacies, and discontents. Coming to grips with those problems would advance his own autonomy. Yet many of us find our "autonomy" at the bottom of a glass.

When we stack the deck, we frequently see things in black and white, not color. Things are either true or false, right or wrong. Again, consider the case of Susan and Bob. She suggests that their life together has become stale and trite. Let us hear Bob's reply.

Bob: Well, you know we don't have the kind of money it takes to live it up.

Susan: Who said anything about living it up?

Bob: Don't think I haven't thought about just getting on a plane and flying somewhere for a week or two. Or going out to some fancy restaurant occasionally and having a first-class meal. Maybe someday we'll be able to do that, but right now—

Susan: But why are your alternatives so unaffordable?

Bob: Because things cost money, that's why.

Susan: Sure, *things* do. But experiences don't.

What is Bob doing? He is stacking the deck. The only alternatives he can visualize are prohibitively expensive. In effect, he is saying: we can do either the inexpensive things we're doing now or those other things we can't afford. The choice is clear-cut, and it promises more boredom. But why not consider other possibilities?

Why is it important for us to seek alternative ideas, beliefs, attitudes, pastimes, and life-styles? Before examining the third way of evading fateful decisions, declining responsibility, let us try to answer this important question.

Reflection   Imagine that you have been sitting next to someone in class all term that you would really like to get to know. Yet for one reason or another you have not made the effort. Describe the rationalizing process you might have gone through to ensure that you never initiated the effort.

Seeking Personal Alternatives

Susan: Tell me something, Bob. How much does it cost to take a walk in the woods? To visit an art gallery? To read a book and discuss it? Look, next month there's going to be a parapsychology exhibit at the Museum of Industry and Science. It's free. Let's go.

Bob: But I don't know anything about parapsychology.

Susan: Well, I don't either. But that's what'll make it fun.

Bob: Fun? How can you enjoy something you don't know anything about?

Susan: By learning about it! By opening yourself up to the possibility of an interest you didn't know you had.

Bob: All right. If it's that important to you, we'll go.

Susan: "If it's that important to me" . . . Bob, what's happening to us? A year ago you wouldn't have said that. A year ago you would have said "Sure, let's go."

Susan is suggesting here more than just a different way to pass time. She is suggesting a way to help discover and enrich self. By being receptive to new possibilities, alternative ways of spending time, we open ourselves to personal insights.

In his book *The Transparent Self*, psychotherapist Sidney Jourard borrows a term from existential-phenomenology literature: *disclosure*. To disclose means to reveal or to show. Self-disclosure is showing ourselves so that others can perceive us. Everything around us is disclosing itself to us by one means or another. It is evident that a large measure of who we are is how we perceive the world around us. But, as Jourard points out, "to perceive is to receive the disclosure of something." Who we are, then, is bound up with how much disclosure of the world we are receiving. If we receive very little—if we are intimidated by novelty and adventure, new ideas and possibilities—we sharply restrict self-development. Susan is suggesting that they open themselves to more disclosure of the world than they are currently open to. In this way they stand a good chance of combating stagnation and boredom. We all do. And there is hardly a better vehicle for opening ourselves up than education.

Right now you are engaged in education, an activity that should be directed to increasing your capacity to receive the world's disclosure. What are you making of it? For some, education is no more than a degree and a job ticket. It is something to "get through." Such people are doing themselves a disservice.

There are several characteristics of well-educated people that give them an advantage over the uneducated. One is that they are equipped to

"Self-disclosure is showing ourselves so that
others can perceive us."

live in a changing environment. In his popular work *Future Shock*, author Alvin Toffler speaks of our need to learn how to survive in a world that changes with frightening speed. Toffler points to the social and psychological consequences of rapid change in a society like ours: the disruption of government, the breakup of cultures, the collapse of family and community life, the growing sense of alienation. These will all put intense stress on the individual. We must be prepared to deal with the obsolescence of our occupational skills, our religious and moral values, and even our language usage. We should anticipate an explosion of goods and services and of life-styles that undermine our very concept of self. How well we are educated will play a large part in determining how well we are able to adjust to such fundamental changes.

Educated people also develop a spirit of cooperative living. The kind of world that Toffler anticipates will demand a greater effort than ever from people to get along with one another. Already we are beginning to feel the pressures resulting from overcrowded living conditions. The temptation to strike out in anger rather than reach out in love will probably grow more intense. We must guard against the inclination to ignore the rights of others, for in so doing we invite violence to our own interests and rights.

In addition, because forecasts indicate that in the future we shall have more leisure time than ever before, we must deal with the problems of spending this free time. This is one of the problems that Susan and Bob are experiencing. Well-educated people are able to entertain themselves. They develop a rewarding inner life and a far-reaching store of interests. Most importantly, they are able to be at ease and to be enriched when alone. Many of us find this very difficult. No sooner are we alone than we must frantically seek diversion. And we rely not only on radio and television to "protect" us from ourselves; frequently we fall into relationships with other people simply because we are lonely, fearful, or unaccustomed to being alone. The basis for such relationships is not one of healthful encounter with another human and ourselves, but primarily evasion of decision-making. Perhaps this is the root of Susan's and Bob's problem. We shall see shortly, when we discuss the third strategy for avoiding fateful decisions: declining responsibility. But first let us conclude this discussion of the importance of education in increasing our capacity to receive the world.

Yes, education is job preparation. Well-educated people are proficient in their profession, trade, or skill. But, as we have seen, a good education means much more than this. It is a way of adjusting to change, learning to live cooperatively, and developing leisure-time activities and interests. Ignoring these vital parts of our education, we diminish our capacity to receive the "disclosure of the world" and increase our capacity to be victimized by it.

Reflection   In what area would you say your current education is most lacking? What can you do about this deficiency?

Declining Responsibility

Frequently today we neither avoid fateful decisions nor stack the cards in favor of one choice or another. Instead, we simply decline responsibility.

Have you ever served on a committee? If you have, you know that one of the wondrous features of a committee is that no single member must ever bear the responsibility for a decision. As a result, no single member must ever take the blame. If things go wrong, individuals can always console themselves with the thought that they would have done differently had they been acting alone. And perhaps they would have. The curious thing about the committee, then, is that a decision is made ˙but nobody makes it. A marvelous way to decline responsibility and autonomy.

Marriage is often like a committee. Although it is a committee of just two, the couple nevertheless reaches a consensus that goes unquestioned if things go well. When things go poorly, partners may be comforted by the knowledge that, acting alone, they would have chosen differently. In effect, as Kaufman points out, "Nobody made any decision at all, and that was one of the main features of the whole arrangement from the start: marriage is a way of avoiding the necessity of having to make fateful decisions."[5] Notice that he does not say that marriage *must* be a way of avoiding fateful decisions. Neither does he say that anyone married is avoiding them. In fact, "getting married can involve the will to incur additional responsibilities and to see a myriad of things in two perspectives."[6] This is also true of the other methods we frequently rely on to avoid decision-making. Education, for example, need not result in a commitment to narrow authority: it can be an experience in thoroughly enriching our self-knowledge and awareness. But frequently it is not, and neither is marriage. Indeed, recent counts indicate that more than one of every two of our marriages ends in divorce. We are led to wonder about our motives for marrying, or for living together —an increasingly popular substitute for marriage.

Some influential motives are our disinclination to "go it alone," our unwillingness to make decisions on our own, and our desire to escape loneliness. A marital arrangement appears to provide relief from these disquieting realities. In it we need not stand alone; we have somebody to lean on. The decisions that once would have consumed us alone now seem to be swallowed up in talk or distraction. "Instead of making a decision, one talks until something 'transpires.'"[7] Again, it need not be this way; but the bromide to the dizziness of decidophobia is there, and, if you are at all concerned with autonomy, you should be alert to it.

This is one of the problems that Susan and Bob are having. It may be the basic one, for it is preventing them from confronting any of their other problems. For too long they have remained silent when they should have spoken; and when they did speak, they had nothing to say to each other.

Susan: Bob, I'm scared.

Bob: Of what?

Susan: That something's happening to us, something I don't like.

Bob: You know, I think I feel it too.

Susan: You do? Oh, God, I'm glad you do, and it's not just me.

Bob: No, no, it's not just you. Something has happened to us. . . . You know, sometimes when I hold you . . .

Susan: Go on.

Bob: It's hard for me to say it.

Susan: It'll be better if you do.

---

[5]Kaufman. *From Decidophobia to Autonomy*, p. 29.

[6]Kaufman. *From Decidophobia to Autonomy*, p. 30.

[7]Kaufman. *From Decidophobia to Autonomy*, p. 29.

Bob:	I'm not so sure. But I want it to be better, I really do. I want it to be the way it was.
Susan:	Then say it.
Bob:	Sometimes when I hold you, I have to remind myself who you are.
Susan:	Oh, God!
Bob:	I'm sorry.
Susan:	No, don't be sorry. I knew.
Bob:	You knew?
Susan:	I feel it too. You've been a stranger to me.
Bob:	And you never said anything.
Susan:	*We* never said anything.
Bob:	But I wanted to. You'll never know how many times I wanted to, and almost did. But every time I thought, "It's for her to say."
Susan:	Funny. I was thinking it was for you to say.
Bob:	Were you?
Susan:	Almost always. Often I thought I was being paranoid, seeing shadows that weren't there. He'll laugh, I thought, or think I'm stupid. No, I won't say anything.
Bob:	I was afraid that just suggesting something was wrong would hurt what we had.
Susan:	Was what we had that flimsy?
Bob:	I don't know.
Susan:	Were you that desperate?
Bob:	I don't understand.
Susan:	What are we doing together, Bob?
Bob:	I don't think I want to talk about that.
Susan:	We must.
Bob:	Why? Why can't we just be happy we're together and not figure out why?
Susan:	We could if we were happy together, but we're not. And I think it's because we're not happy alone.
Bob:	Alone? When are we ever alone?
Susan:	I'm alone all the time.

We are all alone all the time in the sense that ultimately we make the decisions that give shape to our lives. To the degree that we abdicate this responsibility, we have a diminished concept of self. Kaufman's strategies that we have discussed are common ways we avoid this responsibility. Being aware of them will help combat them. But perhaps we can best be aware of them through a lifetime commitment to philosophy.

Reflection   What kind of relationship with another person are you seeking? What are you prepared to bring to it?

PHILOSOPHY AND AUTONOMY

If philosophy proposes to do anything, it is to assist us in making with open eyes decisions that will give shape to our lives. How? By thwarting those obstacles to autonomy that we have just discussed.

First, we saw how we frequently avoid fateful decisions by relying on authority or by drifting. But to philosophize is not to rely on authority as the primary source of claims. In fact, philosophizing demands a healthful skepticism of those very authorities with which we most sympathize, with which we feel the strongest emotional and psychological ties. Why? Because these authorities, through their preferred positions in our minds and hearts, are likely to wield the most persuasive and the least examined influences over our lives, over our autonomy. We are speaking here of home, church or synagogue, school, political institutions, and so forth. Again, this does not mean that these institutions cannot and are not often boons to self-discovery and liberation. But they are not necessarily so. So, if nothing else, philosophy is skeptical, and skepticism is the natural enemy of authority.

We saw that drifting is another way we frequently avoid the dtziness of decidophobia. We said earlier that it is tempting to think philosophizing leads to a kind of paralysis of will that leaves us unable to decide anything. But this is a pedantry that misrepresents philosophy. Yes, if we allow it to do so, philosophy can bog us down in microscopic distinctions that are of no consequence to the major decisions of our life. But this is to miss the forest for the trees. Even at the highest levels of philosophical abstraction, the purpose of microscopic distinctions is to clarify the macroscopic issues. When philosophers forget this, and they frequently do, they too swallow the pill of pedantry to escape the dizziness of decision-making. The fact is that, rather than advancing drifting, philosophizing often begins with a recognition of, distaste for, and attack on drifting. Remember, the philosopher is a seeker. No true seeker is a drifter. Thus, the seeker may at times appear to be drifting, but only because the object of the search still remains unfound. The difference between the seeker and the drifter is that the seeker is searching for something but the drifter is not. Philosophizing always seeks, it never drifts; you cannot philosophize and drift.

". . . it is tempting to think philosophizing leads to a kind of paralysis of will that leaves us unable to decide anything."

Another way to relieve the dizziness of decision-making is to stack the cards in favor of one choice. Philosophizing is the antithesis of this. Indeed, as we just saw, philosophizing "unstacks" the deck so effectively that it can make us pedants if we are not careful. Rather than ignoring inconvenient and disquieting facts, when we philosophize we freely entertain them, because philosophizing demands a commitment to intellectual honesty. This honesty requires an airing of all data relevant to the question at hand, no matter how unsettling those data happen to be. It also demands subscription to those procedures, rational and empirical, that aid a thorough examination of the question.

Finally, we may avoid autonomy by declining responsibility for decision-making. But, again, philosophizing does not allow this, because it recognizes that ultimately each of us—not as a group, committee, company, congress, or marital partnership, but as individuals—must decide the answers to the eternal questions. Plato? Descartes? Sartre? No, they cannot decide it for us. That would be caving in to authority. Look on these and other philosophers as tools for the philosophical mortar of your life—no more, no less. Learn from them, profit by them, grow with them and with all those lives that touch your life.

So far we have seen only what philosophy helps us not to do. Precisely what does philosophy help us *do* to be autonomous? In brief, philosophy opens our eyes.

MAKING DECISIONS WITH OPEN EYES

If you must leave a philosophy course having learned only one thing, the prized possession might be a philosophical attitude.

"Philosophical attitude" finds various definitions: an ability to ask the "big questions," a tolerance of others' opinions, a willingness to exchange viewpoints and ideas, an appreciation of your own and others' limitations, a sensitivity to the many sides of a question. But perhaps a philosophical attitude is best summed up in the following steps we can apply when facing any question, hypothesis, conviction, or belief: (1) clearly defining the issue, (2) evaluating the issue, (3) seeking and weighing alternatives, and (4) choosing the most plausible alternative.

With this philosophical attitude, we are able to make decisions with open eyes. Indeed, we could say that the philosophical attitude epitomizes making with open eyes decisions that give shape to our lives. Let us see how this attitude might function for Susan and Bob.

Susan: So what do you think all this means?

Bob: I don't know.

Susan: Or don't you want to know?

Bob: You're saying we should break up?

Susan: At least for a while, until we find out where we are and who we are.

Bob: Is that what you want?

Susan: It's what I believe is best for us.

Susan's position is clear: she and Bob need to separate. She is convinced that staying together longer will not solve their problem. They need time to withdraw, to do some soul-searching, to find out what they need and want individually and together. He is not convinced.

Bob: But . . .

Susan: What?

Bob: Nothing.

Susan: It'll hurt—that's what you were going to say, wasn't it?

Bob: But it will.

Susan: It will. And at times it will be unbearably lonely.

Bob: Do you realize we may never get back together?

Susan: Yes.

Bob: That one of us may find somebody else?

Susan: But we might also discover each other, as if for the first time. In finding out who we are and what we need, we may rediscover each other, Bob. And then I think we'll have something strong and lasting. Then we'll be able to embrace without clinging, to have without possessing, to love without devouring. I don't think we can do that now, and I want to, and I want to find out how to.

When one side of a question demands change in a life-style, as it does here, the question is especially painful. But the healthy attitude, the philosophical one, is to examine the factors that speak for a position and those that speak against it. Should Susan and Bob separate, Susan believes that they stand a chance of better defining their own wants and needs. From this new place they may rediscover each other and subsequently have a rewarding relationship. On the other side, Bob points out that they will feel terrible pain and loneliness and will risk losing each other forever. There are undoubtedly other considerations that need not concern us, for we are merely concerned with establishing the importance of the evaluative process. Part of this process must involve a consideration of alternatives.

Bob: Look, why can't we work it out together?

Susan: You mean living together?

Bob: Sure. We see the problem now; we're talking about it. That's half the battle, isn't it?

Susan: You know what would happen. In a week, two weeks, a month maybe, we'd fall back into the same old routine.

Bob: But maybe we wouldn't. Maybe we'd resolve it. In any case, we'd be foregoing all the pain we'll cause each other if we separate.

Susan: But don't you see that we'd be falling into the same trap again? One of our problems is that we're not thinking for ourselves. I'm worried about what you're thinking, or not thinking, or should be thinking, when I should be worried about what *I'm* thinking. You're probably doing the same thing. Why didn't I say something sooner? Because I felt you should have. Why didn't you say something sooner? Because you felt I should have. So nothing got said. Instead, we just drifted. I think if we stay together now we're just avoiding getting in touch with ourselves.

The alternatives that face Susan and Bob are whether or not they should remain together at this point. There are compelling arguments for either side. If they stay together, they could conceivably work out their problems without a painful separation. Also, they might not risk losing each other forever. On the other hand, they might slip back into the old syndrome of relying on the other person or on the relationship to decide what they themselves should be deciding. Furthermore, if the problem is one of coming to grips with self, it is unlikely that in struggling to maintain their relationship they will be able to do that. There are, no doubt, considerably more advantages and disadvantages that accompany these alternatives. There may even be more alternatives, such as agreeing to separate only for a month or two, or remaining together but seeking professional counsel. But the point is that they stand the best chance of managing their lives when they candidly examine and evaluate the alternatives available to them.

But it is not just a matter of tallying up alternatives and choosing the most plausible. When the decision is an important one in our lives, emotions are frequently involved. There are times when our head tells us one thing, our heart another. Other times, we must simply postpone a decision until additional data tip the scale. Almost never will we have the luxury of acting in certainty; yet, approaching the problem with a philosophical attitude, we have the comfort of knowing that our decision-making procedure was sound.

CONCLUSIONS

It should be clear that this philosophical attitude does not end with one or more philosophy courses. It may begin with them, but it should never cease with them. Rather, the philosophical attitude is a garden that needs lifelong cultivation to be truly fruitful. And it requires something else: courage—the courage to take from the garden and carry into the market place, the courage to live what we believe.

SUMMARY

We opened this chapter by observing that who and what we are is determined by how well we integrate and transcend our individual legacies. Philosophy can help us in this effort by assisting us in becoming autonomous. Many people try to avoid autonomy by avoiding fateful decisions, stacking the cards in favor of one decision, or declining responsibility. The study of philosophy helps us avoid these obstacles and helps us to make decisions with open eyes. Finally, we saw that, above all, we should take from a philosophy course a philosophical attitude.

MAIN POINTS

1. Whatever the definition of human nature and the perception of self, these are influenced by the social, political, and ethical conventions within which they grow.
2. A great deal of who and what we are is determined by how well we integrate and transcend our individual legacies.
3. Philosophy helps us achieve autonomy.
4. Autonomy, as defined by Walter Kaufman, means "making with open eyes the decisions that give shape to one's life."
5. Decidophobia, according to Kaufman, is "the fear of autonomy."
6. The following are chief obstacles to autonomy: avoiding fateful decisions by relying on authority or drifting, stacking the cards to make one alternative clearly right and remove all risk, and declining responsibility.
7. With respect to stacking the cards, we must constantly be seeking personal alternatives. A sound basis for this search is a good education.
8. Some characteristics of the well-educated person are: an ability to adjust to a changing environment, a spirit of cooperative living, and a capacity for self-entertainment. These characteristics allow us to receive more fully the disclosure of the world and, by so doing, enlarge our own concept of self.
9. Philosophy can be used to fight the obstacles to autonomy.
10. Philosophy helps us make decisions with open eyes by helping us develop a philosophical attitude. This attitude consists of defining an issue, evaluating it, seeking and verifying alternatives, and deciding on the most plausible alternative.

EXERCISE: TOWARD STATING A PERSONAL PHILOSOPHY

It seems fitting that, at the conclusion of your introduction to philosophy, you should in some way state what you think and believe. So, in place of the usual Section Exercises and Additional Exercises, in this last chapter you are invited to attempt such a statement of your personal philosophy.

There are few times in our lives when we are permitted, let alone invited, to state in detail what we believe and why. We don't have this opportunity because other things crowd it out: circumstances, responsibilities, other interests. After a while we come to consider philosophizing a luxury. Do not let this happen.

Accept this invitation to formulate a statement of personal philosophy. There are a number of good reasons for such an undertaking.

First, we have seen that to a great extent we are what we believe. So, if you are interested in knowing who you are, one obvious way to find out is to define your beliefs, values, and attitudes. Another reason is that to a great extent we are as we live. But beliefs almost always determine life-styles. Therefore, examining your beliefs will give you insight into the philosophical basis of your own life-style. Finally, such an examination will probably point out glaring inconsistencies between what you believe and how you are living. These inconsistencies are important to recognize, because for thoughtful, sensitive people they present potential trouble spots in their lives; for when action short-circuits belief, intellectual and emotional sparks often fly. If you operate on one belief-action wave length, you will probably be a lot happier.

Just what does a statement of personal philosophy consist of? First, note the word *personal*. This statement is not intended as a research paper or any kind of project that requires you to present other people's ideas. If other people's ideas find their way into your personal statement, fine. If you wish to support some of your own ideas with sources, fine. But in the last analysis you will have missed the mark if you do not provide a philosophical profile of *yourself*. In brief, from reading your statement, a person who has never met you should know *what, why,* and *how* you think. Let us consider each of these.

By *what* is meant content. Here is an example. Earlier in our study we discussed the problem of marrying an android, a mechanical mate. We used that simple illustration to launch questions, especially questions of reality. Questions of reality are metaphysical in content. If you discuss such questions and assert a position on them, you will be showing what you believe metaphysically. On the other hand, you may be more concerned with ethics, religion, politics, esthetics, epistemology, language, or some other type of content. You are even more likely to be concerned with several. If you are, you may want to emphasize one particular area and then relate others to it. In other words, you may wish to take an ethical bias, or linguistic, or political. You may see this area as vital to your whole world view, and use it as the hub around which you develop other facets of your personal profile. But remember: you are drawing a philosophical profile of yourself. Do not be stingy: provide as much information as necessary to complete the profile.

The *why* of your statement is the justification of your *what*—the defense of the positions you have taken on the content. For example, suppose in your statement you did discuss the problem of the mechanical mate, and you decided you would marry such a creature. You then declared that this decision reflected your materialistic metaphysical position. But do not simply claim this position; *show why* you do. This step is important, because in giving reasons for your beliefs you justify or fail to justify the beliefs to yourself. A lot of people think they believe something until they must convince themselves. Then they frequently argue themselves right out of that position. For the first time in their lives, they look at *why* they believe something, and discover that (1) they don't know why, (2) they're not sure why, (3) they don't really believe it at all, or (4) they don't believe it, but the people around them do and have passed it on to them. Thus, questioning your convictions often reveals a side of you you never knew existed.

Finally, the *how* of your statement. In informing the reader of what your beliefs are and why you hold them, you will be expressing your thought process. You will be showing how you think. In expressing yourself, keep in mind these criteria that you should apply to the development of your ideas:

1. Clarity of presentation: how free of ambiguities and obscurities your statement is.
2. Consistency of presentation: how free of internal contradictions your statement is.
3. Integration of presentation: how well you have incorporated the philosophical problems raised in the course and show signs of going beyond them.
4. Coherence and unity of presentation: how smoothly you connect one part of the statement with other parts, and how well all the parts relate to your central theme.
5. Logic of presentation: how correct and valid your reasoning is, how free of common fallacies it is.

Now, how do you get started? Here is a suggestion, and only a suggestion. Begin with a concrete problem—a problem that is a real one for you. Let us say, for example, that you are bothered by a career choice. You find yourself in college but haven't the foggiest idea why you are there. You could use that problem to launch your statement.

You might begin by asking yourself: What is causing the problem? What is at the root of it? Perhaps it is uncertainty about what is important in your life. On the one hand, you want a good job and all that it brings: wealth, position, prestige. On the other, you suspect that these are shallow values, and that you should be seeking something more substantial—something of more lasting value. Upon self-examination, you may decide that it is the affluence you really want. Now what does that say about you? Probably that you are materialistic, in the common sense of the word. Well, just how far are you prepared to push materialism? Are you ready to accept everything, including yourself, as matter? No, you might think, because you believe in a soul. Just what do you mean by "soul"? Is this belief influencing you at all?

Thus, you have launched your statement of personal philosophy. A good jumping-off point is a problem—any problem. And don't be afraid it is trivial. If it is a problem for you, it cannot be trivial. Then use that problem as a scalpel to open your mind and heart.

Above all, be honest with yourself. Do not mouth platitudes and things you do not really believe. If you do, you will only retreat from the discovery of self. And if there is pain along the way, welcome it; for having beliefs probed and tested is like a visit to the dentist—except that there is no intellectual novocain available.

PAPERBACKS FOR FURTHER READING

Camus, Albert. *The Myth of Sisyphus and Other Essays*. New York: Vintage, 1959. In his classic essay, "Sisyphus," Camus takes up many traditional existential themes dealing with the absurdity and meaninglessness of life. However, Camus's ultimate conclusion is an affirmation, not a rejection, of the human condition.

Frankl, Victor. *Man's Search for Meaning*. New York: Pocket Books, 1963. This is a psychologist's personal account of those who found meaning and purpose to life even amid the horror of Nazi concentration camps, and of those who did not.

Fromm, Erich. *The Art of Loving*. New York: Bantam, 1963. Fromm presents love not as self-renunciation but as self-assertion. We can express ourselves in no more vital a form than in loving.

Fromm, Erich. *Escape from Freedom*. New York: Avon, 1965. This is an account of how we surrender to authority rather than define ourselves through autonomy.

Hemingway, Ernest. *The Old Man and the Sea*. New York: Charles Scribner's Sons, 1962. This is the tale of a man who creates his own meaning, purpose, and destiny within a context of the objectively futile.

Hesse, Hermann. *Steppenwolf*. New York: Bantam, 1969. This book is the story of a man in search of himself, who learns that he can be himself only when he must *not* be something.

May, Rollo. *Man's Search for Himself*. New York: Signet, 1967. May demonstrates how self-integration and self-identity can take root in anxiety, loneliness, and despair.

Miller, Arthur. *Death of a Salesman*. New York: Viking, 1941. This is Miller's brilliant play about a man whose tragedy lies in his never having examined his life.

Glossary

Some of the terms included in this Glossary are not used in the text but are defined here because they are part of the philosopher's working vocabulary.

abstraction   the mental power of separating one part of an entity from its other parts; or of inferring the class from the particular instance

accidental characteristic   a characteristic that is not necessary to make a thing what it is; an accompanying characteristic

act utilitarianism   in normative ethics, the position that an action is moral if it produces the greatest happiness for the most people

agnosticism   a claim of ignorance; the claim that God's existence can be neither proved nor disproved

analogy   a comparison; when you reason *from analogy*, you conclude that, because two or more entities share one aspect, they share another as well

animism   the belief that many spirits fill aspects of nature

anthropomorphism   the attributing of human qualities to nonhuman entities, especially attributing human qualities to God

antinomy   used by Immanuel Kant to refer to contradictory conclusions arrived at through valid deduction

a posteriori   knowledge claims stated in empirically verifiable statements; inductive reasoning

a priori   knowledge that is logically prior to experience; reasoning based on such knowledge

atheism   denial of theism

atman   the Hindu idea of the self after enlightenment; the concept of no self

authority   a common secondary source of knowledge; a source that exists outside the person making the claim and that the person uses as an expert source of information

autonomy   literally, self-rule; "making with open eyes the decisions that give shape to one's life," as defined by Walter Kaufman

383

avidya   in Buddhism, the cause of all suffering and frustration; ignorance or unawareness that leads to clinging

axiology   the study of the general theory of values, including their origin, nature, and classification

axiom   a proposition regarded as self-evident, true

behaviorism   a school of psychology that restricts study of human nature to what can be observed rather than to states of consciousness

bipolarity   a division into two parts

Brahman   the Hindu concept of an impersonal Supreme Being; the source and goal of everything

Categorical Imperative   Immanuel Kant's ethical formula: act as if the maxim (general rule) from which you act were to become a universal law; what is right for one person is also right for everyone in similar circumstances

catharsis   a purging or cleansing of the emotions; used by Aristotle to describe the purifying of the audience through emotional involvement in a play

causality, causation   the relationship of events, or cause and effect

cause   whatever is responsible for or leads to a change, motion, or condition

classification   the process of grouping like things

cognition   the acquiring of knowledge of something; the mental process by which we become aware of the objects of perception and thought

coherence theory   a theory contending that truth is a property of a related group of consistent statements

common sense   the way of looking at things apart from technical or special training

common-sense realism   the epistemological position that does not distinguish between an object and an experience of it

concept   a general idea, to be distinguished from a *percept*, which we have upon experiencing particular entities; thus, we can have a percept when we see particular citizen John Smith, but we have a concept of "man," a universal unexperienced entity

conditioned genesis   the Buddhist formula consisting of twelve factors that summarize the principles of conditionality, relativity, and interdependence

connotation   everything a word suggests, its flavor, including the images and feelings it arouses

consequentialist theory   in ethics, the position that the morality of an action is determined by its consequences

contingent   an entity that may be and also may not be

contract theory   in social philosophy, the doctrine that individuals give up certain liberties and rights to the state, which in turn guarantees such rights as those to life, liberty, and the pursuit of happiness

correspondence theory   a theory contending that truth is an agreement between a proposition and an actual state of affairs

cosmology   the study of the universal world process—the process by which the world unfolds and evolves

critical philosophy   the analysis and definition of basic concepts and the precise expression and criticism of basic beliefs

decidophobia a term coined by Princeton professor of philosophy Walter Kaufman to mean the fear of autonomy

deduction the process of reasoning to logically certain conclusions

defining characteristic a characteristic in whose absence a thing would not be what it is

deism a widespread belief in the seventeenth and eighteenth centuries in a God who, having created the universe, remains apart from it and administers it through natural laws

denotation a definition that is a verbal example of what a word signifies

designation a definition consisting of the defining characteristics of a word

determinism the theory that everything that occurs happens in accordance with some regular pattern or law

dharma in Buddhism, the doctrine whereby self-frustration is ended; the Eightfold Path

dialectic in general, the critical analysis of ideas to determine their meanings, implications, and assumptions; as used by Hegel, a method of reasoning used to synthesize contradictions

disanalogy a difference between things compared that lessens the likelihood of an analogical conclusion

dualism the theory that reality is composed of two different substances, so that neither one can be related to the other; thus: spirit/matter, mind/body, good/evil

duty theory in ethics, the position that the moral action is the one that conforms with obligations accrued in the past, such as the obligations of gratitude, fidelity, or justice

eclecticism the practice of choosing what is thought best from various philosophies

egoism a consequentialist ethical theory that contends we act morally when we act in a way that promotes our own best long-term interests

emergence, emergent evolution the view that, in the development of the universe, new life forms appear that cannot be explained solely through analysis of the previous form

emotivism the metaethical position that ethical statements primarily express surprise, shock, or some other emotion

empathy a psychological and esthetic designation of the motor attitudes, muscular reactions, and feelings we experience when we identify with another person or object

empiricism the doctrine that knowledge has its origins in and derives all of its content from experience

entelechy a nonmaterial power, vital force, or purpose that permits a form to come to realization

entitlement theory a theory of social justice contending that individuals are entitled to the holdings they have acquired without harming anyone in the process

epiphenomenalism the view that matter is primary, that the mind is a secondary phenomenon that accompanies some bodily processes

epistemology   the branch of philosophy that investigates the nature, sources, limitations, and validity of knowledge

essence   that which makes an entity what it is; that which in whose absence a thing would not be itself

esthetics   the branch of philosophy that studies beauty, especially in the arts

ethics   the branch of philosophy that tries to determine the good and right thing to do

eudaemonism   the view that the end of life is happiness—that is, a complete, long-lived kind of well-being; from the Greek *eudaimonia*, "happiness"

existence   actuality

existentialism   a twentieth-century philosophy that denies any essential human nature; each of us creates our own essence through free action

extrasensory perception   the view that the ordinary senses are not the only paths to cognition

fallacy   an incorrect way of reasoning; an argument that tries to persuade psychologically but not logically

false dilemma   an erroneous bipolarity resulting from the existence of intermediate positions between the two presented

fatalism   the view that events are fixed, that humans can do nothing to alter them

finite   limited

formalism   in ethics, the view that moral acts follow from fixed moral principles and do not change because of circumstances

free will   the denial that human acts are completely determined

Gestalt   a psychological view that the whole is not just the sum of its parts

Golden Rule   the ethical rule that holds: Do unto others as you would have them do unto you

hedonism   the view that pleasure is intrinsically worthwhile and is the human's good

humanism   the view that stresses distinctly human values and ideals

human nature   what it essentially means to be of our species; what makes us different from anything else

hypothesis   in general, an assumption, statement, or theory of explanation, the truth of which is under investigation

idealism   in metaphysics, the position that reality is ultimately nonmatter; in epistemology, the position that all we know are our ideas

ideational theory   the theory of word meaning that stresses the emotional impact of words

identity theory   the theory that mental states are really brain states

immanent   indwelling, within the process, as God is frequently thought to be in relation to His creation

immortality   the belief that the self or soul survives physical death

indeterminism   the view that some individual choices are not determined by preceding events

induction   the process of reasoning to probable conclusions

inference   a conclusion arrived at inductively or deductively

infinite   unlimited

infinite regress   the causal or logical relationship of terms in a series that logically can have no first or initiating term

informal fallacies   common argumentative devices used to persuade emotionally or psychologically, but not logically

innate ideas   ideas that, according to some, such as Plato, can never be found in experience but are inborn

instrumentalism   synonymous with John Dewey's pragmatism; the view that emphasizes experience and interprets concepts, beliefs, and attitudes as ways an organism adjusts to its environment

interactionism   the theory that the mind and the body interact; originally associated with Descartes

intuition   a source of knowledge that does not rely immediately on the senses or reason but on direct awareness

judgment   asserting or denying something in the form of a proposition

karma   the Hindu law of sowing and reaping; determines what form and circumstances we assume in each reincarnated state

laissez faire   in economics, politics, and social philosophy, the concept of government noninterference

language   an aspect of human behavior that involves the use of vocal sounds and corresponding written symbols in meaningful patterns to formulate and communicate thoughts and feelings

linguistic analysis   a contemporary form of analytic philosophy claiming that philosophical problems are partially language problems; the purpose of philosophy is to dissolve, not resolve, problems by a rigorous examination of language

logic   the branch of epistemology that studies the methods and principles of correct reasoning

logical empiricism (positivism)   a contemporary form of analytic philosophy that contends meaning is the most important feature of philosophical discourse; there are two kinds of epistemological meaning: (1) that expressed in analytic statements—that is, formal meaning that can be verified by logic and syntax; and (2) empirical—that is, factual meaning that can be verified by sense data

logical positivism   the philosophical school of thought that would restrict meaningful propositions to those that can be empirically verified or to those that state relationships among terms

logos   the term used by classical philosophers to describe the principle of rationality or law that they observed operating in the universe

materialism   the metaphysical position that reality is ultimately composed of matter

maximin rule   the social theory of justice that contends inequality is allowable only insofar as it improves the lot of the worst off in a society

maya   in Buddhism, the world of illusion

mechanism   the view that everything can be explained in terms of laws that govern matter and motion

meliorism   from the Latin meaning "better"; the view that the world is neither all good nor all bad, but can be improved through human effort

mentalism   the view that mind or idea is all that exists

metaethics   the study of the meanings of ethical words and of the sentences in which they appear

metaphysics   the branch of philosophy that studies the nature of reality

metempsychosis   the belief that upon physical death the soul can migrate into another body

monism   the view that reality is reducible to one kind of thing or one explanatory principle

monotheism   the belief in a single God

morals   the conduct or rule of conduct by which people live

mysticism   the philosophy of religion contending that reality can be known only when we surrender our individuality and experience a union with the divine ground of all existence

naïve realism   the view that the world is as we perceive it to be.

naturalism   a version of materialism that rejects supernatural principles and maintains that reality can be explained only in terms of scientifically verifiable concepts; a denial of any fundamental difference between humans and other animals

natural law   (1) a pattern of necessary and universal regularity holding in physical ratio; (2) a moral imperative, a description of what *ought* to happen in human relationships

necessary condition   a way to refer to cause; for example, when B cannot occur in the absence of A, A is said to be a necessary condition of B

new realism   the view that the world is as we perceive it to be

nihilism   the view that nothing exists, that nothing has value; the social view that conditions are so bad that they should be destroyed and replaced by something better

nirvana   in Buddhism, enlightenment that comes when the limited, clinging self is extinguished

nominalism   the view that only particular entities are real and that universals represent detectable likenesses among particulars

nonconsequentialist theory   in ethics, the position that the morality of an action is determined by more than just its consequences

nonnaturalism   the metaethical position that ethical statements defy translation into nonethical language

normative ethics   the reasoned search for the principles of right conduct

objective   a term describing an entity that has a public nature independent of us and our judgments about it

objective idealism   the position that ideas exist in an objective state, associated originally with Plato

objective relativism   the value theory that contends values are relative to human satisfaction but that human needs and what satisfies them are open to empirical examination

obligation   that which we must or are bound to do because of some duty, agreement, contract, promise, or law

omnipotent   all-powerful

omnipresent   capable of being everywhere at once

omniscient   all-knowing

ontology   a subdivision of metaphysics; the theory of the nature of being and existence

ostensive definition   a definition that consists of pointing out an instance of a word's denotation

panentheism   the belief that God is both fixed and changing, inclusive of all possibilities

pantheism   the belief that everything is part of God

parallelism   the theory that physical and mental states do not interact but simply accompany each other

parapsychology   the school of psychology that studies extrasensory powers

perception   the act or process by which we become aware of things

persuasive language   the use of word connotations to persuade

phenomenalism   the belief, associated with Kant, that we can know only appearances (phenomena) and never what is ultimately real (noumena); that the mind has the ability to sort out sense data and provide relationships that hold among them

phenomenology   the philosophical school founded by Edmund Husserl that contends being is the underlying reality; what is ultimately real is our consciousness, which itself is being

philosophy   in its broadest sense the activity undertaken by those deeply concerned with who and what they are and what everything means

pluralism   the view that reality consists of many substances

polytheism   belief in many gods

positivism   the view that only analytic and synthetic propositions are meaningful

postulate   a presupposition used as a basis for establishing a proof

pragmatism   the philosophical school of thought, associated with Dewey, James, and Peirce, that tries to mediate between idealism and materialism by rejecting all absolute first principles, tests truth through workability, and views the universe as pluralistic

predestination   the doctrine that every aspect of our lives has been divinely determined from the beginning of time

primary qualities   according to Locke, the qualities that inhere in an object: size, shape, weight, and so on

probability   the likelihood of an event's happening or of a statement's being true

propaganda   the systematic advancing of a doctrine

proposition   a true or false statement

rationalism   the position that reason alone, without the aid of sense information, is capable of arriving at some knowledge, at some undeniable truths

realism   the doctrine that the objects of our senses exist independently of their being experienced

reason   the capacity for thinking reflectively and making inferences; the process of following relationships from thought to thought and of ultimately drawing conclusions

referential theory   a theory of word meaning contending that words refer to things

relativism   the view that human judgment is conditioned by factors such as acculturation and personal bias

religious belief   in its broadest sense, the belief that there is an unseen order and that we can do no better than to be in harmony with this order

representative realism   the position that distinguishes between an object and one's experience of it; associated with Locke

right   in ethics, acts that conform to moral standards

rights   those things to which we have a just claim

rule utilitarianism   the normative ethical position that contends we should act so that the rule governing our actions produces the greatest happiness for the most people

samsara   in Buddhism, the round of birth and life

scientific method   a way of investigation based on collecting, analyzing, and interpreting sense data to determine the most probable explanation they suggest

secondary qualities   according to Locke, qualities that we impose on an object: color, smell, texture, and so on

self   the individual person, the ego, the knower, that which persists through changes

semantics   the study of the relationship between words and reality, including their linguistic forms, symbolic nature, and effects on human behavior

sense data   images or sense impressions

skepticism   in epistemology, the view that varies between doubting all assumptions until proved and claiming that no knowledge is possible

social philosophy   the application of moral principles to the problems that fall within its sphere, such as freedom, equality, and justice

solipsism   an extreme form of subjective idealism, contending that only "I" exist and that everything else is a product of the subjective consciousness

soul   the immaterial entity that is variously identified with consciousness, mind, or personality

subjective   that which refers to the knower; that which exists in the consciousness but not apart from it

subjective idealism   in epistemology, the position that all we ever know are our own ideas; associated with Berkeley

substance (1) that which is real; (2) essence; (3) the underlying ground in which properties inhere; (4) that which exists in its own right and depends on nothing else

sufficient condition a way to refer to cause; A is said to be a sufficient condition of B if, without exception, whenever A occurs B occurs

tautology a statement whose predicate repeats its subject in whole or in part

teleology the view that maintains the reality of purpose and affirms that the universe either was consciously designed or is working out of partly conscious, partly unconscious purposes

telepathy in ESP, the name given to the phenomenon of thought transfer from one person's mind to another's without normal means of communication

theism the belief in a personal God who intervenes in the lives of His creation

theology the study of God, including religious doctrines

totalitarianism the political view that the state is of paramount importance

universal that which is predictable of many particular entities; thus, "woman" is a universal, since it is predictable of individual women

utilitarianism in ethics, the theory that contends we should act in such a way that our actions produce the greatest happiness for the most people

validity correctness of the reasoning process; characteristic of an argument whose conclusion follows by logical necessity

value an assessment of worth

verification proving or disproving of a proposition

vitalism the view that there is in living organisms an entelechy, or life principle, that provides purpose or direction

word form words considered with respect to their inflections

word order the position of words relative to each other in a sentence

Bibliography

Chapter 1

Allport, Gordon. *Becoming: Basic Considerations for a Psychology of Personality*. New Haven, Conn.: Yale University Press, 1955.

Blanshard, Brand. *The Nature of Thought*. Vol. 1. New York: Macmillan, 1940.

Broad, C. D. *The Mind and Its Place in Nature*. Ch. 3. London: Kegan Paul, 1925.

Bronowski, Jacob. *The Identity of Man*. Garden City, N.Y.: Natural History Press, 1965.

Buber, Martin. *Between Man and Man*. R. G. Smith, trans. London: Kegan Paul, 1947.

Descartes, René. *Selections*. Ralph M. Eaton, Ed. New York: Charles Scribner's Sons, 1927.

Erikson, Erik. *Identity, Youth and Crisis*. New York: W. W. Norton, 1968.

Fromm, Erich. *Escape from Freedom*. New York: Avon, 1965.

Frondizi, Risieri. *The Nature of the Self*. Carbondale: Southern Illinois Univrsity Press, 1971.

Hume, David. "Personal Identity," in *A Treatise of Nature*. Oxford: Oxford University Press, 1955.

Locke, John. *An Essay Concerning Human Understanding*. Bk. II, Ch. 27. A. C. Fraser, Ed. Oxford: Clarendon Press, 1894.

Matson, Floyd. *The Broken Image*. Garden City, N.Y.: Doubleday, 1964.

Niebuhr, Reinhold. *The Nature and Destiny of Man*. New York: Charles Scribner's Sons, 1943.

Rhine, Louisa. *Hidden Channel of the Mind*. New York: Sloane, 1961.

Strawson, P. F. *Individuals*. New York: Anchor, 1963.

Watts, Alan. *The Book*. New York: Vintage, 1972.

Chapter 2

Alston, William P. *Philosophy of Language*. Englewood Cliffs, N.J.: Prentice-Tall, 1966.

393

Austin, John L. *How to Do Things with Words*. New York: Oxford University Press, 1965.

Ayer, Alfred J. *Language, Truth and Logic*. London: Victor Gollancz, 1936.

Black, Max. *Language and Philosophy*. Ithaca, N.Y.: Cornell University Press, 1949.

Chase, Stuart. *The Tyranny of Words*. New York: Harcourt Brace & World, 1938.

Cousins, Norman. "The Environment of Language," in *Introductory Readings on Language*. Wallace L. Anderson and Norman C. Stageberg, Eds. New York: Holt, Rinehart and Winston, 1966.

Hayakawa, S. I. *Language, Thought and Culture*, 3rd ed. New York: Harcourt Brace Jovanovich, 1962.

Kluckhohn, Clyde. "The Gift of Tongues," in *Mirror for Man*. New York: McGraw-Hill, 1949.

Linsky, Leonard, Ed. *Semantics and the Philosophy of Language*. Urbana: University of Illinois, 1952.

Mill, John Stewart. *A System of Logic*. Bk. 1. London: Longmans, Green, 1961.

Pears, David. *Ludwig Wittgenstein*. New York: Viking Press, 1970.

Plato. *Meno*. Benjamin Jowett, trans. New York: Liberal Arts Press, 1957.

Quine, Willard Van Ofman. *Word and Object*. New York: John Wiley & Sons, 1o60.

Whorf, Benjamin. *Language, Thought and Reality*. J. B. Carroll, Ed. New Hork: John Wiley & Sons, 1964.

Tilson, John. *Language and the Pursuit of Truth*. New York: Cambridge University Press, 1956.

Wittgenstein, Ludwig. *Tractatus*. London: Kegan Paul, 1962.

Chapters 3, 4, and 5

Aristotle. *Posterior Analytics*, in *The Basic Works of Aristotle*. Richard McKeon, Ed. G. R. Mure, trans. New York: Random House, 1941.

Ayer, Alfred J. *The Problems of Knowledge*. New York: St. Martin's Press, 1942.

Barry, Vincent E. *Practical Logic*. New York: Holt, Rinehart and Winston, 1976.

Berkeley, George. *Principles of Human Knowledge: Three Dialogues Between Hylas and Philonus*. New York: Philosophy Series of the Modern Student's Library, 1901.

Blanshard, Brand. *The Nature of Thought*. Vol. 2, Chs. 25, 26. New York: Macmillan, 1939.

Copi, Irving. *Introduction to Logic*, 4th ed. New York: Macmillan, 1972.

Descartes, René. "Meditations of First Philosophy," in *Descartes Selections*. Ralph Eaton, Ed. New York: Charles Scribner's Sons, 1927.

Descartes, René. *The Philosophical Works of Descartes*. E. S. Haldane and G. R. T. Ross, trans. Cambridge: Cambridge University Press, 1931.

Dewey, John. *The Quest for Certainty*. New York: Putnam's, 1929.

Hume, David. *Treatise on Human Nature*. L. A. Selby-Bigge, Ed. Oxford: Clarendon Press, 1896.

Hume, David. *An Inquiry Concerning Human Understanding*. Raymond Wilborn, Ed. New York: Liberal Arts Press, 1955.

James, William. *Pragmatism*. New York: Meridian, 1965.

Katz, Jerrold J. *The Problem of Induction and Its Solution*. Chicago: University of Chicago Press, 1962.

Khatchadourian, Haig. *The Coherence Theory of Truth*. Beirut: American University Press, 1961.

Locke, John. *An Essay Concerning Human Understanding*. Bks. 2, 4. New York: Dutton, 1948.

Murphy, Arthur E. "The Pragmatic Theory of Truth," in *The Uses of Reason*. New York: Macmillan, 1943.

Plato. *Apology*. H. N. Fowler, trans. Cambridge, Mass.: Harvard University Press, 1914.

Plato. *Phaedo*. E. F. Church, trans. New York: Liberal Arts Press, 1951.

Plato. *The Republic*. Benjamin Jowett, trans. New York: Random House, 1957.

Price, H. H. *Thinking and Experience*. London: Hutchinson, 1953.

Ritchie, A. D. *George Berkeley*. New York: Barnes & Noble, 1967.

Russell, Bertrand. *Human Knowledge: Its Scope and Limits*. New York: Simon & Schuster, 1948.

Russell, Bertrand. *The Problems of Philosophy*. New York: Oxford University Press, 1912.

Woozley, A. D. *Theory of Knowledge*. London: Allen and Unwin, 1949.

Yolton, John. *John Locke and the War of Ideas*. London: Oxford University Press, 1956.

Chapter 6

Aristotle. *Metaphysics*, in *The Basic Works of Aristotle*. Richard McKeon, Ed. W. D. Ross, trans. New York: Random House, 1941.

Aristotle. *Selections*. W. D. Ross, Ed. New York: Charles Scribner's Sons, 1927.

Ayer, Alfred J. *Language, Truth and Logic*. London: Victor Gollancz, 1936.

Ayer, Alfred J. *Logical Positivism*. Glencoe, Ill.: Free Press, 1959.

Berkeley, George. *A Treatise Concerning the Principles of Human Knowledge*. Colin M. Turbayne, Ed. New York: Liberal Arts Press, 1957.

Bertocci, Peter A., and Richard M. Millard. *Personality and the Good*. New York: McKeon, 1963.

Blanshard, Brand. *Reason and Analysis*. London: Allen and Unwin, 1962.

Brazill, William J. *The Young Hegelians*. New Haven, Conn.: Yale University Press, 1970.

Cornman, J. *Materialism and Sensations*. New Haven, Conn.: Yale University Press, 1971.

Descartes, René. *Meditations on First Philosophy*, 1641, and *Principles of Philosophy*, 1644, in *Descartes Selections*. Ralph Eaton, Ed. New York: Charles Scribner's Sons, 1927.

Harris, E. E. *Nature, Mind and Modern Science*. New York: Humanities Press, 1954.

Heidegger, Martin. *Being and Time*. Edward Robinson, trans. New York: Harper & Row, 1964.

Hume, David. *An Inquiry Concerning Human Understanding*, 1748. New York: Liberal Arts Press, 1955.

Husserl, Edmund. *Phenomenology and the Crisis of Philosophy*. Quentin Lauer, trans. New York: Harper & Row, 1965.

James, William. *Pragmatism*. New York: Meridian, 1965.

Johnson, A. H. *Whitehead's Theory of Reality*. Boston: Beacon Press, 1952.

Kant, Immanuel. *Prolegomena to Any Future Metaphysics*, 1783. Paul Carus, trans. New York: Liberal Arts Press, 1951.

Kierkegaard, Søren. *Fear and Trembling: The Sickness unto Death*. Walter Lourie, trans. New York: Doubleday, 1954.

Krikorian, Yervant H. *Recent Perspectives in American Philosophy*. The Hague: Martinus N. Jhoff, 1973.

Lamprecht, Sterling P. *The Metaphysics of Naturalism*. New York: Appleton-Century-Crofts, 1967.

Lange, F. A. *The History of Materialism*. New York: Humanities Press, 1957.

Marcel, Gabriel. *The Mystery of Being*. G. S. Fraser, trans. Chicago: Henry Regnery, 1950.

Marx, Karl, and Friedrich Engels. *Basic Writings on Politics and Philosophy*. Lewis Feuer, Ed. Garden City, N.Y.: Doubleday, 1959.

Mundle, C. W. K. *A Critique of Linguistic Philosophy*. Oxford: Clarendon Press, 1970.

Peirce, Charles. *Values in a Universe of Chance*. Philip Wiener, Ed. Stanford, Calif.: Stanford University Press, 1958.

Plato. *Phaedo*. E. F. Church, trans. New York: Liberal Arts Press, 1951.

Plato. *The Republic*. Benjamin Jowett, trans. New York: Random House, 1957.

Plato. *Timaeus*. Benjamin Jowett, trans. New York: Liberal Arts Press, 1959.

Pratt, James B. *Personal Realism*. New York: Macmillan, 1937.

Radhakrishnan, S. *An Idealist View of Life*. London: Allen and Unwin, 1951.

Sartre, Jean-Paul. *Being and Nothingness: An Essay on Phenomenological Ontology*. Hazel E. Barnes, trans. New York: Philosophical Library, 1956.

Sartre, Jean-Paul. *Existentialism and Human Emotions*. New York: Philosophical Library, 1957.

Schofield, Robert E. *Mechanism and Materialism: British Natural Philosophy in an Age of Reason*. Princeton, N.J.: Princeton University Press, 1970.

Sellars, Wilfred. *Philosophical Perspectives*. Springfield, Ill.: Charles C Thomas, 1967.

Sellars, Wilfred. *Philosophy for the Future*. New York: Harper & Row, 1949.

Smart, J. J. C. *Philosophy and Scientific Realism*. New York: Humanities Press, 1963.

Taylor, Richard. *Metaphysics*. Englewood Cliffs, N.J.: Prentice-Hall, 1963.

Waismann, Friedrich. *The Principles of Linguistic Philosophy*. London: Macmillan, 1965.

Whitehead, Alfred North. *Process and Reality: An Essay in Cosmology*. New York: Harper & Row, 1960.

Wittgenstein, Ludwig. *Philosophical Investigations*. G. E. Anscombe, trans. Oxford: Blackwell, 1953.

Chapter 7

Asimov, Isaac. *The Intelligent Man's Guide to Science.* New York: Basic Books, 1963.

Barkey, Stephen F. *Induction and Hypothesis.* Ithaca, N.Y.: Cornell University Press, 1957.

Barnett, Lincoln. *The Universe and Dr. Einstein.* New York: New American Library (Mentor Books), 1957.

Boas, George. *The Challenge of Science.* Seattle: University of Washington Press, 1965.

Braithwaite, R. B. *Scientific Explanation.* Cambridge: Cambridge University Press, 1953.

Bunge, Mario. *Causality.* Cambridge: Peter Smith, 1959.

Campbell, Norman R. *What Is Science?* New York: Dover, 1952.

Conant, James B. *Modern Science and Modern Man.* New York: Doubleday, 1953.

Dampier, Sir William Cecil. *A History of Science and Its Relations with Philosophy and Religion.* New York: Cambridge University Press, 1966.

Eddington, Sir Arthur S. *The Nature of the Physical World.* New York: Macmillan, 1937.

Frank, Philipp. *Philosophy of Science.* Englewood Cliffs, N.J.: Prentice-Hall, 1962.

Hart, H. L., and A. Hondre. *Causation and the Law.* Oxford: Oxford University Press, 1958.

Hempel, Norwood Russell. *Aspects of Scientific Explanation.* New York: Free Press, 1965.

Madden, Edward H., Ed. *The Structure of Scientific Thought.* Boston: Houghton Mifflin, 1960.

Mill, John Stuart. *A System of Logic.* London: Longmans, Green, 1959.

Nagel, Ernest. *The Structure of Science.* New York: Harcourt, Brace & World, 1961.

Reichenbach, Hans. *The Rise of Scientific Philosophy.* Berkeley: University of California Press, 1951.

Russell, Bertrand. *The A, B, C's of Relativity,* rev. ed. Felix Pirani, Ed. Fairlawn, N.J.: Essential Books, 1958.

Russell, Bertrand. *Introduction to Mathematical Philosophy.* London: Allen and Unwin, 1919.

Russell, Bertrand. *Religion and Science.* New York: Oxford University Press, 1961.

Salmon, Wesley C. *The Foundations of Scientific Inference.* Pittsburgh: University of Pittsburgh Press, 1967.

Scheffler, Israel. *Science and Subjectivity.* New York: Bobbs-Merrill, 1967.

Werkmeister, W. H. *A Philosophy of Science.* Lincoln: University of Nebraska Press, 1965.

Whitehead, Alfred North. *Process and Reality.* New York: Harper & Row, 1960.

Whitehead, Alfred North. *Science and the Modern World.* New York: The New American Library, 1948.

Chapter 8

Aquinas, Thomas. *Summa Theologica,* in *Basic Writings of Saint Thomas Aquinas.* A. C. Pegis, Ed. New York: Random House, 1945.

Augustine. *City of God.* M. Dods, trans. Edinburgh: T. & T. Clark, 1872.

Augustine. *Confessions.* J. G. Pilkington, trans. New York: Liveright, 1943.

Barth, Karl. *The Humanity of God.* Richmond, Va.: Knox, 1960.

Brightman, Edgar. *A Philosophy of Religion.* Englewood Cliffs, N.J.: Prentice-Hall, 1940.

Burrill, Donald, Ed. *The Cosmological Arguments.* New York: Doubleday, 1967.

Campbell, C. A. *On Selfhood and Godhood.* New York: Macmillan, 1957.

Christian, William A. *Meaning and Truth in Religion.* Princeton, N.J.: Princeton University Press, 1964.

Hick, John. *Arguments for the Existence of God: Philosophy and Religion.* London: Macmillan, 1970.

Hick, John. *Evil and the God of Love.* New York: Harper & Row, 1966.

Kierkegaard, Søren. *Philosophical Fragments.* Princeton, N.J.: Princeton University Press, 1967.

Knox, John. *Myth and Truth: An Essay on the Language of Faith.* Charlottesville: University Press of Virginia, 1965.

Koller, John M. *Oriental Philosophies.* New York: Charles Scribner's Sons, 1970.

Mao Tse-tung. *Four Essays on Philosophy.* Peking: Foreign Language Press, 1960.

Murray, J. C. *The Problem of God, Yesterday and Today.* New Haven, Conn.: Yale University Press, 1964.

Needleman, Jacob. *The New Religions.* Garden City, N.Y.: Doubleday, 1970.

Northrop, F. S. C. *The Meeting of East and West.* New York: Macmillan, 1946.

Novak, Michael. *Belief and Unbelief: A Philosophy of Self-Knowledge.* New York: Macmillan, 1965.

Pegis, Anton C., Ed. *The Basic Writings of Thomas Aquinas.* New York: Random House, 1945.

Pike, Nelsen. *God and Evil.* Englewood Cliffs, N.J.: Prentice-Hall, 1964.

Plating, Alvin. *The Ontological Arguments.* New York: Doubleday, 1961.

Plato. *Apology.* H. N. Fowler, trans. Cambridge, Mass.: Harvard University Press, 1914.

Plato. *Phaedo,* in *The Dialogues of Plato.* B. Jowett, trans. New York: Random House, 1937.

Plato. *Thaetetus,* in *Plato's Cosmology.* F. M. Cornford, trans. New York: Harcourt, Brace & World, 1937.

Radhakrishnan, Sarvepalli. *East and West: The End of Their Separation.* New York: Harper & Row, 1956.

Russell, Bertrand. *Why I Am Not a Christian.* New York: Simon & Schuster, 1957.

Suzuki, D. T. *Zen Buddhism.* William Barrett, Ed. Garden City, N.Y.: Doubleday, 1956.

Teilhard de Chardin. *The Divine Milieu.* New York: Harper & Row, 1964.
The New English Bible with the Apocrypha. Oxford: Oxford University Press, 1970.
Tillich, Paul. *The Future of Religions.* Jerald C. Brower, Ed. New York: Harper & Row, 1966.

Chapter 9

Adler, Alfred. *The Time of Our Lives: The Ethics of Common Sense.* New York: Holt, Rinehart and Winston, 1970.
Aiken, H. D. *Reason and Conduct: New Bearings on Moral Philosophy.* New York: Knopf, 1962.
Aristotle. *The Nicomachean Ethics,* in *The Basic Works of Aristotle.* Richard McKeon, Ed. New York: Random House, 1941.
Blanshard, Brand. *Reason and Goodness.* New York: Macmillan, 1961.
Britton, Karl. *Mill.* Baltimore: Penguin Books, 1953.
Broad, C. D. *Five Types of Ethical Theory.* New York: Harcourt, Brace, 1930.
Bronowski, Jacob. *Science and Human Values.* London: Penguin Books, 1964.
DeWitt Hyde, W. *The Five Great Philosophies of Life.* New York: Macmillan, 1927.
Epicurus. "Letter to Monoecceus," in *Epicurus: The Extant Remains.* C. Bailey, trans. Oxford: Clarendon Press, 1926.
Ewing, A. C. *The Definition of Good.* New York: Humanities Press, 1947.
Fletcher, Joseph. *Situation Ethics: The New Morality.* Philadelphia: Westminster Press, 1966.
Frankena, William. *Ethics,* 2nd ed. Englewood Cliffs, N.J.: Prentice-Hall, 1973.
Fried, Charles. *An Anatomy of Values: Problems of Personal and Social Choice.* Cambridge, Mass.: Harvard University Press, 1970.
Fromm, Erich. *The Art of Loving.* New York: Harper & Row, 1956.
Glass, Bentley. *Science and Ethical Values.* Chapel Hill: University of North Carolina Press, 1965.
Johnson, Ernest F., Ed. *Patterns of Ethics in America Today.* New York: Collier Books, 1962.
Kant, Immanuel. *Foundations of the Metaphysics of Morals.* Lewis White Beck, trans. New York: Bobbs-Merrill, 1959.
Korner, S. *Kant.* Ch. 6. Baltimore: Penguin Books, 1955.
Ladd, J. *Ethical Relativism.* Belmont, Calif.: Wadsworth, 1973.
Lockland, George T. *Grow or Die: The Unifying Principle of Transformation.* New York: Random House, 1973.
Mill, John Stuart. *Utilitarianism.* New York: Bobbs-Merrill, 1957.
Moore, George E. *Principia Ethica.* London: Cambridge University Press, 1903.
Muller, Herbert J. *The Children of Frankenstein.* Bloomington: Indiana University Press, 1970.
Nietzsche, Friedrich. *Genealogy of Morals.* F. Golffing, trans. Garden City, N.Y.: Doubleday, 1956.
Norton, D., and M. Kille. *Philosophies of Love.* San Francisco: Chandler, 1971.
Oraison, Mafe. *Morality for Moderns.* J. F. Bernard, trans. New York: Doubleday, 1972.

Parker, Dewitt. *The Philosophy of Value.* Ann Arbor: University of Michigan Press, 1957.

Plato. *The Republic.* Benjamin Jowett, trans. New York: Random House, 1957.

Rachels, James, Ed. *Moral Problems.* New York: Harper & Row, 1971.

Ramsey, Paul. *Basic Christian Ethics.* New York: Charles Scribner's Sons, 1950.

Ross, W. D. *Foundations of Ethics.* New York: Oxford University Press, 1939.

Ross, W. D. *Kant's Ethical Theory.* Oxford: Clarendon Press, 1954.

Ross, W. D. *The Right and the Good.* Oxford: Clarendon Press, 1930.

Stace, W. T. *The Concept of Morals.* New York: Macmillan, 1965.

Warnock, Mary. *Existential Ethics.* New York: St. Martin's Press, 1968.

Chapter 10

Adler, Alfred. *The Idea of Freedom.* Garden City, N.Y.: Doubleday, 1961.

Arendt, Hannah. *Crises of the Republic.* New York: Harcourt Brace Jovanovich, 1972.

Barth, Alan. *The Price of Liberty.* New York: Viking, 1961.

Benn, S. I., and R. S. Peters. *The Principles of Political Thought: Social Principles and the Democratic State.* London: Allen and Unwin, 1959.

Cahn, Edmond. *The Predicament of Democratic Men.* New York: Macmillan, 1961.

Cranston, Maurice. *Freedom: A New Analysis.* London: Longmans, Green, 1953.

de Beauvoir, Simone. *The Second Sex.* H. M. Parshley, trans. New York: Bantam, 1961.

Devlin, Patrick. *The Enforcement of Morals.* New York: Oxford University Press, 1965.

Hart, H. L. A. *Law, Liberty and Morality.* Stanford, Calif.: Stanford University Press, 1963.

Hobbes, Thomas. *Leviathan,* in *The English Works of Thomas Hobbes.* London: J. Bohn, 1839.

Hook, Sidney. *Political Power and Personal Freedom: Studies in Democracy, Communism and Civil Rights.* New York: Criterion, 1959.

Locke, John. *Of Civil Government.* London: Dent, 1924.

Machiavelli, Niccolo. *The Prince.* T. G. Bergin. New York: Appleton-Century-Crofts, 1947.

Marcuse, Herbert. *One-Dimensional Man.* Boston: Beacon Press, 1964.

Marx, Karl, and Friedrich Engels. *Manifesto of the Communist Party.* F. Engels, Ed. Chicago: Henry Regnery, 1954.

Mill, John Stuart. *The Essential Works of John Stuart Mill.* Max Lerner, Ed. New York: Bantam Books, 1961.

Muller, Herbert J. *Issues of Freedom: Paradoxes and Promises.* New York: Harper & Row, 1960.

Myrdal, Gunnar. *Beyond the Welfare State: Economic Planning and Its International Implications.* New Haven, Conn.: Yale University Press, 1960.

Nathan, N. M. L. *The Concept of Justice.* London: Macmillan, 1971.

Niebuhr, Reinhold. *Faith and History: The Irony of American History.* New York: Charles Scribner's Sons, 1949.

Nietzsche, Friedrich. *Beyond Good and Evil.* Walter Kaufman, trans. New York: Random House, 1966.

Oppenheim, Felix E. *Dimensions of Freedom: An Analysis.* New York: St. Martin's Press, 1961.

Rawls, John. *A Theory of Justice.* Cambridge, Mass.: Harvard University Press, 1971.

Rossiter, Clinton. *Conservatism in America: The Thankless Persuasion,* 2nd ed. New York: Knopf, 1966.

Sorokin, Pitirim A. *The Crisis of Our Age.* New York: Dutton, 1941.

Spengler, Oswald. *Today and Destiny: Vital Excerpts from The Decline of the West.* New York: Knopf, 1940.

Spitz, D. *Patterns of Antidemocratic Thought.* New York: Free Press, 1949.

Sweezy, Paul. *The Theory of Capitalist Development: Principles of Marxian Political Economy.* New York: Oxford University Press, 1942.

Whitehead, Alfred North. *Adventures of Ideas.* New York: The New American Library, 1955.

Williams, Bernard. *Philosophy, Politics and Society,* 2nd series. New York: Barnes & Noble, 1962.

Wise, David. *The Politics of Lying: Government Deception, Secrecy and Power.* New York: Random House, 1963.

Chapter 11

Aristotle. *Poetics,* in *The Basic Works of Aristotle.* Richard McKeon, Ed. Ingram Bywater, trans. New York: Random House, 1941.

Baxandall, Lee. *Radical Perspectives in the Arts.* New York: Penguin Books, 1962.

Beardsley, Monroe. *Aesthetics: From Classical Greece to the Present.* New York: Macmillan, 1966.

Berger, John. *Art and Revolution.* New York: Charles Scribner's Sons, 1970.

Berleant, Arnold. *The Aesthetic Field: A Phenomenology of Aesthetic Experience.* Springfield, Ill.: Charles C Thomas, 1970.

Brown, Merle. *Neo-Idealistic Aesthetics: Croce-Gentile-Collingwood.* Detroit: Wayne University Press, 1966.

Croce, Benedetto. *Aesthetica.* Douglas Hinslie, trans. London: Macmillan, 1909.

Dewey, John. *Art as Experience.* New York: Putnam, 1958.

Ducasse, Curt John. *The Philosophy of Art.* New York: Dover, 1966.

Edman, Irwin. *Arts and the Man: A Short Introduction to Aesthetics.* New York: W. W. Norton, 1939.

Else, Gerald F. *Aristotle's Poetics: The Argument.* Cambridge, Mass.: Harvard University Press, 1957.

Fallico, Arthur B. *Art and Existentialism.* Englewood Cliffs, N.J.: Prentice-Hall, 1962.

Feibleman, James K. *Aesthetics.* New York: Humanities Press, 1949.

Harries, Karsten. *The Meaning of Modern Art.* Evanston, Ill.: Northwestern University Press, 1968.

Hegel, G. W. F. *The Philosophy of Fine Art,* 1832. F. P. B. Osmaston, trans. London: G. Bell, 1920.

Henn, Thomas. *The Harvest of Tragedy*. London: Farber and Farber, 1956.

Hofstadter, Albert. *Truth and Art*. New York: Columbia University Press, 1965.

Kant, Immanuel. *Critique of Judgment*. J. H. Bernard, trans. New York: Hafner, 1951.

Langer, Susanne. *Feeling and Form*. New York: Charles Scribner's Sons, 1953.

Langer, Susanne. *Reflection on Art: A Source Book of Writings by Artists, Critics and Philosophers*. New York: Oxford University Press, 1958.

Munro, Thomas. *Oriental Aesthetics*. Cleveland: Case Western Reserve University Press, 1965.

Newton, Eric. *The Meaning of Beauty*. Baltimore: Penguin, 1962.

Parker, DeWitt H. *The Principles of Aesthetics*. New York: Appleton, 1946.

Plato. *The Republic*. Benjamin Jowett, trans. New York: Random House, 1957.

Santayana, George. *The Sense of Beauty*. New York: Charles Scribner's Sons, 1896.

Sypher, Wylie, Ed. *Comedy*. Garden City, N.Y.: Doubleday, 1956.

Tolstoy, Leo. *What Is Art?* Louise and Aylmer Maude, trans. London: Oxford University Press, 1896.

Tomas, Vincent, Ed. *Creativity in the Arts*. Englewood Cliffs, N.J.: Prentice-Hall, 1964.

Weiss, Paul. *Nine Basic Arts*. Carbondale: Southern Illinois University Press, 1961.

Wittgenstein, Ludwig. *Philosophical Investigations*. G. E. M. Anscombe, trans. New York: Macmillan, 1953.

Chapter 12

Danto, Arthur. *What Philosophy Is*. New York: Harper & Row, 1968.

Frankl, Victor. *Man's Search for Freedom*. New York: Pocket Books, 1965.

Goffman, Erving. *The Presentation of Self in Everyday Life*. New York: Anchor, 1959.

Karl, Frederick R., and Leo Hamalian, Eds. *The Existential Imagination*. Greenwich, Conn.: Faucett, 1963.

Kierkegaard, Søren. *Fear and Trembling*. New York: Anchor, 1954.

Krishnamurti, J. *Think on These Things*. New York: Perennial Library, 1970.

Laing, R. D. *The Divided Self*. Baltimore: Penguin, 1965.

Maslow, Abraham. *Toward a Psychology of Being*. New York: Van Nostrand, 1968.

May, Rollo. *Man's Search for Himself*. New York: Signet, 1967.

Organ, Troy. *The Art of Critical Thinking*. Boston: Houghton Mifflin, 1965.

Pappenheim, Fritz. *The Alienation of Modern Man*. New York: Monthly Review Press, 1959.

Riesman, David. *The Lonely Crowd*. New Haven, Conn.: Yale University Press, 1950.

Thouless, Robert. *How to Think Straight*. New York: Hart, 1959.

Tillich, Paul. *The Dynamics of Faith*. New York: Harper Torchbooks, 1958.

Watts, Alan. *The Wisdom of Insecurity*. New York: Pantheon, 1952.

Wilson, Colin. *The Outsider*. New York: Delta, 1967.

Index